Dive Into Python

MARK PILGRIM

Dive Into Python
Copyright © 2004 by Mark Pilgrim

ISBN (pbk): 1-59059-356-1

Printed and bound in the United States of America 9 8 7 6 5 4 3 2 1

Trademarked names may appear in this book. Rather than use a trademark symbol with every occurrence of a trademarked name, we use the names only in an editorial fashion and to the benefit of the trademark owner, with no intention of infringement of the trademark.

Lead Editor: Chris Mills

Technical Reviewer: Anna Ravenscroft

Editorial Board: Steve Anglin, Dan Appleman, Gary Cornell, Tony Davis, Chris Mills, Steve Rycroft, Dominic Shakeshaft, Jim Sumser, Karen Watterson, Gavin Wray, John Zukowski

Project Manager: Kylie Johnston

Copy Edit Manager: Nicole LeClerc

Copy Editor: Marilyn Smith

Production Manager: Kari Brooks

Production Editor: Katie Stence

Compositor: Kinetic Publishing Services, LLC

Proofreader: Linda Seifert

Indexer: Rebecca Plunkett

Cover Designer: Kurt Krames

Manufacturing Manager: Tom Debolski

Distributed to the book trade in the United States by Springer-Verlag New York, Inc., 175 Fifth Avenue, New York, NY 10010 and outside the United States by Springer-Verlag GmbH & Co. KG, Tiergartenstr. 17, 69112 Heidelberg, Germany.

In the United States: phone 1-800-SPRINGER, e-mail orders@springer-ny.com, or visit http://www.springer-ny.com. Outside the United States: fax +49 6221 345229, e-mail orders@springer.de, or visit http://www.springer.de.

For information on translations, please contact Apress directly at 2560 Ninth Street, Suite 219, Berkeley, CA 94710. Phone 510-549-5930, fax 510-549-5939, e-mail info@apress.com, or visit http://www.apress.com.

The information in this book is distributed on an "as is" basis, without warranty. Although every precaution has been taken in the preparation of this work, neither the author(s) nor Apress shall have any liability to any person or entity with respect to any loss or damage caused or alleged to be caused directly or indirectly by the information contained in this work.

The source code for this book is available to readers at http://www.apress.com in the Downloads section. You will need to answer questions pertaining to this book in order to successfully download the code.

For Ethan

Contents at a Glance

Contents

About the Author

BY DAY, MARK PILGRIM is an accessibility architect. By night, he is a husband and father who lives in North Carolina with his wife, his son, and his dog. He would like to thank his wife and his son, who have been exceedingly patient while he worked on this book. The dog was not all that patient, but two out of three isn't bad. Mark spends his copious free time sunbathing, skydiving, and reading Immanuel Kant's *The Critique of Pure Reason* in the original Klingon.

Introduction

IF YOU ARE a developer interested in getting started quickly with the hottest open-source language, this book is for you. Experience in other languages is recommended but not required. If you have experience in Perl, Java, or Visual Basic, the first few chapters will go even faster. Core programming structures are shared among all languages, and this book contains many analogies to help you become familiar with Python's syntax and move on to higher-level concepts.

But even if you don't have a lot of experience with other modern programming languages, this book is still a good place to start. It won't bore you with long-winded treatises on the history of computer science. You'll get down to business immediately and see how Python's interactive shell is the perfect breeding ground for experimenting with programming concepts before getting your feet wet with actual code.

This book is divided into a series of isolated case studies. Each chapter focuses on a single piece of real code that does something meaningful and useful. As each example brings up related issues, there are digressions to explore them, but the discussion always comes back to the code in the end. This does not mean that every chapter is an island. Many of the later chapters assume you have mastered basic concepts covered in earlier chapters. These cases are clearly marked in the text, with references and quick reviews to get you up and running quickly. Here is an overview of what you'll find in this book:

Chapter 1, Installing Python: No matter what platform you're using, Python runs on your computer. You'll step through how to install it on Windows, Mac OS X, Mac OS 9, Red Hat Linux, and Debian GNU/Linux. After downloading, you can be up and running and experimenting in the Python interactive shell in five minutes.

Chapter 2, Your First Python Program: As promised, you'll dive into your first complete Python program, `odbchelper.py`, and explore every line of it in depth. This will show you how to declare functions, document your code with the Python equivalent of JavaDoc, and test individual functions from the Python interactive shell.

Chapter 3, Native Datatypes: Python has a rich set of native datatypes. You'll learn how to manipulate lists, tuples, and dictionaries; how to format strings; and how to use list comprehensions.

Chapter 4, The Power of Introspection: This chapter explores `apihelper.py`, a short but powerful program that displays information about a module, function, or class from the Python interactive shell. Diving into this program will show you how to define functions with optional arguments, call functions with named arguments, get references to Python objects with the `getattr()` function, and use `lambda` to quickly define one-off functions.

Chapter 5, Objects and Object-Orientation: Python supports first-class objects with a complete inheritance model. This chapter introduces a class, `FileInfo`, that encapsulates reading metadata from different types of files. You'll see how to define classes and create instances of classes. You'll also explore Python's powerful special class methods, which allow you to define behavior in your custom classes that enables you to operate on them as if they were built-in datatypes. This chapter steps through defining a class that behaves like a dictionary, but other special class methods could allow classes to be added and subtracted like numbers, or appended and sliced like lists.

Chapter 6, Exceptions and File Handing: Most modern programming languages have some form of exception handling, and Python is no exception. In this chapter, you'll see how Python's exception handling works. Then you'll use it to safely work with files, directory listings, and other external resources that can fail at any moment.

Chapter 7, Regular Expressions: This chapter introduces the concept of regular expressions, which are a powerful pattern-matching technique. If you have used Perl, this concept will be old hat, but few people use them in other languages (even though all modern programming languages offer regular expression libraries). This chapter steps through a series of mini-studies to explore different forms of regular expression syntax to work with street addresses, Roman numerals, and phone numbers.

Chapter 8, HTML Processing: One of Python's best-kept secrets is `sgmllib`, a built-in library for dealing with HTML and similar forms of markup. This chapter is centered around `dialect.py`, a program that takes HTML pages and transforms the text into different dialects while leaving the HTML markup intact. To understand this will require an in-depth look at Python's `sgmllib`. There are also digressions to learn about dictionary-based string formatting, and the `locals()` and `globals()` functions for accessing all the defined variables in the Python environment as a native data structure.

Chapter 9, XML Processing: This chapter covers Python's built-in XML processing libraries. You'll see kgp.py, a program that takes XML documents that define context-free grammars and parses them to generate randomized output. This will take you through parsing XML documents, accessing arbitrary elements and attributes within them, and reconstructing XML files after they've been parsed. There is also a thorough explanation of Unicode, which is central to XML text processing and is also used within Python to store strings in multiple languages.

Chapter 10, Scripts and Streams: Another one of Python's strengths is the concept of a **file-like object**, which allows you to get data from multiple input sources the same way you would read from a file on disk. This chapter's example is openanything.py, a utility library that lets you handle an in-memory buffer as a file, the output of another running process, or even a remote web page. There is also a discussion of handling command-line arguments and flags in scripts that are run from the command line.

Chapter 11, HTTP Web Services: This chapter dives into HTTP with an expanded version of the openanything.py module introduced in Chapter 10. With HTTP web services, a proper implementation of HTTP is essential, and this chapter will teach you the five features of HTTP you need to know: setting the User-Agent, handling temporary and permanent redirects, taking advantage of the Last-Modified header, using Etags, and supporting compressed data.

Chapter 12, SOAP Web Services: Python comes with a **lot** of libraries (Python fans like to say that it comes with "batteries included"). However, it doesn't yet come with a SOAP library, so the first step to using SOAP web services is to install three libraries: PyXML, fpconst, and SOAPpy. This chapter steps you through that, and then dives into parsing WSDL files and calling remote functions over SOAP. The chapter culminates in a simple program that returns Google search results with the Google SOAP API.

Chapter 13, Unit Testing: Unit testing is the idea that you should write small, independent tests to check each of your functions. Python comes with a unit testing framework, and this chapter will use the example of validating Roman numerals to show you how to write unit tests in Python.

Chapter 14, Test-First Programming: Continuing where Chapter 13 left off, this chapter will explore what it feels like to write code that already has unit tests for it. When all your tests pass, stop coding.

Chapter 15, Refactoring: Continuing where Chapter 14 left off, this final chapter on testing will show how to update your unit tests to handle changing requirements, how to integrate new unit tests to cover newly reported bugs, and how to refactor for performance without worrying about breaking old code.

Chapter 16, Functional Programming: This chapter covers Python's functional programming methods: `map`, `filter`, and `lambda`. Using a sample program to build and run regression test suites, you'll learn about the joys of data-centric programming, dynamically importing modules, and manipulating path information on the command line.

Chapter 17, Dynamic Functions: Python 2.3 introduces a new language feature: *generators*. This chapter uses a staged approach to build the same program in six different ways. By stage six, you'll see how generators can radically reduce your program's complexity, while actually making it more flexible in the long run. Along the way, you'll learn about string substitution with regular expressions, closures, and functions that behave like first-class objects.

Chapter 18, Performance Tuning: Python is an interpreted scripting language, but that doesn't mean you can ignore performance altogether. This chapter explores some common mistakes that can make your program run up to ten times slower than it could. You'll learn how to use the built-in `timeit` module to optimize regular expressions, dictionary lookups, list operations, and string manipulation.

I hope this book makes you love Python as much as I do. Let's dive in.

#### CHAPTER 1

Installing Python

WELCOME TO PYTHON. Let's dive in. In this chapter, you'll install the version of Python that's right for you.

Which Python Is Right for You?

The first thing you need to do with Python is install it. Or do you? If you're using an account on a hosted server, your ISP may have already installed Python. Most popular Linux distributions come with Python in the default installation. Mac OS X 10.2 and later versions come with a command-line version of Python, although you'll probably want to install a version that includes a more Mac-like graphical interface.

Windows does not come with any version of Python, but don't despair! There are several ways to point-and-click your way to Python on Windows.

As you can see already, Python runs on many operating systems. The full list includes Windows, Mac OS, Mac OS X, and all varieties of free UNIX-compatible systems like Linux. There are also versions that run on Sun Solaris, AS/400, Amiga, OS/2, BeOS, and a plethora of other platforms you've probably never even heard of.

What's more, Python programs written on one platform can, with a little care, run on any supported platform. For instance, I regularly develop Python programs on Windows and later deploy them on Linux.

So back to the question that started this section, "Which Python is right for you?" The answer is whichever one runs on the computer you already have.

Python on Windows

On Windows, you have a couple choices for installing Python.

ActiveState makes a Windows installer for Python called ActivePython, which includes a complete version of Python, an IDE with a Python-aware code editor, plus some Windows extensions for Python that allow complete access to Windows-specific services, APIs, and the Windows Registry.

ActivePython is freely downloadable, although it is not open source. It is the IDE I used to learn Python, and I recommend you try it unless you have a specific reason not to use it. One such reason might be that ActiveState is generally several months behind in updating the ActivePython installer when new versions of Python are released. If you absolutely need the latest version of Python, and ActivePython is still a version behind as you read this, you'll want to use the second option for installing Python on Windows.

The second option is the "official" Python installer, distributed by the people who develop Python itself. It is freely downloadable and open source, and it is always current with the latest version of Python.

Option 1: Installing ActivePython

Here is the procedure for installing ActivePython:

1. Download ActivePython from
    `http://www.activestate.com/Products/ActivePython/`.

2. If you are using Windows 95, Windows 98, or Windows Me, you will also need to download and install Windows Installer 2.0, from `http://download.microsoft.com/download/WindowsInstaller/Install/2.0/W9XMe/EN-US/InstMsiA.exe`, before installing ActivePython.

3. Double-click the installer, `ActivePython-2.2.2-224-win32-ix86.msi`.

4. Step through the installer program.

5. If space is tight, you can do a custom installation and deselect the documentation, but I don't recommend this unless you absolutely can't spare the 14MB.

After the installation is complete, close the installer and choose Start ➤ Programs ➤ ActiveState ActivePython 2.2 ➤ PythonWin IDE. You'll see the following:

```
PythonWin 2.2.2 (#37, Nov 26 2002, 10:24:37) [MSC 32 bit (Intel)] on win32.
Portions Copyright 1994-2001 Mark Hammond (mhammond@skippinet.com.au) -
see 'Help/About PythonWin' for further copyright information.
>>>
```

Option 2: Installing Python from Python.org

Here is the procedure for installing Python from `http://www.python.org/`:

1. Download the latest Python Windows installer by going to
    http://www.python.org/ftp/python/ and selecting the highest version
    number listed, and then downloading the .exe installer.

2. Double-click the installer, Python-2.*xxx*.*yyy*.exe. (The name will depend
    on the version of Python available when you read this; at time of writing,
    the latest version was Python 2.3.3.)

3. Step through the installer program.

4. If disk space is tight, you can deselect the HTML Help file, the utility
    scripts (Tools/), and/or the test suite (Lib/test/).

5. If you do not have administrative rights on your machine, you can select
    Advanced Options, and then choose Non-Admin Install. This just affects
    where Registry entries and Start menu shortcuts are created.

After the installation is complete, close the installer and select Start ➤
Programs ➤ Python 2.3 ➤ IDLE (Python GUI). You'll see the following:

```
Python 2.3.2 (#49, Oct  2 2003, 20:02:00) [MSC v.1200 32 bit (Intel)] on win32
Type "copyright", "credits" or "license()" for more information.

****************************************************************
Personal firewall software may warn about the connection IDLE
makes to its subprocess using this computer's internal loopback
interface.  This connection is not visible on any external
interface and no data is sent to or received from the Internet.
****************************************************************

IDLE 1.0
>>>
```

Python on Mac OS X

On Mac OS X, you have two choices for installing Python: install it or don't install
it. You probably want to install it.

Mac OS X 10.2 and later comes with a command-line version of Python preinstalled. If you are comfortable with the command line, you can use this version
for the first third of the book. However, the preinstalled version does not come

with an XML parser, so when you get to the XML chapter, you'll need to install the full version.

Rather than using the preinstalled version, you'll probably want to install the latest version, which also comes with a graphical interactive shell.

Running the Preinstalled Version of Python on Mac OS X

To use the preinstalled version of Python, follow these steps:

1. Open the /Applications folder.

2. Open the Utilities folder.

3. Double-click Terminal to open a terminal window and get to a command line.

4. Type python at the command prompt.

Try it out:

```
Welcome to Darwin!
[localhost:~] you% python
Python 2.2 (#1, 07/14/02, 23:25:09)
[GCC Apple cpp-precomp 6.14] on darwin
Type "help", "copyright", "credits", or "license" for more information.
>>> [press Ctrl+D to get back to the command prompt]
[localhost:~] you%
```

Installing the Latest Version of Python on Mac OS X

Follow these steps to download and install the latest version of Python:

1. Download the MacPython-OSX disk image from
    http://homepages.cwi.nl/~jack/macpython/download.html.

2. If your browser has not already done so, double-click
    MacPython-OSX-2.3-1.dmg to mount the disk image on your desktop.

3. Double-click the installer, MacPython-OSX.pkg.

4. The installer will prompt you for your administrative username and password.

5.   Step through the installer program.

6.   After installation is complete, close the installer and open the /Applications folder.

7.   Open the MacPython-2.3 folder.

8.   Double-click PythonIDE to launch Python.

The MacPython IDE should display a splash screen, and then take you to the interactive shell. If the interactive shell does not appear, select Window ➤ Python Interactive (or press Command-0). The opening screen will show the following information:

```
Python 2.3 (#2, Jul 30 2003, 11:45:28)
[GCC 3.1 20020420 (prerelease)]
Type "copyright", "credits" or "license" for more information.
MacPython IDE 1.0.1
>>>
```

Note that once you install the latest version, the preinstalled version is still present. If you are running scripts from the command line, you need to be aware of which version of Python you are using, which you can check as shown in Listing 1-1.

Listing 1-1. Two Versions of Python

```
[localhost:~] you% python
Python 2.2 (#1, 07/14/02, 23:25:09)
[GCC Apple cpp-precomp 6.14] on darwin
Type "help", "copyright", "credits", or "license" for more information.
>>> [press Ctrl+D to get back to the command prompt]
[localhost:~] you% /usr/local/bin/python
Python 2.3 (#2, Jul 30 2003, 11:45:28)
[GCC 3.1 20020420 (prerelease)] on darwin
Type "help", "copyright", "credits", or "license" for more information.
>>> [press Ctrl+D to get back to the command prompt]
[localhost:~] you%
```

Python on Mac OS 9

Mac OS 9 does not come with any version of Python, but installation is very simple, and there is only one choice.

Follow these steps to install Python on Mac OS 9:

1. Download the `MacPython23full.bin` file from
   `http://homepages.cwi.nl/~jack/macpython/download.html`.

2. If your browser does not decompress the file automatically, double-click `MacPython23full.bin` to decompress the file with Stuffit Expander.

3. Double-click the installer, `MacPython23full`.

4. Step through the installer program.

5. After installation is complete, close the installer and open the `/Applications` folder.

6. Open the `MacPython-OS9 2.3` folder.

7. Double-click `Python IDE` to launch Python.

The MacPython IDE should display a splash screen, and then take you to the interactive shell. If the interactive shell does not appear, select Window ➤ Python Interactive (or press Command-0). You'll see the following:

```
Python 2.3 (#2, Jul 30 2003, 11:45:28)
[GCC 3.1 20020420 (prerelease)]
Type "copyright", "credits" or "license" for more information.
MacPython IDE 1.0.1
>>>
```

Python on RedHat Linux

Installing under UNIX-compatible operating systems such as Linux is easy if you're willing to install a binary package. Prebuilt binary packages are available for most popular Linux distributions, or you can always compile from source.

Download the latest Python RPM by going to `http://www.python.org/ftp/python/` and selecting the `rpms/` directory within that. Then download the RPM with the highest version number. You can install it with the `rpm` command, as shown in Listing 1-2.

Listing 1-2. Installing on RedHat Linux 9

```
localhost:~$ su -
Password: [enter your root password]
[root@localhost root]# wget http://python.org/ftp/python/2.3/rpms/redhat-9/
python2.3-2.3-5pydotorg.i386.rpm
Resolving python.org... done.
Connecting to python.org[194.109.137.226]:80... connected.
HTTP request sent, awaiting response... 200 OK
Length: 7,495,111 [application/octet-stream]
...
[root@localhost root]# rpm -Uvh python2.3-2.3-5pydotorg.i386.rpm
Preparing...                ########################################### [100%]
   1:python2.3             ########################################### [100%]
[root@localhost root]# python                          (1)
Python 2.2.2 (#1, Feb 24 2003, 19:13:11)
[GCC 3.2.2 20030222 (Red Hat Linux 3.2.2-4)] on linux2
Type "help", "copyright", "credits", or "license" for more information.
>>> [press Ctrl+D to exit]
[root@localhost root]# python2.3                       (2)
Python 2.3 (#1, Sep 12 2003, 10:53:56)
[GCC 3.2.2 20030222 (Red Hat Linux 3.2.2-5)] on linux2
Type "help", "copyright", "credits", or "license" for more information.
>>> [press Ctrl+D to exit]
[root@localhost root]# which python2.3                 (3)
/usr/bin/python2.3
```

(1) Whoops! Just typing python gives you the older version of Python—the one that was installed by default. That's not the one you want.

(2) At the time of this writing, the newest version is called python2.3. You'll probably want to change the path on the first line of the sample scripts to point to the newer version.

(3) This is the complete path of the newer version of Python that you just installed. Use this on the #! line (the first line of each script) to ensure that scripts are running under the latest version of Python, and be sure to type python2.3 to get into the interactive shell.

Python on Debian GNU/Linux

If you are lucky enough to be running Debian GNU/Linux, you install Python through the apt command, as shown in Listing 1-3.

Listing 1-3. Installing on Debian GNU/Linux

```
localhost:~$ su -
Password: [enter your root password]
localhost:~# apt-get install python
Reading Package Lists... Done
Building Dependency Tree... Done
The following extra packages will be installed:
  python2.3
Suggested packages:
  python-tk python2.3-doc
The following NEW packages will be installed:
  python python2.3
0 upgraded, 2 newly installed, 0 to remove and 3 not upgraded.
Need to get 0B/2880kB of archives.
After unpacking 9351kB of additional disk space will be used.
Do you want to continue? [Y/n] Y
Selecting previously deselected package python2.3.
(Reading database ... 22848 files and directories currently installed.)
Unpacking python2.3 (from .../python2.3_2.3.1-1_i386.deb) ...
Selecting previously deselected package python.
Unpacking python (from .../python_2.3.1-1_all.deb) ...
Setting up python (2.3.1-1) ...
Setting up python2.3 (2.3.1-1) ...
Compiling python modules in /usr/lib/python2.3 ...
Compiling optimized python modules in /usr/lib/python2.3 ...
localhost:~# exit
logout
localhost:~$ python
Python 2.3.1 (#2, Sep 24 2003, 11:39:14)
[GCC 3.3.2 20030908 (Debian prerelease)] on linux2
Type "help", "copyright", "credits" or "license" for more information.
>>> [press Ctrl+D to exit]
```

Python Installation from Source

If you prefer to build from source, you can download the Python source code from http://www.python.org/ftp/python/. Select the highest version number listed, download the .tgz file, and then do the usual configure, make, make install dance, as shown in Listing 1-4.

Listing 1-4. Installing Python from Source

```
localhost:~$ su -
Password: [enter your root password]
localhost:~# wget http://www.python.org/ftp/python/2.3/Python-2.3.tgz
Resolving www.python.org... done.
Connecting to www.python.org[194.109.137.226]:80... connected.
HTTP request sent, awaiting response... 200 OK
Length: 8,436,880 [application/x-tar]
...
localhost:~# tar xfz Python-2.3.tgz
localhost:~# cd Python-2.3
localhost:~/Python-2.3# ./configure
checking MACHDEP... linux2
checking EXTRAPLATDIR...
checking for --without-gcc... no
...
localhost:~/Python-2.3# make
gcc -pthread -c -fno-strict-aliasing -DNDEBUG -g -O3 -Wall -Wstrict-prototypes
-I. -I./Include  -DPy_BUILD_CORE -o Modules/python.o Modules/python.c
gcc -pthread -c -fno-strict-aliasing -DNDEBUG -g -O3 -Wall -Wstrict-prototypes
-I. -I./Include  -DPy_BUILD_CORE -o Parser/acceler.o Parser/acceler.c
gcc -pthread -c -fno-strict-aliasing -DNDEBUG -g -O3 -Wall -Wstrict-prototypes
-I. -I./Include  -DPy_BUILD_CORE -o Parser/grammar1.o Parser/grammar1.c
...
localhost:~/Python-2.3# make install
/usr/bin/install -c python /usr/local/bin/python2.3
...
localhost:~/Python-2.3# exit
logout
localhost:~$ which python
/usr/local/bin/python
localhost:~$ python
Python 2.3.1 (#2, Sep 24 2003, 11:39:14)
[GCC 3.3.2 20030908 (Debian prerelease)] on linux2
Type "help", "copyright", "credits" or "license" for more information.
>>> [press Ctrl+D to get back to the command prompt]
localhost:~$
```

The Interactive Shell

Now that you have Python installed, what's this interactive shell thing you're running?

It's like this: Python leads a double life. It's an interpreter for scripts that you can run from the command line or run like applications, by double-clicking the scripts. But it's also an interactive shell that can evaluate arbitrary statements and expressions. This is extremely useful for debugging, quick hacking, and testing. I even know some people who use the Python interactive shell in lieu of a calculator!

Launch the Python interactive shell in whatever way works on your platform, and let's dive in with the steps shown in Listing 1-5.

Listing 1-5. First Steps in the Interactive Shell

```
>>> 1 + 1                        (1)
2
>>> print 'hello world'          (2)
hello world
>>> x = 1                        (3)
>>> y = 2
>>> x + y
3
```

(1) The Python interactive shell can evaluate arbitrary Python expressions, including any basic arithmetic expression.

(2) The interactive shell can execute arbitrary Python statements, including the `print` statement.

(3) You can also assign values to variables, and the values will be remembered as long as the shell is open (but not any longer than that).

Summary

You should now have a version of Python installed that works for you.

Depending on your platform, you may have more than one version of Python installed. If so, you need to be aware of your paths. If simply typing `python` on the command line doesn't run the version of Python that you want to use, you may need to enter the full pathname of your preferred version.

Congratulations, and welcome to Python.

#### CHAPTER 2

Your First Python Program

YOU KNOW HOW OTHER books go on and on about programming fundamentals, and finally work up to building a complete, working program? Let's skip all that.

Diving In

Listing 2-1 shows a complete, working Python program. It probably makes absolutely no sense to you. Don't worry about that, because we're going to dissect it line by line. But read through it first and see what, if anything, you can make of it.

> **NOTE** *You can download this code, and all of the other examples used in this book, from the Downloads section of the Apress web site* (http://www. apress.com).

Listing 2-1. odbchelper.py

```python
def buildConnectionString(params):
    """Build a connection string from a dictionary of parameters.

    Returns string."""
    return ";".join(["%s=%s" % (k, v) for k, v in params.items()])

if __name__ == "__main__":
    myParams = {"server":"mpilgrim", \
                "database":"master", \
                "uid":"sa", \
                "pwd":"secret" \
                }
    print buildConnectionString(myParams)
```

Now run this program and see what happens.

- **Running programs on Windows:** In the ActivePython IDE on Windows, you can run the Python program you're editing by choosing File ➤ Run (or pressing Ctrl-R). Output is displayed in the interactive window.

- **Running programs on Mac OS:** In the Python IDE on Mac OS, you can run a Python program by selecting Python ➤ Run window... (or pressing Command-R), but there is an important option you must set first. Open the .py file in the IDE, pop up the options menu by clicking the black triangle in the upper-right corner of the window, and make sure the Run as __main__ option is checked. This is a per-file setting, but you'll only need to do it once per file.

- **Running programs in UNIX:** On UNIX-compatible systems (including Mac OS X), you can run a Python program from the command line. To run the one shown in Listing 2-1, enter python odbchelper.py.

The output of odbchelper.py will look like this:

```
server=mpilgrim;uid=sa;database=master;pwd=secret
```

Declaring Functions

Python has functions like most other languages, but it does not have separate header files like C++ or interface/implementation sections like Pascal. When you need a function, just declare it and code it, like this:

```
def buildConnectionString(params):
```

Note that the keyword def starts the function declaration, followed by the function name, followed by the arguments in parentheses. Multiple arguments (not shown here) are separated with commas.

Also note that the function does not define a return datatype. Python functions do not specify the datatype of their return value; they do not even specify whether or not they return a value. In fact, every Python function returns a value. If the function ever executes a return statement, it will return that value; otherwise, it will return None, the Python null value.

> **NOTE** *Python vs. Visual Basic return values: In Visual Basic, functions (that return a value) start with* function, *and subroutines (that do not return a value) start with* sub. *There are no subroutines in Python. Everything is a function, all functions return a value (even if it's* None*), and all functions start with* def.

The argument, params, does not specify a datatype. In Python, variables are never explicitly typed. Python figures out what type a variable is and keeps track of it internally.

> **NOTE** *Python vs. Java return values: In Java, C++, and other statically typed languages, you must specify the datatype of the function return value and each function argument. In Python, you never explicitly specify the datatype of anything. Based on what value you assign, Python keeps track of the datatype internally.*

How Python's Datatypes Compare to Other Programming Languages

An erudite reader sent me this explanation of how Python compares to other programming languages:

- **Statically typed language:** A language in which types are fixed at compile time. Most statically typed languages enforce this by requiring you to declare all variables with their datatypes before using them. Java and C are statically typed languages.

- **Dynamically typed language:** A language in which types are discovered at execution time; the opposite of statically typed. VBScript and Python are dynamically typed, because they figure out what type a variable is when you first assign it a value.

- **Strongly typed language:** A language in which types are always enforced. Java and Python are strongly typed. If you have an integer, you cannot treat it like a string without explicitly converting it.

- **Weakly typed language:** A language in which types may be ignored; the opposite of strongly typed. VBScript is weakly typed. In VBScript, you can concatenate the string '12' and the integer 3 to get the string '123', and then treat that as the integer 123, all without any explicit conversion.

So Python is both dynamically typed (because it doesn't use explicit datatype declarations) and strongly typed (because once a variable has a datatype, it actually matters).

Documenting Functions

You can document a Python function by giving it a doc string, as shown in Listing 2-2.

Listing 2-2. Defining the buildConnectionString Function's doc string

```
def buildConnectionString(params):
    """Build a connection string from a dictionary of parameters.

    Returns string."""
```

Triple quotes signify a multiline string. Everything between the start and end quotes is part of a single string, including carriage returns and other quote characters. You can use them anywhere, but you'll see them most often used when defining a doc string.

> **NOTE** *Python vs. Perl quoting: Triple quotes are also an easy way to define a string with both single and double quotes, like* qq/.../ *in Perl.*

Everything between the triple quotes is the function's doc string, which documents what the function does. A doc string, if it exists, must be the first thing defined in a function (that is, the first thing after the colon). You don't technically need to give your function a doc string, but you always should. I know you've heard this in every programming class you've ever taken, but Python gives you an added incentive: the doc string is available at runtime as an attribute of the function.

> **NOTE** *Many Python IDEs use the* doc *string to provide context-sensitive documentation, so that when you type a function name, its* doc *string appears as a tooltip. This can be incredibly helpful, but it's only as good as the* doc *strings you write.*

Further Reading on Documentation

Refer to the following for more information about doc strings:

- PEP 257 (http://www.python.org/peps/pep-0257.html) defines doc string conventions.

- *Python Style Guide* (http://www.python.org/doc/essays/styleguide.html) discusses how to write a good doc string.

- *Python Tutorial* (http://www.python.org/doc/current/tut/tut.html) discusses conventions for spacing in doc strings (http://www.python.org/doc/current/tut/node6.html#SECTION006750000000000000000).

Everything Is an Object

In case you missed it, I just said that Python functions have attributes, and that those attributes are available at runtime.

A function, like everything else in Python, is an object.

Open your favorite Python IDE and follow along with the example presented in Listing 2-3.

Listing 2-3. Accessing the buildConnectionString Function's doc string

```
>>> import odbchelper                              (1)
>>> params = {"server":"mpilgrim", "database":"master", "uid":"sa",
"pwd":"secret"}
>>> print odbchelper.buildConnectionString(params)    (2)
server=mpilgrim;uid=sa;database=master;pwd=secret
>>> print odbchelper.buildConnectionString.__doc__    (3)
Build a connection string from a dictionary

Returns string.
```

(1) The first line imports the odbchelper program as a module—a chunk of code that you can use interactively or from a larger Python program. Once you import a module, you can reference any of its public functions, classes, or attributes. Modules can do this to access functionality in other modules, and you can do it in the IDE, too. This is an important concept, and we'll talk more about it in Chapter 4.

(2) When you want to use functions defined in imported modules, you need to include the module name. So, you can't just say buildConnectionString; it must be odbchelper.buildConnectionString. If you've used classes in Java, this should feel vaguely familiar.

(3) Instead of calling the function as you would expect to, you asked for one of the function's attributes: __doc__.

> **NOTE** *Python vs. Perl import:* import *in Python is like* require *in Perl. Once you* import *a Python module, you access its functions with* module.function. *Once you* require *a Perl module, you access its functions with* module::function.

The Import Search Path

Before we go any further, I want to briefly mention the library search path. Python looks in several places when you try to import a module. Specifically, it looks in all the directories defined in sys.path, as you can see in the example in Listing 2-4. This is just a list, and you can easily view it or modify it with standard list methods. (You'll learn more about lists in Chapter 3.)

Listing 2-4. Import Search Path

```
>>> import sys                    (1)
>>> sys.path                      (2)
['', '/usr/local/lib/python2.2', '/usr/local/lib/python2.2/plat-linux2',
'/usr/local/lib/python2.2/lib-dynload', '/usr/local/lib/python2.2/site-packages',
'/usr/local/lib/python2.2/site-packages/PIL',
'/usr/local/lib/python2.2/site-packages/piddle']
>>> sys                           (3)
<module 'sys' (built-in)>
>>> sys.path.append('/my/new/path')        (4)
```

(1) Importing the sys module makes all of its functions and attributes available.

(2) sys.path is a list of directory names that constitute the current search path. (Yours will look different, depending on your operating system, what version of Python you're running, and where it was originally installed.) Python will look through these directories (in this order) for a .py file matching the module name you're trying to import.

(3) Actually, I lied—the truth is more complicated than that, because not all modules are stored as .py files. Some, like the sys module, are built-in modules that are actually baked right into Python itself. Built-in modules behave just like regular modules, but their Python source code is not available, because they are not written in Python! (The sys module is written in C.)

(4) You can add a new directory to Python's search path at runtime by appending the directory name to sys.path, and then Python will look in that directory as well whenever you try to import a module. The effect lasts as long as Python is running. (We'll talk more about append and other list methods in Chapter 3.)

What's an Object?

Everything in Python is an object, and almost everything has attributes and methods. All functions have a built-in attribute __doc__, which returns the doc string defined in the function's source code. The sys module is an object that has (among other things) an attribute called path.

Still, this begs the question. What is an object? Different programming languages define *object* in different ways. In some languages, all objects must have attributes and methods; in others, all objects are subclassable. In Python, the definition is looser; some objects have neither attributes nor methods (more on this in Chapter 3), and not all objects are subclassable (more on this in Chapter 5). But everything is an object in the sense that it can be assigned to a variable or passed as an argument to a function (more on this in Chapter 4).

This is so important that I'm going to repeat it in case you missed it the first few times: Everything in Python is an object. Strings are objects. Lists are objects. Functions are objects. Even modules are objects.

Further Reading on Objects

For more information about Python objects, see the following:

- *Python Reference Manual* (http://www.python.org/doc/current/ref) explains exactly what it means to say that everything in Python is an object (http://www.python.org/doc/current/ref/objects.html), because some people are pedantic and like to discuss this sort of thing at great length.

- eff-bot (http://www.effbot.org/guides) summarizes Python objects (http://www.effbot.org/guides/python-objects.htm).

Indenting Code

Python functions have no explicit begin or end, and no curly braces to mark where the function code starts and stops. The only delimiter is a colon (:) and the indentation of the code itself, as shown in Listing 2-5.

Listing 2-5. Indenting the buildConnectionString Function

```
def buildConnectionString(params):
    """Build a connection string from a dictionary of parameters.

    Returns string."""
    return ";".join(["%s=%s" % (k, v) for k, v in params.items()])
```

Code blocks are defined by their indentation. By *code block*, I mean functions, if statements, for loops, while loops, and so forth. Indenting starts a block, and unindenting ends it. There are no explicit braces, brackets, or keywords. This means that whitespace is significant and must be consistent. In this example, the function code (including the doc string) is indented four spaces. It doesn't need to be four spaces; it just needs to be consistent. The first line that is not indented is outside the function.

Listing 2-6 shows an example of code indentation with if statements.

Listing 2-6. if Statements

```
def fib(n):                          (1)
    print 'n =', n                   (2)
    if n > 1:                        (3)
        return n * fib(n - 1)
    else:                            (4)
        print 'end of the line'
        return 1
```

(1) This is a function named fib that takes one argument, n. All the code within the function is indented.

(2) Printing to the screen is very easy in Python: just use a print statement. print statements can take any datatype, including strings, integers, and other native types like dictionaries and lists that you'll learn about in Chapter 3. You can even mix and match to print several items on one line by using a comma-separated list of values.

Each value is printed on the same line, separated by spaces (the commas don't print). So when `fib` is called with 5, this will print `n = 5`.

(3) `if` statements are a type of code block. If the `if` expression evaluates to true, the indented block is executed; otherwise, it falls to the `else` block.

(4) Of course, `if` and `else` blocks can contain multiple lines, as long as they are all indented the same amount. This `else` block has two lines of code in it. There is no other special syntax for multiline code blocks—just indent and get on with your life.

After some initial protests and several snide analogies to Fortran, you'll make peace with this and start seeing its benefits. One major benefit is that all Python programs look similar, since indentation is a language requirement and not a matter of style. This makes it easier to read and understand other people's Python code.

> **NOTE**   *Python vs. Java statement separation: Python uses carriage returns to separate statements, and a colon and indentation to separate code blocks. C++ and Java use semicolons to separate statements and curly braces to separate code blocks.*

Further Reading on Code Indentation

For more information about Python code indentation, see the following:

- *Python Reference Manual* (http://www.python.org/doc/current/ref) discusses cross-platform indentation issues and shows various indentation errors (http://www.python.org/doc/current/ref/indentation.html).

- *Python Style Guide* (http://www.python.org/doc/essays/styleguide.html) discusses good indentation style.

Testing Modules: The if __name__ Trick

Python modules are objects and have several useful attributes. You can use this to easily test your modules as you write them. Here's an example that uses the `if __name__` trick:

```
if __name__ == "__main__":
```

Some quick observations before we get to the good stuff. First, parentheses are not required around the `if` expression. Second, the `if` statement ends with a colon and is followed by indented code.

> **NOTE** *Python vs. C comparison and assignment: Like C, Python uses == for comparison and = for assignment. Unlike C, Python does not support in-line assignment, so there's no chance of accidentally assigning the value you thought you were comparing.*

So why is this particular `if` statement a trick? Modules are objects, and all modules have a built-in attribute __name__. A module's __name__ depends on how you're using the module. If you `import` the module, then __name__ is the module's filename, without a directory path or file extension. But you can also run the module directly as a stand-alone program, in which case __name__ will be a special default value, __main__.

```
>>> import odbchelper
>>> odbchelper.__name__
'odbchelper'
```

Knowing this, you can design a test suite for your module within the module itself by putting it in this `if` statement. When you run the module directly, __name__ is __main__, so the test suite executes. When you import the module, __name__ is something else, so the test suite is ignored. This makes it easier to develop and debug new modules before integrating them into a larger program.

> **TIP** *if __name__ on Mac OS: On MacPython, there is an additional step to make the* `if __name__` *trick work. Pop up the module's options menu by clicking the black triangle in the upper-right corner of the window, and make sure* `Run as __main__` *is checked.*

Further Reading on Importing Modules

See the following for more information about importing modules:

- *Python Reference Manual* (http://www.python.org/doc/current/ref) discusses the low-level details of importing modules (http://www.python.org/doc/current/ref/import.html).

Summary

Some of the odbchelper.py you saw at the beginning of this chapter should make more sense to you now. You should recognize Python functions. You know that everything in Python is an object. The next chapter will explain the other parts of this sample program.

CHAPTER 3

Native Datatypes

WE'LL GET BACK TO your first Python program (from the previous chapter) in just a minute. But first, a short digression is in order, because you need to know about dictionaries, tuples, and lists (oh my!). If you're a Perl hacker, you can probably skim the bits about dictionaries and lists, but you should still pay attention to the information about tuples.

Introducing Dictionaries

One of Python's built-in datatypes is the dictionary, which defines one-to-one relationships between keys and values.

> **NOTE** *Python vs. Perl dictionaries:* A dictionary in Python is like a hash in Perl. In Perl, variables that store hashes always start with a % character. In Python, variables can be named anything, and Python keeps track of the datatype internally.

> **NOTE** *Python vs. Java dictionaries:* A dictionary in Python is like an instance of the Hashtable class in Java.

> **NOTE** *Python vs. Visual Basic dictionaries:* A dictionary in Python is like an instance of the Scripting.Dictionary object in Visual Basic.

Defining Dictionaries

Listing 3-1 shows an example of a dictionary definition.

Listing 3-1. Defining a Dictionary

```
>>> d = {"server":"mpilgrim", "database":"master"}     (1)
>>> d
{'server': 'mpilgrim', 'database': 'master'}
>>> d["server"]                                         (2)
'mpilgrim'
```

23

```
>>> d["database"]                              (3)
'master'
>>> d["mpilgrim"]                              (4)
Traceback (innermost last):
  File "<interactive input>", line 1, in ?
KeyError: mpilgrim
```

(1) First, you create a new dictionary with two elements and assign it to the variable d. Each element is a key/value pair, and the whole set of elements is enclosed in curly braces.

(2) 'server' is a key, and its associated value, referenced by d["server"], is 'mpilgrim'.

(3) 'database' is a key, and its associated value, referenced by d["database"], is 'master'.

(4) You can get values by key, but you can't get keys by value. So d["server"] is 'mpilgrim', but d["mpilgrim"] raises an exception, because 'mpilgrim' is not a key.

Modifying Dictionaries

Listing 3-2 shows an example of modifying a dictionary.

Listing 3-2. Modifying a Dictionary

```
>>> d
{'server': 'mpilgrim', 'database': 'master'}
>>> d["database"] = "pubs"                     (1)
>>> d
{'server': 'mpilgrim', 'database': 'pubs'}
>>> d["uid"] = "sa"                            (2)
>>> d
{'server': 'mpilgrim', 'uid': 'sa', 'database': 'pubs'}
```

(1) You cannot have duplicate keys in a dictionary. Assigning a value to an existing key will wipe out the old value.

(2) You can add new key/value pairs at any time. This syntax is identical to modifying existing values. (Yes, this will annoy you someday when you think you're adding new values but are actually just modifying the same value over and over, because your key isn't changing the way you think it is.)

Notice that the new element (key 'uid', value 'sa') appears to be in the middle. In fact, it was just a coincidence that the elements appeared to be in order in the first example; it is just as much a coincidence that they appear to be out of order now.

> **NOTE** *Dictionaries are unordered. Dictionaries have no concept of order among elements. It is incorrect to say that the elements are "out of order"; they are simply unordered. This is an important distinction that will annoy you when you want to access the elements of a dictionary in a specific, repeatable order (like alphabetical order by key). There are ways of doing this, but they're not built into the dictionary.*

When working with dictionaries, you need to be aware that dictionary keys are case-sensitive, as demonstrated in Listing 3-3.

Listing 3-3. Dictionary Keys Are Case-Sensitive

```
>>> d = {}
>>> d["key"] = "value"
>>> d["key"] = "other value" (1)
>>> d
{'key': 'other value'}
>>> d["Key"] = "third value" (2)
>>> d
{'Key': 'third value', 'key': 'other value'}
```

(1) Assigning a value to an existing dictionary key simply replaces the old value with a new one.

(2) This is not assigning a value to an existing dictionary key, because strings in Python are case-sensitive, so 'key' is not the same as 'Key'. This creates a new key/value pair in the dictionary. It may look similar to you, but as far as Python is concerned, it's completely different.

Mixing Datatypes in Dictionaries

Listing 3-4 shows an example of mixing datatypes in a dictionary.

Listing 3-4. Mixing Datatypes in a Dictionary

```
>>> d
{'server': 'mpilgrim', 'uid': 'sa', 'database': 'pubs'}
>>> d["retrycount"] = 3                          (1)
>>> d
{'server': 'mpilgrim', 'uid': 'sa', 'database': 'master', 'retrycount': 3}
>>> d[42] = "douglas"                            (2)
>>> d
{'server': 'mpilgrim', 'uid': 'sa', 'database': 'master',
42: 'douglas', 'retrycount': 3}
```

(1) Dictionaries aren't just for strings. Dictionary values can be any datatype, including strings, integers, objects, or even other dictionaries. And within a single dictionary, the values don't all need to be the same type; you can mix and match as needed.

(2) Dictionary keys are more restricted, but they can be strings, integers, and a few other types. You can also mix and match key datatypes within a dictionary.

Deleting Items from Dictionaries

Listing 3-5 shows an example of deleting items from a dictionary.

Listing 3-5. Deleting Items from a Dictionary

```
>>> d
{'server': 'mpilgrim', 'uid': 'sa', 'database': 'master',
42: 'douglas', 'retrycount': 3}
>>> del d[42]                                    (1)
>>> d
{'server': 'mpilgrim', 'uid': 'sa', 'database': 'master', 'retrycount': 3}
>>> d.clear()                                    (2)
>>> d
{}
```

(1) `del` lets you delete individual items from a dictionary by key.

(2) `clear` deletes all items from a dictionary. Note that the set of empty curly braces signifies a dictionary without any items.

Further Reading on Dictionaries

For more information about Python dictionaries, see the following:

- *How to Think Like a Computer Scientist* (`http://www.ibiblio.org/obp/thinkCSpy`) provides information about dictionaries and shows how to use dictionaries to model sparse matrices (`http://www.ibiblio.org/obp/thinkCSpy/chap10.htm`).

- Python Knowledge Base (`http://www.faqts.com/knowledge-base/index.phtml/fid/199`) has a lot of sample code using dictionaries (`http://www.faqts.com/knowledge-base/index.phtml/fid/541`).

- Python Cookbook (`http://www.activestate.com/ASPN/Python/Cookbook`) discusses how to sort the values of a dictionary by key (`http://www.activestate.com/ASPN/Python/Cookbook/Recipe/52306`).

- *Python Library Reference* (`http://www.python.org/doc/current/lib`) summarizes all the dictionary methods (`http://www.python.org/doc/current/lib/typesmapping.html`).

Introducing Lists

Lists are Python's workhorse datatype. If your only experience with lists is arrays in Visual Basic or (God forbid) the datastore in Powerbuilder, brace yourself for Python lists.

> **NOTE** *Python vs. Perl lists: A list in Python is like an array in Perl. In Perl, variables that store arrays always start with the @ character. In Python, variables can be named anything, and Python keeps track of the datatype internally.*

> **NOTE** *Python vs. Java lists: A list in Python is much more than an array in Java (although it can be used as one if that's really all you want out of life). A better analogy would be to the ArrayList class, which can hold arbitrary objects and can expand dynamically as new items are added.*

Defining Lists

Listing 3-6 shows an example of a list definition.

Listing 3-6. Defining a List

```
>>> li = ["a", "b", "mpilgrim", "z", "example"]     (1)
>>> li
['a', 'b', 'mpilgrim', 'z', 'example']
>>> li[0]                                            (2)
'a'
>>> li[4]                                            (3)
'example'
```

(1) First, you define a list of five elements. Note that they retain their original order. This is not an accident. A list is an ordered set of elements enclosed in square brackets.

(2) A list can be used like a zero-based array. The first element of any nonempty list is always li[0].

(3) The last element of this five-element list is li[4], because lists are always zero-based.

Listing 3-7 shows examples of negative indices.

Listing 3-7. Negative List Indices

```
>>> li
['a', 'b', 'mpilgrim', 'z', 'example']
>>> li[-1]                                    (1)
'example'
>>> li[-3]                                    (2)
'mpilgrim'
```

(1) A negative index accesses elements from the end of the list counting backwards. The last element of any nonempty list is always li[-1].

(2) If the negative index is confusing to you, think of it this way: li[-n] == li[len(li) - n]. So in this list, li[-3] == li[5 - 3] == li[2].

Getting a List Subset: Slicing

Listing 3-8 shows an example of slicing a list.

Listing 3-8. Slicing a List

```
>>> li
['a', 'b', 'mpilgrim', 'z', 'example']
>>> li[1:3]                                   (1)
['b', 'mpilgrim']
>>> li[1:-1]                                  (2)
['b', 'mpilgrim', 'z']
>>> li[0:3]                                   (3)
['a', 'b', 'mpilgrim']
```

(1) You can get a subset of a list, called a *slice*, by specifying two indices. The return value is a new list containing all the elements of the list, in order, starting with the first slice index (in this case li[1]), up to but not including the second slice index (in this case li[3]).

(2) Slicing works if one or both of the slice indices is negative. If it helps, you can think of it this way: reading the list from left to right, the first slice index specifies the first element you want, and the second slice index specifies the first element you don't want. The return value is everything in between.

(3) Lists are zero-based, so li[0:3] returns the first three elements of the list, starting at li[0], up to but not including li[3].

You can use some slicing shorthand, as shown in Listing 3-9.

Listing 3-9. Slicing Shorthand

```
>>> li
['a', 'b', 'mpilgrim', 'z', 'example']
>>> li[:3]                                    (1)
['a', 'b', 'mpilgrim']
>>> li[3:]                                    (2) (3)
['z', 'example']
>>> li[:]                                     (4)
['a', 'b', 'mpilgrim', 'z', 'example']
```

(1) If the left slice index is 0, you can leave it out, and 0 is implied. So li[:3] is the same as li[0:3] in Listing 3-8.

(2) Similarly, if the right slice index is the length of the list, you can leave it out. So li[3:] is the same as li[3:5], because this list has five elements.

(3) Note the symmetry here. In this five-element list, li[:3] returns the first three elements, and li[3:] returns the last two elements. In fact, li[:*n*] will always return the first *n* elements, and li[*n*:] will return the rest, regardless of the length of the list.

(4) If both slice indices are left out, all elements of the list are included. But this is not the same as the original li list; it is a new list that happens to have all the same elements. li[:] is shorthand for making a complete copy of a list.

Adding Elements to Lists

Listing 3-10 demonstrates adding elements to a list.

Listing 3-10. Adding Elements to a List

```
>>> li
['a', 'b', 'mpilgrim', 'z', 'example']
>>> li.append("new")                              (1)
>>> li
['a', 'b', 'mpilgrim', 'z', 'example', 'new']
>>> li.insert(2, "new")                           (2)
>>> li

('a', 'b', 'new', 'mpilgrim', 'z', 'example', 'new']
>>> li.extend(["two", "elements"])                (3)
>>> li
['a',* 'b', 'new', 'mpilgrim', 'z', 'example', 'new', 'two', 'elements']
```

(1) append adds a single element to the end of the list.

(2) insert inserts a single element into a list. The numeric argument is the index of the first element that gets bumped out of position. Note that list elements do not need to be unique; there are now two separate elements with the value 'new': li[2] and li[6].

(3) extend concatenates lists. Note that you do not call extend with multiple arguments; you call it with one argument: a list. In this case, that list has two elements.

Listing 3-11 shows the difference between extend and append.

Listing 3-11. The Difference Between Extend and Append

```
>>> li = ['a', 'b', 'c']
>>> li.extend(['d', 'e', 'f'])                    (1)
>>> li
['a', 'b', 'c', 'd', 'e', 'f']
>>> len(li)                                       (2)
6
>>> li[-1]
'f'
>>> li = ['a', 'b', 'c']
>>> li.append(['d', 'e', 'f'])                    (3)
>>> li
['a', 'b', 'c', ['d', 'e', 'f']]
>>> len(li)                                       (4)
4
>>> li[-1]
['d', 'e', 'f']
```

(1) Lists have two methods, extend and append, that look like they do the same thing, but are actually completely different. extend takes a single argument, which is always a list, and adds each of the elements of that list to the original list.

(2) Here, you started with a list of three elements ('a', 'b', and 'c'), and you extended the list with a list of another three elements ('d', 'e', and 'f'), so you now have a list of six elements.

(3) On the other hand, append takes one argument, which can be any datatype, and simply adds it to the end of the list. Here, you're calling the append method with a single argument, which is a list of three elements.

(4) Now your original list, which started as a list of three elements, contains four elements. Why four? Because the last element that you just appended *is itself a list*. Lists can contain any type of data, including other lists. That may be what you want, or maybe not. Don't use append if you mean extend.

Searching Lists

Listing 3-12 shows how to search a list.

Listing 3-12. Searching a List

```
>>> li
['a', 'b', 'new', 'mpilgrim', 'z', 'example', 'new', 'two', 'elements']
>>> li.index("example")                        (1)
5
>>> li.index("new")                            (2)
2
>>> li.index("c")                              (3)
Traceback (innermost last):
  File "<interactive input>", line 1, in ?
ValueError: list.index(x): x not in list
>>> "c" in li                                  (4)
False
```

(1) index finds the *first* occurrence of a value in the list and returns the index.

(2) index finds the first occurrence of a value in the list. In this case, 'new' occurs twice in the list, in li[2] and li[6], but index will return only the first index, 2.

(3) If the value is not found in the list, Python raises an exception. This is notably different from most languages, which will return some invalid index. While this may seem annoying, it is a good thing, because it means your program will crash at the source of the problem, rather than later on when you try to use the invalid index.

(4) To test whether a value is in the list, use in, which returns True if the value is found or False if it is not.

What's True in Python?

Before version 2.2.1, Python had no separate boolean datatype. To compensate for this, Python accepted almost anything in a boolean context (like an if statement), according to the following rules:

- 0 is false; all other numbers are true.

- An empty string ("") is false, all other strings are true.

- An empty list ([ ]) is false; all other lists are true.

- An empty tuple (()) is false; all other tuples are true.

- An empty dictionary ({}) is false; all other dictionaries are true.

These rules still apply in Python 2.2.1 and beyond, but now you can also use an actual boolean, which has a value of True or False. Notice the capitalization; these values, like everything else in Python, are case-sensitive.

Deleting List Elements

Listing 3-13 shows how to delete list elements.

Listing 3-13. Removing Elements from a List

```
>>> li
['a', 'b', 'new', 'mpilgrim', 'z', 'example', 'new', 'two', 'elements']
>>> li.remove("z")                                        (1)
>>> li
['a', 'b', 'new', 'mpilgrim', 'example', 'new', 'two', 'elements']
>>> li.remove("new")                                      (2)
>>> li
['a', 'b', 'mpilgrim', 'example', 'new', 'two', 'elements']
>>> li.remove("c")                                        (3)
Traceback (innermost last):
  File "<interactive input>", line 1, in ?
ValueError: list.remove(x): x not in list
>>> li.pop()                                              (4)
'elements'
>>> li
['a', 'b', 'mpilgrim', 'example', 'new', 'two']
```

(1) remove removes the first occurrence of a value from a list.

(2) remove removes *only* the first occurrence of a value. In this case, 'new' appeared twice in the list, but li.remove("new") removed only the first occurrence.

(3) If the value is not found in the list, Python raises an exception. This mirrors the behavior of the index method.

(4) pop is an interesting beast. It does two things: it removes the last element of the list, and it returns the value that it removed. Note that this is different from li[-1], which returns a value but does not change the list, and different from li.remove(*value*), which changes the list but does not return a value.

Using List Operators

Listing 3-14 demonstrates using list operators.

Listing 3-14. List Operators

```
>>> li = ['a', 'b', 'mpilgrim']
>>> li = li + ['example', 'new']          (1)
>>> li
['a', 'b', 'mpilgrim', 'example', 'new']
>>> li += ['two']                         (2)
>>> li
['a', 'b', 'mpilgrim', 'example', 'new', 'two']
>>> li = [1, 2] * 3                        (3)
>>> li
[1, 2, 1, 2, 1, 2]
```

(1) Lists can also be concatenated with the + operator. *list* = *list* + *otherlist* has the same result as *list*.extend(*otherlist*). But the + operator returns a new (concatenated) list as a value, whereas extend only alters an existing list. This means that extend is faster, especially for large lists.

(2) Python supports the += operator. li += ['two'] is equivalent to li.extend(['two']). The += operator works for lists, strings, and integers, and it can be overloaded to work for user-defined classes as well. (You'll find more on classes in Chapter 5.)

(3) The * operator works on lists as a repeater. li = [1, 2] * 3 is equivalent to li = [1, 2] + [1, 2] + [1, 2], which concatenates the three lists into one.

Further Reading on Lists

For more information about Python lists, refer to the following:

- *How to Think Like a Computer Scientist* (http://www.ibiblio.org/obp/thinkCSpy) provides information about lists and makes an important point about passing lists as function arguments (http://www.ibiblio.org/obp/thinkCSpy/chap08.htm).

- *Python Tutorial* (http://www.python.org/doc/current/tut/tut.html) shows how to use lists as stacks and queues (http://www.python.org/doc/current/tut/node7.html#SECTION007110000000000000000).

- Python Knowledge Base (http://www.faqts.com/knowledge-base/index.phtml/fid/199) answers common questions about lists (http://www.faqts.com/knowledge-base/index.phtml/fid/534) and has a lot of sample code using lists (http://www.faqts.com/knowledge-base/index.phtml/fid/540).

- *Python Library Reference* (http://www.python.org/doc/current/lib) summarizes all the list methods (http://www.python.org/doc/current/lib/typesseq-mutable.html).

Introducing Tuples

A tuple is an immutable list. A tuple cannot be changed in any way once it is created. Listing 3-15 shows an example of defining a tuple.

Listing 3-15. Defining a Tuple

```
>>> t = ("a", "b", "mpilgrim", "z", "example")      (1)
>>> t
('a', 'b', 'mpilgrim', 'z', 'example')
>>> t[0]                                             (2)
'a'
>>> t[-1]                                            (3)
'example'
>>> t[1:3]                                           (4)
('b', 'mpilgrim')
```

(1) A tuple is defined in the same way as a list, except that the whole set of elements is enclosed in parentheses instead of square brackets.

(2) The elements of a tuple have a defined order, just like a list. Tuples indices are zero-based, just like a list, so the first element of a nonempty tuple is always t[0].

(3) Negative indices count from the end of the tuple, just like a list.

(4) Slicing works, too, just as with a list. Note that when you slice a list, you get a new list; when you slice a tuple, you get a new tuple.

Listing 3-16 demonstrates that tuples cannot be changed after they have been created.

Listing 3-16. Tuples Have No Methods

```
>>> t
('a', 'b', 'mpilgrim', 'z', 'example')
>>> t.append("new")                                    (1)
Traceback (innermost last):
  File "<interactive input>", line 1, in ?
AttributeError: 'tuple' object has no attribute 'append'
>>> t.remove("z")                                      (2)
Traceback (innermost last):
  File "<interactive input>", line 1, in ?
AttributeError: 'tuple' object has no attribute 'remove'
>>> t.index("example")                                 (3)
Traceback (innermost last):
  File "<interactive input>", line 1, in ?
AttributeError: 'tuple' object has no attribute 'index'
>>> "z" in t                                           (4)
True
```

(1) You can't add elements to a tuple. Tuples have no append or extend method.

(2) You can't remove elements from a tuple. Tuples have no remove or pop method.

(3) You can't find elements in a tuple. Tuples have no index method.

(4) You can, however, use in to see if an element exists in the tuple.

So what are tuples good for?

Tuples are faster than lists. If you're defining a constant set of values and all you're ever going to do with it is iterate through it, use a tuple instead of a list.

It makes your code safer if you "write-protect" data that does not need to be changed. Using a tuple instead of a list is like having an implied assert statement that shows this data is constant, and that special thought (and a specific function) is required to override that.

Remember that I said that dictionary keys can be integers, strings, and "a few other types"? Tuples are one of those types. Tuples can be used as keys in a dictionary, but lists can't be used this way. Actually, it's more complicated than that. Dictionary keys must be immutable. Tuples themselves are immutable, but if you have a tuple of lists, that counts as mutable and isn't safe to use as a dictionary key. Only tuples of strings, numbers, or other dictionary-safe tuples can be used as dictionary keys.

Tuples are used in string formatting, as you'll see shortly.

> **NOTE** *Tuples can be converted into lists, and vice versa. The built-in* tuple *function takes a list and returns a tuple with the same elements, and the* list *function takes a tuple and returns a list. In effect,* tuple *freezes a list, and* list *thaws a tuple.*

Further Reading on Tuples

For more information about tuples, refer to the following:

- *How to Think Like a Computer Scientist* (http://www.ibiblio.org/obp/thinkCSpy) provides information about tuples and shows how to concatenate tuples (http://www.ibiblio.org/obp/thinkCSpy/chap10.htm).

- Python Knowledge Base (http://www.faqts.com/knowledge-base/index.phtml/ fid/199) shows how to sort a tuple (http://www.faqts.com/knowledge-base/ view.phtml/aid/4553/fid/587).

- *Python Tutorial* (http://www.python.org/doc/current/tut/tut.html) shows how to define a tuple with one element (http://www.python.org/doc/current/ tut/node7.html#SECTION007300000000000000000).

Declaring Variables

Now that you know something about dictionaries, tuples, and lists (oh my!), let's get back to our sample program from Chapter 2, odbchelper.py.

Python has local and global variables like most other languages, but it has no explicit variable declarations. Variables spring into existence by being assigned a value, and they are automatically destroyed when they go out of scope. Listing 3-17 demonstrates variable declaration.

Listing 3-17. Defining the myParams Variable

```
if __name__ == "__main__":
    myParams = {"server":"mpilgrim", \
                "database":"master", \
                "uid":"sa", \
                "pwd":"secret" \
                }
```

Notice the indentation. An if statement is a code block and needs to be indented just like a function.

Also notice that the variable assignment is one command split over several lines, with a backslash (\) serving as a line-continuation marker.

Writing Multiline Commands

When a command is split among several lines with the line-continuation marker (\), the continued lines can be indented in any manner; Python's normally stringent indentation rules do not apply. If your Python IDE auto-indents the continued line, you should probably accept its default, unless you have a burning reason not to use it.

Strictly speaking, expressions in parentheses, straight brackets, or curly braces (like `defining a dictionary`) can be split into multiple lines with or without the line-continuation character (\). I like to include the backslash even when it's not required, because I think it makes the code easier to read, but that's a matter of style.

Referencing Variables

You never declared the variable `myParams`; you just assigned a value to it. This is like VBScript without the `option explicit` option. Luckily, unlike VBScript, Python will not allow you to reference a variable that has never been assigned a value; trying to do so will raise an exception, as shown in Listing 3-18.

Listing 3-18. Referencing an Unbound Variable

```
>>> x
Traceback (innermost last):
  File "<interactive input>", line 1, in ?
NameError: There is no variable named 'x'
>>> x = 1
>>> x
1
```

You will thank Python for this one day.

Assigning Multiple Values at Once

One of the cooler programming shortcuts in Python is using sequences to assign multiple values at once, as shown in Listing 3-19.

Listing 3-19. Assigning Multiple Values at Once

```
>>> v = ('a', 'b', 'e')
>>> (x, y, z) = v                                    (1)
>>> x
'a'
```

```
>>> y
'b'
>>> z
'e'
```

(1) v is a tuple of three elements, and (x, y, z) is a tuple of three variables. Assigning one to the other assigns each of the values of v to each of the variables, in order.

This has all sorts of uses. I often want to assign names to a range of values. In C, you would use enum and manually list each constant and its associated value, which seems especially tedious when the values are consecutive. In Python, you can use the built-in range function with multivariable assignment to quickly assign consecutive values, as shown in Listing 3-20.

Listing 3-20. Assigning Consecutive Values

```
>>> range(7)                                                          (1)
[0, 1, 2, 3, 4, 5, 6]
>>> (MONDAY, TUESDAY, WEDNESDAY, THURSDAY, FRIDAY, SATURDAY, SUNDAY) = range(7) (2)
>>> MONDAY                                                            (3)
0
>>> TUESDAY
1
>>> SUNDAY
6
```

(1) The built-in range function returns a list of integers. In its simplest form, it takes an upper limit and returns a zero-based list counting up to but not including the upper limit. (If you like, you can pass other parameters to specify a base other than 0 and a step other than 1.) You can print range.__doc__ for details.)

(2) MONDAY, TUESDAY, WEDNESDAY, THURSDAY, FRIDAY, SATURDAY, and SUNDAY are the variables you're defining. (This example came from the calendar module, a fun little module that prints calendars, like the UNIX program cal. The calendar module defines integer constants for days of the week.)

(3) Now each variable has its value: MONDAY is 0, TUESDAY is 1, and so forth.

You can also use multivariable assignment to build functions that return multiple values, simply by returning a tuple of all the values. The caller can treat it as a tuple or assign the values to individual variables. Many standard Python libraries do this, including the os module, which we'll discuss in Chapter 6.

Further Reading on Variables

For more information about Python variables, refer to the following:

- *Python Reference Manual* (http://www.python.org/doc/current/ref) shows examples of when you can skip the line-continuation character (http://www.python.org/doc/current/ref/implicit-joining.html) and when you must use it (http://www.python.org/doc/current/ref/explicit-joining.html).

- *How to Think Like a Computer Scientist* (http://www.ibiblio.org/obp/thinkCSpy) shows how to use multivariable assignment to swap the values of two variables (http://www.ibiblio.org/obp/thinkCSpy/chap09.htm).

Formatting Strings

Python supports formatting values into strings, as shown in Listing 3-21. Although this can include very complicated expressions, the most basic usage is to insert values into a string with the %s placeholder.

> **NOTE** **Python vs. C string formatting:** *String formatting in Python uses the same syntax as the* sprintf *function in C.*

Listing 3-21. Introducing String Formatting

```
>>> k = "uid"
>>> v = "sa"
>>> "%s=%s" % (k, v)                          (1)
'uid=sa'
```

(1) The whole expression evaluates to a string. The first %s is replaced by the value of k; the second %s is replaced by the value of v. All other characters in the string (in this case, the equal sign) stay as they are.

Notice that (k, v) is a tuple. I told you they were good for something.

You might be thinking that this is a lot of work just to do simple string concatenation, and you would be right, except that string formatting isn't just concatenation, as demonstrated in Listing 3-22. It's not even just formatting. It's also type coercion.

Listing 3-22. String Formatting vs. Concatenating

```
>>> uid = "sa"
>>> pwd = "secret"
>>> print pwd + " is not a good password for " + uid          (1)
secret is not a good password for sa
>>> print "%s is not a good password for %s" % (pwd, uid)      (2)
secret is not a good password for sa
>>> userCount = 6
>>> print "Users connected: %d" % (userCount, )               (3) (4)
Users connected: 6
>>> print "Users connected: " + userCount                     (5)
Traceback (innermost last):
  File "<interactive input>", line 1, in ?
TypeError: cannot concatenate 'str' and 'int' objects
```

(1) + is the string concatenation operator.

(2) In this trivial case, string formatting accomplishes the same result as concatenation.

(3) (userCount,) is a tuple with one element. Yes, the syntax is a little strange, but there's a good reason for it: It's unambiguously a tuple. In fact, you can always include a comma after the last element when defining a list, tuple, or dictionary, but the comma is required when defining a tuple with one element. If the comma weren't required, Python wouldn't know whether (userCount) was a tuple with one element or just the value of userCount.

(4) String formatting works with integers by specifying %d instead of %s.

(5) Trying to concatenate a string with a nonstring raises an exception. Unlike string formatting, string concatenation works only when everything is already a string.

As with printf in C, string formatting in Python is like a Swiss Army knife. There are options galore, and modifier strings to specially format many different types of values, as shown in Listing 3-23.

Listing 3-23. Formatting Numbers

```
>>> print "Today's stock price: %f" % 50.4625       (1)
50.462500
>>> print "Today's stock price: %.2f" % 50.4625      (2)
50.46
>>> print "Change since yesterday: %+.2f" % 1.5      (3)
+1.50
```

(1) The `%f` string formatting option treats the value as a decimal and prints it to six decimal places.

(2) The `.2` modifier of the `%f` option truncates the value to two decimal places.

(3) You can even combine modifiers. Adding the `+` modifier displays a plus or minus sign before the value. Note that the `.2` modifier is still in place and is padding the value to exactly two decimal places.

Further Reading on String Formatting

For more information on string formatting, refer to the following:

- *Python Library Reference* (`http://www.python.org/doc/current/lib`) summarizes all the string formatting format characters (`http://www.python.org/doc/current/lib/typesseq-strings.html`).

- *Effective AWK Programming* (`http://www-gnats.gnu.org:8080/cgi-bin/info2www?(gawk)Top`) discusses all the format characters (`http://www-gnats.gnu.org:8080/cgi-bin/info2www?(gawk)Control+Letters`) and advanced string-formatting techniques such as specifying width, precision, and zero-padding (`http://www-gnats.gnu.org:8080/cgi-bin/info2www?(gawk)Format+Modifiers`).

Mapping Lists

One of the most powerful features of Python is the list comprehension, which provides a compact way of mapping a list into another list by applying a function to each of the elements of the list, as shown in Listing 3-24.

Listing 3-24. Introducing List Comprehensions

```
>>> li = [1, 9, 8, 4]
>>> [elem*2 for elem in li]          (1)
[2, 18, 16, 8]
>>> li                               (2)
[1, 9, 8, 4]
>>> li = [elem*2 for elem in li]     (3)
>>> li
[2, 18, 16, 8]
```

(1) To make sense of this, look at it from right to left. `li` is the list you're mapping. Python loops through `li` one element at a time, temporarily assigning the value of each element to the variable `elem`. Python then applies the function `elem*2` and appends that result to the returned list.

(2) Note that list comprehensions do not change the original list.

(3) It is safe to assign the result of a list comprehension to the variable that you're mapping. Python constructs the new list in memory, and when the list comprehension is complete, it assigns the result to the variable.

Here are the list comprehensions in the `buildConnectionString` function that we declared in Chapter 2.

```
["%s=%s" % (k, v) for k, v in params.items()]
```

Notice that you're calling the `items` function of the `params` dictionary. This function returns a list of tuples of all the data in the dictionary. Listing 3-25 demonstrates the `items` function, along with the `keys` and `values` functions.

Listing 3-25. The keys, values, and items Functions

```
>>> params = {"server":"mpilgrim", "database":"master", "uid":"sa", "pwd":"secret"}
>>> params.keys()                                    (1)
['server', 'uid', 'database', 'pwd']
>>> params.values()                                  (2)
['mpilgrim', 'sa', 'master', 'secret']
>>> params.items()                                   (3)
[('server', 'mpilgrim'), ('uid', 'sa'), ('database', 'master'), ('pwd', 'secret')]
```

(1) The `keys` method of a dictionary returns a list of all the keys. The list is not in the order in which the dictionary was defined (remember that elements in a dictionary are unordered), but it is a list.

(2) The `values` method returns a list of all the values. The list is in the same order as the list returned by `keys`, so `params.values()[n]` == `params[params.keys()[n]]` for all values of n.

(3) The `items` method returns a list of tuples of the form (`key, value`). The list contains all the data in the dictionary.

Now let's see what `buildConnectionString` does. As shown in Listing 3-26, it takes a list, `params.items()`, and maps it to a new list by applying string formatting to each element. The new list will have the same number of elements as `params.items()`, but each element in the new list will be a string that contains both a key and its associated value from the `params` dictionary.

Listing 3-26. List Comprehensions in buildConnectionString, Step by Step

```
>>> params = {"server":"mpilgrim", "database":"master", "uid":"sa", "pwd":"secret"}
>>> params.items()
```

```
[('server', 'mpilgrim'), ('uid', 'sa'), ('database', 'master'), ('pwd', 'secret')]
>>> [k for k, v in params.items()]                    (1)
['server', 'uid', 'database', 'pwd']
>>> [v for k, v in params.items()]                    (2)
['mpilgrim', 'sa', 'master', 'secret']
>>> ["%s=%s" % (k, v) for k, v in params.items()]      (3)
['server=mpilgrim', 'uid=sa', 'database=master', 'pwd=secret']
```

(1) Note that you're using two variables to iterate through the `params.items()` list. This is another use of multivariable assignment. The first element of `params.items()` is (`'server'`, `'mpilgrim'`), so in the first iteration of the list comprehension, k will get `'server'` and v will get `'mpilgrim'`. In this case, you're ignoring the value of v and including only the value of k in the returned list, so this list comprehension ends up being equivalent to `params.keys`.

(2) Here, you're doing the same thing, but ignoring the value of k, so this list comprehension ends up being equivalent to `params.values()`.

(3) Combining the previous two examples with some simple string formatting, you get a list of strings that include both the key and value of each element of the dictionary. This looks suspiciously like the output of the program. All that remains is to join the elements in this list into a single string.

Further Reading on List Comprehensions

For more information about list mapping, refer to the following:

- *Python Tutorial* (http://www.python.org/doc/current/tut/tut.html) discusses another way to map lists using the built-in map function (http://www.python.org/doc/current/tut/node7.html#SECTION007130000000000000000) and shows how to do nested list comprehensions (http://www.python.org/doc/current/tut/node7.html#SECTION007140000000000000000).

Joining Lists and Splitting Strings

Suppose that you have a list of key/value pairs in the form *key=value*, and you want to join them into a single string. To join any list of strings into a single string, use the join method of a string object.

Here is an example of joining a list from the buildConnectionString function:

```
return ";".join(["%s=%s" % (k, v) for k, v in params.items()])
```

One interesting note before we continue. I keep repeating that functions are objects, strings are objects... everything is an object. You might have thought I meant that string *variables* are objects. But no, look closely at this example. and you'll see that the string ";" itself is an object, and you are calling its `join` method.

The `join` method joins the elements of the list into a single string, with each element separated by a semicolon. The delimiter doesn't need to be a semicolon; it doesn't even need to be a single character. It can be any string.

> **CAUTION**   *You cannot join nonstrings.*

`join` works only on lists of strings; it does not do any type coercion. Joining a list that has one or more nonstring elements will raise an exception.

Listing 3-27 shows the string returned by the `odbchelper` function.

Listing 3-27. Output of odbchelper.py

```
>>> params = {"server":"mpilgrim", "database":"master", "uid":"sa", "pwd":"secret"}
>>> ["%s=%s" % (k, v) for k, v in params.items()]
['server=mpilgrim', 'uid=sa', 'database=master', 'pwd=secret']
>>> ";".join(["%s=%s" % (k, v) for k, v in params.items()])
'server=mpilgrim;uid=sa;database=master;pwd=secret'
```

This string is then returned from the `odbchelper` function and printed by the calling block, which gives you the output that you marveled at when you started reading this chapter.

Historical Note on String Methods

When I first learned Python, I expected `join` to be a method of a list, which would take the delimiter as an argument. Many people feel the same way, and there's a story behind the `join` method. Prior to Python 1.6, strings didn't have all these useful methods. There was a separate `string` module that contained all the string functions; each function took a string as its first argument. The functions were deemed important enough to put onto the strings themselves, which made sense for functions like `lower`, `upper`, and `split`. But many hard-core Python programmers objected to the new `join` method, arguing that it should be a method of the list instead, or that it shouldn't move at all but simply stay a part of the old `string` module (which still has a lot of useful stuff in it). I use the new `join` method exclusively, but you will see code written either way, and if it really bothers you, you can use the old `string.join` function instead.

You're probably wondering whether there's an analogous method to split a string into a list. And, of course, there is. It's called `split` and demonstrated in Listing 3-28.

Listing 3-28. Splitting a String

```
>>> li = ['server=mpilgrim', 'uid=sa', 'database=master', 'pwd=secret']
>>> s = ";".join(li)
>>> s
'server=mpilgrim;uid=sa;database=master;pwd=secret'
>>> s.split(";")                                          (1)
['server=mpilgrim', 'uid=sa', 'database=master', 'pwd=secret']
>>> s.split(";", 1)                                       (2)
['server=mpilgrim', 'uid=sa;database=master;pwd=secret']
```

(1) `split` reverses `join` by splitting a string into a multielement list. Note that the delimiter (;) is stripped out completely; it does not appear in any of the elements of the returned list.

(2) `split` takes an optional second argument, which is the number of times to split. (Ooooooh, optional arguments...) You'll learn how to do this in your own functions in the next chapter.

> **TIP** `anystring.split(delimiter, 1)` *is a useful technique when you want to search a string for a substring, and then work with everything before the substring (which ends up in the first element of the returned list) and everything after it (which ends up in the second element).*

Further Reading on String Methods

For more information about using strings, refer to the following:

- Python Knowledge Base (http://www.faqts.com/knowledge-base/index.phtml/ fid/199) answers common questions about strings (http://www.faqts.com/knowledge-base/index.phtml/fid/480) and has a lot of sample code using strings (http://www.faqts.com/knowledge-base/ index.phtml/fid/539).

- *Python Library Reference* (http://www.python.org/doc/current/lib) summarizes all the string methods (http://www.python.org/doc/current/ lib/string-methods.html) and documents the string module (http:// www.python.org/doc/current/lib/module-string.html).

- *The Whole Python FAQ* (http://www.python.org/doc/FAQ.html) explains why join is a string method (http://www.python.org/cgi-bin/ faqw.py?query=4.96&querytype=simple&casefold=yes&req=search) instead of a list method.

Summary

The odbchelper.py program from Chapter 2 and its output should now make perfect sense.

```
def buildConnectionString(params):
    """Build a connection string from a dictionary of parameters.

    Returns string."""
    return ";".join(["%s=%s" % (k, v) for k, v in params.items()])

if __name__ == "__main__":
    myParams = {"server":"mpilgrim", \
                "database":"master", \
                "uid":"sa", \
                "pwd":"secret" \
                }
    print buildConnectionString(myParams)
```

Here is the output of odbchelper.py:

```
server=mpilgrim;uid=sa;database=master;pwd=secret
```

Before diving into the next chapter, make sure you're comfortable doing all of these things:

- Using the Python IDE to test expressions interactively

- Writing Python programs and running them from within your IDE or from the command line

- Importing modules and calling their functions

- Declaring functions and using doc strings, local variables, and proper indentation

- Defining dictionaries, tuples, and lists

- Accessing attributes and methods of any object, including strings, lists, dictionaries, functions, and modules

- Concatenating values through string formatting

- Mapping lists into other lists using list comprehensions

- Splitting strings into lists and joining lists into strings

CHAPTER 4

The Power of Introspection

THIS CHAPTER COVERS ONE of Python's strengths: introspection. As you know, everything in Python is an object, and introspection is code looking at other modules and functions in memory as objects, getting information about them, and manipulating them. Along the way, you'll define functions with no name, call functions with arguments out of order, and reference functions whose names you don't even know ahead of time.

Diving In

Listing 4-1 is a complete, working Python program. You should understand a good deal about it just by looking at it. The numbered lines illustrate concepts covered in the previous chapters. Don't worry if the rest of the code looks intimidating; you'll learn all about it in this chapter.

> **NOTE** *You can download all of the examples presented in this book from the Downloads section of the Apress web site (*http://www.apress.com*).*

Listing 4-1. apihelper.py

```
def info(object, spacing=10, collapse=1):               (1) (2) (3)
    """Print methods and doc strings.

    Takes module, class, list, dictionary, or string."""
    methodList = [method for method in dir(object) if callable(getattr(object,
method))]
    processFunc = collapse and (lambda s: " ".join(s.split())) or (lambda s: s)
    print "\n".join(["%s %s" %
                     (method.ljust(spacing),
                      processFunc(str(getattr(object, method).__doc__)))
                     for method in methodList])

if __name__ == "__main__":                              (4) (5)
    print info.__doc__
```

(1) This module has one function, `info`. According to its function declaration, it takes three parameters: `object`, `spacing`, and `collapse`. The last two are actually optional parameters, as you'll see shortly.

(2) The `info` function has a multiline `doc` string that succinctly describes the function's purpose. Note that no return value is mentioned; this function will be used solely for its effects, rather than its value.

(3) Code within the function is indented.

(4) The `if __name__` trick allows this program do something useful when run by itself, without interfering with its use as a module for other programs. In this case, the program simply prints the `doc` string of the `info` function.

(5) `if` statements use `==` for comparison, and parentheses are not required.

The `info` function is designed to be used by you, the programmer, while working in the Python IDE. It takes any object that has functions or methods (like a module, which has functions, or a list, which has methods) and prints the functions and their `doc` strings. Listing 4-2 shows an example of using the info function.

Listing 4-2. Sample Use of apihelper.py

```
>>> from apihelper import info
>>> li = []
>>> info(li)
append      L.append(object) -- append object to end
count       L.count(value) -> integer -- return number of occurrences of value
extend      L.extend(list) -- extend list by appending list elements
index       L.index(value) -> integer -- return index of first occurrence of value
insert      L.insert(index, object) -- insert object before index
pop         L.pop([index]) -> item -- remove and return item at index (default last)
remove      L.remove(value) -- remove first occurrence of value
reverse     L.reverse() -- reverse *IN PLACE*
sort        L.sort([cmpfunc]) -- sort *IN PLACE*; if given, cmpfunc(x, y) -> -1, 0, 1
```

By default, the output is formatted to be easy to read. Multiline `doc` strings are collapsed into a single long line, but this option can be changed by specifying 0 for the *collapse* argument. If the function names are longer than ten characters, you can specify a larger value for the *spacing* argument to make the output easier to read, as demonstrated in Listing 4-3.

Listing 4-3. Advanced Use of apihelper.py

```
>>> import odbchelper
>>> info(odbchelper)
buildConnectionString Build a connection string from a dictionary Returns string.
>>> info(odbchelper, 30)
```

```
buildConnectionString          Build a connection string from a dictionary
Returns string.
>>> info(odbchelper, 30, 0)
buildConnectionString          Build a connection string from a dictionary

    Returns string.
```

Using Optional and Named Arguments

Python allows function arguments to have default values; if the function is called without the argument, the argument gets its default value. Futhermore, arguments can be specified in any order by using named arguments. Stored procedures in SQL Server Transact/SQL can do this, so if you're a SQL Server scripting guru, you can skim this part.

Here is an example of info, a function with two optional arguments:

```
def info(object, spacing=10, collapse=1):
```

spacing and collapse are optional, because they have default values defined. object is required, because it has no default value. If info is called with only one argument, spacing defaults to 10 and collapse defaults to 1. If info is called with two arguments, collapse still defaults to 1.

Say you want to specify a value for collapse but want to accept the default value for spacing. In most languages, you would be out of luck, because you would need to call the function with three arguments. But in Python, arguments can be specified by name, in any order, as shown in Listing 4-4.

Listing 4-4. Valid Calls of info

```
info(odbchelper)                        (1)
info(odbchelper, 12)                    (2)
info(odbchelper, collapse=0)            (3)
info(spacing=15, object=odbchelper)     (4)
```

(1) With only one argument, spacing gets its default value of 10 and collapse gets its default value of 1.

(2) With two arguments, collapse gets its default value of 1.

(3) Here, you are naming the collapse argument explicitly and specifying its value. spacing still gets its default value of 10.

(4) Even required arguments (like object, which has no default value) can be named, and named arguments can appear in any order.

This looks totally whacked until you realize that arguments are simply a dictionary. The "normal" method of calling functions without argument names is actually just a shorthand where Python matches up the values with the argument names in the order they're specified in the function declaration. And most of the time, you'll call functions the normal way, but you always have the additional flexibility if you need it.

> **NOTE** *The only thing you need to do to call a function is specify a value (somehow) for each required argument; the manner and order in which you do that is up to you.*

Further Reading on Optional Arguments

For more information about Python function arguments, refer to the following:

- *Python Tutorial* (http://www.python.org/doc/current/tut/tut.html) discusses exactly when and how default arguments are evaluated (http://www.python.org/doc/current/tut/node6.html#SECTION006710000000000000000), which matters when the default value is a list or an expression with side effects.

Using type, str, dir, and Other Built-in Functions

Python has a small set of extremely useful built-in functions. All other functions are partitioned off into modules. This was actually a conscious design decision, to keep the core language from getting bloated like other scripting languages (cough cough, Visual Basic).

The type Function

The type function, shown in Listing 4-5, returns the datatype of any arbitrary object. The possible types are listed in the types module. This is useful for helper functions that can handle several types of data.

Listing 4-5. Introducing type

```
>>> type(1)                                    (1)
<type 'int'>
>>> li = []
>>> type(li)                                   (2)
<type 'list'>
>>> import odbchelper
>>> type(odbchelper)                           (3)
```

```
<type 'module'>
>>> import types                                    (4)
>>> type(odbchelper) == types.ModuleType
True
```

(1) type takes anything—and I mean anything—and returns its datatype.
Integers, strings, lists, dictionaries, tuples, functions, classes, modules, and even
types are acceptable.

(2) type can take a variable and return its datatype.

(3) type also works on modules.

(4) You can use the constants in the types module to compare types of
objects. This is what the info function does, as you'll see shortly.

The str Function

The str function, shown in Listing 4-6, coerces data into a string. Every datatype
can be coerced into a string.

Listing 4-6. Introducing str

```
>>> str(1)                                          (1)
'1'
>>> horsemen = ['war', 'pestilence', 'famine']
>>> horsemen
['war', 'pestilence', 'famine']
>>> horsemen.append('Powerbuilder')
>>> str(horsemen)                                   (2)
"['war', 'pestilence', 'famine', 'Powerbuilder']"
>>> str(odbchelper)                                 (3)
"<module 'odbchelper' from 'c:\\docbook\\dip\\py\\odbchelper.py'>"
>>> str(None)                                       (4)
'None'
```

(1) For simple datatypes like integers, you would expect str to work, because
almost every language has a function to convert an integer to a string.

(2) However, str works on any object of any type. Here, it works on a list that
you've constructed in bits and pieces.

(3) str also works on modules. Note that the string representation of the module includes the pathname of the module on disk, so yours will be different.

(4) A subtle but important behavior of str is that it works on None, the Python
null value. It returns the string 'None'. We'll use this to our advantage in the info
function, as you'll see shortly.

The dir Function

At the heart of our info function is the powerful dir function, shown in Listing 4-7. dir returns a list of the attributes and methods of any object: modules, functions, strings, lists, dictionaries—pretty much anything.

Listing 4-7. Introducing dir

```
>>> li = []
>>> dir(li)                                    (1)
['append', 'count', 'extend', 'index', 'insert',
'pop', 'remove', 'reverse', 'sort']
>>> d = {}
>>> dir(d)                                     (2)
['clear', 'copy', 'get', 'has_key', 'items', 'keys',
'setdefault', 'update', 'values']
>>> import odbchelper
>>> dir(odbchelper)                            (3)
['__builtins__', '__doc__', '__file__', '__name__', 'buildConnectionString']
```

(1) li is a list, so dir(li) returns a list of all the methods of a list. Note that the returned list contains the names of the methods as strings, not the methods themselves.

(2) d is a dictionary, so dir(d) returns a list of the names of dictionary methods. At least one of these, keys, should look familiar.

(3) This is where it really gets interesting. odbchelper is a module, so dir(odbchelper) returns a list of all kinds of stuff defined in the module, including built-in attributes, like __name__, __doc__, and whatever other attributes and methods you define. In this case, odbchelper has only one user-defined method, the buildConnectionString function described in Chapters 2 and 3.

The callable Function

The callable function, shown in Listing 4-8, takes any object and returns True if the object can be called or False otherwise. Callable objects include functions, class methods, and even classes themselves. (You'll find more on classes in Chapter 5.)

Listing 4-8. Introducing callable

```
>>> import string
>>> string.punctuation                              (1)
'!"#$%&\'()*+,-./:;<=>?@[\\]^_`{|}~'
>>> string.join                                     (2)
<function join at 00C55A7C>
>>> callable(string.punctuation)                    (3)
False
>>> callable(string.join)                           (4)
True
>>> print string.join.__doc__                       (5)
join(list [,sep]) -> string

    Return a string composed of the words in list, with
    intervening occurrences of sep.  The default separator is a
    single space.

    (joinfields and join are synonymous)
```

(1) The functions in the string module are deprecated (although many people still use the join function), but the module contains a lot of useful constants like this string.punctuation, which contains all the standard punctuation characters.

(2) string.join is a function that joins a list of strings.

(3) string.punctuation is not callable; it is a string. (A string does have callable methods, but the string itself is not callable.)

(4) string.join is callable; it's a function that takes two arguments.

(5) Any callable object may have a doc string. By using the callable function on each of an object's attributes, you can determine which attributes you care about (methods, functions, and classes) and which you want to ignore (constants and so on) without knowing anything about the object ahead of time.

The __builtin__ Module

type, str, dir, and all the rest of Python's built-in functions are grouped into a special module called __builtin__. (That's two underscores before and after.)

If it helps, you can think of Python automatically executing from __builtin__ import * on startup, which imports all the "built-in" functions into the namespace so you can use them directly. The advantage of thinking like this is that you can access all the built-in functions and attributes as a group by getting information about the __builtin__ module. And guess what, Python has a function for that: info. Try it yourself as shown in Listing 4-9, and skim through the list now. We'll dive into some of the more important functions later. (Some of the built-in error classes, like AttributeError, should already look familiar.)

Listing 4-9. Built-in Attributes and Functions

```
>>> from apihelper import info
>>> import __builtin__
>>> info(__builtin__, 20)
ArithmeticError     Base class for arithmetic errors.
AssertionError      Assertion failed.
AttributeError      Attribute not found.
EOFError            Read beyond end of file.
EnvironmentError    Base class for I/O related errors.
Exception           Common base class for all exceptions.
FloatingPointError  Floating point operation failed.
IOError             I/O operation failed.

[...snip...]
```

> **NOTE** *Python comes with excellent reference manuals, which you should peruse thoroughly to learn about all the modules Python has to offer. But unlike with most languages, for which you would find yourself referring back to the manuals or man pages to remind yourself how to use these modules, Python is largely self-documenting.*

Further Reading on Built-in Functions

For more information about Python's built-in functions, refer to the following:

- *Python Library Reference* (http://www.python.org/doc/current/lib) documents all the built-in functions (http://www.python.org/doc/current/lib/built-in-funcs.html) and all the built-in exceptions (http://www.python.org/doc/current/lib/module-exceptions.html).

Getting Object References with getattr

You already know that Python functions are objects. What you don't know is that you can get a reference to a function without knowing its name until runtime by using the getattr function, as shown in Listing 4-10.

Listing 4-10. Introducing getattr

```
>>> li = ["Larry", "Curly"]
>>> li.pop                                        (1)
<built-in method pop of list object at 010DF884>
```

```
>>> getattr(li, "pop")                            (2)
<built-in method pop of list object at 010DF884>
>>> getattr(li, "append")("Moe")                  (3)
>>> li
["Larry", "Curly", "Moe"]
>>> getattr({}, "clear")                          (4)
<built-in method clear of dictionary object at 00F113D4>
>>> getattr((), "pop")                            (5)
Traceback (innermost last):
  File "<interactive input>", line 1, in ?
AttributeError: 'tuple' object has no attribute 'pop'
```

(1) This gets a reference to the pop method of the list. Note that this is not calling the pop method; that would be li.pop(). This is the method itself.

(2) This also returns a reference to the pop method, but this time, the method name is specified as a string argument to the getattr function. getattr is an incredibly useful built-in function that returns any attribute of any object. In this case, the object is a list and the attribute is the pop method.

(3) In case it hasn't sunk in just how incredibly useful this is, try this: the return value of getattr *is* the method, which you can then call just as if you had said li.append("Moe") directly. But you didn't call the function directly; you specified the function name as a string instead.

(4) getattr also works on dictionaries.

(5) In theory, getattr would work on tuples, except that tuples have no methods, so getattr will raise an exception no matter what attribute name you give.

getattr with Modules

getattr isn't just for built-in datatypes. It also works on modules, as demonstrated in Listing 4-11.

Listing 4-11. getattr in apihelper.py

```
>>> import odbchelper
>>> odbchelper.buildConnectionString             (1)
<function buildConnectionString at 00D18DD4>
>>> getattr(odbchelper, "buildConnectionString")  (2)
<function buildConnectionString at 00D18DD4>
>>> object = odbchelper
>>> method = "buildConnectionString"
>>> getattr(object, method)                       (3)
<function buildConnectionString at 00D18DD4>
>>> type(getattr(object, method))                 (4)
<type 'function'>
```

```
>>> import types
>>> type(getattr(object, method)) == types.FunctionType
True
>>> callable(getattr(object, method))                       (5)
True
```

(1) This returns a reference to the buildConnectionString function in the odbchelper module, which you studied in Chapters 2 and 3. (The hex address you see is specific to my machine; your output will be different.)

(2) Using getattr, you can get the same reference to the same function. In general, getattr(*object*, *"attribute"*) is equivalent to *object.attribute*. If *object* is a module, then *attribute* can be anything defined in the module: a function, class, or global variable.

(3) And this is what you actually use in the info function. object is passed into the function as an argument; method is a string that is the name of a method or function.

(4) In this case, method is the name of a function, which you can prove by getting its type.

(5) Since method is a function, it is callable.

getattr As a Dispatcher

A common usage pattern of getattr is as a dispatcher. For example, if you had a program that could output data in a variety of different formats, you could define separate functions for each output format and use a single dispatch function to call the right one.

For example, let's imagine a program that prints site statistics in HTML, XML, and plain text formats. The choice of output format could be specified on the command line or stored in a configuration file. A statsout module defines three functions: output_html, output_xml, and output_text. Then the main program defines a single output function, as shown in Listing 4-12.

Listing 4-12. Creating a Dispatcher with getattr

```
import statsout

def output(data, format="text"):                              (1)
    output_function = getattr(statsout, "output_%s" % format) (2)
    return output_function(data)                              (3)
```

(1) The output function takes one required argument, data, and one optional argument, format. If format is not specified, it defaults to text, and you'll end up calling the plain text output function.

(2) You concatenate the `format` argument with `"output_"` to produce a function name, and then go get that function from the `statsout` module. This allows you to easily extend the program later to support other output formats, without changing this dispatch function. Just add another function to `statsout` named, for instance, `output_pdf`, and pass `"pdf"` as the `format` into the `output` function.

(3) Now you can simply call the `output` function in the same way as any other function. The `output_function` variable is a reference to the appropriate function from the `statsout` module.

Did you see the bug in the previous example? This is a very loose coupling of strings and functions, and there is no error checking. What happens if the user passes in a format that doesn't have a corresponding function defined in `statsout`? Well, `getattr` will return `None`, which will be assigned to `output_function` instead of a valid function, and the next line that attempts to call that function will crash and raise an exception. That's bad.

Luckily, `getattr` takes an optional third argument, a default value, as demonstrated in Listing 4-13.

Listing 4-13. getattr Default Values

```
import statsout

def output(data, format="text"):
    output_function = getattr(statsout, "output_%s" % format,
statsout.output_text)
    return output_function(data)                              (1)
```

(1) This function call is guaranteed to work, because you added a third argument to your call to `getattr`. The third argument is a default value that is returned if the attribute or method specified by the second argument wasn't found.

As you can see, `getattr` is quite powerful. It's the heart of introspection, and you'll see even more powerful examples of it in later chapters.

Filtering Lists

As you know, Python has powerful capabilities for mapping lists into other lists, via list comprehensions (discussed in Chapter 3). This can be combined with a filtering mechanism, where some elements in the list are mapped while others are skipped entirely. Here is the list filtering sytax:

```
[mapping-expression for element in source-list if filter-expression]
```

This is an extension of the list comprehensions that you know and love. The first two-thirds are the same; the last part, starting with the `if`, is the filter expression. A filter expression can be any expression that evaluates true or false (which in Python can be almost anything). Any element for which the filter expression evaluates true will be included in the mapping. All other elements are ignored, so they are never put through the mapping expression and are not included in the output list. Listing 4-14 demonstrates list filtering.

Listing 4-14. Introducing List Filtering

```
>>> li = ["a", "mpilgrim", "foo", "b", "c", "b", "d", "d"]
>>> [elem for elem in li if len(elem) > 1]            (1)
['mpilgrim', 'foo']
>>> [elem for elem in li if elem != "b"]              (2)
['a', 'mpilgrim', 'foo', 'c', 'd', 'd']
>>> [elem for elem in li if li.count(elem) == 1]      (3)
['a', 'mpilgrim', 'foo', 'c']
```

(1) The mapping expression here is simple (it just returns the value of each element), so concentrate on the filter expression. As Python loops through the list, it runs each element through the filter expression. If the filter expression is true, the element is mapped and the result of the mapping expression is included in the returned list. Here, you are filtering out all the one-character strings, so you're left with a list of all the longer strings.

(2) Here, you are filtering out a specific value, b. Note that this filters all occurrences of b, since each time it comes up, the filter expression will be false.

(3) count is a list method that returns the number of times a value occurs in a list. You might think that this filter would eliminate duplicates from a list, returning a list containing only one copy of each value in the original list. But it doesn't, because values that appear twice in the original list (in this case, b and d) are excluded completely. There are ways of eliminating duplicates from a list, but filtering is not the solution.

Now let's get back to this line from apihelper.py:

```
methodList = [method for method in dir(object) if callable(getattr(object, method))]
```

This looks complicated, and it is complicated, but the basic structure is the same. The whole filter expression returns a list, which is assigned to the methodList variable. The first half of the expression is the list mapping part. The mapping expression is an identity expression, which returns the value of each element. dir(object) returns a list of object's attributes and methods—that's the list you're mapping. So the only new part is the filter expression after the if.

The filter expression looks scary, but it's not. You already know about callable, getattr, and in. As you saw in the previous section, the expression getattr(object, method) returns a function object if object is a module and method is the name of a function in that module.

So this expression takes an object (named `object`). Then it gets a list of the names of the object's attributes, methods, functions, and a few other things. Then it filters that list to weed out all the stuff that you don't care about. You do the weeding out by taking the name of each attribute/method/function and getting a reference to the real thing, via the `getattr` function. Then you check to see if that object is callable, which will be any methods and functions, both built-in (like the `pop` method of a list) and user-defined (like the `buildConnectionString` function of the `odbchelper` module). You don't care about other attributes, like the `__name__` attribute that's built into every module.

Further Reading on Filtering Lists

For more information about list filtering in Python, refer to the following:

- *Python Tutorial* (`http://www.python.org/doc/current/tut/tut.html`) discusses another way to filter lists using the built-in `filter` function (`http://www.python.org/doc/current/tut/node7.html#SECTION007130000000000000000`).

Understanding the Peculiar Nature of *and* and *or*

In Python, `and` and `or` perform boolean logic as you would expect, but they do not return boolean values; instead, they return one of the actual values they are comparing. Listing 4-15 shows the use of `and`.

Listing 4-15. Introducing and

```
>>> 'a' and 'b'                          (1)
'b'
>>> '' and 'b'                           (2)
''
>>> 'a' and 'b' and 'c'                   (3)
'c'
```

(1) When using `and`, values are evaluated in a boolean context from left to right. 0, `''`, `[]`, `()`, `{}`, and `None` are false in a boolean context; everything else is true. Well, almost everything. By default, instances of classes are true in a boolean context, but you can define special methods in your class to make an instance evaluate to false. You'll learn all about classes and special methods in Chapter 5. If all values are true in a boolean context, `and` returns the last value. In this case, `and` evaluates `'a'`, which is true, then `'b'`, which is true, and returns `'b'`.

(2) If any value is false in a boolean context, and returns the first false value. In this case, `' '` is the first false value.

(3) All values are true, so and returns the last value, `'c'`.

Listing 4-16 shows the use of or.

Listing 4-16. Introducing or

```
>>> 'a' or 'b'                                    (1)
'a'
>>> '' or 'b'                                     (2)
'b'
>>> '' or [] or {}                                (3)
{}
>>> def sidefx():
...     print "in sidefx()"
...     return 1
>>> 'a' or sidefx()                               (4)
'a'
```

(1) When using or, values are evaluated in a boolean context from left to right, just like and. If any value is true, or returns that value immediately. In this case, `'a'` is the first true value.

(2) or evaluates `' '`, which is false, then `'b'`, which is true, and returns `'b'`.

(3) If all values are false, or returns the last value. or evaluates `' '`, which is false, then `[]`, which is false, then `{}`, which is false, and returns `{}`.

(4) Note that or evaluates values only until it finds one that is true in a boolean context, and then it ignores the rest. This distinction is important if some values can have side effects. Here, the function `sidefx` is never called, because or evaluates `'a'`, which is true, and returns `'a'` immediately.

Using the and-or Trick

If you're a C hacker, you are certainly familiar with the *bool* ? a : b expression, which evaluates to a if *bool* is true, and b otherwise. Because of the way and and or work in Python, you can accomplish the same thing, as shown in Listing 4-17.

Listing 4-17. Introducing the and-or Trick

```
>>> a = "first"
>>> b = "second"
>>> 1 and a or b                                  (1)
'first'
>>> 0 and a or b                                  (2)
'second'
```

(1) This syntax looks similar to the *bool* ? a : b expression in C. The entire expression is evaluated from left to right, so the and is evaluated first. 1 and 'first' evaluates to 'first', and then 'first' or 'second' evaluates to 'first'.

(2) 0 and 'first' evaluates to False, and then 0 or 'second' evaluates to 'second'.

However, since this Python expression is simply boolean logic, and not a special construct of the language, there is one extremely important difference between this and-or trick in Python and the *bool* ? a : b syntax in C. If the value of a is false, the expression will not work as you would expect it to, as shown in Listing 4-18. (Can you tell I was bitten by this? More than once?)

Listing 4-18. When the and-or Trick Fails

```
>>> a = ""
>>> b = "second"
>>> 1 and a or b                                    (1)
'second'
```

(1) Since a is an empty string, which Python considers false in a boolean context, 1 and '' evaluates to '', and then '' or 'second' evaluates to 'second'. Oops! That's not what you wanted.

The and-or trick, *bool* and a or b, will not work like the C expression *bool* ? a : b when a is false in a boolean context.

The real trick behind the and-or trick, then, is to make sure that the value of a is *never* false. One common way of doing this is to turn a into [a] and b into [b], and then take the first element of the returned list, which will be either a or b. Listing 4-19 shows how to use the and-or trick safely.

Listing 4-19. Using the and-or Trick Safely

```
>>> a = ""
>>> b = "second"
>>> (1 and [a] or [b])[0]                           (1)
''
```

(1) Since [a] is a nonempty list, it is never false. Even if a is 0 or '', or some other false value, the list [a] is true because it has one element.

By now, this trick may seem like more trouble than it's worth. You could, after all, accomplish the same thing with an if statement, so why go through all this fuss? Well, in many cases, you are choosing between two constant values, so you can use the simpler syntax and not worry, because you know that the a value will always be true. And even if you need to use the more complicated safe form, there are good reasons to do so. For example, there are some cases in Python where if statements are not allowed, such as in lambda functions (described next).

Further Reading on the and-or Trick

For more information about the and-or trick, refer to the following:

- Python Cookbook (http://www.activestate.com/ASPN/Python/Cookbook) discusses alternatives to the and-or trick (http://www.activestate.com/ASPN/Python/Cookbook/Recipe/52310).

Using lambda Functions

Python supports an interesting syntax that lets you define one-line mini-functions on the fly. Borrowed from Lisp, these so-called lambda functions can be used anywhere a function is required. Listing 4-20 shows some lambda functions.

Listing 4-20. Introducing lambda Functions

```
>>> def f(x):
...     return x*2
...
>>> f(3)
6
>>> g = lambda x: x*2                                    (1)
>>> g(3)
6
>>> (lambda x: x*2)(3)                                   (2)
6
```

(1) This is a lambda function that accomplishes the same thing as the normal function above it. Note the abbreviated syntax here: there are no parentheses around the argument list, and the return keyword is missing (it is implied, since the entire function can be only one expression). Also, the function has no name, but it can be called through the variable it is assigned to.

(2) You can use a lambda function without even assigning it to a variable. This may not be the most useful thing in the world, but it just goes to show that a lambda is just an in-line function.

To generalize, a lambda function is a function that takes any number of arguments (including optional arguments) and returns the value of a single expression. lambda functions cannot contain commands, and they cannot contain more than one expression. Don't try to squeeze too much into a lambda function; if you need something more complex, define a normal function instead and make it as long as you want.

> **NOTE** lambda *functions are a matter of style. Using them is never required; anywhere you could use them, you could define a separate normal function and use that instead. I use them in places where I want to encapsulate specific, nonreusable code without littering my code with a lot of little one-line functions.*

Real-World lambda Functions

Here are the lambda functions in apihelper.py:

```
processFunc = collapse and (lambda s: " ".join(s.split())) or (lambda s: s)
```

Notice that this uses the simple form of the and-or trick, which is okay, because a lambda function is always true in a boolean context. (That doesn't mean that a lambda function can't return a false value. The function is always true; its return value could be anything.)

Also notice that you're using the split function with no arguments. You've already seen it used with one or two arguments, but without any arguments, it splits on whitespace, as shown in Listing 4-21.

Listing 4-21. split Without Arguments

```
>>> s = "this    is\na\ttest"                    (1)
>>> print s
this    is
a        test
>>> print s.split()                              (2)
['this', 'is', 'a', 'test']
>>> print " ".join(s.split())                    (3)
'this is a test'
```

(1) This is a multiline string, defined by escape characters instead of triple quotes. \n is a carriage return, and \t is a tab character.

(2) split without any arguments splits on whitespace. So three spaces, a carriage return, and a tab character are all the same.

(3) You can normalize whitespace by splitting a string with split and then rejoining it with join, using a single space as a delimiter. This is what the info function does to collapse multiline doc strings into a single line.

So what is the info function actually doing with these lambda functions, splits, and and-or tricks?

```
processFunc = collapse and (lambda s: " ".join(s.split())) or (lambda s: s)
```

processFunc is now a function, but which function it is depends on the value of the collapse variable. If collapse is true, processFunc(*string*) will collapse whitespace; otherwise, processFunc(*string*) will return its argument unchanged.

To do this in a less robust language, like Visual Basic, you would probably create a function that took a string and a *collapse* argument and used an if statement to decide whether to collapse the whitespace or not, then returned the appropriate value. This would be inefficient, because the function would need to handle every possible case. Every time you called it, it would need to decide whether to collapse whitespace before it could give you what you wanted. In Python, you can take that decision logic out of the function and define a lambda function that is custom-tailored to give you exactly (and only) what you want. This is more efficient, more elegant, and less prone to those nasty oh-I-thought-those-arguments-were-reversed kinds of errors.

Further Reading on lambda Functions

For more information about lambda functions, refer to the following:

- Python Knowledge Base (http://www.faqts.com/knowledge-base/index.phtml/fid/199) discusses using lambda to call functions indirectly (http://www.faqts.com/knowledge-base/view.phtml/aid/6081/fid/241).

- *Python Tutorial* (http://www.python.org/doc/current/tut/tut.html) shows how to access outside variables from inside a lambda function (http://www.python.org/doc/current/tut/node6.html#SECTION006740000000000000000).

- PEP 227 (http://python.sourceforge.net/peps/pep-0227.html) explains how this will change in future versions of Python.

- *The Whole Python FAQ* (http://www.python.org/doc/FAQ.html) has examples of obfuscated one-liners using lambda (http://www.python.org/cgi-bin/faqw.py?query=4.15&querytype=simple&casefold=yes&req=search).

Putting It All Together

The last line of code, the only one we haven't deconstructed yet, is the one that does all the work. But by now, the work is easy, because everything you need is already set up just the way you want it. All the dominos are in place, and it's time to knock them down.

This is the meat of apihelper.py:

```
print "\n".join(["%s %s" %
                (method.ljust(spacing),
                 processFunc(str(getattr(object, method).__doc__)))
                for method in methodList])
```

Note that this is one command, split over multiple lines, but it doesn't use the line continuation character (\). Remember when I said that some expressions can be split into multiple lines without using a backslash? A list comprehension is one of those expressions, since the entire expression is contained in square brackets.

Now, let's take it from the end and work backwards. The `for method in methodList` shows that this is a list comprehension. As you know, `methodList` is a list of all the methods you care about in `object`. So you're looping through that list with method, as demonstrated in Listing 4-22.

Listing 4-22. Getting a doc string Dynamically

```
>>> import odbchelper
>>> object = odbchelper                          (1)
>>> method = 'buildConnectionString'             (2)
>>> getattr(object, method)                      (3)
<function buildConnectionString at 010D6D74>
>>> print getattr(object, method).__doc__        (4)
Build a connection string from a dictionary of parameters.

    Returns string.
```

(1) In the `info` function, `object` is the object you're getting help on, passed in as an argument.

(2) As you're looping through `methodList`, `method` is the name of the current method.

(3) Using the `getattr` function, you're getting a reference to the *method* function in the *object* module.

(4) Now printing the actual `doc string` of the method is easy.

The next piece of the puzzle is the use of `str` around the `doc string`. As you may recall, `str` is a built-in function that coerces data into a string. But a `doc string` is always a string, so why bother with the `str` function? The answer is that not every function has a `doc string`, and if it doesn't, its `__doc__` attribute is `None`, as you can see in Listing 4-23.

Listing 4-23. Why Use str on a doc string?

```
>>> >>> def foo(): print 2
>>> >>> foo()
2
```

```
>>> >>> foo.__doc__                              (1)
>>> foo.__doc__ == None                          (2)
True
>>> str(foo.__doc__)                             (3)
'None'
```

(1) You can easily define a function that has no doc string, so its __doc__ attribute is None. Confusingly, if you evaluate the __doc__ attribute directly, the Python IDE prints nothing at all, which makes sense if you think about it but is still unhelpful.

(2) You can verify that the value of the __doc__ attribute is actually None by comparing it directly.

(3) The str function takes the null value and returns a string representation of it, 'None'.

> **NOTE** *Python vs. SQL null value comparisons: In SQL, you must use* IS NULL *instead of* = NULL *to compare a null value. In Python, you can use either* == None *or* is None, *but* is None *is faster.*

Once you are guaranteed to have a string, you can pass the string to processFunc, which you have already defined as a function that either does or doesn't collapse whitespace. Now you see why it was important to use str to convert a None value into a string representation. processFunc is assuming a string argument and calling its split method, which would crash if you passed it None, because None doesn't have a split method.

Stepping back even further, you see that you're using string formatting again to concatenate the return value of processFunc with the return value of method's ljust method. This is a new string method that you haven't seen before. Listing 4-24 demonstrates the use of the ljust method.

Listing 4-24. Introducing ljust

```
>>> s = 'buildConnectionString'
>>> s.ljust(30)                                  (1)
'buildConnectionString         '
>>> s.ljust(20)                                  (2)
'buildConnectionString'
```

(1) ljust pads the string with spaces to the given length. This is what the info function uses to make two columns of output and line up all the doc strings in the second column.

(2) If the given length is smaller than the length of the string, ljust will simply return the string unchanged. It never truncates the string.

You're almost finished. Given the padded method name from the `ljust` method and the (possibly collapsed) `doc` string from the call to `processFunc`, you concatenate the two and get a single string. Since you're mapping `methodList`, you end up with a list of strings. Using the `join` method of the string `"\n"`, you join this list into a single string, with each element of the list on a separate line, and print the result, as shown in Listing 4-25.

Listing 4-25. Printing a List

```
>>> li = ['a', 'b', 'c']
>>> print "\n".join(li)                          (1)
a
b
c
```

(1) This is also a useful debugging trick when you're working with lists. And in Python, you're always working with lists.

That's the last piece of the puzzle. You should now understand this code:

```
print "\n".join(["%s %s" %
                (method.ljust(spacing),
                 processFunc(str(getattr(object, method).__doc__)))
               for method in methodList])
```

Summary

The `apihelper.py` program and its output should now make perfect sense.

```
def info(object, spacing=10, collapse=1):
    """Print methods and doc strings.

    Takes module, class, list, dictionary, or string."""
    methodList = [method for method in dir(object) if callable(getattr(object, method))]
    processFunc = collapse and (lambda s: " ".join(s.split())) or (lambda s: s)
    print "\n".join(["%s %s" %
                    (method.ljust(spacing),
                     processFunc(str(getattr(object, method).__doc__)))
                   for method in methodList])

if __name__ == "__main__":
    print info.__doc__
```

Here's the output of apihelper.py:

```
>>> from apihelper import info
>>> li = []
>>> info(li)
append      L.append(object) -- append object to end
count       L.count(value) -> integer -- return number of occurrences of value
extend      L.extend(list) -- extend list by appending list elements
index       L.index(value) -> integer -- return index of first occurrence of value
insert      L.insert(index, object) -- insert object before index
pop         L.pop([index]) -> item -- remove and return item at index (default last)
remove      L.remove(value) -- remove first occurrence of value
reverse     L.reverse() -- reverse *IN PLACE*
sort        L.sort([cmpfunc]) -- sort *IN PLACE*; if given, cmpfunc(x, y) -> -1, 0, 1
```

Before diving into the next chapter, make sure you're comfortable doing all of these things:

- Defining and calling functions with optional and named arguments

- Using str to coerce any arbitrary value into a string representation

- Using getattr to get references to functions and other attributes dynamically

- Extending the list comprehension syntax to do list filtering

- Recognizing the and-or trick and using it safely

- Defining lambda functions

- Assigning functions to variables and calling the function by referencing the variable.

I can't emphasize enough the last point about assigning functions to variables and referencing those variables, because it's vital to advancing your understanding of Python. You'll see more complex applications of this concept throughout this book.

CHAPTER 5

Objects and Object-Orientation

THIS CHAPTER, and pretty much every chapter after this, deals with object-oriented Python programming.

Diving In

Listing 5-1 shows a complete, working Python program. Read the doc strings of the module, the classes, and the functions to get an overview of what this program does and how it works. As usual, don't worry about the stuff you don't understand; that's what the rest of the chapter (and the next chapter) is for.

> **NOTE** *If you have not already done so, you can download this and the other examples used in this book from the Downloads section of the Apress web site (*http://www.apress.com*).*

Listing 5-1. fileinfo.py

```
"""Framework for getting filetype-specific metadata.

Instantiate appropriate class with filename.  Returned object acts like a
dictionary, with key-value pairs for each piece of metadata.
    import fileinfo
    info = fileinfo.MP3FileInfo("/music/ap/mahadeva.mp3")
    print "\\n".join(["%s=%s" % (k, v) for k, v in info.items()])

Or use listDirectory function to get info on all files in a directory.
    for info in fileinfo.listDirectory("/music/ap/", [".mp3"]):
        ...

Framework can be extended by adding classes for particular file types, e.g.
HTMLFileInfo, MPGFileInfo, DOCFileInfo.  Each class is completely responsible for
parsing its files appropriately; see MP3FileInfo for example.
"""
```

```
import os
import sys
from UserDict import UserDict

def stripnulls(data):
    "strip whitespace and nulls"
    return data.replace("\00", "").strip()

class FileInfo(UserDict):
    "store file metadata"
    def __init__(self, filename=None):
        UserDict.__init__(self)
        self["name"] = filename

class MP3FileInfo(FileInfo):
    "store ID3v1.0 MP3 tags"
    tagDataMap = {"title"   : (  3,  33, stripnulls),
                  "artist"  : ( 33,  63, stripnulls),
                  "album"   : ( 63,  93, stripnulls),
                  "year"    : ( 93,  97, stripnulls),
                  "comment" : ( 97, 126, stripnulls),
                  "genre"   : (127, 128, ord)}

    def __parse(self, filename):
        "parse ID3v1.0 tags from MP3 file"
        self.clear()
        try:
            fsock = open(filename, "rb", 0)
            try:
                fsock.seek(-128, 2)
                tagdata = fsock.read(128)
            finally:
                fsock.close()
            if tagdata[:3] == "TAG":
                for tag, (start, end, parseFunc) in self.tagDataMap.items():
                    self[tag] = parseFunc(tagdata[start:end])
        except IOError:
            pass

    def __setitem__(self, key, item):
        if key == "name" and item:
            self.__parse(item)
        FileInfo.__setitem__(self, key, item)
```

```
def listDirectory(directory, fileExtList):
    "get list of file info objects for files of particular extensions"
    fileList = [os.path.normcase(f) for f in os.listdir(directory)]
    fileList = [os.path.join(directory, f) for f in fileList \
                if os.path.splitext(f)[1] in fileExtList]
    def getFileInfoClass(filename, module=sys.modules[FileInfo.__module__]):
        "get file info class from filename extension"
        subclass = "%sFileInfo" % os.path.splitext(filename)[1].upper()[1:]
        return hasattr(module, subclass) and getattr(module, subclass) or FileInfo
    return [getFileInfoClass(f)(f) for f in fileList]


if __name__ == "__main__":
    for info in listDirectory("/music/_singles/", [".mp3"]):            (1)
        print "\n".join(["%s=%s" % (k, v) for k, v in info.items()])
        print
```

(1) This program's output depends on the files on your hard drive. To get meaningful output, you'll need to change the directory path to point to a directory of MP3 files on your own machine.

This is the output I got on my machine. Your output will be different, unless, by some startling coincidence, you share my exact taste in music.

```
album=
artist=Ghost in the Machine
title=A Time Long Forgotten (Concept
genre=31
name=/music/_singles/a_time_long_forgotten_con.mp3
year=1999
comment=http://mp3.com/ghostmachine

album=Rave Mix
artist=***DJ MARY-JANE***
title=HELLRAISER****Trance from Hell
genre=31
name=/music/_singles/hellraiser.mp3
year=2000
comment=http://mp3.com/DJMARYJANE

album=Rave Mix
artist=***DJ MARY-JANE***
title=KAIRO****THE BEST GOA
genre=31
name=/music/_singles/kairo.mp3
```

```
year=2000
comment=http://mp3.com/DJMARYJANE

album=Journeys
artist=Masters of Balance
title=Long Way Home
genre=31
name=/music/_singles/long_way_home1.mp3
year=2000
comment=http://mp3.com/MastersofBalan

album=
artist=The Cynic Project
title=Sidewinder
genre=18
name=/music/_singles/sidewinder.mp3
year=2000
comment=http://mp3.com/cynicproject

album=Digitosis@128k
artist=VXpanded
title=Spinning
genre=255
name=/music/_singles/spinning.mp3
year=2000
comment=http://mp3.com/artists/95/vxp
```

Importing Modules Using from module import

Python has two ways of importing modules. Both are useful, and you should
know when to use each. One way, import *module*, you've already seen in Chapter 2.
The other way accomplishes the same thing, but it has subtle and important
differences.

Here is the basic from *module* import syntax:

```
from UserDict import UserDict
```

This is similar to the import *module* syntax that you know and love, but with an
important difference: the attributes and methods of the imported module types
are imported directly into the local namespace, so they are available directly,
without qualification by module name. You can import individual items or use
from *module* import * to import everything.

Listing 5-2 demonstrates the differences between the methods for importing modules.

Listing 5-2. import module vs. from module import

```
>>> import types
>>> types.FunctionType                          (1)
<type 'function'>
>>> FunctionType                                (2)
Traceback (innermost last):
  File "<interactive input>", line 1, in ?
NameError: There is no variable named 'FunctionType'
>>> from types import FunctionType              (3)
>>> FunctionType                                (4)
<type 'function'>
```

(1) The types module contains no methods; it just has attributes for each Python object type. Note that the attribute, FunctionType, must be qualified by the module name, types.

(2) FunctionType by itself has not been defined in this namespace; it exists only in the context of types.

(3) This syntax imports the attribute FunctionType from the types module directly into the local namespace.

(4) Now FunctionType can be accessed directly, without reference to types. When should you use from *module* import?

- If you will be accessing attributes and methods often and don't want to type the module name over and over, use from *module* import.

- If you want to selectively import some attributes and methods but not others, use from *module* import.

- If the module contains attributes or functions with the same name as ones in your module, you must use import *module*, rather than from *module* import, to avoid name conflicts.

Other than these guidelines, it's just a matter of style, and you will see Python code written both ways.

> **CAUTION** *Use* `from module import *` *sparingly, because it makes it difficult to determine where a particular function or attribute came from, and that makes debugging and refactoring more difficult.*

Further Reading on Module Importing Techniques

For more information about the Python methods for importing modules, refer to the following:

- effbot (http://www.effbot.org/guides/) has more to say on `import` *module* vs. `from` *module* `import` (http://www.effbot.org/guides/import-confusion.htm).

- *Python Tutorial* (http://www.python.org/doc/current/tut/tut.html) discusses advanced import techniques, including `from` *module* `import *` (http://www.python.org/doc/current/tut/node8.html#SECTION008410000000000000000).

Defining Classes

Python is fully object-oriented: you can define your own classes, inherit from your own or built-in classes, and instantiate the classes you've defined.

Defining a class in Python is simple. As with functions, there is no separate interface definition. You can just define the class and start coding. A Python class starts with the reserved word `class`, followed by the class name. Technically, that's all that's required, since a class doesn't need to inherit from any other class, as in the simple example shown in Listing 5-3.

Listing 5-3. The Simplest Python Class

```
class Loaf:            (1)
    pass               (2) (3)
```

(1) The name of this class is `Loaf`, and it doesn't inherit from any other class. Class names are usually capitalized, `EachWordLikeThis`, but this is only a convention, not a requirement.

(2) This class doesn't define any methods or attributes, but syntactically, there needs to be something in the definition, so this example uses `pass`. This is a Python reserved word that just means "move along; nothing to see here".

It's a statement that does nothing, and it's a good placeholder when you're stubbing out functions or classes.

(3) You probably guessed this, but everything in a class is indented, just like the code within a function, if statement, for loop, and so forth. The first thing not indented is not in the class.

> **NOTE** ***Python vs. Java pass:*** *The* pass *statement in Python is like an empty set of braces ({}) in Java or C.*

Of course, realistically, most classes will be inherited from other classes, and they will define their own class methods and attributes. But as you've just seen, there is nothing that a class absolutely must have, other than a name. In particular, C++ programmers may find it odd that Python classes don't have explicit constructors and destructors. Python classes do have something similar to a constructor: the __init__ method.

Listing 5-4 shows how the FileInfo class in the sample program (fileinfo.py) is defined.

Listing 5-4. Defining the FileInfo Class

```
from UserDict import UserDict

class FileInfo(UserDict):   (1)
```

(1) In Python, the ancestor of a class is simply listed in parentheses immediately after the class name. So, the FileInfo class is inherited from the UserDict class (which was imported from the UserDict module). UserDict is a class that acts like a dictionary, allowing you to essentially subclass the dictionary datatype and add your own behavior. (The similar classes UserList and UserString allow you to subclass lists and strings.) There is a bit of black magic behind this, which I will demystify later in this chapter when we explore the UserDict class in more depth.

> **NOTE** ***Python vs. Java ancestors:*** *In Python, the ancestor of a class is simply listed in parentheses immediately after the class name. There is no special keyword like* extends *in Java.*

Python also supports multiple inheritance. In the parentheses following the class name, you can list as many ancestor classes as you like, separated by commas.

Initializing and Coding Classes

Listing 5-5 shows the initialization of the FileInfo class using the __init__ method.

Listing 5-5. Initializing the FileInfo Class

```
class FileInfo(UserDict):
    "store file metadata"                           (1)
    def __init__(self, filename=None):              (2) (3) (4)
```

(1) Classes can (and should) have doc strings, just like modules and functions.

(2) __init__ is called immediately after an instance of the class is created. It would be tempting but incorrect to call this the constructor of the class. It's tempting, because it looks like a constructor (by convention, __init__ is the first method defined for the class), acts like one (it's the first piece of code executed in a newly created instance of the class), and even sounds like one (*"init"* certainly suggests a constructor-ish nature). It's incorrect, because the object has already been constructed by the time __init__ is called, and you already have a valid reference to the new instance of the class. But __init__ is the closest thing you're going to get to a constructor in Python, and it fills much the same role.

(3) The first argument of every class method, including __init__, is always a reference to the current instance of the class. By convention, this argument is always named self. In the __init__ method, self refers to the newly created object; in other class methods, it refers to the instance whose method was called. Although you need to specify self explicitly when defining the method, you do *not* specify it when calling the method; Python will add it for you automatically.

(4) __init__ methods can take any number of arguments, and just like functions, the arguments can be defined with default values, making them optional to the caller. In this case, filename has a default value of None, which is the Python null value.

> **NOTE** *Python vs. Java self: By convention, the first argument of any Python class method (the reference to the current instance) is called* self. *This argument fills the role of the reserved word* this *in C++ or Java, but* self *is not a reserved word in Python, merely a naming convention. Nonetheless, please don't call it anything but* self; *this is a very strong convention.*

Listing 5-6 shows the coding for the FileInfo class.

Listing 5-6. Coding the FileInfo Class

```
class FileInfo(UserDict):
    "store file metadata"
    def __init__(self, filename=None):
```

```
    UserDict.__init__(self)                    (1)
    self["name"] = filename                    (2)
                                               (3)
```

(1) Some pseudo-object-oriented languages like Powerbuilder have a concept of "extending" constructors and other events, where the ancestor's method is called automatically before the descendant's method is executed. Python does not do this; you must always explicitly call the appropriate method in the ancestor class.

(2) I told you that this class acts like a dictionary, and here is the first sign of it. You're assigning the argument `filename` as the value of this object's `name` key.

(3) Note that the __init__ method never returns a value.

Knowing When to Use self and _init_

When defining your class methods, you *must* explicitly list `self` as the first argument for each method, including __init__. When you call a method of an ancestor class from within your class, you *must* include the `self` argument. But when you call your class method from outside, you do not specify anything for the `self` argument; you skip it entirely, and Python automatically adds the instance reference for you.

I am aware that this is confusing at first. It's not really inconsistent, but it may appear inconsistent because it relies on a distinction (between bound and unbound methods) that you don't know about yet.

Whew, I realize that's a lot to absorb, but you'll get the hang of it. All Python classes work the same way, so once you've learn one, you've learned them all.

If you forget everything else, remember this one thing, because I promise it will trip you up: __init__ methods are optional, but when you define one, you must remember to explicitly call the ancestor's __init__ method (if it defines one). This is more generally true: Whenever a descendant wants to extend the behavior of the ancestor, the descendant method must explicitly call the ancestor method at the proper time, with the proper arguments.

Further Reading on Python Classes

For more information about Python classes, refer to the following:

- *Learning to Program* (http://www.freenetpages.co.uk/hp/alan.gauld) has a gentle introduction to classes (http://www.freenetpages.co.uk/hp/alan.gauld/tutclass.htm).

- *How to Think Like a Computer Scientist* (http://www.ibiblio.org/obp/thinkCSpy) shows how to use classes to model compound datatypes (http://www.ibiblio.org/obp/thinkCSpy/chap12.htm).

- *Python Tutorial* (http://www.python.org/doc/current/tut/tut.html) has an in-depth look at classes, namespaces, and inheritance (http://www.python.org/doc/current/tut/node11.html).

- Python Knowledge Base (http://www.faqts.com/knowledge-base/index.phtml/fid/199) answers common questions about classes (http://www.faqts.com/knowledge-base/index.phtml/fid/242).

Instantiating Classes

Instantiating classes in Python is straightforward, as shown in Listing 5-7. To instantiate a class, simply call the class as if it were a function, passing the arguments that the __init__ method defines. The return value will be the newly created object.

Listing 5-7. Creating a FileInfo Instance

```
>>> import fileinfo
>>> f = fileinfo.FileInfo("/music/_singles/kairo.mp3")    (1)
>>> f.__class__                                           (2)
<class fileinfo.FileInfo at 010EC204>
>>> f.__doc__                                             (3)
'store file metadata'
>>> f                                                     (4)
{'name': '/music/_singles/kairo.mp3'}
```

(1) You are creating an instance of the FileInfo class (defined in the fileinfo module) and assigning the newly created instance to the variable f. You are passing one parameter, /music/_singles/kairo.mp3, which will end up as the filename argument in FileInfo's __init__ method.

(2) Every class instance has a built-in attribute, __class__, which is the object's class. (Note that the representation of this includes the physical address of the instance on my machine; your representation will be different.) Java programmers may be familiar with the Class class, which contains methods like getName and getSuperclass to get metadata information about an object. In Python, this kind of metadata is available directly on the object itself through attributes like __class__, __name__, and __bases__.

(3) You can access the instance's doc string just as with a function or a module. All instances of a class share the same doc string.

(4) Remember when the __init__ method assigned its filename argument to self["name"]? Well, here's the result. The arguments you pass when you create the class instance get sent right along to the __init__ method (along with the object reference, self, which Python adds for free).

> **NOTE** *Python vs. Java instantiating classes:* In Python, simply call a class as if it were a function to create a new instance of the class. There is no explicit new *operator like C++ or Java.*

Garbage Collection

If creating new instances is easy, destroying them is even easier. In general, there is no need to explicitly free instances, because they are freed automatically when the variables assigned to them go out of scope. Memory leaks are rare in Python, as demonstrated in Listing 5-8.

Listing 5-8. Trying to Implement a Memory Leak

```
>>> def leakmem():
...     f = fileinfo.FileInfo('/music/_singles/kairo.mp3')      (1)
...
>>> for i in range(100):
...     leakmem()                                               (2)
```

(1) Every time the leakmem function is called, you are creating an instance of FileInfo and assigning it to the variable f, which is a local variable within the function. Then the function ends without ever freeing f, so you would expect a memory leak, but you would be wrong. When the function ends, the local variable f goes out of scope. At this point, there are no longer any references to the newly created instance of FileInfo (since you never assigned it to anything other than f), so Python destroys the instance for you.

(2) No matter how many times you call the leakmem function, it will never leak memory, because every time, Python will destroy the newly created FileInfo class before returning from leakmem.

The technical term for this form of garbage collection is *"reference counting."* Python keeps a list of references to every instance created. In the example in Listing 5-8, there was only one reference to the FileInfo instance: the local variable f. When the function ends, the variable f goes out of scope, so the reference count drops to 0, and Python destroys the instance automatically.

In previous versions of Python, there were situations where reference counting failed, and Python couldn't clean up after you. If you created two instances that referenced each other (for instance, a doubly linked list, where each node has a pointer to the previous and next node in the list), neither instance would ever be destroyed automatically because Python (correctly) believed that there was always a reference to each instance. Python 2.0 has an additional form of garbage collection called *"mark-and-sweep,"* which is smart enough to notice this virtual gridlock and clean up circular references correctly.

As a former philosophy major, it disturbs me to think that things disappear when no one is looking at them, but that's exactly what happens in Python. In general, you can simply forget about memory management and let Python clean up after you.

Further Reading on Class Instantiation

For more information about Python's class instantiation and garbage collection, refer to the following:

- *Python Library Reference* (http://www.python.org/doc/current/lib) summarizes built-in attributes like __class__ (http://www.python.org/doc/current/lib/specialattrs.html).

- *Python Library Reference* (http://www.python.org/doc/current/lib/) documents the gc module (http://www.python.org/doc/current/lib/module-gc.html), which gives you low-level control over Python's garbage collection.

Exploring UserDict: A Wrapper Class

As you've seen, FileInfo is a class that acts like a dictionary. To explore this further, let's look at the UserDict class in the UserDict module, which is the ancestor of our FileInfo class. This is nothing special; the class is written in Python and stored in a .py file, just like your code. In particular, it's stored in the lib directory in your Python installation.

> **TIP** *In the ActivePython IDE on Windows, you can quickly open any module in your library path by selecting File ➤ Locate, or by pressing Ctrl-L.*

Listing 5-9 shows the definition of the UserDict class.

Listing 5-9. Defining the UserDict Class

```
class UserDict:                               (1)
    def __init__(self, dict=None):            (2)
        self.data = {}                        (3)
        if dict is not None: self.update(dict) (4) (5)
```

(1) Note that UserDict is a base class, not inherited from any other class.
(2) This is the __init__ method that you overrode in the FileInfo class. Notice that the argument list in this ancestor class is different than in the

descendant. That's okay; each subclass can have its own set of arguments, as long as it calls the ancestor with the correct arguments. Here, the ancestor class has a way to define initial values (by passing a dictionary in the dict argument), which FileInfo does not use.

(3) Python supports data attributes (called "*instance variables*" in Java and Powerbuilder, and "*member variables*" in C++). Data attributes are pieces of data held by a specific instance of a class. In this case, each instance of UserDict will have a data attribute data. To reference this attribute from code outside the class, you qualify it with the instance name, *instance*.data, in the same way that you qualify a function with its module name. To reference a data attribute from within the class, you use self as the qualifier. By convention, all data attributes are initialized to reasonable values in the __init__ method. However, this is not required, since data attributes, like local variables, spring into existence when they are first assigned a value.

(4) The update method is a dictionary duplicator: it copies all the keys and values from one dictionary to another. This does *not* clear the target dictionary first; if the target dictionary already has some keys, the ones from the source dictionary will be overwritten, but others will be left untouched. Think of update as a merge function, not a copy function.

(5) This is a syntax you may not have seen before (I haven't used it in the examples in this book). It's an if statement, but instead of having an indented block starting on the next line, there is just a single statement on the same line, after the colon. This is perfectly legal syntax, which is just a shortcut you can use when you have only one statement in a block. (It's like specifying a single statement without braces in C++.) You can use this syntax, or you can have indented code on subsequent lines, but you can't do both for the same block.

> **NOTE** *Python vs. Java function overloading: Java and Powerbuilder support function overloading by argument list—one class can have multiple methods with the same name but a different number of arguments, or arguments of different types. Other languages (most notably PL/SQL) even support function overloading by argument name—one class can have multiple methods with the same name and the same number of arguments of the same type but different argument names. Python supports neither of these; it has no form of function overloading whatsoever. Methods are defined solely by their name, and there can be only one method per class with a given name. So, if a descendant class has an __init__ method, it always overrides the ancestor __init__ method, even if the descendant defines it with a different argument list. The same rule applies to any other method.*

Guido, the original author of Python, explains method overriding this way:

Derived classes may override methods of their base classes. Because methods have no special privileges when calling other methods of the same object, a method of a base class that calls another method defined in the same base class, may in fact end up calling a method of a derived class that overrides it. (For C++ programmers: all methods in Python are effectively virtual.)

If that doesn't make sense to you (it confuses the hell out of me), feel free to ignore it. I just thought I would pass it along.

> **CAUTION**   *Always assign an initial value to all of an instance's data attributes in the* __init__ *method. It will save you hours of debugging later, tracking down* AttributeError *exceptions because you're referencing uninitialized (and therefore nonexistent) attributes.*

Listing 5-10 shows how to use UserDict's normal methods.

Listing 5-10. UserDict Normal Methods

```
def clear(self): self.data.clear()           (1)
def copy(self):                              (2)
    if self.__class__ is UserDict:           (3)
        return UserDict(self.data)
    import copy                              (4)
    return copy.copy(self)
def keys(self): return self.data.keys()      (5)
def items(self): return self.data.items()
def values(self): return self.data.values()
```

(1) clear is a normal class method; it is publicly available to be called by anyone at any time. Notice that clear, like all class methods, has self as its first argument. (Remember that you don't include self when you call the method; it's something that Python adds for you.) Also note the basic technique of this wrapper class: store a real dictionary (data) as a data attribute, define all the methods that a real dictionary has, and have each class method redirect to the corresponding method on the real dictionary. (In case you've forgotten, a dictionary's clear method deletes all of its keys and their associated values.)

(2) The copy method of a real dictionary returns a new dictionary that is an exact duplicate of the original (all the same key/value pairs). But UserDict can't simply redirect to self.data.copy, because that method returns a real dictionary, and what you want is to return a new instance that is the same class as self.

(3) You use the __class__ attribute to see if self is a UserDict; if so, you're golden, because you know how to copy a UserDict: just create a new UserDict and give it the real dictionary that you've squirreled away in `self.data`. Then you immediately return the new `UserDict`; you don't even get to the `import copy` on the next line.

(4) If `self.__class__` is not `UserDict`, then `self` must be some subclass of `UserDict` (like maybe `FileInfo`), in which case, life gets trickier. `UserDict` doesn't know how to make an exact copy of one of its descendants; there could, for instance, be other data attributes defined in the subclass, so you would need to iterate through them and make sure to copy all of them. Luckily, Python comes with a module to do exactly this, and it's called `copy`. I won't go into the details here (though it's a wicked cool module, if you're ever inclined to dive into it on your own). Suffice it to say that `copy` can copy arbitrary Python objects, and that's how you're using it here.

(5) The rest of the methods are straightforward, redirecting the calls to the built-in methods on `self.data`.

> **NOTE** *In versions of Python prior to 2.2, you could not directly subclass built-in datatypes like strings, lists, and dictionaries. To compensate for this, Python comes with wrapper classes that mimic the behavior of these built-in datatypes:* `UserString`, `UserList`, *and* `UserDict`. *Using a combination of normal and special methods, the* `UserDict` *class does an excellent imitation of a dictionary. In Python 2.2 and later, you can inherit classes directly from built-in datatypes like* `dict`. *An example of this is given in the examples that come with this book, in* `fileinfo_fromdict.py`.

In Python, you can inherit directly from the `dict` built-in datatype, as shown in Listing 5-11. There are three differences here, compared with the `UserDict` version.

Listing 5-11. Inheriting Directly from the Built-in Datatype dict

```
class FileInfo(dict):                            (1)
    "store file metadata"
    def __init__(self, filename=None):           (2)
        self["name"] = filename
```

(1) The first difference is that you don't need to import the `UserDict` module, since `dict` is a built-in datatype and is always available. The second is that you are inheriting from `dict` directly, instead of from `UserDict.UserDict`.

(2) The third difference is subtle but important. Because of the way `UserDict` works internally, it requires you to manually call its `__init__` method to properly initialize its internal data structures. `dict` does not work like this; it is not a wrapper, and it requires no explicit initialization.

Further Reading on UserDict

For more information about the UserDict module, refer to the following:

- *Python Library Reference* (http://www.python.org/doc/current/lib) documents the UserDict module (http://www.python.org/doc/current/lib/module-UserDict.html) and the copy module (http://www.python.org/doc/current/lib/module-copy.html).

Using Special Class Methods

In addition to normal class methods, there are a number of special methods that Python classes can define. Instead of being called directly by your code (like normal methods), special methods are called for you by Python in particular circumstances or when specific syntax is used.

As you saw in the previous section, normal methods go a long way toward wrapping a dictionary in a class. But normal methods alone are not enough, because there are a lot of things you can do with dictionaries besides call methods on them.

Getting and Setting Items

For starters, you can get and set items with a syntax that doesn't include explicitly invoking methods. This is where special class methods come in: they provide a way to map non-method-calling syntax into method calls. Listing 5-12 demonstrates the __getitem__ special method.

Listing 5-12. The __getitem__ Special Method

```
    def __getitem__(self, key): return self.data[key]
>>> f = fileinfo.FileInfo("/music/_singles/kairo.mp3")
>>> f
{'name':'/music/_singles/kairo.mp3'}
>>> f.__getitem__("name")                           (1)
'/music/_singles/kairo.mp3'
>>> f["name"]                                       (2)
'/music/_singles/kairo.mp3'
```

(1) The __getitem__ special method looks simple enough. Like the normal methods clear, keys, and values, it just redirects to the dictionary to return its value. But how does it get called? Well, you can call __getitem__ directly, but in practice, you would not actually do that; I'm just doing it here to show you how it works. The right way to use __getitem__ is to get Python to call it for you.

(2) This looks just like the syntax you would use to get a dictionary value, and, in fact, it returns the value you would expect. But here's the missing link: under the covers, Python has converted this syntax to the method call f.__getitem__("name"). That's why __getitem__ is a special class method: not only can you call it yourself, you can get Python to call it for you by using the right syntax.

Of course, Python has a __setitem__ special method to go along with __getitem__, as shown in Listing 5-13.

Listing 5-13. The __setitem__ Special Method

```
    def __setitem__(self, key, item): self.data[key] = item

>>> f
{'name':'/music/_singles/kairo.mp3'}
>>> f.__setitem__("genre", 31)                    (1)
>>> f
{'name':'/music/_singles/kairo.mp3', 'genre':31}
>>> f["genre"] = 32                               (2)
>>> f
{'name':'/music/_singles/kairo.mp3', 'genre':32}
```

(1) Like the __getitem__ method, __setitem__ simply redirects to the real dictionary self.data to do its work. And like __getitem__, you would not ordinarily call it directly like this; Python calls __setitem__ for you when you use the right syntax.

(2) This looks like regular dictionary syntax, except that f is really a class that's trying very hard to masquerade as a dictionary, and __setitem__ is an essential part of that masquerade. This line of code actually calls f.__setitem__("genre", 32) under the covers.

__setitem__ is a special class method because it gets called for you, but it's still a class method. Just as easily as the __setitem__ method was defined in UserDict, you can redefine it in your descendant class to override the ancestor method. This allows you to define classes that act like dictionaries in some ways, but define their own behavior above and beyond the built-in dictionary.

This concept is the basis of the entire framework we're studying in this chapter. Each file type can have a handler class that knows how to get metadata from a particular type of file. Once some attributes (like the file's name and location) are known, the handler class knows how to derive other attributes automatically. This is done by overriding the __setitem__ method, checking for particular keys, and adding additional processing when they are found.

For example, MP3FileInfo is a descendant of FileInfo. When an MP3FileInfo's name is set, it doesn't just set the name key (like the ancestor FileInfo does); it also looks in the file itself for MP3 tags and populates a whole set of keys. Listing 5-14 shows how this works.

Listing 5-14. Overriding __setitem__ in MP3FileInfo

```
def __setitem__(self, key, item):            (1)
    if key == "name" and item:               (2)
        self.__parse(item)                    (3)
    FileInfo.__setitem__(self, key, item)     (4)
```

(1) Notice that this __setitem__ method is defined exactly the same way as the ancestor method. This is important, since Python will be calling the method for you, and Python expects it to be defined with a certain number of arguments. (Technically speaking, the names of the arguments don't matter; only the number of arguments is important.)

(2) Here's the crux of the entire MP3FileInfo class: if you're assigning a value to the name key, you want to do something extra.

(3) The extra processing you do for name items is encapsulated in the __parse method. This is another class method defined in MP3FileInfo, and when you call it, you qualify it with self. Just calling __parse would look for a normal function defined outside the class, which is not what you want. Calling self.__parse will look for a class method defined within the class. This isn't anything new; you reference data attributes the same way.

(4) After doing your extra processing, you want to call the ancestor method. Remember that this is never done for you in Python; you must do it manually. Note that you're calling the immediate ancestor, FileInfo, even though it doesn't have a __setitem__ method. That's okay, because Python will walk up the ancestor tree until it finds a class with the method you're calling, so this line of code will eventually find and call the __setitem__ defined in UserDict.

> **NOTE** *When accessing data attributes within a class, you need to qualify the attribute name:* self.attribute. *When calling other methods within a class, you need to qualify the method name:* self.method.

Listing 5-15 demonstrates how to set an MP3FileInfo's name.

Listing 5-15. Setting an MP3FileInfo's Name

```
>>> import fileinfo
>>> mp3file = fileinfo.MP3FileInfo()                        (1)
>>> mp3file
{'name':None}
>>> mp3file["name"] = "/music/_singles/kairo.mp3"           (2)
>>> mp3file
{'album': 'Rave Mix', 'artist': '***DJ MARY-JANE***', 'genre': 31,
'title': 'KAIRO****THE BEST GOA', 'name': '/music/_singles/kairo.mp3',
```

```
'year': '2000', 'comment': 'http://mp3.com/DJMARYJANE'}
>>> mp3file["name"] = "/music/_singles/sidewinder.mp3"          (3)
>>> mp3file
{'album': '', 'artist': 'The Cynic Project', 'genre': 18, 'title': 'Sidewinder',
'name': '/music/_singles/sidewinder.mp3', 'year': '2000',
'comment': 'http://mp3.com/cynicproject'}
```

(1) First, you create an instance of MP3FileInfo, without passing it a filename. (You can get away with this because the filename argument of the __init__ method is optional.) Since MP3FileInfo has no __init__ method of its own, Python walks up the ancestor tree and finds the __init__ method of FileInfo. This __init__ method manually calls the __init__ method of UserDict and then sets the name key to filename, which is None, since you didn't pass a filename. Thus, mp3file initially looks like a dictionary with one key, name, whose value is None.

(2) Now the real fun begins. Setting the name key of mp3file triggers the __setitem__ method on MP3FileInfo (not UserDict), which notices that you're setting the name key with a real value and calls self.__parse. Although you haven't traced through the __parse method yet, you can see from the output that it sets several other keys: album, artist, genre, title, year, and comment.

(3) Modifying the name key will go through the same process again: Python calls __setitem__, which calls self.__parse, which sets all the other keys.

Using Advanced Special Class Methods

Python has more special methods than just __getitem__ and __setitem__. Some of them let you emulate functionality that you may not even know about. Listing 5-16 shows some of the other special methods in UserDict.

Listing 5-16. More Special Methods in UserDict

```
def __repr__(self): return repr(self.data)                      (1)
def __cmp__(self, dict):                                        (2)
    if isinstance(dict, UserDict):
        return cmp(self.data, dict.data)
    else:
        return cmp(self.data, dict)
def __len__(self): return len(self.data)                        (3)
def __delitem__(self, key): del self.data[key]                  (4)
```

(1) __repr__ is a special method that is called when you call repr(*instance*). The repr function is a built-in function that returns a string representation of an object. It works on any object, not just class instances. You're already intimately familiar with repr, and you don't even know it. In the interactive window, when you type just a variable name and press the Enter key, Python uses repr to display the variable's value. Go create a dictionary d with some data, and then print repr(d) to see for yourself.

(2) __cmp__ is called when you compare class instances. In general, you can compare any two Python objects, not just class instances, by using ==. There are rules that define when built-in datatypes are considered equal; for instance, dictionaries are equal when they have all the same keys and values, and strings are equal when they are the same length and contain the same sequence of characters. For class instances, you can define the __cmp__ method and code the comparison logic yourself, and then you can use == to compare instances of your class, and Python will call your __cmp__ special method for you.

(3) __len__ is called when you call len(*instance*). The len function is a built-in function that returns the length of an object. It works on any object that could reasonably be thought of as having a length. The len of a string is its number of characters; the len of a dictionary is its number of keys; the len of a list or tuple is its number of elements. For class instances, define the __len__ method and code the length calculation yourself, and then call len(*instance*), and Python will call your __len__ special method for you.

(4) __delitem__ is called when you call del *instance*[*key*], which you may remember as the way to delete individual items from a dictionary. When you use del on a class instance, Python calls the __delitem__ special method for you.

> **NOTE** *Python vs. Java equality and identity: In Java, you determine whether two string variables reference the same physical memory location by using* str1 == str2. *This is called object identity, and it is written in Python as* str1 is str2. *To compare string values in Java, you would use* str1.equals(str2); *in Python, you would use* str1 == str2. *Java programmers who have been taught to believe that the world is a better place because == in Java compares by identity instead of by value may have a difficult time adjusting to Python's lack of such "gotchas."*

At this point, you may be thinking, "All this work just to do something in a class that I can do with a built-in datatype." And it's true that life would be easier (and the entire UserDict class would be unnecessary) if you could inherit from built-in datatypes like a dictionary. But even if you could, special methods would still be useful, because they can be used in any class, not just wrapper classes like UserDict.

Special methods mean that *any class* can store key/value pairs like a dictionary, just by defining the __setitem__ method. *Any class* can act like a sequence, just by defining the __getitem__ method. Any class that defines the __cmp__ method can be compared with ==. And if your class represents something that has a length, don't define a GetLength method—define the __len__ method and use len(*instance*).

> **NOTE**   *While other object-oriented languages only let you define the physical model of an object ("this object has a* GetLength *method"), Python's special class methods like* __len__ *allow you to define the logical model of an object ("this object has a length").*

Python has a lot of other special methods. A whole set of them lets classes act like numbers, allowing you to add, subtract, and do other arithmetic operations on class instances. (The canonical example of this is a class that represents complex numbers—numbers with both real and imaginary components.) The __call__ method lets a class act like a function, allowing you to call a class instance directly. And there are other special methods that allow classes to have read-only and write-only data attributes; we'll talk more about those in later chapters.

Further Reading on Special Class Methods

For more information about Python's special class methods, refer to the following:

- *Python Reference Manual* (http://www.python.org/doc/current/ref) documents all of the special class methods (http://www.python.org/doc/current/ref/specialnames.html).

Introducing Class Attributes

You already know about data attributes, which are variables owned by a specific instance of a class. Python also supports class attributes, which are variables owned by the class itself. Listing 5-17 demonstrates the use of class attributes.

Listing 5-17. Introducing Class Attributes

```
class MP3FileInfo(FileInfo):
    "store ID3v1.0 MP3 tags"
    tagDataMap = {"title"   : (  3,  33, stripnulls),
                  "artist"  : ( 33,  63, stripnulls),
                  "album"   : ( 63,  93, stripnulls),
                  "year"    : ( 93,  97, stripnulls),
                  "comment" : ( 97, 126, stripnulls),
                  "genre"   : (127, 128, ord)}
>>> import fileinfo
>>> fileinfo.MP3FileInfo                            (1)
<class fileinfo.MP3FileInfo at 01257FDC>
>>> fileinfo.MP3FileInfo.tagDataMap                 (2)
{'title': (3, 33, <function stripnulls at 0260C8D4>),
```

```
'genre': (127, 128, <built-in function ord>),
'artist': (33, 63, <function stripnulls at 0260C8D4>),
'year': (93, 97, <function stripnulls at 0260C8D4>),
'comment': (97, 126, <function stripnulls at 0260C8D4>),
'album': (63, 93, <function stripnulls at 0260C8D4>)}
>>> m = fileinfo.MP3FileInfo()                    (3)
>>> m.tagDataMap
{'title': (3, 33, <function stripnulls at 0260C8D4>),
'genre': (127, 128, <built-in function ord>),
'artist': (33, 63, <function stripnulls at 0260C8D4>),
'year': (93, 97, <function stripnulls at 0260C8D4>),
'comment': (97, 126, <function stripnulls at 0260C8D4>),
'album': (63, 93, <function stripnulls at 0260C8D4>)}
```

(1) MP3FileInfo is the class itself, not any particular instance of the class.

(2) tagDataMap is a class attribute—literally, an attribute of the class. It is available before creating any instances of the class.

(3) Class attributes are available both through direct reference to the class and through any instance of the class.

> **NOTE** *Python vs. Java attribute definition: In Java, both static variables (called class attributes in Python) and instance variables (called data attributes in Python) are defined immediately after the class definition (one with the* static *keyword; one without). In Python, only class attributes can be defined here; data attributes are defined in the* __init__ *method.*

Class attributes can be used as class-level constants (which is how you use them in MP3FileInfo), but they are not really constants. You can also change them, as shown in Listing 5-18.

> **NOTE** *There are no constants in Python. Everything can be changed if you try hard enough. This fits with one of the core principles of Python: bad behavior should be discouraged but not banned. If you really want to change the value of* None, *you can do it, but don't come running to me when your code is impossible to debug.*

Listing 5-18. Modifying Class Attributes

```
>>> class counter:
...     count = 0                           (1)
...     def __init__(self):
...         self.__class__.count += 1       (2)
...
>>> counter
<class __main__.counter at 010EAECC>
>>> counter.count                           (3)
0
>>> c = counter()
>>> c.count                                 (4)
1
>>> counter.count
1
>>> d = counter()                           (5)
>>> d.count
2
>>> c.count
2
>>> counter.count
2
```

(1) count is a class attribute of the counter class.

(2) __class__ is a built-in attribute of every class instance (of every class). It is a reference to the class that self is an instance of (in this case, the counter class).

(3) Because count is a class attribute, it is available through direct reference to the class, before you have created any instances of the class.

(4) Creating an instance of the class calls the __init__ method, which increments the class attribute count by 1. This affects the class itself, not just the newly created instance.

(5) Creating a second instance will increment the class attribute count again. Notice how the class attribute is shared by the class and all instances of the class.

Using Private Functions

Like most languages, Python has the concept of private elements:

- Private functions, which cannot be called from outside their module

- Private class methods, which cannot be called from outside their class

- Private attributes, which cannot be accessed from outside their class

Unlike in most languages, whether a Python function, method, or attribute is private or public is determined entirely by its name. If the name of a Python function, class method, or attribute starts with (but doesn't end with) two underscores, it's private; everything else is public. Python has no concept of *protected* class methods (accessible only in their own class and descendant classes). Class methods are either private (accessible only in their own class) or public (accessible from anywhere).

In `MP3FileInfo`, there are two methods: `__parse` and `__setitem__`. As we have already discussed, `__setitem__` is a special method; normally, you would call it indirectly by using the dictionary syntax on a class instance, but it is public, and you could call it directly (even from outside the `fileinfo` module) if you had a really good reason. However, `__parse` is private, because it has two underscores at the beginning of its name. Listing 5-19 demonstrates what happens when you try to call a private method outside its class.

> **CAUTION** *In Python, all special methods (like* `__setitem__`*) and built-in attributes (like* `__doc__`*) follow a standard naming convention: they both start with and end with two underscores. Don't name your own methods and attributes this way, because it will only confuse you (and others) later.*

Listing 5-19. Trying to Call a Private Method

```
>>> import fileinfo
>>> m = fileinfo.MP3FileInfo()
>>> m.__parse("/music/_singles/kairo.mp3")          (1)
Traceback (innermost last):
  File "<interactive input>", line 1, in ?
AttributeError: 'MP3FileInfo' instance has no attribute '__parse'
```

(1) If you try to call a private method, Python will raise a slightly misleading exception, saying that the method does not exist. Of course, it does exist, but it's private, so it's not accessible outside the class.

Strictly speaking, private methods are accessible outside their class, just not *easily* accessible. Nothing in Python is truly private; internally, the names of private methods and attributes are mangled and unmangled on the fly to make them seem inaccessible by their given names. You can access the `__parse` method of the `MP3FileInfo` class by the name `_MP3FileInfo__parse`. Acknowledge that this is interesting, but promise to never, ever do it in real code. Private methods are private for a reason, but like many other things in Python, their privateness is ultimately a matter of convention, not force.

Further Reading on Private Functions

For more information about Python's private functions, refer to the following:

- *Python Tutorial* (`http://www.python.org/doc/current/tut/tut.html`) discusses the inner workings of private variables (`http://www.python.org/doc/current/tut/node11.html#SECTION0011600000000000000000`).

Summary

That's it for the hard-core object trickery. You'll see a real-world application of special class methods in Chapter 12, which uses __getattr__ to create a proxy to a remote web service.

The next chapter will continue using the code sample presented in Listing 5-1 to explore other Python concepts, such as exceptions, file objects, and `for` loops.

Before you dive into the next chapter, make sure you're comfortable doing all of these things:

- Importing modules using either `import` *module* or *from module* `import`

- Defining and instantiating classes

- Defining __init__ methods and other special class methods, and understanding when they are called

- Subclassing `UserDict` to define classes that act like dictionaries

- Defining data attributes and class attributes, and understanding the difference between them

- Defining private attributes and methods

Exceptions and File Handling

IN THIS CHAPTER, you will dive into exceptions, file objects, for loops, and the os and sys modules. If you've used exceptions in another programming language, you can skim the first section to get a sense of Python's syntax. Be sure to tune in again for file handling.

Handling Exceptions

Like many other programming languages, Python has exception handling via try...except blocks.

> **NOTE**   *Python vs. Java exception handling: Python uses* try...except *to handle exceptions and* raise *to generate them. Java and C++ use* try...catch *to handle exceptions and* throw *to generate them.*

Exceptions are everywhere in Python. Virtually every module in the standard Python library uses them, and Python itself will raise them in a lot of different circumstances. You've already seen them repeatedly throughout this book.

- Accessing a nonexistent dictionary key will raise a KeyError exception.

- Searching a list for a nonexistent value will raise a ValueError exception.

- Calling a nonexistent method will raise an AttributeError exception.

- Referencing a nonexistent variable will raise a NameError exception.

- Mixing datatypes without coercion will raise a TypeError exception.

In each of these cases, you were simply playing around in the Python IDE—an error occurred, the exception was printed (depending on your IDE, perhaps in an intentionally jarring shade of red), and that was that. This is called an *unhandled* exception. When the exception was raised, there was no code to explicitly notice it and deal with it, so it bubbled its way back to the default behavior built in to Python, which is to spit out some debugging information and give up. In the IDE, that's no big deal. But what if that happened while your actual Python program was running? The entire program would come to a screeching halt.

An exception doesn't need to result in a complete program crash, though. Exceptions, when raised, can be *handled*. Sometimes an exception is really because you have a bug in your code (like accessing a variable that doesn't exist), but many times, an exception is something you can anticipate. If you're opening a file, it might not exist. If you're connecting to a database, it might be unavailable, or you might not have the correct security credentials to access it. If you know a line of code might raise an exception, you should handle the exception using a try...except block, as shown in the example in Listing 6-1.

Listing 6-1. Opening a Nonexistent File

```
>>> fsock = open("/notthere", "r")              (1)
Traceback (innermost last):
  File "<interactive input>", line 1, in ?
IOError: [Errno 2] No such file or directory: '/notthere'
>>> try:
...     fsock = open("/notthere")               (2)
... except IOError:                             (3)
...     print "The file does not exist, exiting gracefully"
... print "This line will always print"         (4)
The file does not exist, exiting gracefully
This line will always print
```

(1) Using the built-in open function, you can try to open a file for reading (more on open in the next section). But the file doesn't exist, so this raises the IOError exception. Since you haven't provided any explicit check for an IOError exception, Python just prints out some debugging information about what happened and gives up.

(2) You're trying to open the same nonexistent file, but this time, you're doing it within a try...except block.

(3) When the open method raises an IOError exception, you're ready for it. The except IOError: line catches the exception and executes your own block of code, which, in this case, just prints a more pleasant error message.

(4) Once an exception has been handled, processing continues normally on the first line after the try...except block. Note that this line will always print, whether or not an exception occurs. If you really did have a file called notthere in your root directory, the call to open would succeed, the except clause would be ignored, and this line would still be executed.

Exceptions may seem unfriendly (after all, if you don't catch the exception, your entire program will crash), but consider the alternative. Would you rather get back an unusable file object to a nonexistent file? You would need to check its validity somehow anyway, and if you forgot, somewhere down the line, your program would give you strange errors that you would need to trace back to the source. I'm sure you've experienced this and you know it's not fun. With exceptions, errors occur immediately, and you can handle them in a standard way at the source of the problem.

Using Exceptions for Other Purposes

There are a lot of other uses for exceptions besides handling actual error conditions. A common use in the standard Python library is to try to import a module, and then check whether it worked. Importing a module that does not exist will raise an ImportError exception. You can use this to define multiple levels of functionality based on which modules are available at runtime, or to support multiple platforms (where platform-specific code is separated into different modules).

> **NOTE** *You can also define your own exceptions by creating a class that inherits from the built-in* Exception *class, and then raise your exceptions with the* raise *command. See the "Further Reading on Exception Handling" section later in this chapter if you're interested in doing this.*

Listing 6-2 demonstrates how to use an exception to support platform-specific functionality. This code comes from the getpass module, a wrapper module for getting a password from the user. Getting a password is accomplished differently on UNIX, Windows, and Mac OS platforms, but this code encapsulates all of those differences.

Listing 6-2. Supporting Platform-Specific Functionality

```
# Bind the name getpass to the appropriate function
try:
    import termios, TERMIOS                    (1)
except ImportError:
    try:
```

```
            import msvcrt                              (2)
    except ImportError:
        try:
            from EasyDialogs import AskPassword        (3)
        except ImportError:
            getpass = default_getpass                  (4)
        else:                                          (5)
            getpass = AskPassword
    else:
        getpass = win_getpass
else:
    getpass = unix_getpass
```

(1) termios is a UNIX-specific module that provides low-level control over the input terminal. If this module is not available (because it's not on your system or your system doesn't support it), the import fails, and Python raises an ImportError, which you catch.

(2) Okay, you didn't have termios, so let's try msvcrt, which is a Windows-specific module that provides an API to many useful functions in the Microsoft Visual C++ runtime services. If this import fails, Python will raise an ImportError, which you catch.

(3) If the first two didn't work, you try to import a function from EasyDialogs, which is a Mac OS–specific module that provides functions to pop up dialog boxes of various types. Once again, if this import fails, Python will raise an ImportError, which you catch.

(4) None of these platform-specific modules is available (which is possible, since Python has been ported to a lot of different platforms), so you need to fall back on a default password input function (which is defined elsewhere in the getpass module). Notice what you're doing here: assigning the function default_getpass to the variable getpass. If you read the official getpass documentation, it tells you that the getpass module defines a getpass function. It does this by binding getpass to the correct function for your platform. Then when you call the getpass function, you're really calling a platform-specific function that this code has set up for you. You don't need to know or care which platform your code is running on—just call getpass, and it will always do the right thing.

(5) A try...except block can have an else clause, like an if statement. If no exception is raised during the try block, the else clause is executed afterwards. In this case, that means that the from EasyDialogs import AskPassword import worked, so you should bind getpass to the AskPassword function. Each of the other try...except blocks has similar else clauses to bind getpass to the appropriate function when you find an import that works.

Further Reading on Exception Handling

For more information about exception handling in Python, refer to the following:

- *Python Tutorial* (http://www.python.org/doc/current/tut/tut.html) discusses defining and raising your own exceptions, and handling multiple exceptions at once (http://www.python.org/doc/current/tut/node10.html#SECTION0010400000000000000000).

- *Python Library Reference* (http://www.python.org/doc/current/lib/) summarizes all the built-in exceptions (http://www.python.org/doc/current/lib/module-exceptions.html), documents the getpass module (http://www.python.org/doc/current/lib/module-getpass.html), and documents the traceback module, which provides low-level access to exception attributes after an exception is raised (http://www.python.org/doc/current/lib/module-traceback.html).

- *Python Reference Manual* (http://www.python.org/doc/current/ref/) discusses the inner workings of the try...except block (http://www.python.org/doc/current/ref/try.html).

Working with File Objects

Python has a built-in function, open, for opening a file on disk. As shown in Listing 6-3, open returns a file object, which has methods and attributes for getting information about and manipulating the opened file.

Listing 6-3. Opening a File

```
>>> f = open("/music/_singles/kairo.mp3", "rb")        (1)
>>> f                                                  (2)
<open file '/music/_singles/kairo.mp3', mode 'rb' at 010E3988>
>>> f.mode                                             (3)
'rb'
>>> f.name                                             (4)
'/music/_singles/kairo.mp3'
```

(1) The open method can take up to three parameters: a filename, a mode, and a buffering parameter. Only the first one, the filename, is required; the other two are optional. If not specified, the file is opened for reading in text mode.

Here, you are opening the file for reading in binary mode. (print open.__doc__ displays a great explanation of all the possible modes.)

(2) The open function returns an object (by now, this should not surprise you). A file object has several useful attributes.

(3) The mode attribute of a file object tells you in which mode the file was opened.

(4) The name attribute of a file object tells you the name of the file that the file object has open.

Reading Files

After you open a file, the first thing you'll want to do is read from it, as shown in Listing 6-4.

Listing 6-4. Reading a File

```
>>> f
<open file '/music/_singles/kairo.mp3', mode 'rb' at 010E3988>
>>> f.tell()                                    (1)
0
>>> f.seek(-128, 2)                             (2)
>>> f.tell()                                    (3)
7542909
>>> tagData = f.read(128)                        (4)
>>> tagData
'TAGKAIRO****THE BEST GOA        ***DJ MARY-JANE***
Rave Mix                2000http://mp3.com/DJMARYJANE      \037'
>>> f.tell()                                    (5)
7543037
```

(1) A file object maintains state about the file it has open. The tell method of a file object tells you your current position in the open file. Since you haven't done anything with this file yet, the current position is 0, which is the beginning of the file.

(2) The seek method of a file object moves to another position in the open file. The second parameter specifies what the first one means: 0 means move to an absolute position (counting from the start of the file), 1 means move to a relative position (counting from the current position), and 2 means move to a position relative to the end of the file. Since the MP3 tags you're looking for are stored at the end of the file, you use 2 and tell the file object to move to a position 128 bytes from the end of the file.

(3) The tell method confirms that the current file position has moved.

(4) The read method reads a specified number of bytes from the open file and returns a string with the data that was read. The optional parameter specifies the maximum number of bytes to read. If no parameter is specified, read will read until the end of the file. (You could have simply said read() here, since you know your location in the file and you are, in fact, reading the last 128 bytes.) The read data is assigned to the tagData variable, and the current position is updated based on how many bytes were read.

(5) The tell method confirms that the current position has moved. If you do the math, you'll see that after reading 128 bytes, the position has been incremented by 128.

Closing Files

Open files consume system resources, and depending on the file mode, other programs may not be able to access them. It's important to close files as soon as you're finished with them, as shown in Listing 6-5.

Listing 6-5. Closing a File

```
>>> f
<open file '/music/_singles/kairo.mp3', mode 'rb' at 010E3988>
>>> f.closed                              (1)
False
>>> f.close()                             (2)
>>> f
<closed file '/music/_singles/kairo.mp3', mode 'rb' at 010E3988>
>>> f.closed                              (3)
True
>>> f.seek(0)                             (4)
Traceback (innermost last):
  File "<interactive input>", line 1, in ?
ValueError: I/O operation on closed file
>>> f.tell()
Traceback (innermost last):
  File "<interactive input>", line 1, in ?
ValueError: I/O operation on closed file
>>> f.read()
Traceback (innermost last):
  File "<interactive input>", line 1, in ?
ValueError: I/O operation on closed file
>>> f.close()                             (5)
```

(1) The closed attribute of a file object indicates whether the object has a file open or not. In this case, the file is still open (closed is False).

(2) To close a file, call the close method of the file object. This frees the lock (if any) that you were holding on the file, flushes buffered writes (if any) that the system had not gotten around to actually writing yet, and releases the system resources.

(3) The closed attribute confirms that the file is closed.

(4) Just because a file is closed doesn't mean that the file object ceases to exist. The variable f will continue to exist until it goes out of scope or is manually deleted. However, none of the methods that manipulate an open file will work once the file has been closed; they all raise an exception.

(5) Calling close on a file object whose file is already closed does *not* raise an exception; it fails silently.

Handling I/O Errors

Now you've seen enough to understand the file-handling code in the fileinfo.py sample code from the previous chapter. Listing 6-6 shows how to safely open and read from a file and gracefully handle errors.

Listing 6-6. File Objects in MP3FileInfo

```
    try:                                        (1)
        fsock = open(filename, "rb", 0)         (2)
        try:
            fsock.seek(-128, 2)                 (3)
            tagdata = fsock.read(128)           (4)
        finally:                                (5)
            fsock.close()

        .

        .

        .

    except IOError:                             (6)
        pass
```

(1) Because opening and reading files is risky and may raise an exception, all of this code is wrapped in a try...except block. (Hey, isn't standardized indentation great? This is where you start to appreciate it.)

(2) The open function may raise an IOError. (Maybe the file doesn't exist.)

(3) The seek method may raise an IOError. (Maybe the file is smaller than 128 bytes.)

(4) The read method may raise an IOError. (Maybe the disk has a bad sector, or it's on a network drive and the network just went down.)

(5) This is new: a try...finally block. Once the file has been opened successfully by the open function, you want to make absolutely sure that you close it, even if an exception is raised by the seek or read method. That's what a try...finally block is for: code in the finally block will *always* be executed, even if something in the try block raises an exception. Think of it as code that gets executed on the way out, regardless of what happened before.

(6) At last, you handle your IOError exception. This could be the IOError exception raised by the call to open, seek, or read. Here, you really don't care, because all you're going to do is ignore it silently and continue. (Remember that pass is a Python statement that does nothing.) That's perfectly legal— "handling" an exception can mean explicitly doing nothing. It still counts as handled, and processing will continue normally on the next line of code after the try...except block.

Writing to Files

As you would expect, you can also write to files in much the same way that you read from them. There are two basic file modes:

- Append mode will add data to the end of the file.

- Write mode will overwrite the file.

Either mode will create the file automatically if it doesn't already exist, so there's never a need for any sort of fiddly "if the log file doesn't exist yet, create a new empty file just so we can open it for the first time" logic. Just open it and start writing.

Listing 6-7 demonstrates writing to files.

Listing 6-7. Writing to Files

```
>>> logfile = open('test.log', 'w')              (1)
>>> logfile.write('test succeeded')              (2)
>>> logfile.close()
>>> print file('test.log').read()                (3)
test succeeded
>>> logfile = open('test.log', 'a')              (4)
>>> logfile.write('line 2')
>>> logfile.close()
>>> print file('test.log').read()                (5)
test succeededline 2
```

(1) We start boldly by either creating the new file test.log or overwriting the existing file, and opening the file for writing. (The second parameter, "w", means open the file for writing.) Yes, that's all as dangerous as it sounds. I hope you didn't care about the previous contents of that file, because they are gone now.

(2) You can add data to the newly opened file with the write method of the file object returned by open.

(3) file is a synonym for open. This one-liner opens the file, reads its contents, and prints them.

(4) You happen to know that test.log exists (since you just finished writing to it), so you can open it and append to it. (The "a" parameter means open the file for appending.) Actually, you could do this even if the file didn't exist, because opening the file for appending will create the file if necessary. But appending will *never* harm the existing contents of the file.

(5) As you can see, both the original line you wrote and the second line you appended are now in test.log. Also note that carriage returns are not included. Since you didn't write them explicitly to the file either time, the file doesn't include them. You can write a carriage return with the "\n" character. Since you didn't do this, everything you wrote to the file ended up jammed together on the same line.

Further Reading on File Handling

For more information about working with Python file objects, refer to the following:

- *Python Tutorial* (http://www.python.org/doc/current/tut/tut.html) discusses reading and writing files, including how to read a file one line at a time into a list (http://www.python.org/doc/current/tut/node9.html#SECTION009210000000000000000).

- effbot (http://www.effbot.org/guides/) discusses efficiency and performance of various ways of reading a file (http://www.effbot.org/guides/readline-performance.htm).

- Python Knowledge Base (http://www.faqts.com/knowledge-base/index.phtml/fid/199) answers common questions about files (http://www.faqts.com/knowledge-base/index.phtml/fid/552).

- *Python Library Reference* (http://www.python.org/doc/current/lib) summarizes all the file object methods (http://www.python.org/doc/current/lib/bltin-file-objects.html).

Iterating with for Loops

Like most other languages, Python has for loops. The only reason you haven't seen them until now is that Python is good at so many other things that you don't need them as often.

Most other languages don't have a powerful list datatype like Python's, so you end up doing a lot of manual work, specifying a start, end, and step to define a range of integers, characters, or other entities you might iterate through. But in Python, a for loop simply iterates over a list, the same way list comprehensions work, as shown in Listing 6-8.

Listing 6-8. Introducing the for Loop

```
>>> li = ['a', 'b', 'e']
>>> for s in li:                        (1)
...     print s                         (2)
a
b
e
>>> print "\n".join(li)                 (3)
a
b
e
```

(1) The syntax for a for loop is similar to list comprehensions. li is a list, and s will take the value of each element in turn, starting from the first element.

(2) Like an if statement, or any other indented block, a for loop can have any number of lines of code in it.

(3) This is the reason you haven't seen the for loop yet: you haven't needed it yet. It's amazing how often you use for loops in other languages when all you really want is a join or a list comprehension.

Doing a "normal" (by Visual Basic standards) counter for loop is also simple, as shown in Listing 6-9.

Listing 6-9. Simple Counters

```
>>> for i in range(5):                  (1)
...     print i
0
1
2
3
4
>>> li = ['a', 'b', 'c', 'd', 'e']
>>> for i in range(len(li)):            (2)
...     print li[i]
a
b
c
d
e
```

(1) As you saw in Chapter 3's Listing 3-20, "Assigning Consecutive Values," range produces a list of integers, which you then loop through. I know it looks a bit odd, but it is occasionally (and I stress *occasionally*) useful to have a counter loop.

(2) Don't ever do this. This is Visual Basic–style thinking. Break out of it. Just iterate through the list, as shown in the previous example.

Listing 6-10 shows an example of a for loop that iterates through a dictionary.

Listing 6-10. Iterating Through a Dictionary

```
>>> import os
>>> for k, v in os.environ.items():      (1) (2)
...     print "%s=%s" % (k, v)
USERPROFILE=C:\Documents and Settings\mpilgrim
OS=Windows_NT
COMPUTERNAME=MPILGRIM
USERNAME=mpilgrim

[...snip...]
>>> print "\n".join(["%s=%s" % (k, v) for k, v in os.environ.items()])      (3)
USERPROFILE=C:\Documents and Settings\mpilgrim
OS=Windows_NT
COMPUTERNAME=MPILGRIM
USERNAME=mpilgrim

[...snip...]
```

(1) os.environ is a dictionary of the environment variables defined on your system. In Windows, these are your user and system variables accessible from MS-DOS. In UNIX, they are the variables exported in your shell's startup scripts. In Mac OS, there is no concept of environment variables, so this dictionary is empty.

(2) os.environ.items() returns a list of tuples: [(*key1*, *value1*), (*key2*, *value2*), ...]. The for loop iterates through this list. In the first round, it assigns *key1* to k and *value1* to v, so k = USERPROFILE and v = C:\Documents and Settings\mpilgrim. In the second round, k gets the second key, OS, and v gets the corresponding value, Windows_NT.

(3) With multivariable assignment and list comprehensions, you can replace the entire for loop with a single statement. Whether you actually do this in real code is a matter of personal coding style. I like it because it clearly shows that I'm mapping a dictionary into a list, and then joining the list into a single string. Other programmers prefer to write this out as a for loop. The output is the same in either case, although this version is slightly faster, because there is only one print statement instead of many.

Now, we can look at the `for` loop in `MP3FileInfo`, shown in Listing 6-11, from the sample `fileinfo.py` program introduced in Chapter 5.

Listing 6-11. for Loop in MP3FileInfo

```
tagDataMap = {"title"   : (  3,   33, stripnulls),
              "artist"  : ( 33,  63, stripnulls),
              "album"   : ( 63,  93, stripnulls),
              "year"    : ( 93,  97, stripnulls),
              "comment" : ( 97, 126, stripnulls),
              "genre"   : (127, 128, ord)}                    (1)
              .
              .
              .

    if tagdata[:3] == "TAG":
        for tag, (start, end, parseFunc) in self.tagDataMap.items():   (2)
            self[tag] = parseFunc(tagdata[start:end])                  (3)
```

(1) `tagDataMap` is a class attribute that defines the tags you're looking for in an MP3 file. Tags are stored in fixed-length fields. Once you read the last 128 bytes of the file, bytes 3 through 32 of those are always the song title, 33 through 62 are always the artist name, 63 through 92 are the album name, and so forth. Note that `tagDataMap` is a dictionary of tuples, and each tuple contains two integers and a function reference.

(2) This looks complicated, but it's not. The structure of the `for` variables matches the structure of the elements of the list returned by `items`. Remember that `items` returns a list of tuples of the form (*key, value*). The first element of that list is ("title", (3, 33, <function stripnulls>)), so the first time around the loop, `tag` gets "title", `start` gets 3, `end` gets 33, and `parseFunc` gets the function `stripnulls`.

(3) Now that you've extracted all the parameters for a single MP3 tag, saving the tag data is easy. You slice `tagdata` from `start` to `end` to get the actual data for this tag, call `parseFunc` to postprocess the data, and assign this as the value for the key `tag` in the pseudo-dictionary `self`. After iterating through all the elements in `tagDataMap`, `self` has the values for all the tags, and you know what that looks like.

Using `sys.modules`

Modules, like everything else in Python, are objects. Once imported, you can always get a reference to a module through the global dictionary `sys.modules`, introduced in Listing 6-12.

Listing 6-12. Introducing sys.modules

```
>>> import sys                                      (1)
>>> print '\n'.join(sys.modules.keys())            (2)
win32api
os.path
os
exceptions
__main__
ntpath
nt
sys
__builtin__
site
signal
UserDict
stat
```

(1) The sys module contains system-level information, like the version of Python you're running (sys.version or sys.version_info), and system-level options, such as the maximum allowed recursion depth (sys.getrecursionlimit() and sys.setrecursionlimit()).

(2) sys.modules is a dictionary containing all the modules that have ever been imported since Python was started. The key is the module name, and the value is the module object. Note that this includes more than just the modules *your* program has imported. Python preloads some modules on startup, and if you're using a Python IDE, sys.modules contains all the modules imported by all the programs you've run within the IDE.

Listing 6-13 demonstrates how to use sys.modules.

Listing 6-13. Using sys.modules

```
>>> import fileinfo                                 (1)
>>> print '\n'.join(sys.modules.keys())
win32api
os.path
os
fileinfo
exceptions
__main__
ntpath
nt
sys
__builtin__
site
```

```
signal
UserDict
stat
>>> fileinfo
<module 'fileinfo' from 'fileinfo.pyc'>
>>> sys.modules["fileinfo"]                          (2)
<module 'fileinfo' from 'fileinfo.pyc'>
```

(1) As new modules are imported, they are added to sys.modules. This explains why importing the same module twice is very fast: Python has already loaded and cached the module in sys.modules, so importing the second time is simply a dictionary lookup.

(2) Given the name (as a string) of any previously imported module, you can get a reference to the module itself through the sys.modules dictionary.

Listing 6-14 shows how to use the _module_ class attribute with the sys.modules dictionary to get a reference to the module in which a class is defined.

Listing 6-14. The _module_ Class Attribute

```
>>> from fileinfo import MP3FileInfo
>>> MP3FileInfo._module_                             (1)
'fileinfo'
>>> sys.modules[MP3FileInfo._module_]                (2)
<module 'fileinfo' from 'fileinfo.pyc'>
```

(1) Every Python class has a built-in class attribute _module_, which is the name of the module in which the class is defined.

(2) Combining this with the sys.modules dictionary, you can get a reference to the module in which a class is defined.

Now, you're ready to see how sys.modules is used in fileinfo.py, the sample program introduced in the previous chapter. Listing 6-15 shows that portion of the code.

Listing 6-15. sys.modules in fileinfo.py

```
def getFileInfoClass(filename, module=sys.modules[FileInfo._module_]):   (1)
    "get file info class from filename extension"
    subclass = "%sFileInfo" % os.path.splitext(filename)[1].upper()[1:]  (2)
    return hasattr(module, subclass) and getattr(module, subclass) or FileInfo   (3)
```

(1) This is a function with two arguments: filename is required, but module is optional and defaults to the module that contains the FileInfo class. This looks inefficient, because you might expect Python to evaluate the sys.modules expression every time the function is called. In fact, Python evaluates default

111

expressions only once: the first time the module is imported. As you'll see later, you never call this function with a module argument, so module serves as a function-level constant.

(2) We'll plow through this line later, after we dive into the os module. For now, take it on faith that subclass ends up as the name of a class, like MP3FileInfo.

(3) You already know about getattr, which gets a reference to an object by name. hasattr is a complementary function that checks whether an object has a particular attribute; in this case, whether a module has a particular class (although it works for any object and any attribute, just like getattr). In English, this line of code says, "If this module has the class named by subclass, then return it; otherwise, return the base class FileInfo."

Further Reading on Modules

For more information on Python modules, refer to the following:

- *Python Tutorial* (http://www.python.org/doc/current/tut/tut.html) discusses exactly when and how default arguments are evaluated (http://www.python.org/doc/current/tut/node6.html#SECTION006710000000000000000).

- *Python Library Reference* (http://www.python.org/doc/current/lib) documents the sys module (http://www.python.org/doc/current/lib/module-sys.html).

Working with Directories

The os.path module has several functions for manipulating files and directories. Here, we'll look at handling pathnames and listing the contents of a directory. Listing 6-16 demonstrates how to construct pathnames.

Listing 6-16. Constructing Pathnames

```
>>> import os
>>> os.path.join("c:\\music\\ap\\", "mahadeva.mp3")    (1) (2)
'c:\\music\\ap\\mahadeva.mp3'
>>> os.path.join("c:\\music\\ap", "mahadeva.mp3")      (3)
'c:\\music\\ap\\mahadeva.mp3'
>>> os.path.expanduser("~")                            (4)
'c:\\Documents and Settings\\mpilgrim\\My Documents'
>>> os.path.join(os.path.expanduser("~"), "Python")    (5)
'c:\\Documents and Settings\\mpilgrim\\My Documents\\Python'
```

(1) os.path is a reference to a module—which module depends on your platform. Just as getpass encapsulates differences between platforms by setting getpass to a platform-specific function, os encapsulates differences between platforms by setting path to a platform-specific module.

(2) The join function of os.path constructs a pathname out of one or more partial pathnames. In this case, it simply concatenates strings. (Note that dealing with pathnames on Windows is annoying because the backslash character must be escaped.)

(3) In this slightly less trivial case, join will add an extra backslash to the pathname before joining it to the filename. I was overjoyed when I discovered this, since addSlashIfNecessary is one of the stupid little functions I always have to write when building up my toolbox in a new language. *Do not* write this stupid little function in Python; smart people have already taken care of it for you.

(4) expanduser will expand a pathname that uses ~ to represent the current user's home directory. This works on any platform where users have a home directory, like Windows, UNIX, and Mac OS X; it has no effect on Mac OS.

(5) Combining these techniques, you can easily construct pathnames for directories and files under the user's home directory.

Listing 6-17 shows how to split pathnames.

Listing 6-17. Splitting Pathnames

```
>>> os.path.split("c:\\music\\ap\\mahadeva.mp3")                    (1)
('c:\\music\\ap', 'mahadeva.mp3')
>>> (filepath, filename) = os.path.split("c:\\music\\ap\\mahadeva.mp3")   (2)
>>> filepath                                                        (3)
'c:\\music\\ap'
>>> filename                                                        (4)
'mahadeva.mp3'
>>> (shortname, extension) = os.path.splitext(filename)             (5)
>>> shortname
'mahadeva'
>>> extension
'.mp3'
```

(1) The split function splits a full pathname and returns a tuple containing the path and filename. Remember when I said you could use multivariable assignment to return multiple values from a function? Well, split is such a function.

(2) You assign the return value of the split function into a tuple of two variables. Each variable receives the value of the corresponding element of the returned tuple.

(3) The first variable, filepath, receives the value of the first element of the tuple returned from split: the file path.

(4) The second variable, `filename`, receives the value of the second element of the tuple returned from `split`: the filename.

(5) `os.path` also contains a function `splitext`, which splits a filename and returns a tuple containing the filename and the file extension. You use the same technique to assign each of them to separate variables.

Listing Directories

Listing 6-18 demonstrates how to get a list of directories, using `os.listdir`.

Listing 6-18. Listing Directories

```
>>> os.listdir("c:\\music\\_singles\\")          (1)
['a_time_long_forgotten_con.mp3', 'hellraiser.mp3',
'kairo.mp3', 'long_way_home1.mp3', 'sidewinder.mp3',
'spinning.mp3']
>>> dirname = "c:\\"
>>> os.listdir(dirname)                          (2)
['AUTOEXEC.BAT', 'boot.ini', 'CONFIG.SYS', 'cygwin',
'docbook', 'Documents and Settings', 'Incoming',
'Inetpub', 'IO.SYS', 'MSDOS.SYS', 'Music',
'NTDETECT.COM', 'ntldr', 'pagefile.sys',
'Program Files', 'Python20', 'RECYCLER',
'System Volume Information', 'TEMP', 'WINNT']
>>> [f for f in os.listdir(dirname)
... if os.path.isfile(os.path.join(dirname, f))]  (3)
['AUTOEXEC.BAT', 'boot.ini', 'CONFIG.SYS', 'IO.SYS',
'MSDOS.SYS', 'NTDETECT.COM', 'ntldr', 'pagefile.sys']
>>> [f for f in os.listdir(dirname) if
... os.path.isdir(os.path.join(dirname, f))]      (4)
['cygwin', 'docbook', 'Documents and Settings',
'Incoming', 'Inetpub', 'Music', 'Program Files',
'Python20', 'RECYCLER', 'System Volume Information',
'TEMP', 'WINNT']
```

(1) The `listdir` function takes a pathname and returns a list of the contents of the directory.

(2) `listdir` returns both files and folders, with no indication of which is which.

(3) You can use list filtering and the `isfile` function of the `os.path` module to separate the files from the folders. `isfile` takes a pathname and returns 1 if the path represents a file or 0 otherwise. Here, you're using `os.path.join` to ensure a full pathname, but `isfile` also works with a partial path, relative to the current working directory. You can use `os.getcwd()` to get the current working directory.

(4) os.path also has an isdir function, which returns 1 if the path represents a directory or 0 otherwise. You can use this to get a list of the subdirectories within a directory.

The two lines of code shown in Listing 6-19 combine everything you've learned so far about the os module, and then some.

Listing 6-19. Listing Directories in fileinfo.py

```
def listDirectory(directory, fileExtList):
    "get list of file info objects for files of particular extensions"
    fileList = [os.path.normcase(f)
                for f in os.listdir(directory)]          (1) (2)
    fileList = [os.path.join(directory, f)
                for f in fileList
                if os.path.splitext(f)[1] in fileExtList]   (3) (4) (5)
```

(1) os.listdir(directory) returns a list of all the files and folders in directory.

(2) Iterating through the list with f, you use os.path.normcase(f) to normalize the case according to operating system defaults. normcase is a useful little function that compensates for case-insensitive operating systems that think that mahadeva.mp3 and mahadeva.MP3 are the same file. For instance, on Windows and Mac OS, normcase will convert the entire filename to lowercase; on UNIX-compatible systems, it will return the filename unchanged.

(3) Iterating through the normalized list with f again, you use os.path.splitext(f) to split each filename into name and extension.

(4) For each file, you see if the extension is in the list of file extensions you care about (fileExtList, which was passed to the listDirectory function).

(5) For each file you care about, you use os.path.join(directory, f) to construct the full pathname of the file, and then return a list of the full pathnames.

> **NOTE** *Whenever possible, you should use the functions in os and os.path for file, directory, and path manipulations. These modules are wrappers for platform-specific modules, so functions like os.path.split work on UNIX, Windows, Mac OS, and any other platform supported by Python.*

There is one other way to get the contents of a directory, shown in Listing 6-20. It's very powerful, and it uses the sort of wildcards that you may already be familiar with from working on the command line.

Listing 6-20. Listing Directories with glob

```
>>> os.listdir("c:\\music\\_singles\\")              (1)
['a_time_long_forgotten_con.mp3', 'hellraiser.mp3', 'kairo.mp3',
'long_way_home1.mp3', 'sidewinder.mp3', 'spinning.mp3']
>>> import glob
>>> glob.glob('c:\\music\\_singles\\*.mp3')          (2)
['c:\\music\\_singles\\a_time_long_forgotten_con.mp3',
'c:\\music\\_singles\\hellraiser.mp3',
'c:\\music\\_singles\\kairo.mp3',
'c:\\music\\_singles\\long_way_home1.mp3',
'c:\\music\\_singles\\sidewinder.mp3',
'c:\\music\\_singles\\spinning.mp3']
>>> glob.glob('c:\\music\\_singles\\s*.mp3')         (3)
['c:\\music\\_singles\\sidewinder.mp3',
'c:\\music\\_singles\\spinning.mp3']
>>> glob.glob('c:\\music\\*\\*.mp3')                  (4)
```

(1) As you saw earlier, os.listdir simply takes a directory path and lists all files and directories in that directory.

(2) The glob module, on the other hand, takes a wildcard and returns the full path of all files and directories matching the wildcard. Here, the wildcard is a directory path plus *.mp3, which will match all .mp3 files. Note that each element of the returned list already includes the full path of the file.

(3) If you want to find all the files in a specific directory that start with *s* and end with *.mp3*, you can do that, too.

(4) Now consider this scenario: you have a music directory, with several subdirectories within it, with .mp3 files within each subdirectory. You can get a list of all of those with a single call to glob, by using two wildcards at once. One wildcard is the "*.mp3" (to match .mp3 files), and one wildcard is *within the directory path itself*, to match any subdirectory within c:\music. That's a crazy amount of power packed into one deceptively simple-looking function!

Further Reading on the os Module

For more information about the os module, refer to the following:

- Python Knowledge Base (http://www.faqts.com/knowledge-base/index.phtml/fid/199) answers questions about the os module (http://www.faqts.com/knowledge-base/index.phtml/fid/240).

- *Python Library Reference* (http://www.python.org/doc/current/lib) documents the os module (http://www.python.org/doc/current/lib/module-os.html) and the os.path module (http://www.python.org/doc/current/lib/module-os.path.html).

Putting It All Together

Once again, all the dominos are in place. You've seen how each line of code works. Now let's step back and see how it all fits together. Take a look at Listing 6-21.

Listing 6-21. listDirectory

```
def listDirectory(directory, fileExtList):                      (1)
    "get list of file info objects for files of particular extensions"
    fileList = [os.path.normcase(f) for f in os.listdir(directory)]
    fileList = [os.path.join(directory, f) for f in fileList \
                if os.path.splitext(f)[1] in fileExtList]        (2)
    def getFileInfoClass(filename, \
        module=sys.modules[FileInfo.__module__]):                (3)
        "get file info class from filename extension"
        subclass = "%sFileInfo" % \
            os.path.splitext(filename)[1].upper()[1:]            (4)
        return hasattr(module, subclass) and \
            getattr(module, subclass) or FileInfo                (5)
    return [getFileInfoClass(f)(f) for f in fileList]            (6)
```

(1) listDirectory is the main attraction of this entire module. It takes a directory (like c:\music_singles\ in my case) and a list of interesting file extensions (like ['.mp3']), and returns a list of class instances that act like dictionaries that contain metadata about each interesting file in that directory. And it does it in just a few straightforward lines of code.

(2) As you saw in the previous section, this line of code gets a list of the full pathnames of all the files in directory that have an interesting file extension (as specified by fileExtList).

(3) Old-school Pascal programmers may be familiar with these, but most people give me a blank stare when I tell them that Python supports *nested functions*—literally, functions within functions. The nested function getFileInfoClass can be called only from the function in which it is defined, listDirectory. As with any other function, you don't need an interface declaration or anything fancy; just define the function and code it.

(4) Now that you've seen the os module, this line should make more sense. It gets the extension of the file (os.path.splitext(filename)[1]), forces it to uppercase (.upper()), slices off the dot ([1:]), and constructs a class name out of it with string formatting. So, c:\music\ap\mahadeva.mp3 becomes .mp3 becomes .MP3 becomes MP3 becomes MP3FileInfo.

(5) Having constructed the name of the handler class that would handle this file, you check to see if that handler class actually exists in this module. If it does, you return the class; otherwise, you return the base class FileInfo. This is a very important point: *this function returns a class*—not an instance of a class, but the class itself.

(6) For each file in our interesting files list (fileList), you call getFileInfoClass with the filename (f). Calling getFileInfoClass(f) returns a class. You don't know exactly which class, but you don't care. You then create an instance of this class (whatever it is) and pass the filename (f again), to the __init__ method. As you saw earlier in this chapter, the __init__ method of FileInfo sets self["name"], which triggers __setitem__, which is overridden in the descendant (MP3FileInfo) to parse the file appropriately to pull out the file's metadata. You do all that for each interesting file and return a list of the resulting instances.

Note that listDirectory is completely generic. It doesn't know ahead of time which types of files it will be getting, or which classes are defined that could potentially handle those files. It inspects the directory for the files to process, and then introspects its own module to see what special handler classes (like MP3FileInfo) are defined. You can extend this program to handle other types of files simply by defining an appropriately named class: HTMLFileInfo for HTML files, DOCFileInfo for Word .doc files, and so forth. listDirectory will handle them all, without modification, by handing off the real work to the appropriate classes and collating the results.

Summary

The fileinfo.py program introduced at the beginning of the previous chapter should now make perfect sense.

```
"""Framework for getting filetype-specific metadata.

Instantiate appropriate class with filename.  Returned object acts like a
dictionary, with key-value pairs for each piece of metadata.
    import fileinfo
    info = fileinfo.MP3FileInfo("/music/ap/mahadeva.mp3")
    print "\\n".join(["%s=%s" % (k, v) for k, v in info.items()])

Or use listDirectory function to get info on all files in a directory.
    for info in fileinfo.listDirectory("/music/ap/", [".mp3"]):
        ...
```

Framework can be extended by adding classes for particular file types, e.g.
HTMLFileInfo, MPGFileInfo, DOCFileInfo. Each class is completely responsible for
parsing its files appropriately; see MP3FileInfo for example.
"""

```python
import os
import sys
from UserDict import UserDict

def stripnulls(data):
    "strip whitespace and nulls"
    return data.replace("\00", "").strip()

class FileInfo(UserDict):
    "store file metadata"
    def __init__(self, filename=None):
        UserDict.__init__(self)
        self["name"] = filename

class MP3FileInfo(FileInfo):
    "store ID3v1.0 MP3 tags"
    tagDataMap = {"title"   : (  3,  33, stripnulls),
                  "artist"  : ( 33,  63, stripnulls),
                  "album"   : ( 63,  93, stripnulls),
                  "year"    : ( 93,  97, stripnulls),
                  "comment" : ( 97, 126, stripnulls),
                  "genre"   : (127, 128, ord)}

    def __parse(self, filename):
        "parse ID3v1.0 tags from MP3 file"
        self.clear()
        try:
            fsock = open(filename, "rb", 0)
            try:
                fsock.seek(-128, 2)
                tagdata = fsock.read(128)
            finally:
                fsock.close()
            if tagdata[:3] == "TAG":
                for tag, (start, end, parseFunc) in self.tagDataMap.items():
                    self[tag] = parseFunc(tagdata[start:end])
        except IOError:
            pass

    def __setitem__(self, key, item):
```

```
            if key == "name" and item:
                self.__parse(item)
            FileInfo.__setitem__(self, key, item)

    def listDirectory(directory, fileExtList):
        "get list of file info objects for files of particular extensions"
        fileList = [os.path.normcase(f) for f in os.listdir(directory)]
        fileList = [os.path.join(directory, f) for f in fileList \
                        if os.path.splitext(f)[1] in fileExtList]
        def getFileInfoClass(filename, module=sys.modules[FileInfo.__module__]):
            "get file info class from filename extension"
            subclass = "%sFileInfo" % os.path.splitext(filename)[1].upper()[1:]
            return hasattr(module, subclass) and getattr(module, subclass) or FileInfo
        return [getFileInfoClass(f)(f) for f in fileList]

if __name__ == "__main__":
    for info in listDirectory("/music/_singles/", [".mp3"]):
        print "\n".join(["%s=%s" % (k, v) for k, v in info.items()])
        print
```

Before diving into the next chapter, make sure you're comfortable doing the following:

- Catching exceptions with try...except

- Protecting external resources with try...finally

- Reading from files

- Assigning multiple values at once in a for loop

- Using the os module for all your cross-platform file manipulation needs

- Dynamically instantiating classes of unknown type by treating classes as objects and passing them around

CHAPTER 7

Regular Expressions

REGULAR EXPRESSIONS ARE a powerful and standardized way of searching, replacing, and parsing text with complex patterns of characters. If you've used regular expressions in other languages (like Perl), the syntax will be very familiar, so you might want to just read the summary of the re module (http://www.python.org/doc/current/lib/module-re.html) to get an overview of the available functions and their arguments.

Diving In

Strings have methods for searching (index, find, and count), replacing (replace), and parsing (split), but they are limited to the simplest of cases. The search methods look for a single, hard-coded substring, and they are always case-sensitive. To do case-insensitive searches of a string s, you must call s.lower() or s.upper() and make sure your search strings are the appropriate case to match. The replace and split methods have the same limitations.

If what you're trying to do can be accomplished with string functions, you should use them. They're fast and simple and easy to read, and there's a lot to be said for fast, simple, readable code. But if you find yourself using a lot of different string functions with if statements to handle special cases, or if you're combining them with split and join and list comprehensions in weird unreadable ways, you may need to move up to regular expressions.

Although the regular expression syntax is tight and unlike normal code, the result can end up being *more* readable than a hand-rolled solution that uses a long chain of string functions. There are even ways of embedding comments within regular expressions to make them practically self-documenting.

Case Study: Street Addresses

This series of examples was inspired by a real-life problem I had in my day job several years ago, when I needed to scrub and standardize street addresses exported from a legacy system before importing them into a newer system. (See, I don't just make this stuff up; it's actually useful.) Listing 7-1 shows how I approached the problem.

Listing 7-1. Matching at the End of a String

```
>>> s = '100 NORTH MAIN ROAD'
>>> s.replace('ROAD', 'RD.')                    (1)
'100 NORTH MAIN RD.'
>>> s = '100 NORTH BROAD ROAD'
>>> s.replace('ROAD', 'RD.')                    (2)
'100 NORTH BRD. RD.'
>>> s[:-4] + s[-4:].replace('ROAD', 'RD.')      (3)
'100 NORTH BROAD RD.'
>>> import re                                    (4)
>>> re.sub('ROAD$', 'RD.', s)                    (5) (6)
'100 NORTH BROAD RD.'
```

(1) My goal is to standardize a street address so that 'ROAD' is always abbreviated as 'RD.'. At first glance, I thought this was simple enough that I could just use the string method replace. After all, all the data was already uppercase, so case mismatches would not be a problem. And the search string, 'ROAD', was a constant. And in this deceptively simple example, s.replace does indeed work.

(2) Life, unfortunately, is full of counterexamples, and I quickly discovered this one. The problem here is that 'ROAD' appears twice in the address: once as part of the street name 'BROAD' and once as its own word. The replace method sees these two occurrences and blindly replaces both of them; meanwhile, I see my addresses getting destroyed.

(3) To solve the problem of addresses with more than one 'ROAD' substring, you could resort to something like this: only search and replace 'ROAD' in the last four characters of the address (s[-4:]), and leave the string alone (s[:-4]). But you can see that this is already getting unwieldy. For example, the pattern is dependent on the length of the string you're replacing (if you were replacing 'STREET' with 'ST.', you would need to use s[:-6] and s[-6:].replace(...)). Would you like to come back in six months and debug this? I know I wouldn't.

(4) It's time to move up to regular expressions. In Python, all functionality related to regular expressions is contained in the re module.

(5) Take a look at the first parameter: 'ROAD$'. This is a simple regular expression that matches 'ROAD' only when it occurs at the end of a string. The $ means "end of the string." (There is a corresponding character, the caret ^, which means "beginning of the string.")

(6) Using the re.sub function, you search the string s for the regular expression 'ROAD$' and replace it with 'RD.'. This matches the ROAD at the end of the string s, but does *not* match the ROAD that's part of the word BROAD, because that's in the middle of s.

Continuing with my story of scrubbing addresses, I soon discovered that the previous example—matching 'ROAD' at the end of the address—was not good enough, because not all addresses included a street designation; some just ended with the street name. Most of the time, I got away with it, but if the street name were 'BROAD', then the regular expression would match 'ROAD' at the end of the string as part of the word 'BROAD', which is not what I wanted. Listing 7-2 shows the resolution.

Listing 7-2. Matching Whole Words

```
>>> s = '100 BROAD'
>>> re.sub('ROAD$', 'RD.', s)
'100 BRD.'
>>> re.sub('\\bROAD$', 'RD.', s)              (1)
'100 BROAD'
>>> re.sub(r'\bROAD$', 'RD.', s)              (2)
'100 BROAD'
>>> s = '100 BROAD ROAD APT. 3'
>>> re.sub(r'\bROAD$', 'RD.', s)              (3)
'100 BROAD ROAD APT. 3'
>>> re.sub(r'\bROAD\b', 'RD.', s)             (4)
'100 BROAD RD. APT 3'
```

(1) What I really wanted was to match 'ROAD' when it was at the end of the string *and* it was its own whole word, not a part of some larger word. To express this in a regular expression, you use \b, which means "a word boundary must occur right here." In Python, this is complicated by the fact that the \ character in a string must itself be escaped. This is sometimes referred to as the backslash plague, and it is one reason why regular expressions are easier in Perl than in Python. On the downside, Perl mixes regular expressions with other syntax, so if you have a bug, it may be hard to tell whether it's a bug in syntax or a bug in your regular expression.

(2) To work around the backslash plague, you can use what is called a raw string, by prefixing the string with the letter r. This tells Python that nothing in this string should be escaped; '\t' is a tab character, but r'\t' is really the backslash character \ followed by the letter t. I recommend always using raw strings when dealing with regular expressions; otherwise, things get too confusing too quickly (and regular expressions get confusing quickly enough all by themselves).

(3) *sigh* Unfortunately, I soon found more cases that contradicted my logic. In this case, the street address contained the word 'ROAD' as a whole word by itself, but it wasn't at the end, because the address had an apartment number after the street designation. Because 'ROAD' isn't at the very end of the string, it doesn't match, so the entire call to re.sub ends up replacing nothing at all, and you get the original string back, which is not what you want.

(4) To solve this problem, remove the $ character and add another \b. Now, the regular expression reads "match 'ROAD' when it's a whole word by itself anywhere in the string, whether at the end, the beginning, or somewhere in the middle."

Case Study: Roman Numerals

You've most likely seen Roman numerals, even if you didn't recognize them. You may have seen them in copyrights of old movies and television shows ("Copyright MCMXLVI" instead of "Copyright 1946"), or on the dedication walls of libraries or universities ("established MDCCCLXXXVIII" instead of "established 1888"). You may also have seen them in outlines and bibliographical references. It's a system of representing numbers that really does date back to the ancient Roman empire (hence the name).

In Roman numerals, there are seven characters that are repeated and combined in various ways to represent numbers:

I = 1

V = 5

X = 10

L = 50

C = 100

D = 500

M = 1000

The following are some general rules for constructing Roman numerals:

- Characters are additive. I is 1, II is 2, and III is 3. VI is 6 (literally, 5 and 1), VII is 7, and VIII is 8.

- The tens characters (I, X, C, and M) can be repeated up to three times. At 4, you need to subtract from the next highest fives character. You can't represent 4 as IIII; instead, it is represented as IV (1 less than 5). The number 40 is written as XL (10 less than 50), 41 as XLI, 42 as XLII, 43 as XLIII, and then 44 as XLIV (10 less than 50, then 1 less than 5).

- Similarly, at 9, you need to subtract from the next highest tens character: 8 is VIII, but 9 is IX (1 less than 10), not VIIII (since the I character cannot be repeated four times). The number 90 is XC; 900 is CM.

- The fives characters cannot be repeated. The number 10 is always represented as X, never as VV. The number 100 is always C, never LL.

- Roman numerals are always written highest to lowest, and read left to right, so the order of the characters matters very much. DC is 600; CD is a completely different number (400, or 100 less than 500). CI is 101; IC is not even a valid Roman numeral (because you can't subtract 1 directly from 100; you would need to write it as XCIX, for 10 less than 100, then 1 less than 10).

Checking for Thousands

What would it take to validate that an arbitrary string is a valid Roman numeral? Let's take it one digit at a time. Since Roman numerals are always written highest to lowest, let's start with the highest: the thousands place. For numbers 1,000 and higher, the thousands are represented by a series of M characters. Listing 7-3 shows how to use regular expressions to check for thousands.

Listing 7-3. Checking for Thousands

```
>>> import re
>>> pattern = '^M?M?M?$'                    (1)
>>> re.search(pattern, 'M')                 (2)
<SRE_Match object at 0106FB58>
>>> re.search(pattern, 'MM')                (3)
<SRE_Match object at 0106C290>
>>> re.search(pattern, 'MMM')               (4)
<SRE_Match object at 0106AA38>
>>> re.search(pattern, 'MMMM')              (5)
>>> re.search(pattern, '')                  (6)
<SRE_Match object at 0106F4A8>
```

(1) This pattern has three parts:

- ^ to match what follows only at the beginning of the string. If this were not specified, the pattern would match no matter where the M characters were, which is not what you want. You want to make sure that the M characters, if they're there, are at the beginning of the string.

- M? to optionally match a single M character. Since this is repeated three times, you're matching anywhere from 0 to 3 M characters in a row.

- $ to match what precedes only at the end of the string. When combined with the ^ character at the beginning, this means that the pattern must match the entire string, with no other characters before or after the M characters.

(2) The essence of the re module is the search function, which takes a regular expression (pattern) and a string ('M') to try to match against the regular expression. If a match is found, search returns an object that has various methods to describe the match; if no match is found, search returns None, the Python null value. All you care about at the moment is whether the pattern matches, which you can tell by just looking at the return value of search. 'M' matches this regular expression, because the first optional M matches, and the second and third optional M characters are ignored.

(3) 'MM' matches because the first and second optional M characters match and the third M is ignored.

(4) 'MMM' matches because all three M characters match.

(5) 'MMMM' does not match. All three M characters match, but then the regular expression insists on the string ending (because of the $ character), and the string doesn't end yet (because of the fourth M). So search returns None.

(6) Interestingly, an empty string also matches this regular expression, since all the M characters are optional.

Checking for Hundreds

The hundreds place is more difficult than the thousands, because there are several mutually exclusive ways it could be expressed, depending on its value.

100 = C

200 = CC

300 = CCC

400 = CD

500 = D

600 = DC

700 = DCC

800 = DCCC

900 = CM

So there are four possible patterns:

- CM

- CD

- Zero to three C characters (zero if the hundreds place is 0)

- D, followed by zero to three C characters

The last two patterns can be combined: an optional D, followed by zero to three C characters.

Listing 7-4 shows how to use regular expressions to validate the hundreds place of a Roman numeral.

Listing 7-4. Checking for Hundreds

```
>>> import re
>>> pattern = '^M?M?M?(CM|CD|D?C?C?C?)$'        (1)
>>> re.search(pattern, 'MCM')                   (2)
<SRE_Match object at 01070390>
>>> re.search(pattern, 'MD')                    (3)
<SRE_Match object at 01073A50>
>>> re.search(pattern, 'MMMCCC')                (4)
<SRE_Match object at 010748A8>
>>> re.search(pattern, 'MCMC')                  (5)
>>> re.search(pattern, '')                      (6)
<SRE_Match object at 01071D98>
```

(1) This pattern starts out the same as the one in Listing 7-3, checking for the beginning of the string (^), then the thousands place (M?M?M?). Then it has the new part, in parentheses, which defines a set of three mutually exclusive patterns, separated by vertical bars: CM, CD, and D?C?C?C? (which is an optional D followed by zero to three optional C characters). The regular expression parser checks for each of these patterns in order (from left to right), takes the first one that matches, and ignores the rest.

(2) 'MCM' matches because the first M matches, the second and third M characters are ignored, and the CM matches (so the CD and D?C?C?C? patterns are never even considered). MCM is the Roman numeral representation of 1900.

(3) 'MD' matches because the first M matches, the second and third M characters are ignored, and the D?C?C?C? pattern matches D (each of the 3 C characters are optional and are ignored). MD is the Roman numeral representation of 1500.

(4) 'MMMCCC' matches because all three M characters match, and the D?C?C?C? pattern matches CCC (the D is optional and is ignored). MMMCCC is the Roman numeral representation of 3300.

(5) 'MCMC' does not match. The first M matches, the second and third M characters are ignored, and the CM matches, but then the $ does not match because you're not at the end of the string yet (you still have an unmatched C character). The C does *not* match as part of the D?C?C?C? pattern, because the mutually exclusive CM pattern has already matched.

(6) Interestingly, an empty string still matches this pattern, because all the M characters are optional and ignored, and the empty string matches the D?C?C?C? pattern where all the characters are optional and ignored.

Whew! See how quickly regular expressions can get nasty? And we've only covered the thousands and hundreds places of Roman numerals. But if you followed all that, the tens and ones places are easy, because they're exactly the same pattern. But let's look at another way to express the pattern.

Using the {n,m} Syntax

In the previous section, we were dealing with a pattern where the same character could be repeated up to three times. There is another way to express this in regular expressions, which some people find more readable. First look at the method we already used, in Listing 7-5.

Listing 7-5. The Old Way: Every Character Optional

```
>>> import re
>>> pattern = '^M?M?M?$'
>>> re.search(pattern, 'M')                          (1)
<_sre.SRE_Match object at 0x008EE090>
>>> pattern = '^M?M?M?$'
>>> re.search(pattern, 'MM')                         (2)
<_sre.SRE_Match object at 0x008EEB48>
>>> pattern = '^M?M?M?$'
>>> re.search(pattern, 'MMM')                        (3)
<_sre.SRE_Match object at 0x008EE090>
>>> re.search(pattern, 'MMMM')                       (4)
>>>
```

(1) This matches the start of the string, then the first optional M, but not the second and third M (but that's okay because they're optional), and then the end of the string.

(2) This matches the start of the string, then the first and second optional M, but not the third M (but that's okay because it's optional), and then the end of the string.

(3) This matches the start of the string, then all three optional M characters, and then the end of the string.

(4) This matches the start of the string, then all three optional M characters, but then *does not match* the end of string (because there is still one unmatched M), so the pattern does not match and returns None.

Listing 7-6 shows the alternative way to express repeated characters.

Listing 7-6. The New Way: From n to m

```
>>> pattern = '^M{0,3}$'                          (1)
>>> re.search(pattern, 'M')                        (2)
<_sre.SRE_Match object at 0x008EEB48>
>>> re.search(pattern, 'MM')                       (3)
<_sre.SRE_Match object at 0x008EE090>
>>> re.search(pattern, 'MMM')                      (4)
<_sre.SRE_Match object at 0x008EEDA8>
>>> re.search(pattern, 'MMMM')                     (5)
>>>
```

(1) This pattern says, "Match the start of the string, then anywhere from 0 to 3 M characters, and then the end of the string." The 0 and 3 can be any numbers; if you want to match at least one but no more than three M characters, you could say M{1,3}.

(2) This matches the start of the string, then one M out of a possible three, and then the end of the string.

(3) This matches the start of the string, then two Ms out of a possible three, and then the end of the string.

(4) This matches the start of the string, then three Ms out of a possible four, and then the end of the string.

(5) This matches the start of the string, then three Ms out of a possible four, but then does not match the end of the string. The regular expression allows for only up to three M characters before the end of the string, but you have four, so the pattern does not match and returns None.

> **NOTE** *There is no way to programmatically determine that two regular expressions are equivalent. The best you can do is write a lot of test cases to make sure they behave the same way on all relevant inputs. You'll learn more about writing test cases in Chapter 13.*

Checking for Tens and Ones

Now let's expand our Roman numeral regular expression to cover the tens and ones place. Listing 7-7 shows the check for tens.

Listing 7-7. Checking for Tens

```
>>> pattern = '^M?M?M?M?(CM|CD|D?C?C?C?)(XC|XL|L?X?X?X?)$'
>>> re.search(pattern, 'MCMXL')                    (1)
<_sre.SRE_Match object at 0x008EEB48>
```

```
>>> re.search(pattern, 'MCML')                    (2)
<_sre.SRE_Match object at 0x008EEB48>
>>> re.search(pattern, 'MCMLX')                   (3)
<_sre.SRE_Match object at 0x008EEB48>
>>> re.search(pattern, 'MCMLXXX')                 (4)
<_sre.SRE_Match object at 0x008EEB48>
>>> re.search(pattern, 'MCMLXXXX')                (5)
>>>
```

(1) This matches the start of the string, then the first optional M, then CM, then XL, and then the end of the string. Remember that the (A|B|C) syntax means "match exactly one of A, B, or C." You match XL, so you ignore the XC and L?X?X?X? choices, and then move on to the end of the string. MCML is the Roman numeral representation of 1940.

(2) This matches the start of the string, then the first optional M, then CM, and then L?X?X?X?. Of the L?X?X?X?, it matches the L and skips all three optional X characters. Then you move to the end of the string. MCML is the Roman numeral representation of 1950.

(3) This matches the start of the string, then the first optional M, then CM, then the optional L and the first optional X, skips the second and third optional X, and then the end of the string. MCMLX is the Roman numeral representation of 1960.

(4) This matches the start of the string, then the first optional M, then CM, then the optional L and all three optional X characters, and then the end of the string. MCMLXXX is the Roman numeral representation of 1980.

(5) This matches the start of the string, then the first optional M, then CM, then the optional L and all three optional X characters, then *fails to match* the end of the string because there is still one more X unaccounted for. So, the entire pattern fails to match and returns None. MCMLXXXX is not a valid Roman numeral.

The expression for the ones place follows the same pattern. I'll spare you the details and show you the end result:

```
>>> pattern = '^M?M?M?M?(CM|CD|D?C?C?C?)(XC|XL|L?X?X?X?)(IX|IV|V?I?I?I?)$'
```

Okay, so what does that look like using this alternate {n,m} syntax? Listing 7-8 shows the new syntax.

Listing 7-8. Validating Roman Numerals with {n,m}

```
>>> pattern = '^M{0,4}(CM|CD|D?C{0,3})(XC|XL|L?X{0,3})(IX|IV|V?I{0,3})$'
>>> re.search(pattern, 'MDLV')                    (1)
<_sre.SRE_Match object at 0x008EEB48>
>>> re.search(pattern, 'MMDCLXVI')                (2)
<_sre.SRE_Match object at 0x008EEB48>
```

```
>>> re.search(pattern, 'MMMMDCCCLXXXVIII')          (3)
<_sre.SRE_Match object at 0x008EEB48>
>>> re.search(pattern, 'I')                          (4)
<_sre.SRE_Match object at 0x008EEB48>
```

(1) This matches the start of the string, then one of a possible four M characters, and then D?C{0,3}. Of that, it matches the optional D and zero of three possible C characters. Moving on, it matches L?X{0,3} by matching the optional L and zero of three possible X characters. Then it matches V?I{0,3} by matching the optional V and zero of three possible I characters, and finally, the end of the string. MDLV is the Roman numeral representation of 1555.

(2) This matches the start of the string, then two of a possible four M characters; then the D?C{0,3} with a D and one of three possible C characters; then L?X{0,3} with an L and one of three possible X characters; then V?I{0,3} with a V and one of three possible I characters; and then the end of the string. MMDCLXVI is the Roman numeral representation of 2666.

(3) This matches the start of the string; then four out of four M characters; then D?C{0,3} with a D and three out of three C characters; then L?X{0,3} with an L and three out of three X characters; then V?I{0,3} with a V and three out of three I characters; and then the end of the string. MMMMDCCCLXXXVIII is the Roman numeral representation of 3888, and it's the longest Roman numeral you can write without extended syntax.

(4) Watch closely. (I feel like a magician. "Watch closely, kids, I'm going to pull a rabbit out of my hat.") This matches the start of the string; then zero out of four M characters; then matches D?C{0,3} by skipping the optional D and matching zero out of three C characters; then matches L?X{0,3} by skipping the optional L and matching zero out of three X characters; then matches V?I{0,3} by skipping the optional V and matching one out of three I characters; and then the end of the string. Whoa.

If you followed all that and understood it on the first try, you're doing better than I did. Now imagine trying to understand someone else's regular expressions, in the middle of a critical function of a large program. Or even imagine coming back to your own regular expressions a few months later. I've done it, and it's not a pretty sight.

In the next section. we'll explore an alternate syntax that can help keep your expressions maintainable.

Verbose Regular Expressions

So far, we've been dealing with what I'll call "compact" regular expressions. As you've seen, they are difficult to read, and even if you figure out what one does, that's no guarantee that you'll be able to understand it six months later. What we really need is inline documentation.

Python allows you to do this with something called *verbose regular expressions.* A verbose regular expression is different from a compact regular expression in two ways:

- Whitespace is ignored. Spaces, tabs, and carriage returns are not matched as spaces, tabs, and carriage returns. They're not matched at all. (If you want to match a space in a verbose regular expression, you'll need to escape it by putting a backslash in front of it.)

- Comments are ignored. A comment in a verbose regular expression is just like a comment in Python code: it starts with a # character and goes until the end of the line. In this case, it's a comment within a multiline string instead of within your source code, but it works the same way.

This will be more clear with an example. Let's revisit the compact regular expression we've been working with, and make it a verbose regular expression. Listing 7-9 shows how.

Listing 7-9. Regular Expressions with Inline Comments

```
>>> pattern = """
    ^                   # beginning of string
    M{0,4}              # thousands - 0 to 4 M's
    (CM|CD|D?C{0,3})    # hundreds - 900 (CM), 400 (CD), 0-300 (0 to 3 C's),
                        #            or 500-800 (D, followed by 0 to 3 C's)
    (XC|XL|L?X{0,3})    # tens - 90 (XC), 40 (XL), 0-30 (0 to 3 X's),
                        #        or 50-80 (L, followed by 0 to 3 X's)
    (IX|IV|V?I{0,3})    # ones - 9 (IX), 4 (IV), 0-3 (0 to 3 I's),
                        #        or 5-8 (V, followed by 0 to 3 I's)
    $                   # end of string
    """
>>> re.search(pattern, 'M', re.VERBOSE)                        (1)
<_sre.SRE_Match object at 0x008EEB48>
>>> re.search(pattern, 'MCMLXXXIX', re.VERBOSE)                 (2)
<_sre.SRE_Match object at 0x008EEB48>
>>> re.search(pattern, 'MMMMDCCCLXXXVIII', re.VERBOSE)          (3)
<_sre.SRE_Match object at 0x008EEB48>
>>> re.search(pattern, 'M')                                    (4)
```

(1) The most important thing to remember when using verbose regular expressions is that you need to pass an extra argument when working with them: re.VERBOSE is a constant defined in the re module that signals that the pattern should be treated as a verbose regular expression. As you can see, this pattern has quite a bit of whitespace (all of which is ignored), and several comments (all of which are ignored). Once you ignore the whitespace and the comments, this is

exactly the same regular expression as you saw in the previous section, but it's a lot more readable.

(2) This matches the start of the string, then one of a possible four Ms, then CM, then L and three of a possible three X characters, then IX, and then the end of the string.

(3) This matches the start of the string, then four of a possible four Ms, then D and three of a possible three Cs, then L and three of a possible three Xs, then V and three of a possible three Is, and then the end of the string.

(4) This does not match. Why? Because it doesn't have the re.VERBOSE flag, so the re.search function is treating the pattern as a compact regular expression, with significant whitespace and literal hash marks. Python can't auto-detect whether a regular expression is verbose. Python assumes every regular expression is compact unless you explicitly state that it is verbose.

Case Study: Parsing Phone Numbers

So far, we've concentrated on matching whole patterns. Either the pattern matches or it doesn't. But regular expressions are much more powerful than that. When a regular expression *does* match, you can pick out specific pieces of it. You can find out what matched where.

This example came from another real-world problem I encountered, again from a previous day job. The problem: parsing an American phone number. The client wanted to be able to enter the number free-form (in a single field), but then wanted to store the area code, trunk, number, and, optionally, an extension separately in the company's database. I scoured the Web and found many examples of regular expressions that purported to do this, but none of them were permissive enough.

Here are the phone number formats I needed to be able to accept:

- 800-555-1212
- 800 555 1212
- 800.555.1212
- (800) 555-1212
- 1-800-555-1212
- 800-555-1212-1234
- 800-555-1212x1234
- 800-555-1212 ext. 1234
- work 1-(800) 555.1212 #1234

Quite a variety! In each of these cases, I needed to know that the area code was 800, the trunk was 555, and the rest of the phone number was 1212. For those with an extension, I needed to know that the extension was 1234.

Let's work through developing a solution for phone number parsing. Listing 7-10 shows a first step.

Listing 7-10. Finding Numbers

```
>>> phonePattern = re.compile(r'^(\d{3})-(\d{3})-(\d{4})$')        (1)
>>> phonePattern.search('800-555-1212').groups()                  (2)
('800', '555', '1212')
>>> phonePattern.search('800-555-1212-1234')                      (3)
>>>
```

(1) Always read regular expressions from left to right. This one matches the beginning of the string, and then (\d{3}). What's \d{3}? Well, the {3} means "match exactly thee numeric digits"; it's a variation on the {n,m} syntax you saw earlier. \d means "any numeric digit" (0 through 9). Putting it in parentheses means "match exactly three numeric digits, and *then remember them as a group that I can ask for later*." Then match a literal hyphen. Then match another group of exactly three digits. Then match another literal hyphen. Then match another group of exactly four digits. Then match the end of the string.

(2) To get access to the groups that the regular expression parser remembered along the way, use the groups() method on the object that the search function returns. It will return a tuple of however many groups were defined in the regular expression. In this case, you defined three groups: one with three digits, one with three digits, and one with four digits.

(3) This regular expression is not the final answer, because it doesn't handle a phone number with an extension on the end. For that, you'll need to expand our regular expression.

Listing 7-11 shows an expanded regular expression to find the extension as well.

Listing 7-11. Finding the Extension

```
>>> phonePattern = re.compile(r'^(\d{3})-(\d{3})-(\d{4})-(\d+)$')  (1)
>>> phonePattern.search('800-555-1212-1234').groups()             (2)
('800', '555', '1212', '1234')
>>> phonePattern.search('800 555 1212 1234')                      (3)
>>>
>>> phonePattern.search('800-555-1212')                           (4)
>>>
```

(1) This regular expression is almost identical to the previous one. Just as before, you match the beginning of the string, then a remembered group of three digits, then a hyphen, then a remembered group of three digits, then a hyphen, and then a remembered group of four digits. What's new is that you then match another hyphen, and a remembered group of one or more digits, and then the end of the string.

(2) The groups() method now returns a tuple of four elements, since your regular expression now defines four groups to remember.

(3) Unfortunately, this regular expression is not the final answer either, because it assumes that the different parts of the phone number are separated by hyphens. What if they're separated by spaces, or commas, or dots? You need a more general solution to match several different types of separators.

(4) Oops! Not only does this regular expression not do everything you want, it's actually a step backwards, because now you can't parse phone numbers *without* an extension. That's not what you wanted at all; if the extension is there, you want to know what it is, but if it's not there, you still want to know what the different parts of the main number are.

Listing 7-12 shows the regular expression to handle separators between the different parts of the phone number.

Listing 7-12. Handling Different Separators

```
>>> phonePattern = re.compile(r'^(\d{3})\D+(\d{3})\D+(\d{4})\D+(\d+)$')   (1)
>>> phonePattern.search('800 555 1212 1234').groups()                     (2)
('800', '555', '1212', '1234')
>>> phonePattern.search('800-555-1212-1234').groups()                     (3)
('800', '555', '1212', '1234')
>>> phonePattern.search('80055512121234')                                 (4)
>>>
>>> phonePattern.search('800-555-1212')                                   (5)
>>>
```

(1) Okay, hang on to your hat. You're matching the beginning of the string, then a group of three digits, and then \D+. What the heck is that? Well, \D matches any character *except* a numeric digit, and + means "one or more." So \D+ matches one or more characters that are not digits. This is what you're using instead of a literal hyphen, to try to match different separators.

(2) Using \D+ instead of - means you can now match phone numbers where the parts are separated by spaces instead of hyphens.

(3) Of course, phone numbers separated by hyphens still work, too.

(4) Unfortunately, this is still not the final answer, because it assumes that a separator exists. What if the phone number is entered without any spaces or hyphens at all?

(5) Oops! This still has not fixed the problem of requiring extensions. Now you have two problems, but you can solve both of them with the same technique.

Listing 7-13 shows the regular expression for handling phone numbers without separators.

Listing 7-13. Handling Numbers Without Separators

```
>>> phonePattern = re.compile(r'^(\d{3})\D*(\d{3})\D*(\d{4})\D*(\d*)$')    (1)
>>> phonePattern.search('80055512121234').groups()                        (2)
('800', '555', '1212', '1234')
>>> phonePattern.search('800.555.1212 x1234').groups()                    (3)
('800', '555', '1212', '1234')
>>> phonePattern.search('800-555-1212').groups()                          (4)
('800', '555', '1212', '')
>>> phonePattern.search('(800)5551212 x1234')                             (5)
>>>
```

(1) The only change you've made since that last step is changing all the + characters to * characters. Instead of \D+ between the parts of the phone number, you now match on \D*. Remember that + means "one or more"? Well, * means "zero or more." So, now you should be able to parse phone numbers even when there is no separator character at all.

(2) Lo and behold, it actually works. Why? You matched the beginning of the string, then a remembered group of three digits (800), then zero nonnumeric characters, then a remembered group of three digits (555), then zero nonnumeric characters, then a remembered group of four digits (1212), then zero nonnumeric characters, then a remembered group of an arbitrary number of digits (1234), and then the end of the string.

(3) Other variations work now, too: dots instead of hyphens and both a space and an *x* before the extension.

(4) Finally, you've solved the other long-standing problem: extensions are optional again. If no extension is found, the groups() method still returns a tuple of four elements, but the fourth element is just an empty string.

(5) I hate to be the bearer of bad news, but you're not finished yet. What's the problem here? There's an extra character before the area code, but the regular expression assumes that the area code is the first thing at the beginning of the string. No problem—you can use the same technique of "zero or more nonnumeric characters" to skip over the leading characters before the area code.

Listing 7-14 shows how to handle leading characters in phone numbers.

Listing 7-14. Handling Leading Characters

```
>>> phonePattern = re.compile(r'^\D*(\d{3})\D*(\d{3})\D*(\d{4})\D*(\d*)$')  (1)
>>> phonePattern.search('(800)5551212 ext. 1234').groups()                 (2)
('800', '555', '1212', '1234')
>>> phonePattern.search('800-555-1212').groups()                           (3)
('800', '555', '1212', '')
>>> phonePattern.search('work 1-(800) 555.1212 #1234')                     (4)
>>>
```

(1) This is the same as in Listing 7-13, except now you're matching \D*, zero or more nonnumeric characters, before the first remembered group (the area code). Notice that you're not remembering these nonnumeric characters (they're not in parentheses). If you find them, you'll just skip over them, and then start remembering the area code whenever you get to it.

(2) Okay, you can successfully parse the phone number, even with the leading left parenthesis before the area code. (The right parenthesis after the area code is already handled; it's treated as a nonnumeric separator and matched by the \D* after the first remembered group.)

(3) Just a sanity check to make sure you haven't broken anything that used to work. Since the leading characters are entirely optional, this matches the beginning of the string, then zero nonnumeric characters, then a remembered group of three digits (800), then one nonnumeric character (the hyphen), then a remembered group of three digits (555), then one nonnumeric character (the hyphen), then a remembered group of four digits (1212), then zero nonnumeric characters, then a remembered group of zero digits, and then the end of the string.

(4) This is where regular expressions make me want to gouge my eyes out with a blunt object. Why doesn't this phone number match? Because there's a 1 before the area code, but you assumed that all the leading characters before the area code were nonnumeric characters (\D*). Aargh.

Let's back up for a second. So far the regular expressions have all matched from the beginning of the string. But now you see that there may be an indeterminate amount of stuff at the beginning of the string that you want to ignore. Rather than trying to match it all just so you can skip over it, let's take a different approach: don't explicitly match the beginning of the string at all. This approach is shown in Listing 7-15.

Listing 7-15. Phone Number, Wherever I May Find Ye

```
>>> phonePattern = re.compile(r'(\d{3})\D*(\d{3})\D*(\d{4})\D*(\d*)$')    (1)
>>> phonePattern.search('work 1-(800) 555.1212 #1234').groups()          (2)
('800', '555', '1212', '1234')
>>> phonePattern.search('800-555-1212')                                  (3)
('800', '555', '1212', '')
>>> phonePattern.search('80055512121234')                                (4)
('800', '555', '1212', '1234')
```

(1) Note the lack of ^ in this regular expression. You are not matching the beginning of the string anymore. There's nothing that says you must match the entire input with your regular expression. The regular expression engine will do the hard work of figuring out where the input string starts to match and go from there.

(2) Now you can successfully parse a phone number that includes leading characters and a leading digit, plus any number of any kind of separators around each part of the phone number.

(3) Sanity check: this still works.

(4) That still works, too.

See how quickly a regular expression can get out of control? Take a quick glance at any of the previous iterations. Can you tell the difference between one and the next?

While you still understand the final answer (and it is our final answer; if you've discovered a case it doesn't handle, I don't want to know about it), let's write it out as a verbose regular expression, before you forget why you made the choices you made. Listing 7-16 shows the final version.

Listing 7-16. Parsing Phone Numbers (Final Version)

```
>>> phonePattern = re.compile(r'''
                # don't match beginning of string, number can start anywhere
    (\d{3})     # area code is 3 digits (e.g. '800')
    \D*         # optional separator is any number of non-digits
    (\d{3})     # trunk is 3 digits (e.g. '555')
    \D*         # optional separator
    (\d{4})     # rest of number is 4 digits (e.g. '1212')
    \D*         # optional separator
    (\d*)       # extension is optional and can be any number of digits
    $           # end of string
    ''', re.VERBOSE)
>>> phonePattern.search('work 1-(800) 555.1212 #1234').groups()      (1)
('800', '555', '1212', '1234')
>>> phonePattern.search('800-555-1212')                              (2)
('800', '555', '1212', '')
```

(1) Other than being spread out over multiple lines, this is exactly the same regular expression as the last step, so it's no surprise that it parses the same inputs.

(2) Final sanity check: yes, this still works. I think we're finished.

Further Reading on Regular Expressions

For more information about regular expressions, refer to the following:

- Regular Expression HOWTO (http://py-howto.sourceforge.net/regex/regex.html) teaches about regular expressions and how to use them in Python.

- *Python Library Reference* (http://www.python.org/doc/current/lib) summarizes the re module (http://www.python.org/doc/current/lib/module-re.html).

Summary

This is just the tiniest tip of the iceberg of what regular expressions can do. In other words, even though you're completely overwhelmed by them now, believe me, you ain't seen nothing yet.

You should now be familiar with the following techniques:

- ^ matches the beginning of a string.

- $ matches the end of a string.

- \b matches a word boundary.

- \d matches any numeric digit.

- \D matches any nonnumeric character.

- *x*? matches an optional *x* character (in other words, it matches *x* zero or one times).

- *x** matches *x* zero or more times.

- *x*+ matches *x* one or more times.

- *x*{n,m} matches *x* character at least *n* times, but not more than *m* times.

- (a|b|c) matches either a or b or c.

- (*x*) in general is a remembered group. You can get the value of what matched by using the groups() method of the object returned by re.search.

Regular expressions are extremely powerful, but they are not the correct solution for every problem. You should learn enough about them to know when they are appropriate, when they will solve your problems, and when they will cause more problems than they solve.

Some people, when confronted with a problem, think, "I know, I'll use regular expressions." Now they have two problems.

—Jamie Zawinski, in comp.emacs.xemacs

CHAPTER 8

HTML Processing

I OFTEN SEE QUESTIONS on comp.lang.python (http://groups.google.com/ groups?group=comp.lang.python) like these:

- How can I list all the headers/images/links in my HTML document?

- How do I parse/translate/munge the text of my HTML document but leave the tags alone?

- How can I add/remove/quote attributes of all my HTML tags at once?

This chapter will answer all of these questions.

Diving In

Here is a complete, working Python program in two parts. The first part, BaseHTMLProcessor.py, shown in Listing 8-1, is a generic tool to help you process HTML files by walking through the tags and text blocks. Read the doc strings and comments to get an overview of what's going on. Most of it will seem like magic, because it's not obvious how any of these class methods ever get called. Don't worry—all will be revealed in due time.

> **NOTE** *If you have not already done so, you can download this and other examples used in this book from the Downloads section of the Apress web site (http://www.apress.com).*

Listing 8-1. BaseHTMLProcessor.py

```python
from sgmllib import SGMLParser
import htmlentitydefs

class BaseHTMLProcessor(SGMLParser):
    def reset(self):
        # extend (called by SGMLParser.__init__)
        self.pieces = []
        SGMLParser.reset(self)
```

```
def unknown_starttag(self, tag, attrs):
    # called for each start tag
    # attrs is a list of (attr, value) tuples
    # e.g. for <pre class="screen">, tag="pre", attrs=[("class", "screen")]
    # Ideally we would like to reconstruct original tag and attributes, but
    # we may end up quoting attribute values that weren't quoted in the source
    # document, or we may change the type of quotes around the attribute value
    # (single to double quotes).
    # Note that improperly embedded non-HTML code (like client-side Javascript)
    # may be parsed incorrectly by the ancestor, causing runtime script errors.
    # All non-HTML code must be enclosed in HTML comment tags (<!-- code -->)
    # to ensure that it will pass through this parser unaltered
    # (in handle_comment).
    strattrs = "".join([' %s="%s"' % (key, value) for key, value in attrs])
    self.pieces.append("<%(tag)s%(strattrs)s>" % locals())

def unknown_endtag(self, tag):
    # called for each end tag, e.g. for </pre>, tag will be "pre"
    # Reconstruct the original end tag.
    self.pieces.append("</%(tag)s>" % locals())

def handle_charref(self, ref):
    # called for each character reference, e.g. for " ", ref will be "160"
    # Reconstruct the original character reference.
    self.pieces.append("&#%(ref)s;" % locals())

def handle_entityref(self, ref):
    # called for each entity reference, e.g. for "&copy;", ref will be "copy"
    # Reconstruct the original entity reference.
    self.pieces.append("&%(ref)s" % locals())
    # standard HTML entities are closed with a semicolon;
    # other entities are not
    if htmlentitydefs.entitydefs.has_key(ref):
        self.pieces.append(";")

def handle_data(self, text):
    # called for each block of plain text, i.e. outside of any tag and
    # not containing any character or entity references
    # Store the original text verbatim.
    self.pieces.append(text)

def handle_comment(self, text):
    # called for each HTML comment, e.g. <!-- insert Javascript code here -->
    # Reconstruct the original comment.
```

```
        # It is especially important that the source document enclose client-side
        # code (like Javascript) within comments so it can pass through this
        # processor undisturbed; see comments in unknown_starttag for details.
        self.pieces.append("<!--%(text)s-->" % locals())

    def handle_pi(self, text):
        # called for each processing instruction, e.g. <?instruction>
        # Reconstruct original processing instruction.
        self.pieces.append("<?%(text)s>" % locals())

    def handle_decl(self, text):
        # called for the DOCTYPE, if present, e.g.
        # <!DOCTYPE html PUBLIC "-//W3C//DTD HTML 4.01 Transitional//EN"
        #      "http://www.w3.org/TR/html4/loose.dtd">
        # Reconstruct original DOCTYPE
        self.pieces.append("<!%(text)s>" % locals())

    def output(self):
        """Return processed HTML as a single string"""
        return "".join(self.pieces)
```

The second part, dialect.py, shown in Listing 8-2, is an example of how to use BaseHTMLProcessor.py to translate the text of an HTML document but leave the tags alone.

Listing 8-2. dialect.py

```
import re
from BaseHTMLProcessor import BaseHTMLProcessor

class Dialectizer(BaseHTMLProcessor):
    subs = ()

    def reset(self):
        # extend (called from __init__ in ancestor)
        # Reset all data attributes
        self.verbatim = 0
        BaseHTMLProcessor.reset(self)

    def start_pre(self, attrs):
        # called for every <pre> tag in HTML source
        # Increment verbatim mode count, then handle tag like normal
        self.verbatim += 1
        self.unknown_starttag("pre", attrs)
```

```python
    def end_pre(self):
        # called for every </pre> tag in HTML source
        # Decrement verbatim mode count
        self.unknown_endtag("pre")
        self.verbatim -= 1

    def handle_data(self, text):
        # override
        # called for every block of text in HTML source
        # If in verbatim mode, save text unaltered;
        # otherwise process the text with a series of substitutions
        self.pieces.append(self.verbatim and text or self.process(text))

    def process(self, text):
        # called from handle_data
        # Process text block by performing series of regular expression
        # substitutions (actual substitions are defined in descendant)
        for fromPattern, toPattern in self.subs:
            text = re.sub(fromPattern, toPattern, text)
        return text

class ChefDialectizer(Dialectizer):
    """convert HTML to Swedish Chef-speak

    based on the classic chef.x, copyright (c) 1992, 1993 John Hagerman
    """
    subs = ((r'a([nu])', r'u\1'),
            (r'A([nu])', r'U\1'),
            (r'a\B', r'e'),
            (r'A\B', r'E'),
            (r'en\b', r'ee'),
            (r'\Bew', r'oo'),
            (r'\Be\b', r'e-a'),
            (r'\be', r'i'),
            (r'\bE', r'I'),
            (r'\Bf', r'ff'),
            (r'\Bir', r'ur'),
            (r'(\w*?)i(\w*?)$', r'\1ee\2'),
            (r'\bow', r'oo'),
            (r'\bo', r'oo'),
            (r'\bO', r'Oo'),
            (r'the', r'zee'),
            (r'The', r'Zee'),
```

```
                (r'th\b', r't'),
                (r'\Btion', r'shun'),
                (r'\Bu', r'oo'),
                (r'\BU', r'Oo'),
                (r'v', r'f'),
                (r'V', r'F'),
                (r'w', r'w'),
                (r'W', r'W'),
                (r'([a-z])[.]', r'\1.  Bork Bork Bork!'))

class FuddDialectizer(Dialectizer):
    """convert HTML to Elmer Fudd-speak"""
    subs = ((r'[rl]', r'w'),
            (r'qu', r'qw'),
            (r'th\b', r'f'),
            (r'th', r'd'),
            (r'n[.]', r'n, uh-hah-hah-hah.'))

class OldeDialectizer(Dialectizer):
    """convert HTML to mock Middle English"""
    subs = ((r'i([bcdfghjklmnpqrstvwxyz])e\b', r'y\1'),
            (r'i([bcdfghjklmnpqrstvwxyz])e', r'y\1\1e'),
            (r'ick\b', r'yk'),
            (r'ia([bcdfghjklmnpqrstvwxyz])', r'e\1e'),
            (r'e[ea]([bcdfghjklmnpqrstvwxyz])', r'e\1e'),
            (r'([bcdfghjklmnpqrstvwxyz])y', r'\1ee'),
            (r'([bcdfghjklmnpqrstvwxyz])er', r'\1re'),
            (r'([aeiou])re\b', r'\1r'),
            (r'ia([bcdfghjklmnpqrstvwxyz])', r'i\1e'),
            (r'tion\b', r'cioun'),
            (r'ion\b', r'ioun'),
            (r'aid', r'ayde'),
            (r'ai', r'ey'),
            (r'ay\b', r'y'),
            (r'ay', r'ey'),
            (r'ant', r'aunt'),
            (r'ea', r'ee'),
            (r'oa', r'oo'),
            (r'ue', r'e'),
            (r'oe', r'o'),
            (r'ou', r'ow'),
            (r'ow', r'ou'),
            (r'\bhe', r'hi'),
            (r've\b', r'veth'),
            (r'se\b', r'e'),
```

```
                    (r"'s\b", r'es'),
                    (r'ic\b', r'ick'),
                    (r'ics\b', r'icc'),
                    (r'ical\b', r'ick'),
                    (r'tle\b', r'til'),
                    (r'll\b', r'l'),
                    (r'ould\b', r'olde'),
                    (r'own\b', r'oune'),
                    (r'un\b', r'onne'),
                    (r'rry\b', r'rye'),
                    (r'est\b', r'este'),
                    (r'pt\b', r'pte'),
                    (r'th\b', r'the'),
                    (r'ch\b', r'che'),
                    (r'ss\b', r'sse'),
                    (r'([wybdp])\b', r'\1e'),
                    (r'([rnt])\b', r'\1\1e'),
                    (r'from', r'fro'),
                    (r'when', r'whan'))

    def translate(url, dialectName="chef"):
        """fetch URL and translate using dialect

        dialect in ("chef", "fudd", "olde")"""
        import urllib
        sock = urllib.urlopen(url)
        htmlSource = sock.read()
        sock.close()
        parserName = "%sDialectizer" % dialectName.capitalize()
        parserClass = globals()[parserName]
        parser = parserClass()
        parser.feed(htmlSource)
        parser.close()
        return parser.output()

    def test(url):
        """test all dialects against URL"""
        for dialect in ("chef", "fudd", "olde"):
            outfile = "%s.html" % dialect
            fsock = open(outfile, "wb")
            fsock.write(translate(url, dialect))
            fsock.close()
            import webbrowser
            webbrowser.open_new(outfile)
```

```
if __name__ == "__main__":
    test("http://diveintopython.org/odbchelper_list.html")
```

Running this script will translate *Introducing lists* into mock Swedish chef–speak (from The Muppets), mock Elmer Fudd–speak (from Bugs Bunny cartoons), and mock Middle English (loosely based on Chaucer's *The Canterbury Tales*). Sample output of each of these dialects is available online:

- **Swedish chef–speak:**
  http://diveintopython.org/native_data_types/chef.html

- **Elmer Fudd–speak:**
  http://diveintopython.org/native_data_types/fudd.html

- **Mock Middle English:**
  http://diveintopython.org/native_data_types/olde.html

If you look at the HTML source of the output pages, you'll see that all the HTML tags and attributes are untouched, but the text between the tags has been "translated" into the mock language. If you look closer, you'll see that, in fact, only the titles and paragraphs were translated; the code listings and screen examples were left untouched.

```
<div class="abstract">
<p>Lists awe <span class="application">Pydon</span>'s wowkhowse datatype.
If youw onwy expewience wif wists is awways in
<span class="application">Visuaw Basic</span> ow (God fowbid) de datastowe
in <span class="application">Powewbuiwdew</span>, bwace youwsewf fow
<span class="application">Pydon</span> wists.</p>
</div>
```

Introducing Python's `sgmllib.py`

HTML processing is broken into three steps: breaking down the HTML into its constituent pieces, fiddling with the pieces, and reconstructing the pieces into HTML again. The first step is done by `sgmllib.py`, a part of the standard Python library.

The key to understanding this chapter is to realize that HTML is not just text; it is structured text. The structure is derived from the more-or-less-hierarchical sequence of start tags and end tags. Usually you don't work with HTML this way; you work with it *textually* in a text editor or *visually* in a web browser or web-authoring tool. `sgmllib.py` presents HTML *structurally*.

`sgmllib.py` contains one important class: `SGMLParser`, which parses HTML into useful pieces, like start tags and end tags. As soon as it succeeds in breaking down some data into a useful piece, it calls a method on itself based on what it found.

In order to use the parser, you subclass the SGMLParser class and override these methods. This is what I meant when I said that it presents HTML *structurally*: the structure of the HTML determines the sequence of method calls and the arguments passed to each method.

SGMLParser parses HTML into eight kinds of data and calls a separate method for each of them:

- **Start tag:** An HTML tag that starts a block, like <html>, <head>, <body>, or <pre>, or a stand-alone tag like <br> or <img>. When it finds a start tag *tagname*, SGMLParser will look for a method called start_*tagname* or do_*tagname*. For instance, when it finds a <pre> tag, it will look for a start_pre or do_pre method. If it finds the method, SGMLParser calls it with a list of the tag's attributes; otherwise, it calls unknown_starttag with the tag name and list of attributes.

- **End tag:** An HTML tag that ends a block, like </html>, </head>, </body>, or </pre>. When it finds an end tag, SGMLParser will look for a method called end_*tagname*. If it finds the method, SGMLParser calls it; otherwise, it calls unknown_endtag with the tag name.

- **Character reference:** An escaped character referenced by its decimal or hexadecimal equivalent, like . When it finds the reference, SGMLParser calls handle_charref with the text of the decimal or hexadecimal character equivalent.

- **Entity reference:** An HTML entity, like ©. When it finds the reference, SGMLParser calls handle_entityref with the name of the HTML entity.

- **Comment:** An HTML comment, enclosed in <!-- ... -->. When it finds the comment, SGMLParser calls handle_comment with the body of the comment.

- **Processing instruction:** An HTML processing instruction, enclosed in <? ... >. When it finds the instruction, SGMLParser calls handle_pi with the body of the processing instruction.

- **Declaration:** An HTML declaration, such as a DOCTYPE, enclosed in <! ... >. When it finds the declaration, SGMLParser calls handle_decl with the body of the declaration.

- **Text data:** A block of text—anything that doesn't fit into the other seven categories. When it finds text data, SGMLParser calls handle_data with the text.

> **NOTE**   *Python 2.0 had a bug where* SGMLParser *would not recognize declarations at all (*handle_decl *would never be called), which meant that* DOCTYPE*s were silently ignored. This is fixed in Python 2.1.*

sgmllib.py comes with a test suite to demonstrate how it works. You can run sgmllib.py, passing the name of an HTML file on the command line, and it will print the tags and other elements as it parses them. It does this by subclassing the SGMLParser class and defining unknown_starttag, unknown_endtag, handle_data, and other methods that simply print their arguments.

> **TIP**   *In the ActivePython IDE on Windows, you can specify command-line arguments in the Run Script dialog box. Separate multiple arguments with spaces.*

Here is a snippet from the table of contents of the HTML version of this book. Of course your paths may vary. (If you haven't downloaded the HTML version of the book, you can do so at http://diveintopython.org.)

```
c:\python23\lib> type "c:\downloads\diveintopython\html\toc\index.html"

<!DOCTYPE html
  PUBLIC "-//W3C//DTD HTML 4.01//EN" "http://www.w3.org/TR/html4/strict.dtd">
<html lang="en">
  <head>
    <meta http-equiv="Content-Type" content="text/html; charset=ISO-8859-1">

    <title>Dive Into Python</title>
    <link rel="stylesheet" href="diveintopython.css" type="text/css">

... rest of file omitted for brevity ...
```

Running this through the test suite of sgmllib.py yields this output:

```
c:\python23\lib> python sgmllib.py
    "c:\downloads\diveintopython\html\toc\index.html"
data: '\n\n'
start tag: <html lang="en" >
data: '\n   '
start tag: <head>
data: '\n      '
```

```
start tag: <meta http-equiv="Content-Type" content="text/html;
charset=ISO-8859-1" >
data: '\n    \n        '
start tag: <title>
data: 'Dive Into Python'
end tag: </title>
data: '\n        '
start tag: <link rel="stylesheet" href="diveintopython.css" type="text/css" >
data: '\n        '
```

... rest of output omitted for brevity ...

Here's the roadmap for the rest of the chapter:

- Subclass SGMLParser to create classes that extract interesting data from HTML documents.

- Subclass SGMLParser to create BaseHTMLProcessor, which overrides all eight handler methods and uses them to reconstruct the original HTML from the pieces.

- Subclass BaseHTMLProcessor to create Dialectizer, which adds some methods to process specific HTML tags specially and overrides the handle_data method to provide a framework for processing the text blocks between the HTML tags.

- Subclass Dialectizer to create classes that define text-processing rules used by Dialectizer.handle_data.

- Write a test suite that grabs a real web page from http://diveintopython.org and processes it.

Along the way, you'll also learn about locals(), globals(), and dictionary-based string formatting.

Extracting Data from HTML Documents

To extract data from HTML documents, subclass the SGMLParser class and define methods for each tag or entity you want to capture.

Retrieving HTML from a Web Page

The first step to extracting data from an HTML document is getting some HTML. If you have some HTML lying around on your hard drive, you can use file functions to read it, but the real fun begins when you get HTML from live web pages.

Listing 8-3 introduces Python's `urlib` module.

Listing 8-3. Introducing urllib

```
>>> import urllib                                            (1)
>>> sock = urllib.urlopen("http://diveintopython.org/")      (2)
>>> htmlSource = sock.read()                                 (3)
>>> sock.close()                                             (4)
>>> print htmlSource                                         (5)
<!DOCTYPE html PUBLIC "-//W3C//DTD HTML 4.01 Transitional//EN"
"http://www.w3.org/TR/html4/loose.dtd"><html><head>
    <meta http-equiv='Content-Type' content='text/html; charset=ISO-8859-1'>
  <title>Dive Into Python</title>
<link rel='stylesheet' href='diveintopython.css' type='text/css'>
<link rev='made' href='mailto:mark@diveintopython.org'>
<meta name='keywords'
content='Python, Dive Into Python, tutorial, object-oriented,
programming, documentation, book, free'>
<meta name='description'
content='Python from novice to pro'>
</head>
<body bgcolor='white' text='black' link='#0000FF' vlink='#840084'
alink='#0000FF'>
<table cellpadding='0' cellspacing='0' border='0' width='100%'>
<tr><td class='header' width='1%' valign='top'>diveintopython.org</td>
<td width='99%' align='right'><hr size='1' noshade></td></tr>
<tr><td class='tagline'
colspan='2'>Python for experienced programmers</td></tr>

[...snip...]
```

(1) The `urllib` module is part of the standard Python library. It contains functions for getting information about and actually retrieving data from Internet-based URLs (mainly web pages).

(2) The simplest use of `urllib` is to retrieve the entire text of a web page using the `urlopen` function. Opening a URL is similar to opening a file. The return value of `urlopen` is a file-like object, which has some of the same methods as a file object.

(3) The simplest thing to do with the file-like object returned by urlopen is read, which reads the entire HTML of the web page into a single string. The object also supports readlines, which reads the text line by line into a list.

(4) When you're finished with the object, make sure to close it, just as you close a normal file object.

(5) You now have the complete HTML of the home page of http://diveintopython.org in a string, and you're ready to parse it.

Parsing HTML

Listing 8-4 shows how you can subclass SGMLParser to define classes that catch specific tags.

Listing 8-4. Introducing urllister.py

```
from sgmllib import SGMLParser

class URLLister(SGMLParser):
    def reset(self):                                    (1)
        SGMLParser.reset(self)
        self.urls = []

    def start_a(self, attrs):                           (2)
        href = [v for k, v in attrs if k=='href']       (3) (4)
        if href:
            self.urls.extend(href)
```

(1) reset is called by the __init__ method of SGMLParser, and it can also be called manually once an instance of the parser has been created. So, if you need to do any initialization, do it in reset, not in __init__, so that it will be reinitialized properly when someone reuses a parser instance.

(2) start_a is called by SGMLParser whenever it finds an <a> tag. The tag may contain an href attribute, and/or other attributes, like name or title. The attrs parameter is a list of tuples, [(*attribute*, *value*), (*attribute*, *value*), ...]. Or it may be just an <a>, a valid (if useless) HTML tag, in which case attrs would be an empty list.

(3) You can find out whether this <a> tag has an href attribute with a simple multivariable list comprehension.

(4) String comparisons like k=='href' are always case-sensitive, but that's safe in this case, because SGMLParser converts attribute names to lowercase while building attrs.

Listing 8-5 shows how to use urllister.py to create a list of all the links on the web page.

Listing 8-5. Using urllister.py

```
>>> import urllib, urllister
>>> usock = urllib.urlopen("http://diveintopython.org/")
>>> parser = urllister.URLLister()
>>> parser.feed(usock.read())                    (1)
>>> usock.close()                                (2)
>>> parser.close()                               (3)
>>> for url in parser.urls: print url            (4)
toc/index.html
#download
#languages
toc/index.html
appendix/history.html
download/diveintopython-html-5.0.zip
download/diveintopython-pdf-5.0.zip
download/diveintopython-word-5.0.zip
download/diveintopython-text-5.0.zip
download/diveintopython-html-flat-5.0.zip
download/diveintopython-xml-5.0.zip
download/diveintopython-common-5.0.zip


... rest of output omitted for brevity ...
```

(1) Call the feed method, defined in SGMLParser, to get HTML into the parser. It takes a string, which is what usock.read() returns.

(2) As with files, you should close your URL objects as soon as you're finished with them.

(3) You should close your parser object, too, but for a different reason. You've read all the data and fed it to the parser, but the feed method isn't guaranteed to have actually processed all the HTML you give it; it may buffer it, waiting for more. Be sure to call close to flush the buffer and force everything to be fully parsed.

(4) Once the parser is closed, the parsing is complete, and parser.urls contains a list of all the linked URLs in the HTML document. (Your output may look different, if the download links have been updated by the time you read this.)

The technical term for a parser like SGMLParser is a *consumer*; it consumes HTML and breaks it down into small, structured pieces. Presumably, the name feed was chosen to fit into the whole "consumer" motif. Personally, it makes me think of an exhibit in the zoo where there's just a dark cage with no trees or plants or evidence of life of any kind. If you stand perfectly still and look really closely, you can make out two beady eyes staring back at you from the far-left corner, but you convince yourself that's just your mind playing tricks on you. And the only way you can tell that the whole scene isn't just an empty cage is a small innocuous sign on the railing that reads, "Do not feed the parser." But maybe that's just me. In any event, it's an interesting mental image.

Processing HTML

SGMLParser doesn't produce anything by itself. It parses and parses and parses, and it calls a method for each interesting thing it finds, but the methods don't do anything. As you saw in the previous section, you can subclass SGMLParser to define classes that catch specific tags and produce useful things, like a list of all the links on a web page. Now, you'll take this one step further by defining a class that catches everything SGMLParser throws at it and reconstructs the complete HTML document. In technical terms, this class will be an HTML *producer*.

BaseHTMLProcessor, shown in Listing 8-6, subclasses SGMLParser and provides all eight essential handler methods: unknown_starttag, unknown_endtag, handle_charref, handle_entityref, handle_comment, handle_pi, handle_decl, and handle_data.

Listing 8-6. Introducing BaseHTMLProcessor

```
class BaseHTMLProcessor(SGMLParser):
    def reset(self):                                (1)
        self.pieces = []
        SGMLParser.reset(self)

    def unknown_starttag(self, tag, attrs):         (2)
        strattrs = "".join([' %s="%s"' % (key, value) for key, value in attrs])
        self.pieces.append("<%(tag)s%(strattrs)s>" % locals())

    def unknown_endtag(self, tag):                  (3)
        self.pieces.append("</%(tag)s>" % locals())

    def handle_charref(self, ref):                  (4)
        self.pieces.append("&#%(ref)s;" % locals())

    def handle_entityref(self, ref):                (5)
        self.pieces.append("&%(ref)s" % locals())
        if htmlentitydefs.entitydefs.has_key(ref):
            self.pieces.append(";")

    def handle_data(self, text):                    (6)
        self.pieces.append(text)

    def handle_comment(self, text):                 (7)
        self.pieces.append("<!--%(text)s-->" % locals())
```

```
def handle_pi(self, text):                              (8)
    self.pieces.append("<?%(text)s>" % locals())

def handle_decl(self, text):
    self.pieces.append("<!%(text)s>" % locals())
```

(1) reset, called by SGMLParser.__init__, initializes self.pieces as an empty list before calling the ancestor method. self.pieces is a data attribute that will hold the pieces of the HTML document you're constructing. Each handler method will reconstruct the HTML that SGMLParser parsed, and each method will append that string to self.pieces. Note that self.pieces is a list. You might be tempted to define it as a string and just keep appending each piece to it. That would work, but Python is much more efficient at dealing with lists.

> **NOTE** *The reason Python is better at lists than strings is that lists are mutable but strings are immutable. This means that appending to a list just adds the element and updates the index. Since strings cannot be changed after they are created, code like* s = s + newpiece *will create an entirely new string out of the concatenation of the original and the new piece, and then throw away the original string. This involves a lot of expensive memory management, and the amount of effort involved increases as the string gets longer, so doing* s = s + newpiece *in a loop is deadly. In technical terms, appending* n *items to a list is* O(n)*, while appending* n *items to a string is* O(n^2)*.*

(2) Since BaseHTMLProcessor does not define any methods for specific tags (like the start_a method in URLLister), SGMLParser will call unknown_starttag for every start tag. This method takes the tag (tag) and the list of attribute name/value pairs (attrs), reconstructs the original HTML, and appends it to self.pieces. The string formatting here is a little strange; we'll untangle that (and also the odd-looking locals() function) later in this chapter.

(3) Reconstructing end tags is much simpler: just take the tag name and wrap it in the </...> brackets.

(4) When SGMLParser finds a character reference, it calls handle_charref with the bare reference. If the HTML document contains the reference , ref will be 160. Reconstructing the original complete character reference just involves wrapping ref in &#...; characters.

(5) Entity references are similar to character references, but without the hash mark. Reconstructing the original entity reference requires wrapping ref in &...; characters. Actually, as an erudite reader pointed out to me, it's slightly more complicated than this. Only certain standard HTML entities end in a semicolon; other similar-looking entities do not. Luckily for us, the set of standard HTML entities is defined in a dictionary in a Python module called htmlentitydefs. Hence, you have the extra if statement.

(6) Blocks of text are simply appended to `self.pieces` unaltered.

(7) HTML comments are wrapped in `<!--...-->` characters.

(8) Processing instructions are wrapped in `<?...>` characters.

The HTML specification requires that all non-HTML (like client-side JavaScript) must be enclosed in HTML comments, but not all web pages do this properly (and all modern web browsers are forgiving if they don't). `BaseHTMLProcessor` is not forgiving; if the script is improperly embedded, it will be parsed as if it were HTML. For instance, if the script contains less-than and equal signs, `SGMLParser` may incorrectly think that it has found tags and attributes. `SGMLParser` always converts tags and attribute names to lowercase, which may break the script, and `BaseHTMLProcessor` always encloses attribute values in double quotes (even if the original HTML document used single quotes or no quotes), which will certainly break the script. Always protect your client-side script within HTML comments.

Listing 8-7 shows `BaseHTMLProcessor`'s output.

Listing 8-7. BaseHTMLProcessor Output

```
def output(self):                              (1)
    """Return processed HTML as a single string"""
    return "".join(self.pieces)                (2)
```

(1) This is the one method in `BaseHTMLProcessor` that is never called by the ancestor `SGMLParser`. Since the other handler methods store their reconstructed HTML in `self.pieces`, this function is needed to join all those pieces into one string. As noted earlier, Python is great at lists and mediocre at strings, so you create the complete string only when someone explicitly asks for it.

(2) If you prefer, you could use the `join` method of the `string` module instead: `string.join(self.pieces, "")`.

Further Reading on HTML Processing

For more information about processing HTML data, refer to the following:

- W3C (`http://www.w3.org`) discusses character and entity references (`http://www.w3.org/TR/REC-html40/charset.html#entities`).

- *Python Library Reference* (`http://www.python.org/doc/current/lib`) confirms your suspicions that the `htmlentitydefs` module is exactly what it sounds like (`http://www.python.org/doc/current/lib/module-htmlentitydefs.html`).

Understanding locals() and globals()

Let's digress from HTML processing for a minute and talk about how Python handles variables. Python has two built-in functions that provide dictionary-based access to local and global variables: locals() and globals().

Remember locals()? You first saw it here:

```
def unknown_starttag(self, tag, attrs):
    strattrs = "".join([' %s="%s"' % (key, value) for key, value in attrs])
    self.pieces.append("<%(tag)s%(strattrs)s>" % locals())
```

No, wait, we can't talk about locals() yet. First, we need to talk about namespaces. This is dry stuff, but it's important, so pay attention.

Python uses what are called *namespaces* to keep track of variables. A namespace is just like a dictionary where the keys are names of variables and the dictionary values are the values of those variables. In fact, you can access a namespace as a Python dictionary, as you'll see in a minute.

At any particular point in a Python program, there are several namespaces available:

- Each function has its own namespace, called the *local namespace*, which keeps track of the function's variables, including function arguments and locally defined variables.

- Each module has its own namespace, called the *global namespace*, which keeps track of the module's variables, including functions, classes, any other imported modules, and module-level variables and constants.

- A built-in namespace, accessible from any module, holds built-in functions and exceptions.

When a line of code asks for the value of a variable x, Python will search for that variable in all the available namespaces, in order:

1. Local namespace, specific to the current function or class method. If the function defines a local variable x, or has an argument x, Python will use this and stop searching.

2. Global namespace, specific to the current module. If the module has defined a variable, function, or class called x, Python will use that and stop searching.

3. Built-in namespace, global to all modules. As a last resort, Python will assume that x is the name of built-in function or variable.

If Python doesn't find *x* in any of these namespaces, it gives up and raises a NameError with the message There is no variable named 'x', which you saw back in Chapter 3's Listing 3-18, "Referencing an Unbound Variable," but you didn't appreciate how much work Python was doing before giving you that error.

> **NOTE** *Python 2.2 introduced a subtle but important change that affects the namespace search order: nested scopes. In versions of Python prior to 2.2, when you reference a variable within a nested function or* lambda *function, Python will search for that variable in the current (nested or* lambda*) function's namespace, and then in the module's namespace. Python 2.2 will search for the variable in the current (nested or* lambda*) function's namespace, then in the parent function's namespace, and then in the module's namespace. Python 2.1 can work either way; by default, it works like Python 2.0, but you can add the following line of code at the top of your module to make your module work like Python 2.2:* from __future__ import nested_scopes.

Are you confused yet? Don't despair! This is really cool, I promise. Like many things in Python, namespaces are *directly accessible at runtime*. How is that possible? Well, the local namespace is accessible via the built-in locals() function, and the global (module-level) namespace is accessible via the built-in globals() function.

Introducing locals()

Listing 8-8 demonstrates how the locals() dictionary works.

Listing 8-8. Introducing locals()

```
>>> def foo(arg):              (1)
...     x = 1
...     print locals()
...
>>> foo(7)                     (2)
{'arg': 7, 'x': 1}
>>> foo('bar')                 (3)
{'arg': 'bar', 'x': 1}
```

   (1) The function foo has two variables in its local namespace: arg, whose value is passed in to the function, and x, which is defined within the function.
   (2) locals() returns a dictionary of name/value pairs. The keys of this dictionary are the names of the variables as strings; the values of the dictionary are the

actual values of the variables. So calling foo with 7 prints the dictionary containing the function's two local variables: arg (7) and x (1).

(3) Remember that Python has dynamic typing, so you could just as easily pass a string in for arg; the function (and the call to locals()) would still work just as well. locals() works with all variables of all datatypes.

Introducing globals()

What locals() does for the local (function) namespace, globals() does for the global (module) namespace. globals() is more exciting, though, because a module's namespace is more exciting (can you tell that I don't get out much?). Not only does the module's namespace include module-level variables and constants, it includes all the functions and classes defined in the module. Plus, it includes anything that was imported into the module.

Remember the difference between from *module* import and import *module* (explained in Chapter 5)? With import *module*, the module itself is imported, but it retains its own namespace, which is why you need to use the module name to access any of its functions or attributes: *module.function*. But with from *module* import, you're actually importing specific functions and attributes from another module into your own namespace, which is why you can access them directly without referencing their original module. With the globals() function, you can actually see this happen.

Look at the following block of code at the bottom of BaseHTMLProcessor.py:

```
if __name__ == "__main__":
    for k, v in globals().items():
        print k, "=", v
```

Just so you don't get intimidated, remember that you've seen all this before. The globals() function returns a dictionary, and you're iterating through the dictionary using the items method and multivariable assignment. The only thing new here is the globals() function.

Running the script from the command line gives the output shown in Listing 8-9 (note that your output may be slightly different, depending on your platform and where you installed Python).

Listing 8-9. BaseHTMLProcessor Output for Command-Line Execution

```
c:\docbook\dip\py> python BaseHTMLProcessor.py

SGMLParser = sgmllib.SGMLParser                     (1)
htmlentitydefs = <module 'htmlentitydefs'
from 'C:\Python23\lib\htmlentitydefs.py'>           (2)
```

```
BaseHTMLProcessor = __main__.BaseHTMLProcessor          (3)
__name__ = __main__                                     (4)
... rest of output omitted for brevity...
```

(1) SGMLParser was imported from sgmllib, using from *module* import. That means that it was imported directly into our module's namespace, and here it is.

(2) Contrast this with htmlentitydefs, which was imported using import. That means that the htmlentitydefs module itself is in your namespace, but the entitydefs variable defined within htmlentitydefs is not.

(3) This module defines only one class, BaseHTMLProcessor, and here it is. Note that the value here is the class itself, not a specific instance of the class.

(4) Remember the if __name__ trick (introduced in Chapter 4)? When running a module (as opposed to importing it from another module), the built-in __name__ attribute is a special value, __main__. Since you ran this module as a script from the command line, __name__ is __main__, which is why the little test code to print the globals() was executed.

> **NOTE** *Using the* locals() *and* globals() *functions, you can get the value of arbitrary variables dynamically, providing the variable name as a string. This mirrors the functionality of the* getattr *function, which allows you to access arbitrary functions dynamically by providing the function name as a string.*

There is one other important difference between the locals() and globals() functions, which you should learn now before it bites you. (Well, it will bite you anyway, but at least then you'll remember learning it.) That difference is that locals() is read-only, but globals() is not read-only, as demonstrated in Listing 8-10.

Listing 8-10. locals() Is Read-Only: globals() Is Not

```
def foo(arg):
    x = 1
    print locals()                      (1)
    locals()["x"] = 2                    (2)
    print "x=",x                         (3)

z = 7
print "z=",z
foo(3)
globals()["z"] = 8                       (4)
print "z=",z                             (5)
```

(1) Since foo is called with 3, this will print {'arg': 3, 'x': 1}. This should not be a surprise.

(2) locals() is a function that returns a dictionary, and here you are setting a value in that dictionary. You might think that this would change the value of the local variable x to 2, but it doesn't. locals() does not actually return the local namespace; it returns a copy. So, changing it does nothing to the value of the variables in the local namespace.

(3) This prints x= 1, not x= 2.

(4) After being burned by locals(), you might think that this *wouldn't* change the value of z, but it does. Due to internal differences in how Python is implemented (which I would rather not go into, since I don't fully understand them myself), globals() returns the actual global namespace, not a copy: the exact opposite behavior of locals(). So, any changes to the dictionary returned by globals() directly affect your global variables.

(5) This prints z= 8, not z= 7.

Using Dictionary-based String Formatting

Why did we talk about locals() and globals()? So we can talk about dictionary-based string formatting. As you recall from Chapter 3, regular string formatting provides an easy way to insert values into strings. Values are listed in a tuple and inserted in order into the string in place of each formatting marker. Although this is efficient, it is not always the easiest code to read, especially when multiple values are being inserted. You can't simply scan through the string in one pass and understand what the result will be; you're constantly switching between reading the string and reading the tuple of values.

An alternative form of string formatting uses dictionaries instead of tuples of values, as demonstrated in Listing 8-11.

Listing 8-11. Introducing Dictionary-based String Formatting

```
>>> params = {"server":"mpilgrim", "database":"master", "uid":"sa",
"pwd":"secret"}
>>> "%(pwd)s" % params                                    (1)
'secret'
>>> "%(pwd)s is not a good password for %(uid)s" % params   (2)
'secret is not a good password for sa'
>>> "%(database)s of mind, %(database)s of body" % params   (3)
'master of mind, master of body'
```

(1) Instead of a tuple of explicit values, this form of string formatting uses a dictionary, params. And instead of a simple %s marker in the string, the marker contains a name in parentheses. This name is used as a key in the params dictionary and substitutes the corresponding value, secret, in place of the %(pwd)s marker.

(2) Dictionary-based string formatting works with any number of named keys. Each key must exist in the given dictionary, or the formatting will fail with a KeyError.

(3) You can even specify the same key twice; each occurrence will be replaced with the same value.

So why would you use dictionary-based string formatting? Well, it does seem like overkill to set up a dictionary of keys and values simply to do string formatting in the next line. This approach is most useful when you happen to have a dictionary of meaningful keys and values—like locals()—already. You can see this in the dictionary-based string formatting in BaseHTMLProcessor.py:

```
def handle_comment(self, text):
    self.pieces.append("<!--%(text)s-->" % locals())
```

Using the built-in locals() function is the most common use of dictionary-based string formatting. It means that you can use the names of local variables within your string (in this case, text, which was passed to the class method as an argument) and each named variable will be replaced by its value. If text is 'Begin page footer', the string formatting "<!--%(text)s-->" % locals() will resolve to the string '<!--Begin page footer-->'.

Listing 8-12 demonstrates more dictionary-based string formatting.

Listing 8-12. More Dictionary-based String Formatting

```
def unknown_starttag(self, tag, attrs):
    strattrs = "".join([' %s="%s"' % (key, value) for key, value in attrs])  (1)
    self.pieces.append("<%(tag)s%(strattrs)s>" % locals())                   (2)
```

(1) When this method is called, attrs is a list of key/value tuples, just like the items of a dictionary, which means you can use multivariable assignment to iterate through it. This should be a familiar pattern by now, but there's a lot going on here, so let's break it down:

- Suppose attrs is [('href', 'index.html'), ('title', 'Go to home page')].

- In the first round of the list comprehension, key will get 'href', and value will get 'index.html'.

- The string formatting ' %s="%s"' % (key, value) will resolve to ' href="index.html"'. This string becomes the first element of the list comprehension's return value.

- In the second round, `key` will get `'title'`, and `value` will get `'Go to home page'`.

- The string formatting will resolve to `' title="Go to home page"'`.

- The list comprehension returns a list of these two resolved strings, and `strattrs` will join both elements of this list together to form `' href="index.html" title="Go to home page"'`.

(2) Now, using dictionary-based string formatting, you insert the value of `tag` and `strattrs` into a string. So, if `tag` is `'a'`, the final result will be `'<a href="index.html" title="Go to home page">'`, and that is what is appended to `self.pieces`.

> **CAUTION** *Using dictionary-based string formatting with* `locals()` *is a convenient way of making complex string-formatting expressions more readable, but it comes at a price. There is a slight performance hit in making the call to* `locals()`, *since* `locals()` *builds a copy of the local namespace.*

Quoting Attribute Values

A common question on comp.lang.python (`http://groups.google.com/ groups?group=comp.lang.python`) is, "I have a bunch of HTML documents with unquoted attribute values, and I want to properly quote them all. How can I do this?"

Okay, I admit that it's not that common a question. It's not up there with "What editor should I use to write Python code?" (answer: Emacs) or "Is Python better or worse than Perl?" (answer: "Perl is worse than Python because people wanted it worse." Larry Wall, October 14, 1998). But questions about HTML processing pop up in one form or another about once a month, and among those questions, this is a popular one. Unquoted attribute values are easy to fix by feeding HTML through `BaseHTMLProcessor`.

`BaseHTMLProcessor` consumes HTML (since it's descended from `SGMLParser`) and produces equivalent HTML, but the HTML output is not identical to the input. Tags and attribute names will end up in lowercase, even if they started in uppercase or mixed case, and attribute values will be enclosed in double quotes, even if they started in single quotes or with no quotes at all. It is this last side effect that you can take advantage of to fix unquoted attribute values, as shown in Listing 8-13.

Listing 8-13. Quoting Attribute Values

```
>>> htmlSource = """                              (1)
...     <html>
...     <head>
...     <title>Test page</title>
...     </head>
...     <body>
...     <ul>
...     <li><a href=index.html>Home</a></li>
...     <li><a href=toc.html>Table of contents</a></li>
...     <li><a href=history.html>Revision history</a></li>
...     </body>
...     </html>
...     """
>>> from BaseHTMLProcessor import BaseHTMLProcessor
>>> parser = BaseHTMLProcessor()
>>> parser.feed(htmlSource)                       (2)
>>> print parser.output()                         (3)
<html>
<head>
<title>Test page</title>
</head>
<body>
<ul>
<li><a href="index.html">Home</a></li>
<li><a href="toc.html">Table of contents</a></li>
<li><a href="history.html">Revision history</a></li>
</body>
</html>
```

(1) Note that the attribute values of the href attributes in the <a> tags are not properly quoted. Also note that you're using triple quotes for something other than a doc string—and directly in the IDE, no less. They're very useful.

(2) Feed the parser.

(3) Using the output function defined in BaseHTMLProcessor, you get the output as a single string, complete with quoted attribute values. While this may seem anticlimactic, think about how much has actually happened here: SGMLParser parsed the entire HTML document, breaking it down into tags, refs, data, and so forth. BaseHTMLProcessor used those elements to reconstruct pieces of HTML (which are still stored in parser.pieces, if you want to see them). Finally, you called parser.output, which joined all the pieces of HTML into one string.

Parsing HTML One Tag at a Time

Dialectizer is a simple (and silly) descendant of BaseHTMLProcessor. It runs blocks of text through a series of substitutions, but it makes sure that anything within a <pre>...</pre> block passes through unaltered.

To handle the <pre> blocks, two methods are defined in Dialectizer: start_pre and end_pre, as shown in Listing 8-14.

Listing 8-14. Handling Specific Tags

```
def start_pre(self, attrs):                 (1)
    self.verbatim += 1                      (2)
    self.unknown_starttag("pre", attrs)     (3)

def end_pre(self):                          (4)
    self.unknown_endtag("pre")              (5)
    self.verbatim -= 1                      (6)
```

(1) start_pre is called every time SGMLParser finds a <pre> tag in the HTML source. (In a minute, you'll see exactly how this happens.) The method takes a single parameter, attrs, which contains the attributes of the tag (if any). attrs is a list of key/value tuples, just like unknown_starttag takes.

(2) In the reset method, you initialize a data attribute that serves as a counter for <pre> tags. Every time you hit a <pre> tag, you increment the counter. Every time you hit a </pre> tag, you'll decrement the counter. You could just use this as a flag and set it to 1 and reset it to 0, but it's just as easy to do it this way, and this handles the odd (but possible) case of nested <pre> tags. In a minute, you'll see how this counter is put to good use.

(3) That's it—that's the only special processing you do for <pre> tags. Now, you pass the list of attributes along to unknown_starttag so it can do the default processing.

(4) end_pre is called every time SGMLParser finds a </pre> tag. Since end tags cannot contain attributes, the method takes no parameters.

(5) First, you want to do the default processing, just like any other end tag.

(6) Second, you decrement your counter to signal that this <pre> block has been closed.

At this point, it's worth digging a little further into SGMLParser. I've claimed repeatedly (and you've taken it on faith so far) that SGMLParser looks for and calls specific methods for each tag, if they exist. For instance, you just saw the definition of start_pre and end_pre to handle <pre> and </pre>. But how does this happen? Well, it's not magic; it's just good Python coding. Listing 8-15 demonstrates how this works.

Listing 8-15. SGMLParser

```
def finish_starttag(self, tag, attrs):                    (1)
    try:
        method = getattr(self, 'start_' + tag)            (2)
    except AttributeError:                                (3)
        try:
            method = getattr(self, 'do_' + tag)           (4)
        except AttributeError:
            self.unknown_starttag(tag, attrs)             (5)
            return -1
        else:
            self.handle_starttag(tag, method, attrs)      (6)
            return 0
    else:
        self.stack.append(tag)
        self.handle_starttag(tag, method, attrs)
        return 1                                          (7)

def handle_starttag(self, tag, method, attrs):
    method(attrs)                                         (8)
```

(1) At this point, SGMLParser has already found a start tag and parsed the attribute list. The only thing left to do is figure out whether there is a specific handler method for this tag or you should fall back on the default method (unknown_starttag).

(2) The "magic" of SGMLParser is nothing more than our old friend, getattr. What you may not have realized before is that getattr will find methods defined in descendants of an object as well as the object itself. Here the object is self, the current instance. So if tag is 'pre', this call to getattr will look for a start_pre method on the current instance, which is an instance of the Dialectizer class.

(3) getattr raises an AttributeError if the method it's looking for doesn't exist in the object (or any of its descendants), but that's okay, because you wrapped the call to getattr inside a try...except block and explicitly caught the AttributeError.

(4) Since you didn't find a start_*xxx* method, you'll also look for a do_*xxx* method before giving up. This alternate naming scheme is generally used for stand-alone tags, like <br>, which have no corresponding end tag. But you can use either naming scheme; as you can see, SGMLParser tries both for every tag. (You shouldn't define both a start_*xxx* and do_*xxx* handler method for the same tag, though; only the start_*xxx* method will get called.)

(5) This is another AttributeError, which means that the call to getattr failed with do_*xxx*. Since you found neither a start_*xxx* nor a do_*xxx* method for this tag, you catch the exception and fall back on the default method, unknown_starttag.

(6) Remember that try...except blocks can have an else clause, which is called if no exception is raised during the try...except block. Logically, that means that you *did* find a do_*xxx* method for this tag, so you're going to call it.

(7) By the way, don't worry about these different return values; in theory, they mean something, but they're never actually used. Don't worry about the self.stack.append(tag) either; SGMLParser keeps track internally of whether your start tags are balanced by appropriate end tags, but it doesn't do anything with this information either. In theory, you could use this module to validate that your tags were fully balanced, but it's probably not worth it.

(8) start_*xxx* and do_*xxx* methods are not called directly; the tag, method, and attributes are passed to this function, handle_starttag, so that descendants can override it and change the way *all* start tags are dispatched. You don't need that level of control, so you just let this method do its thing, which is to call the method (start_*xxx* or do_*xxx*) with the list of attributes. Remember that method is a function, returned from getattr, and functions are objects. (I know you're getting tired of hearing it, and I promise I'll stop saying it as soon as we stop finding new ways of using it to our advantage.) Here, the function object is passed into this dispatch method as an argument, and this method turns around and calls the function. At this point, you don't need to know what the function is, what it's named, or where it's defined. The only thing you need to know about the function is that it is called with one argument: attrs.

Now back to our regularly scheduled program: Dialectizer. When we left, we were in the process of defining specific handler methods for <pre> and </pre> tags. There's only one thing left to do: process text blocks with your predefined substitutions. For that, you need to override the handle_data method, as shown in Listing 8-16.

Listing 8-16. Overriding the handle_data Method

```
def handle_data(self, text):                                        (1)
    self.pieces.append(self.verbatim and text or self.process(text))  (2)
```

(1) handle_data is called with only one argument: the text to process.

(2) In the ancestor BaseHTMLProcessor, the handle_data method simply appended the text to the output buffer, self.pieces. Here, the logic is only slightly more complicated. If you're in the middle of a <pre>...</pre> block, self.verbatim will be some value greater than 0, and you want to put the text in the output buffer unaltered. Otherwise, you will call a separate method to process the substitutions, and then put the result of that into the output buffer. In Python, this is a one-liner, using the and-or trick.

You're close to completely understanding Dialectizer. The only missing link is the nature of the text substitutions themselves. If you know any Perl, you know that when complex text substitutions are required, the only real solution is regular expressions. The classes later in dialect.py define a series of regular expressions that operate on the text between the HTML tags. But we just had a whole chapter on regular expressions. You don't really want to slog through regular expressions again, do you? Let's not.

Putting It All Together

It's time to put everything you've learned so far to good use. I hope you were paying attention. Listing 8-17 gets you started.

Listing 8-17. The translate Function, Part 1

```
def translate(url, dialectName="chef"):          (1)
    import urllib                                 (2)
    sock = urllib.urlopen(url)                    (3)
    htmlSource = sock.read()
    sock.close()
```

(1) The translate function has an optional argument dialectName, which is a string that specifies the dialect you'll be using. You'll see how this is used in a minute.

(2) Hey, wait a minute—there's an import statement in this function! That's perfectly legal in Python. You're used to seeing import statements at the top of a program, which means that the imported module is available anywhere in the program. But you can also import modules within a function, which means that the imported module is only available within the function. If you have a module that is used in only one function, this is an easy way to make your code more modular. (When you find that your weekend hack has turned into an 800-line work of art and decide to split it up into a dozen reusable modules, you'll appreciate this.)

(3) Now you get the source of the given URL.

Now for the second part of the translate function, in Listing 8-18.

Listing 8-18. The translate Function, Part 2: Curiouser and Curiouser

```
    parserName = "%sDialectizer" % dialectName.capitalize()    (1)
    parserClass = globals()[parserName]                        (2)
    parser = parserClass()                                     (3)
```

(1) capitalize is a string method you haven't seen before. It simply capitalizes the first letter of a string and forces everything else to lowercase. Combined with some string formatting, you've taken the name of a dialect and transformed it into the name of the corresponding Dialectizer class. If dialectName is the string 'chef', parserName will be the string 'ChefDialectizer'.

(2) We have the name of a class as a string (parserName), and we have the global namespace as a dictionary (globals()). Combined, we can get a reference to the class which the string names. (Remember, classes are objects, and they can be assigned to variables just like any other object.) If `parserName` is the string `'ChefDialectizer'`, `parserClass` will be the class `ChefDialectizer`.

(3) Finally, you have a class object (`parserClass`), and you want an instance of the class. Well, you already know how to do that: call the class as you call a function. The fact that the class is being stored in a local variable makes absolutely no difference. You just call the local variable in the same way you call a function, and out pops an instance of the class. If `parserClass` is the class `ChefDialectizer`, `parser` will be an instance of the class `ChefDialectizer`.

Why bother? After all, there are only three `Dialectizer` classes. Why not just use a `case` statement? (Well, there's no `case` statement in Python, but why not just use a series of `if` statements?) You want to do this for one reason: extensibility. The `translate` function has absolutely no idea how many `Dialectizer` classes you've defined.

Imagine that you define a new `FooDialectizer` tomorrow—translate would still work by passing `'foo'` as the `dialectName`.

Even better, imagine putting `FooDialectizer` in a separate module and importing it with `from` *module* `import`. You've already seen that this includes it in `globals()`, so `translate` would still work without modification, even though `FooDialectizer` was in a separate file.

Now imagine that the name of the dialect is coming from somewhere outside the program, maybe from a database or from a user-inputted value on a form. You can use any number of server-side Python scripting architectures to dynamically generate web pages. This function could take a URL and a dialect name (both strings) in the query string of a web page request, and output the "translated" web page.

> **NOTE** *You thought I was kidding about the server-side scripting idea. So did I, until I found this web-based dialectizer:* `http://rinkworks.com/dialect/`. *Unfortunately, source code does not appear to be available.*

Finally, imagine a `Dialectizer` framework with a plug-in architecture. You could put each `Dialectizer` class in a separate file, leaving only the `translate` function in `dialect.py`. Assuming a consistent naming scheme, the `translate` function could dynamically import the appropiate class from the appropriate file, given nothing but the dialect name. (You haven't seen dynamic importing yet, but I promise to cover it in Chapter 16.) To add a new dialect, you would simply add an appropriately named file in the plug-ins directory (like `foodialect.py`, which contains the `FooDialectizer` class). Calling the `translate` function with the dialect name `'foo'` would find the module `foodialect.py`, import the class `FooDialectizer`, and away you go.

Let's continue with the third and final part of the `translate` function, in Listing 8-19.

Listing 8-19. The translate Function, Part 3

```
parser.feed(htmlSource)                                          (1)
parser.close()                                                   (2)
return parser.output()                                           (3)
```

(1) After all that imagining, this is going to seem pretty boring, but the `feed` function is what does the entire transformation. You had the entire HTML source in a single string, so you needed to call `feed` only once. However, you can call `feed` as often as you want, and the parser will just keep parsing. So, if you were worried about memory usage (or you knew you were going to be dealing with very large HTML pages), you could set this up in a loop, where you read a few bytes of HTML and fed it to the parser. The result would be the same.

(2) Because `feed` maintains an internal buffer, you should always call the parser's `close` method when you're finished (even if you fed it all at once, as we did here). Otherwise, you may find that your output is missing the last few bytes.

(3) Remember that `output` is the function defined in `BaseHTMLProcessor` that joins all the pieces of output you've buffered and returns them in a single string.

And just like that, you've "translated" a web page, given nothing but a URL and the name of a dialect.

Summary

Python provides you with a powerful tool, `sgmllib.py`, to manipulate HTML by turning its structure into an object model. You can use this tool in many different ways:

- Parsing the HTML, looking for something specific

- Aggregating the results, like the URL lister

- Altering the structure along the way, like the attribute quoter

- Transforming the HTML into something else by manipulating the text while leaving the tags alone, like the `Dialectizer`

After working through this chapter's examples, you should be comfortable using `locals()` and `globals()` to access namespaces, as well as formatting strings using dictionary-based substitutions.

CHAPTER 9

XML Processing

THIS CHAPTER AND THE next chapter are about XML processing in Python. It would be helpful if you already knew what an XML document looks like—that it's made up of structured tags to form a hierarchy of elements, and so on. If this doesn't make sense to you, there are many XML tutorials that can explain the basics (http://directory.google.com/Top/Computers/Data_Formats/Markup_Languages/XML/Resources/FAQs,_Help,_and_Tutorials/).

If you're not particularly interested in XML, you should still read these chapters, because they cover important topics like Python packages, Unicode, command-line arguments, and how to use getattr for method dispatching.

Being a philosophy major is not required, although if you have ever had the misfortune of being subjected to the writings of Immanuel Kant, you will appreciate the sample program a lot more than if you majored in something useful, like computer science.

There are two basic ways to work with XML. One is called SAX (for Simple API for XML), and it works by reading the XML a bit at a time and calling a method for each element it finds. (If you read Chapter 8, this should sound familiar, because that's how the sgmllib module works.) The other is called DOM (for Document Object Model), and it works by reading in the entire XML document at once and creating an internal representation of it using native Python classes linked in a tree structure. Python has standard modules for both kinds of parsing, but this chapter will deal only with using the DOM.

Diving In

Listing 9-1 is a complete Python program that generates pseudo-random output based on a context-free grammar defined in an XML format. We'll examine both the program's input and its output in depth throughout this and the next chapter.

> **NOTE** *If you have not already done so, you can download this and the other examples used in this book from the Downloads section of the Apress web site (http://www.apress.com).*

Listing 9-1. kgp.py

```
"""Kant Generator for Python

Generates mock philosophy based on a context-free grammar

Usage: python kgp.py [options] [source]

Options:
  -g ..., --grammar=...   use specified grammar file or URL
  -h, --help              show this help
  -d                      show debugging information while parsing

Examples:
  kgp.py                  generates several paragraphs of Kantian philosophy
  kgp.py -g husserl.xml   generates several paragraphs of Husserl
  kpg.py "<xref id='paragraph'/>"  generates a paragraph of Kant
  kgp.py template.xml     reads from template.xml to decide what to generate
"""
from xml.dom import minidom
import random
import toolbox
import sys
import getopt


_debug = 0


class NoSourceError(Exception): pass

class KantGenerator:
    """generates mock philosophy based on a context-free grammar"""

    def __init__(self, grammar, source=None):
        self.loadGrammar(grammar)
        self.loadSource(source and source or self.getDefaultSource())
        self.refresh()

    def _load(self, source):
        """load XML input source, return parsed XML document

        - a URL of a remote XML file
        - a filename of a local XML file
        - standard input ("-")
        - the actual XML document, as a string
        """
```

```
        sock = toolbox.openAnything(source)
        xmldoc = minidom.parse(sock).documentElement
        sock.close()
        return xmldoc

    def loadGrammar(self, grammar):
        """load context-free grammar"""
        self.grammar = self._load(grammar)
        self.refs = {}
        for ref in self.grammar.getElementsByTagName("ref"):
            self.refs[ref.attributes["id"].value] = ref

    def loadSource(self, source):
        """load source"""
        self.source = self._load(source)

    def getDefaultSource(self):
        """guess default source of the current grammar

        The default source will be one of the <ref>s that is not
        cross-referenced.  This sounds complicated but it's not.
        Example: The default source for kant.xml is
        "<xref id='section'/>", because 'section' is the one <ref>
        that is not <xref>'d anywhere in the grammar.
        In most grammars, the default source will produce the
        longest (and most interesting) output.
        """
        xrefs = {}
        for xref in self.grammar.getElementsByTagName("xref"):
            xrefs[xref.attributes["id"].value] = 1
        xrefs = xrefs.keys()
        standaloneXrefs = [e for e in self.refs.keys() if e not in xrefs]
        if not standaloneXrefs:
            raise NoSourceError, "can't guess source, and no source specified"
        return '<xref id="%s"/>' % random.choice(standaloneXrefs)

    def reset(self):
        """reset parser"""
        self.pieces = []
        self.capitalizeNextWord = 0

    def refresh(self):
        """reset output buffer, reparse entire source file, and return output
```

```
          Since parsing involves a good deal of randomness, this is an
          easy way to get new output without having to reload a grammar file
          each time.
          """
          self.reset()
          self.parse(self.source)
          return self.output()

      def output(self):
          """output generated text"""
          return "".join(self.pieces)

      def randomChildElement(self, node):
          """choose a random child element of a node

          This is a utility method used by do_xref and do_choice.
          """
          choices = [e for e in node.childNodes
                        if e.nodeType == e.ELEMENT_NODE]
          chosen = random.choice(choices)
          if _debug:
              sys.stderr.write('%s available choices: %s\n' % \
                  (len(choices), [e.toxml() for e in choices]))
              sys.stderr.write('Chosen: %s\n' % chosen.toxml())
          return chosen

      def parse(self, node):
          """parse a single XML node

          A parsed XML document (from minidom.parse) is a tree of nodes
          of various types.  Each node is represented by an instance of the
          corresponding Python class (Element for a tag, Text for
          text data, Document for the top-level document).  The following
          statement constructs the name of a class method based on the type
          of node we're parsing ("parse_Element" for an Element node,
          "parse_Text" for a Text node, etc.) and then calls the method.
          """
          parseMethod = getattr(self, "parse_%s" % node.__class__.__name__)
          parseMethod(node)

      def parse_Document(self, node):
          """parse the document node
```

```
        The document node by itself isn't interesting (to us), but
        its only child, node.documentElement, is: it's the root node
        of the grammar.
        """
        self.parse(node.documentElement)

    def parse_Text(self, node):
        """parse a text node

        The text of a text node is usually added to the output buffer
        verbatim.  The one exception is that <p class='sentence'> sets
        a flag to capitalize the first letter of the next word.  If
        that flag is set, we capitalize the text and reset the flag.
        """
        text = node.data
        if self.capitalizeNextWord:
            self.pieces.append(text[0].upper())
            self.pieces.append(text[1:])
            self.capitalizeNextWord = 0
        else:
            self.pieces.append(text)

    def parse_Element(self, node):
        """parse an element

        An XML element corresponds to an actual tag in the source:
        <xref id='...'>, <p chance='...'>, <choice>, etc.
        Each element type is handled in its own method.  As we did in
        parse(), we construct a method name based on the name of the
        element ("do_xref" for an <xref> tag, etc.) and
        call the method.
        """
        handlerMethod = getattr(self, "do_%s" % node.tagName)
        handlerMethod(node)

    def parse_Comment(self, node):
        """parse a comment

        The grammar can contain XML comments, but we ignore them
        """
        pass

    def do_xref(self, node):
        """handle <xref id='...'> tag
```

```
            An <xref id='...'> tag is a cross-reference to a <ref id='...'>
            tag.  <xref id='sentence'/> evaluates to a randomly chosen child of
            <ref id='sentence'>.
            """
            id = node.attributes["id"].value
            self.parse(self.randomChildElement(self.refs[id]))

    def do_p(self, node):
        """handle <p> tag

        The <p> tag is the core of the grammar.  It can contain almost
        anything: freeform text, <choice> tags, <xref> tags, even other
        <p> tags.  If a "class='sentence'" attribute is found, a flag
        is set and the next word will be capitalized.  If a "chance='X'"
        attribute is found, there is an X% chance that the tag will be
        evaluated (and therefore a (100-X)% chance that it will be
        completely ignored)
        """
        keys = node.attributes.keys()
        if "class" in keys:
            if node.attributes["class"].value == "sentence":
                self.capitalizeNextWord = 1
        if "chance" in keys:
            chance = int(node.attributes["chance"].value)
            doit = (chance > random.randrange(100))
        else:
            doit = 1
        if doit:
            for child in node.childNodes: self.parse(child)

    def do_choice(self, node):
        """handle <choice> tag

        A <choice> tag contains one or more <p> tags.  One <p> tag
        is chosen at random and evaluated; the rest are ignored.
        """
        self.parse(self.randomChildElement(node))

def usage():
    print __doc__

def main(argv):
    grammar = "kant.xml"
    try:
        opts, args = getopt.getopt(argv, "hg:d", ["help", "grammar="])
```

```
        except getopt.GetoptError:
            usage()
            sys.exit(2)
        for opt, arg in opts:
            if opt in ("-h", "--help"):
                usage()
                sys.exit()
            elif opt == '-d':
                global _debug
                _debug = 1
            elif opt in ("-g", "--grammar"):
                grammar = arg

        source = "".join(args)

        k = KantGenerator(grammar, source)
        print k.output()

if __name__ == "__main__":
    main(sys.argv[1:])
```

Listing 9-2 shows toolbox.py, which is a helper module that kgp.py uses to be able to treat remote and local input sources in the same way.

Listing 9-2. toolbox.py

```
"""Miscellaneous utility functions"""

def openAnything(source):
    """URI, filename, or string --> stream

    This function lets you define parsers that take any input source
    (URL, pathname to local or network file, or actual data as a string)
    and deal with it in a uniform manner.  Returned object is guaranteed
    to have all the basic stdio read methods (read, readline, readlines).
    Just .close() the object when you're done with it.

    Examples:
    >>> from xml.dom import minidom
    >>> sock = openAnything("http://localhost/kant.xml")
    >>> doc = minidom.parse(sock)
    >>> sock.close()
    >>> sock = openAnything("c:\\inetpub\\wwwroot\\kant.xml")
    >>> doc = minidom.parse(sock)
    >>> sock.close()
```

```
>>> sock = openAnything("<ref id='conjunction'><text>" +
.... "and</text><text>or</text></ref>")
>>> doc = minidom.parse(sock)
>>> sock.close()
"""
if hasattr(source, "read"):
    return source

if source == '-':
    import sys
    return sys.stdin

# try to open with urllib (if source is http, ftp, or file URL)
import urllib
try:
    return urllib.urlopen(source)
except (IOError, OSError):
    pass

# try to open with native open function (if source is pathname)
try:
    return open(source)
except (IOError, OSError):
    pass

# treat source as string
import StringIO
return StringIO.StringIO(str(source))
```

Run the program kgp.py by itself, and it will parse the default XML-based grammar, in kant.xml, and print several paragraphs' worth of philosophy in the style of Immanuel Kant. Here's an example of its output:

```
    As is shown in the writings of Hume, our a priori concepts, in
reference to ends, abstract from all content of knowledge; in the study
of space, the discipline of human reason, in accordance with the
principles of philosophy, is the clue to the discovery of the
Transcendental Deduction.  The transcendental aesthetic, in all
theoretical sciences, occupies part of the sphere of human reason
concerning the existence of our ideas in general; still, the
never-ending regress in the series of empirical conditions constitutes
the whole content for the transcendental unity of apperception.  What
```

we have alone been able to show is that, even as this relates to the
architectonic of human reason, the Ideal may not contradict itself, but
it is still possible that it may be in contradictions with the
employment of the pure employment of our hypothetical judgements, but
natural causes (and I assert that this is the case) prove the validity
of the discipline of pure reason. As we have already seen, time (and
it is obvious that this is true) proves the validity of time, and the
architectonic of human reason, in the full sense of these terms,
abstracts from all content of knowledge. I assert, in the case of the
discipline of practical reason, that the Antinomies are just as
necessary as natural causes, since knowledge of the phenomena is a
posteriori.

The discipline of human reason, as I have elsewhere shown, is by
its very nature contradictory, but our ideas exclude the possibility of
the Antinomies. We can deduce that, on the contrary, the pure
employment of philosophy, on the contrary, is by its very nature
contradictory, but our sense perceptions are a representation of, in
the case of space, metaphysics. The thing in itself is a
representation of philosophy. Applied logic is the clue to the
discovery of natural causes. However, what we have alone been able to
show is that our ideas, in other words, should only be used as a canon
for the Ideal, because of our necessary ignorance of the conditions.

This is, of course, complete gibberish. Well, it's not complete gibberish. It is syntactically and grammatically correct (although very verbose; Kant wasn't what you would call a get-to-the-point kind of guy). Some of it may actually be true (or at least the sort of thing that Kant would have agreed with), some of it is blatantly false, and most of it is simply incoherent. But all of it is in the style of Immanuel Kant. (As I said at the beginning of the chapter, this is much, much funnier if you are now or have ever been a philosophy major.)

The interesting thing about this program is that there is nothing Kant-specific about it. All the content in the previous example was derived from the grammar file, kant.xml. If you tell the program to use a different grammar file (which you can specify on the command line), the output will be completely different. Here's a simpler example of the output from kgp.py:

```
[you@localhost kgp]$ python kgp.py -g binary.xml
00101001
[you@localhost kgp]$ python kgp.py -g binary.xml
10110100
```

We will take a closer look at the structure of the grammar file later in this chapter. For now, all you need to know is that the grammar file defines the structure of the output, and the kgp.py program reads through the grammar and makes random decisions about which words to plug in where.

Importing Python Packages

Actually parsing an XML document is very simple: it just takes one line of code. However, before we get to that line of code, we need to take a short detour to talk about packages. Here is a sneak peek at loading an XML document:

```
>>> from xml.dom import minidom
>>> xmldoc = minidom.parse('~/diveintopython/common/py/kgp/binary.xml')
```

This is a syntax you haven't seen before. It looks almost like the from *module* import you know and love, but the dot (.) in the syntax gives it away as something above and beyond a simple import. In fact, xml is what is known as a *package*, dom is a nested package within xml, and minidom is a module within xml.dom.

That sounds complicated, but it's really not. Looking at the actual implementation may help. Packages are little more than directories of modules; nested packages are subdirectories. The modules within a package (or a nested package) are still just .py files, as always, except that they're in a subdirectory instead of the main lib/ directory of your Python installation. Listing 9-3 shows the file layout of a package.

Listing 9-3. File Layout of a Package

```
Python23/            root Python installation (home of the executable)
|
+--lib/              library directory (home of the standard library modules)
   |
   +-- xml/          xml package (really just a directory with other stuff in it)
        |
        +--sax/      xml.sax package (again, just a directory)
        |
        +--dom/      xml.dom package (contains minidom.py)
        |
        +--parsers/  xml.parsers package (used internally)
```

So when you say from xml.dom import minidom, Python figures out that you mean, "Look in the xml directory for a dom directory, and look in *that* for the minidom module, and import it as minidom." But Python is even smarter than that. Not only can you import entire modules contained within a package, but you can also selectively import specific classes or functions from a module contained within a package. You can also import the package itself as a module. The syntax is all the same. Python figures out what you mean, based on the file layout of the package, and automatically does the right thing.

Listing 9-4 demonstrates importing a package.

Listing 9-4. Packages Are Modules, Too

```
>>> from xml.dom import minidom                          (1)
>>> minidom
<module 'xml.dom.minidom' from 'C:\Python23\lib\xml\dom\minidom.pyc'>
>>> minidom.Element
<class xml.dom.minidom.Element at 01095744>
>>> from xml.dom.minidom import Element                  (2)
>>> Element
<class xml.dom.minidom.Element at 01095744>
>>> minidom.Element
<class xml.dom.minidom.Element at 01095744>
>>> from xml import dom                                   (3)
>>> dom
<module 'xml.dom' from 'C:\Python23\lib\xml\dom\__init__.pyc'>
>>> import xml                                            (4)
>>> xml
<module 'xml' from 'C:\Python23\lib\xml\__init__.pyc'>
```

(1) Here, you're importing a module (minidom) from a nested package (xml.dom). The result is that minidom is imported into your namespace, and in order to reference classes within the minidom module (like Element), you need to preface them with the module name.

(2) Here, you are importing a class (Element) from a module (minidom) from a nested package (xml.dom). The result is that Element is imported directly into your namespace. Note that this does not interfere with the previous import; the Element class can now be referenced in two ways (but it's all still the same class).

(3) Here, you are importing the dom package (a nested package of xml) as a module in and of itself. Any level of a package can be treated as a module, as you'll see in a moment. It can even have its own attributes and methods, just like the modules you've seen before.

(4) Here, you are importing the root-level xml package as a module.

So how can a package (which is just a directory on disk) be imported and treated as a module (which is always a file on disk)? The answer is the magical __init__.py file. You see, packages are not simply directories; they are directories with a specific file, __init__.py, inside. This file defines the attributes and methods of the package. For instance, xml.dom contains a Node class, which is defined in xml/dom/__init__.py. When you import a package as a module (like dom from xml), you're really importing its __init__.py file.

> **NOTE** *A package is a directory with the special __init__.py file in it. The __init__.py file defines the attributes and methods of the package. It doesn't need to define anything; it can just be an empty file, but it must exist. But if __init__.py doesn't exist, the directory is just a directory, not a package, and it can't be imported or contain modules or nested packages.*

So why bother with packages? Well, they provide a way to logically group related modules. Instead of having an `xml` package with `sax` and `dom` packages inside, the authors could have chosen to put all the `sax` functionality in `xmlsax.py` and all the `dom` functionality in `xmldom.py`, or even put all of it in a single module. But that would have been unwieldy (as of this writing, the XML package has more than 3,000 lines of code) and difficult to manage (separate source files mean multiple people can work on different areas simultaneously).

If you ever find yourself writing a large subsystem in Python (or, more likely, when you realize that your small subsystem has grown into a large one), invest some time designing a good package architecture. It's one of the many things Python is good at, so take advantage of it.

Parsing XML

As I was saying, actually parsing an XML document is very simple: it just takes one line of code. Where you go from there is up to you. Take a look at Listing 9-5.

Listing 9-5. Loading an XML Document (For Real This Time)

```
>>> from xml.dom import minidom                                         (1)
>>> xmldoc = minidom.parse('~/diveintopython/common/py/kgp/binary.xml')  (2)
>>> xmldoc                                                              (3)
<xml.dom.minidom.Document instance at 010BE87C>
>>> print xmldoc.toxml()                                               (4)
<?xml version="1.0" ?>
<grammar>
<ref id="bit">
  <p>0</p>
  <p>1</p>
</ref>
<ref id="byte">
  <p><xref id="bit"/><xref id="bit"/><xref id="bit"/><xref id="bit"/>\
<xref id="bit"/><xref id="bit"/><xref id="bit"/><xref id="bit"/></p>
</ref>
</grammar>
```

(1) As you saw in the previous section, this imports the `minidom` module from the `xml.dom` package.

(2) Here is the one line of code that does all the work: `minidom.parse` takes one argument and returns a parsed representation of the XML document. The argument can be many things; in this case, it's simply a filename of an XML document on my local disk. (To follow along, you'll need to change the path to point to your downloaded examples directory.) But you can also pass a file object, or even a file-like object. We'll take advantage of this flexibility later, in Chapter 10.

(3) The object returned from `minidom.parse` is a `Document` object, a descendant of the `Node` class. This `Document` object is the root level of a complex tree-like structure of interlocking Python objects that completely represent the XML document you passed to `minidom.parse`.

(4) `toxml` is a method of the `Node` class (and is therefore available on the `Document` object you got from `minidom.parse`). `toxml` prints the XML that this `Node` represents. For the `Document` node, this prints the entire XML document.

Now that you have an XML document in memory, you can start traversing through it, as shown in Listing 9-6.

Listing 9-6. Getting Child Nodes

```
>>> xmldoc.childNodes                                    (1)
[<DOM Element: grammar at 17538908>]
>>> xmldoc.childNodes[0]                                 (2)
<DOM Element: grammar at 17538908>
>>> xmldoc.firstChild                                    (3)
<DOM Element: grammar at 17538908>
```

(1) Every `Node` has a `childNodes` attribute, which is a list of the `Node` objects. A `Document` always has only one child node: the root element of the XML document (in this case, the `grammar` element).

(2) To get the first (and in this case, the only) child node, just use regular list syntax. Remember that there is nothing special going on here; this is just a regular Python list of regular Python objects.

(3) Since getting the first child node of a node is a useful and common activity, the `Node` class has a `firstChild` attribute, which is synonymous with `childNodes[0]`. (There is also a `lastChild` attribute, which is synonymous with `childNodes[-1]`.)

Listing 9-7 shows what you can do with the `toxml` method.

Listing 9-7. toxml Works on Any Node

```
>>> grammarNode = xmldoc.firstChild
>>> print grammarNode.toxml()                            (1)
```

```
<grammar>
<ref id="bit">
  <p>0</p>
  <p>1</p>
</ref>
<ref id="byte">
  <p><xref id="bit"/><xref id="bit"/><xref id="bit"/><xref id="bit"/>\
<xref id="bit"/><xref id="bit"/><xref id="bit"/><xref id="bit"/></p>
</ref>
</grammar>
```

(1) Since the toxml method is defined in the Node class, it is available on any XML node, not just the Document element.

Now, let's see what you can do with child nodes, as shown in Listing 9-8.

Listing 9-8. Child Nodes Can Be Text

```
>>> grammarNode.childNodes                         (1)
[<DOM Text node "\n">, <DOM Element: ref at 17533332>, \
<DOM Text node "\n">, <DOM Element: ref at 17549660>, <DOM Text node "\n">]
>>> print grammarNode.firstChild.toxml()           (2)


>>> print grammarNode.childNodes[1].toxml()        (3)
<ref id="bit">
  <p>0</p>
  <p>1</p>
</ref>
>>> print grammarNode.childNodes[3].toxml()        (4)
<ref id="byte">
  <p><xref id="bit"/><xref id="bit"/><xref id="bit"/><xref id="bit"/>\
<xref id="bit"/><xref id="bit"/><xref id="bit"/><xref id="bit"/></p>
</ref>
>>> print grammarNode.lastChild.toxml()            (5)
```

(1) Looking at the XML in binary.xml, you might think that grammar has only two child nodes: the two ref elements. But you're missing something: the carriage returns! After the '<grammar>' and before the first '<ref>' is a carriage return, and this text counts as a child node of the grammar element. Similarly, there is a carriage return after each '</ref>'; these also count as child nodes. So grammar.childNodes is actually a list of five objects: three Text objects and two Element objects.

(2) The first child is a Text object representing the carriage return after the '<grammar>' tag and before the first '<ref>' tag.

(3) The second child is an Element object representing the first ref element.

(4) The fourth child is an Element object representing the second ref element.

(5) The last child is a Text object representing the carriage return after the '</ref>' end tag and before the '</grammar>' end tag.

Listing 9-9 demonstrates how you can drill down through the child nodes.

Listing 9-9. Drilling Down All the Way to Text

```
>>> grammarNode
<DOM Element: grammar at 19167148>
>>> refNode = grammarNode.childNodes[1]              (1)
>>> refNode
<DOM Element: ref at 17987740>
>>> refNode.childNodes                               (2)
[<DOM Text node "\n">, <DOM Text node "  ">, <DOM Element: p at 19315844>, \
<DOM Text node "\n">, <DOM Text node "  ">, \
<DOM Element: p at 19462036>, <DOM Text node "\n">]
>>> pNode = refNode.childNodes[2]
>>> pNode
<DOM Element: p at 19315844>
>>> print pNode.toxml()                              (3)
<p>0</p>
>>> pNode.firstChild                                 (4)
<DOM Text node "0">
>>> pNode.firstChild.data                            (5)
u'0'
```

(1) As you saw in Listing 9-8, the first ref element is grammarNode.childNodes[1], since childNodes[0] is a Text node for the carriage return.

(2) The ref element has its own set of child nodes, one for the carriage return, a separate one for the spaces, one for the p element, and so forth.

(3) You can even use the toxml method here, deeply nested within the document.

(4) The p element has only one child node (you can't tell that from this example, but look at pNode.childNodes if you don't believe me), and it is a Text node for the single character '0'.

(5) The .data attribute of a Text node gives you the actual string that the text node represents. But what is that 'u' in front of the string? The answer to that deserves its own section.

Dealing with Unicode

Unicode is a system to represent characters from all the world's different languages. When Python parses an XML document, all data is stored in memory as Unicode.

Historical Note on Unicode

Before Unicode, there were separate character-encoding systems for each language, each using the same numbers (0–255) to represent that language's characters. Some languages (like Russian) have multiple conflicting standards about how to represent the same characters; other languages (like Japanese) have so many characters that they require multiple-byte character sets.

Exchanging documents between systems was difficult because there was no way for a computer to tell for certain which character-encoding scheme the document author had used; the computer saw only numbers, and the numbers could mean different things. Then think about trying to store these documents in the same place (like in the same database table); you would need to store the character encoding alongside each piece of text, and make sure to pass it around whenever you passed the text around.

Then think about multilingual documents, with characters from multiple languages in the same document. They typically used escape codes to switch modes; poof, we're in Russian koi8-r mode, so character 241 means this; poof, now we're in Mac Greek mode, so character 241 means something else; and so on. These are the problems that Unicode was designed to solve.

Unicode itself comes in several flavors. The most common encoding, called UTF-16, represents each character as a 2-byte number, from 0 to 65535. Each 2-byte number represents a unique character used in at least one of the world's languages. (Characters that are used in multiple languages have the same numeric code.) There is exactly one number per character, and exactly one character per number. Unicode data is never ambiguous.

> **NOTE** *Unicode now has been extended to handle ancient Chinese, Korean, and Japanese texts, which had so many different characters that the 2-byte Unicode system could not represent them all. Python 2.4 will support these extended encodings out of the box. You can download the support libraries for earlier versions of Python at http://cjkpython.i18n.org/.*

Of course, there is still the matter of all these legacy encoding systems, such as 7-bit ASCII, which stores English characters as numbers ranging from 0 to 127 (65 is capital *A*, 97 is lowercase *a*, and so forth). English has a very simple alphabet, so it can be completely expressed in 7-bit ASCII. Western European languages like French, Spanish, and German all use an encoding system called ISO-8859-1 (also called Latin-1), which uses the 7-bit ASCII characters for the numbers 0 through 127, but then extends into the 128–255 range for characters like *n*-with-a-tilde-over-it (241) and *u*-with-two-dots-over-it (252). And Unicode uses the same characters as 7-bit ASCII for 0 through 127, and the same characters as ISO-8859-1 for 128 through 255, and then extends from there into characters for other languages with the remaining numbers, 256 through 65535.

When dealing with Unicode data, you may, at some point, need to convert the data back into one of these other legacy encoding systems. For instance, you might need to integrate with some other computer system that expects its data in a specific 1-byte encoding scheme, print data to a non-Unicode-aware terminal or printer, or store data in an XML document that explicitly specifies the encoding scheme.

And on that note, let's get back to Python.

Using Unicode

Python has had Unicode support throughout the language since version 2.0. The XML package uses Unicode to store all parsed XML data, but you can use Unicode anywhere, as demonstrated in Listing 9-10.

Listing 9-10. Introducing Unicode

```
>>> s = u'Dive in'                          (1)
>>> s
u'Dive in'
>>> print s                                 (2)
Dive in
```

(1) To create a Unicode string instead of a regular ASCII string, add the letter u before the string. Note that this particular string doesn't have any non-ASCII characters. That's fine; Unicode is a superset of ASCII (a very large superset at that), so any regular ASCII string can also be stored as Unicode.

(2) When printing a string, Python will attempt to convert it to your default encoding, which is usually ASCII (more on the default encoding in a minute). Since this Unicode string is made up of characters that are also ASCII characters, printing it has the same result as printing a normal ASCII string. The conversion is seamless, and if you didn't know that s was a Unicode string, you would never notice the difference.

The real advantage of Unicode, of course, is its ability to represent non-ASCII characters, as demonstrated in Listing 9-11.

Listing 9-11. Storing Non-ASCII Characters

```
>>> s = u'La Pe\xf1a'                           (1)
>>> print s                                     (2)
Traceback (innermost last):
  File "<interactive input>", line 1, in ?
UnicodeError: ASCII encoding error: ordinal not in range(128)
>>> print s.encode('latin-1')                   (3)
La Peña
```

(1) Here, you have the Spanish *ñ* (*n* with a tilde over it). The Unicode character code for the tilde-*n* is 0xf1 in hexadecimal (241 in decimal), which you can type like this: \xf1.

(2) Remember that I said that the print function attempts to convert a Unicode string to ASCII so it can print it? Well, that's not going to work here, because this Unicode string contains non-ASCII characters, so Python raises a UnicodeError error.

(3) Here's where the conversion from Unicode to other encoding schemes comes in. s is a Unicode string, but print can print only a regular string. To solve this problem, you call the encode method, which is available for every Unicode string, to convert the Unicode string to a regular string in the given encoding scheme, which you pass as a parameter. In this case, you're using latin-1 (also known as iso-8859-1), which includes the tilde-*n* (whereas the default ASCII encoding scheme does not; it includes only characters numbered 0 through 127).

Setting the Default Encoding

Remember I said Python usually converted Unicode to ASCII whenever it needed to make a regular string out of a Unicode string? Well, this default encoding scheme is an option that you can customize. Listing 9-12 shows a file you can use to set Python's default encoding.

Listing 9-12. sitecustomize.py

```
# sitecustomize.py                              (1)
# this file can be anywhere in your Python path,
# but it usually goes in ${pythondir}/lib/site-packages/
import sys
sys.setdefaultencoding('iso-8859-1')           (2)
```

(**1**) sitecustomize.py is a special script. Python will try to import it on startup, so any code in it will be run automatically. As the comment mentions, it can go anywhere (as long as import can find it), but it usually goes in the site-packages directory within your Python lib directory.

(**2**) setdefaultencoding function sets, well, the default encoding. This is the encoding scheme that Python will try to use whenever it needs to auto-coerce a Unicode string into a regular string.

After you change setdefaultencoding in your sitecustomize.py file as shown in Listing 9-12, and restart Python, you can see the effects, as shown in Listing 9-13.

Listing 9-13. Effects of Setting the Default Encoding

```
>>> import sys
>>> sys.getdefaultencoding()                    (1)
'iso-8859-1'
>>> s = u'La Pe\xf1a'
>>> print s                                     (2)
La Peña
```

(**1**) If your default encoding still says 'ascii', you didn't set up your sitecustomize.py properly, or you didn't restart Python. The default encoding can be changed only during Python startup; you can't change it later.

> **NOTE** *Due to some wacky programming tricks, you can't even call* sys.setdefaultencoding *after Python has started up. If you dig into* site.py *and search for* setdefaultencoding, *you'll see that the module actually deletes the function at runtime... after calling it exactly once!*

(**2**) Now that the default encoding scheme includes all the characters you use in your string, Python has no problem auto-coercing the string and printing it.

Specifying Encoding in .py Files

If you are going to be storing non-ASCII strings within your Python code, you'll need to specify the encoding of each individual .py file by putting an encoding declaration at the top of each file. This declaration defines the .py file to be UTF-8:

```
#!/usr/bin/env python
# -*- coding: UTF-8 -*-
```

Now, what about XML? Well, every XML document is in a specific encoding. Again, ISO-8859-1 is a popular encoding for data in Western European languages. KOI8-R is popular for Russian texts. The encoding, if specified, is in the header of the XML document, as shown in the example in Listing 9-14 (russiansample.xml is included with this book's sample code, in the kgp directory).

Listing 9-14. russiansample.xml

```
<?xml version="1.0" encoding="koi8-r"?>         (1)
<preface>
<title> Предисловие </title>                    (2)
</preface>
```

(1) This is a sample extract from a real Russian XML document—part of a Russian translation of this very book. Note the encoding, koi8-r, specified in the header.

(2) These are Cyrillic characters that, as far as I know, spell the Russian word for *Preface*. If you open this file in a regular text editor, the characters will most likely look like gibberish, because they're encoded using the koi8-r encoding scheme, but they're being displayed in iso-8859-1.

Listing 9-15 shows what happens when you specify an encoding scheme.

Listing 9-15. Parsing russiansample.xml

```
>>> from xml.dom import minidom
>>> xmldoc = minidom.parse('russiansample.xml')
>>> title = xmldoc.getElementsByTagName('title')[0].firstChild.data
>>> title                                       (1)
u'\u041f\u0440\u0435\u0434\u0438\u0441\u043b\u043e\u0432\u0438\u0435'
>>> print title                                 (2)
Traceback (innermost last):
  File "<interactive input>", line 1, in ?
UnicodeError: ASCII encoding error: ordinal not in range(128)
>>> convertedtitle = title.encode('koi8-r')     (3)
>>> convertedtitle
'\xf0\xd2\xc5\xc4\xc9\xd3\xcc\xcf\xd7\xc9\xc5'
>>> print convertedtitle                        (4)
Предисловие
```

(1) Note that the text data of the title tag (now in the title variable) is stored in Unicode.

(2) Printing the title is not possible, because this Unicode string contains non-ASCII characters, so Python can't convert it to ASCII, because that doesn't make sense.

(3) You can, however, explicitly convert it to koi8-r, in which case, you get a (regular, not Unicode) string of single-byte characters (f0, d2, c5, and so forth) that are the koi8-r-encoded versions of the characters in the original Unicode string.

(4) Printing the koi8-r-encoded string will probably show gibberish on your screen, because your Python IDE is interpreting those characters as iso-8859-1, not koi8-r. But at least they do print. And, if you look carefully, you'll see that it's the same gibberish that you saw when you opened the original XML document in a non-Unicode-aware text editor. Python converted it from koi8-r into Unicode when it parsed the XML document, and you've just converted it back.

Although Unicode itself is a bit intimidating if you've never seen it before, Unicode data is really easy to handle in Python. If your XML documents are all 7-bit ASCII (like the examples in this chapter), you will literally never think about Unicode. Python will convert the ASCII data in the XML documents into Unicode while parsing and auto-coerce it back to ASCII whenever necessary, and you'll never even notice. But if you need to deal with non-ASCII characters, Python is ready.

Further Reading on Unicode

For more information about Unicode, refer to the following:

- Unicode.org, the home page of the Unicode standard (http://www.unicode.org) includes a brief, technical introduction to Unicode (http://www.unicode.org/standard/principles.html).

- *Unicode Tutorial* has some more examples of how to use Python's Unicode functions, including how to force Python to coerce Unicode into ASCII, even when it doesn't really want to (http://www.reportlab.com/i18n/python_unicode_tutorial.html).

- PEP 263 goes into detail about how and when to define a character encoding in your .py files (http://www.python.org/peps/pep-0263.html).

Searching for XML Elements

Traversing XML documents by stepping through each node can be tedious. If you're looking for something in particular, buried deep within your XML document, there is a shortcut you can use to find it quickly: getElementsByTagName.

For the examples in this section, we'll use the binary.xml grammar file, which is shown in Listing 9-16.

Listing 9-16. binary.xml

```
<?xml version="1.0"?>
<!DOCTYPE grammar PUBLIC
"-//diveintopython.org//DTD Kant Generator Pro v1.0//EN"
"kgp.dtd">
<grammar>
<ref id="bit">
  <p>0</p>
  <p>1</p>
</ref>
<ref id="byte">
  <p><xref id="bit"/><xref id="bit"/><xref id="bit"/><xref id="bit"/>\
<xref id="bit"/><xref id="bit"/><xref id="bit"/><xref id="bit"/></p>
</ref>
</grammar>
```

binary.xml has two refs: 'bit' and 'byte'. A bit is either a '0' or '1', and a byte is 8 bits.

Listing 9-17 demonstrates how to find elements in binary.xml.

Listing 9-17. Introducing getElementsByTagName

```
>>> from xml.dom import minidom
>>> xmldoc = minidom.parse('binary.xml')
>>> reflist = xmldoc.getElementsByTagName('ref')       (1)
>>> reflist
[<DOM Element: ref at 136138108>, <DOM Element: ref at 136144292>]
>>> print reflist[0].toxml()
<ref id="bit">
  <p>0</p>
  <p>1</p>
</ref>
>>> print reflist[1].toxml()
<ref id="byte">
  <p><xref id="bit"/><xref id="bit"/><xref id="bit"/><xref id="bit"/>\
<xref id="bit"/><xref id="bit"/><xref id="bit"/><xref id="bit"/></p>
</ref>
```

(1) getElementsByTagName takes one argument: the name of the element you wish to find. It returns a list of Element objects, corresponding to the XML elements that have that name. In this case, you find two ref elements.

Listing 9-18 continues with the search example.

Listing 9-18. Every Element Is Searchable

```
>>> firstref = reflist[0]                              (1)
>>> print firstref.toxml()
<ref id="bit">
  <p>0</p>
  <p>1</p>
</ref>
>>> plist = firstref.getElementsByTagName("p")         (2)
>>> plist
[<DOM Element: p at 136140116>, <DOM Element: p at 136142172>]
>>> print plist[0].toxml()                             (3)
<p>0</p>
>>> print plist[1].toxml()
<p>1</p>
```

(1) Continuing from the example in Listing 9-17, the first object in the reflist is the 'bit' ref element.

(2) You can use the same getElementsByTagName method on this Element to find all the <p> elements within the 'bit' ref element.

(3) Just as before, the getElementsByTagName method returns a list of all the elements it found. In this case, you have two: one for each bit.

And Listing 9-19 finishes up the search example.

Listing 9-19. Searching Is Actually Recursive

```
>>> plist = xmldoc.getElementsByTagName("p")           (1)
>>> plist
[<DOM Element: p at 136140116>,
<DOM Element: p at 136142172>,
<DOM Element: p at 136146124>]
>>> plist[0].toxml()                                   (2)
'<p>0</p>'
>>> plist[1].toxml()
'<p>1</p>'
>>> plist[2].toxml()                                   (3)
'<p><xref id="bit"/><xref id="bit"/><xref id="bit"/><xref id="bit"/>\
<xref id="bit"/><xref id="bit"/><xref id="bit"/><xref id="bit"/></p>'
```

(1) Note carefully the difference between this example and the example in Listing 9-18. Previously, you were searching for p elements within firstref. Here, you are searching for p elements within xmldoc, the root-level object that represents the entire XML document. This *does* find the p elements nested within the ref elements within the root grammar element.

(2) The first two p elements are within the first ref (the 'bit' ref).

(3) The last p element is the one within the second ref (the 'byte' ref).

Accessing XML Element Attributes

XML elements can have one or more attributes, and it is incredibly simple to access them once you have parsed an XML document.

For this section, you'll be using the binary.xml grammar file in Listing 9-16 in the previous section. Listing 9-20 shows how to access XML element attributes in that file.

> **NOTE** *This section may be a little confusing, because of some overlapping terminology. Elements in an XML document have attributes, and Python objects also have attributes. When you parse an XML document, you get a bunch of Python objects that represent all the pieces of the XML document, and some of these Python objects represent attributes of the XML elements. But the (Python) objects that represent the (XML) attributes also have (Python) attributes, which are used to access various parts of the (XML) attribute that the object represents. I told you it was confusing.*

Listing 9-20. Accessing XML Element Attributes

```
>>> xmldoc = minidom.parse('binary.xml')
>>> reflist = xmldoc.getElementsByTagName('ref')
>>> bitref = reflist[0]
>>> print bitref.toxml()
<ref id="bit">
  <p>0</p>
  <p>1</p>
</ref>
>>> bitref.attributes                               (1)
<xml.dom.minidom.NamedNodeMap instance at 0x81e0c9c>
>>> bitref.attributes.keys()                        (2) (3)
[u'id']
>>> bitref.attributes.values()                      (4)
[<xml.dom.minidom.Attr instance at 0x81d5044>]
>>> bitref.attributes["id"]                         (5)
<xml.dom.minidom.Attr instance at 0x81d5044>
```

(1) Each `Element` object has an attribute called `attributes`, which is a `NamedNodeMap` object. This sounds scary, but it's not, because a `NamedNodeMap` is an object that acts like a dictionary, so you already know how to use it.

(2) Treating the `NamedNodeMap` as a dictionary, you can get a list of the names of the attributes of this element by using `attributes.keys()`. This element has only one attribute: `'id'`.

(3) Attribute names, like all other text in an XML document, are stored in Unicode.

(4) Again treating the `NamedNodeMap` as a dictionary, you can get a list of the values of the attributes by using `attributes.values()`. The values are themselves objects, of type `Attr`. You'll see how to get useful information out of this object in the next example.

(5) Still treating the `NamedNodeMap` as a dictionary, you can access an individual attribute by name, using normal dictionary syntax. (Readers who have been paying extra-close attention will already know how the `NamedNodeMap` class accomplishes this neat trick: by defining a __getitem__ special method, as described in Chapter 5. Other readers can take comfort in the fact that they don't need to understand how it works in order to use it effectively.)

Listing 9-21 shows how to use an `Attr` object to access individual XML attributes.

Listing 9-21. Accessing Individual XML Attributes

```
>>> a = bitref.attributes["id"]
>>> a
<xml.dom.minidom.Attr instance at 0x81d5044>
>>> a.name                                    (1)
u'id'
>>> a.value                                   (2)
u'bit'
```

(1) The `Attr` object completely represents a single XML attribute of a single XML element. The name of the attribute (the same name as you used to find this object in the `bitref.attributes` `NamedNodeMap` pseudo-dictionary) is stored in `a.name`.

(2) The actual text value of this XML attribute is stored in `a.value`.

> **NOTE** *Like dictionaries, attributes of an XML element have no ordering. Attributes may happen to be listed in a certain order in the original XML document, and the* Attr *objects may happen to be listed in a certain order when the XML document is parsed into Python objects, but these orders are arbitrary and should carry no special meaning. You should always access individual attributes by name, as you do the keys of a dictionary.*

Summary

Okay, that's it for the hard-core XML stuff. The next chapter will continue to use these same sample programs, but focus on other aspects that make the program more flexible: using streams for input processing, using getattr for method dispatching, and using command-line flags to allow users to reconfigure the program without changing the code.

Before moving on to the next chapter, make sure you're comfortable doing all of these things:

- Parsing XML documents using xml.dom.minidom

- Searching a parsed XML document

- Accessing arbitrary element attributes and element children

- Organizing complex libraries into packages

- Converting Unicode strings to different character encodings

CHAPTER 10

Scripts and Streams

THIS CHAPTER CONTINUES the coverage of XML processing we began in Chapter 9. One of Python's greatest strengths is its dynamic binding, and one powerful use of dynamic binding is the *file-like object*. You'll see how what this has to do with XML processing in this chapter.

Abstracting Input Sources

Many functions that require an input source could simply take a filename, open the file for reading, read it, and close it when they're done. But they don't. Instead, they take a file-like object.

In the simplest case, a file-like object is any object that has a read method with an optional size parameter, which returns a string. When called without a size parameter, the file-like object reads everything there is to read from the input source and returns all the data as a single string. When called with a size parameter, the file-like object reads that much from the input source and returns that much data; when called again, it picks up where it left off and returns the next chunk of data. This is how reading from real files works. The difference is that you're not limited to real files.

The input source could be anything: a file on disk, a web page, or even a hard-coded string. As long as you pass a file-like object to the function, and the function simply calls the object's read method, the function can handle any kind of input source, without requiring specific code for each kind.

Parsing XML from Local Files and Remote URLs

In case you're wondering how this relates to XML processing, minidom.parse is one such function that can take a file-like object. Listing 10-1 shows an example.

> **NOTE** *If you have not already done so, you can download this and the other examples used in this book from the Downloads section of the Apress web site* (http://www.apress.com).

Listing 10-1. Parsing XML from a File

```
>>> from xml.dom import minidom
>>> fsock = open('binary.xml')                    (1)
>>> xmldoc = minidom.parse(fsock)                  (2)
>>> fsock.close()                                  (3)
>>> print xmldoc.toxml()                           (4)
<?xml version="1.0" ?>
<grammar>
<ref id="bit">
  <p>0</p>
  <p>1</p>
</ref>
<ref id="byte">
  <p><xref id="bit"/><xref id="bit"/><xref id="bit"/><xref id="bit"/>\
<xref id="bit"/><xref id="bit"/><xref id="bit"/><xref id="bit"/></p>
</ref>
</grammar>
```

(1) First, you open the file on disk. This gives you a file object.

(2) You pass the file object to minidom.parse, which calls the read method of fsock and reads the XML document from the file on disk.

(3) Be sure to call the close method of the file object after you're finished with it. minidom.parse will not do this for you.

(4) Calling the toxml() method on the returned XML document prints the entire document.

Well, that all seems like a colossal waste of time. After all, you've already seen that minidom.parse can simply take the filename and do all the opening and closing nonsense automatically. And it's true that if you know you're just going to be parsing a local file, you can pass the filename, and minidom.parse is smart enough to do the right thing. But Listing 10-2 shows how similar, and easy, it is to parse an XML document straight from the Internet.

Listing 10-2. Parsing XML from a URL

```
>>> import urllib
>>> usock = urllib.urlopen('http://slashdot.org/slashdot.rdf')  (1)
>>> xmldoc = minidom.parse(usock)                               (2)
>>> usock.close()                                               (3)
>>> print xmldoc.toxml()
<?xml version="1.0" ?>
<rdf:RDF xmlns="http://my.netscape.com/rdf/simple/0.9/"
 xmlns:rdf="http://www.w3.org/1999/02/22-rdf-syntax-ns#">
```

```
<channel>
<title>Slashdot</title>
<link>http://slashdot.org/</link>
<description>News for nerds, stuff that matters</description>
</channel>

<image>
<title>Slashdot</title>
<url>http://images.slashdot.org/topics/topicslashdot.gif</url>
<link>http://slashdot.org/</link>
</image>

<item>
<title>To HDTV or Not to HDTV?</title>
<link>http://slashdot.org/article.pl?sid=01/12/28/0421241</link>
</item>
```

[...snip...]

(1) As you saw in a previous chapter, urlopen takes a web page URL and returns a file-like object. Most important, this object has a read method that returns the HTML source of the web page. By the way, this URL is real, and it really is XML. It's an XML representation of the current headlines on Slashdot (http://slashdot.org), a technical news and gossip site.

(2) Now, you pass the file-like object to minidom.parse, which obediently calls the read method of the object and parses the XML data that the read method returns. The fact that this XML data is now coming straight from a web page is completely irrelevant. minidom.parse doesn't know or care about web pages; it just knows about file-like objects.

(3) As soon as you're finished with it, be sure to close the file-like object that urlopen gives you.

Parsing XML from Strings

You've seen that you can use the minidom.parse function for parsing both local files and remote URLs. However, for parsing strings, you use a different function, as shown in Listing 10-3.

Listing 10-3. Parsing XML from a String (Easy But Inflexible Way)

```
>>> contents = "<grammar><ref id='bit'><p>0</p><p>1</p></ref></grammar>"
>>> xmldoc = minidom.parseString(contents)              (1)
>>> print xmldoc.toxml()
<?xml version="1.0" ?>
<grammar><ref id="bit"><p>0</p><p>1</p></ref></grammar>
```

(1) minidom has a method, parseString, which takes an entire XML document as a string and parses it. You can use this instead of minidom.parse if you know you already have your entire XML document in a string.

This means that if you want to be able to take input from a file, URL, or string, you'll need special logic to check whether it's a string, and if it is, call the parseString function instead of the parse function—how unsatisfying.

If there were a way to turn a string into a file-like object, you could simply pass this object to minidom.parse. And, in fact, there is a module specifically designed for doing just that: StringIO, introduced in Listing 10-4.

Listing 10-4. Introducing StringIO

```
>>> contents = "<grammar><ref id='bit'><p>0</p><p>1</p></ref></grammar>"
>>> import StringIO
>>> ssock = StringIO.StringIO(contents)                    (1)
>>> ssock.read()                                           (2)
"<grammar><ref id='bit'><p>0</p><p>1</p></ref></grammar>"
>>> ssock.read()                                           (3)
''
>>> ssock.seek(0)                                          (4)
>>> ssock.read(15)                                         (5)
'<grammar><ref i'
>>> ssock.read(15)
"d='bit'><p>0</p"
>>> ssock.read()
'><p>1</p></ref></grammar>'
>>> ssock.close()                                          (6)
```

(1) The StringIO module contains a single class, also called StringIO, which allows you to turn a string into a file-like object. The StringIO class takes the string as a parameter when creating an instance.

(2) Now, you have a file-like object, and you can do all sorts of file-like things with it. One of these things is read, which returns the original string.

(3) Calling read again returns an empty string. This is how real file objects work, too. Once you read the entire file, you can't read any more without explicitly seeking to the beginning of the file. The StringIO object works the same way.

(4) You can explicitly seek to the beginning of the string, just like seeking through a file, by using the seek method of the StringIO object.

(5) You can also read the string in chunks, by passing a size parameter to the read method.

(6) At any time, read will return the rest of the string that you haven't read yet. All of this is exactly how file objects work; hence the term *file-like object*.

Now, let's look at parsing from a string using StringIO, as shown in Listing 10-5.

Listing 10-5. Parsing XML from a String (File-like Object Way)

```
>>> contents = "<grammar><ref id='bit'><p>0</p><p>1</p></ref></grammar>"
>>> ssock = StringIO.StringIO(contents)
>>> xmldoc = minidom.parse(ssock)                    (1)
>>> ssock.close()
>>> print xmldoc.toxml()
<?xml version="1.0" ?>
<grammar><ref id="bit"><p>0</p><p>1</p></ref></grammar>
```

(1) Now, you can pass the file-like object (really a StringIO) to minidom.parse, which will call the object's read method and happily parse away, never knowing that its input came from a hard-coded string.

Opening Anything

So, now you know how to use a single function, minidom.parse, to parse an XML document stored on a web page, in a local file, or in a hard-coded string. For a web page, you use urlopen to get a file-like object; for a local file, you use open; and for a string, you use StringIO. Now let's take it one step further and generalize *these* differences as well, as shown in Listing 10-6.

Listing 10-6. Introducing openAnything

```
def openAnything(source):                              (1)
    # try to open with urllib (if source is http, ftp, or file URL)
    import urllib
    try:
        return urllib.urlopen(source)                  (2)
    except (IOError, OSError):
        pass

    # try to open with native open function (if source is pathname)
    try:
        return open(source)                            (3)
    except (IOError, OSError):
        pass

    # treat source as string
    import StringIO
    return StringIO.StringIO(str(source))              (4)
```

(1) The openAnything function takes a single parameter, source, and returns a file-like object. source is a string of some sort: a URL (like 'http://slashdot.org/slashdot.rdf'), a full or partial pathname to a local file (like 'binary.xml'), or a string that contains actual XML data to be parsed.

(2) First, you see whether source is a URL. You do this through brute force: you try to open it as a URL and silently ignore errors caused by trying to open something that is not a URL. This is actually elegant in the sense that, if urllib ever supports new types of URLs in the future, you will also support them without recoding. If urllib is able to open source, the return kicks you out of the function immediately, and the following try statements never execute.

(3) On the other hand, if urllib yelled at you and told you that source wasn't a valid URL, you assume it's a path to a file on disk and try to open it. Again, you don't do anything fancy to check whether source is a valid filename (the rules for valid filenames vary wildly between different platforms anyway, so you would probably get them wrong anyway). Instead, you just blindly open the file and silently trap any errors.

(4) By this point, you have to assume that source is a string that has hard-coded data in it (since nothing else worked), so you use StringIO to create a file-like object out of it and return that. (In fact, since you're using the str function, source doesn't even need to be a string; it could be any object, and you'll use its string representation, as defined by its __str__ special method.)

Now, you can use this openAnything function in conjunction with minidom.parse to make a function that takes a source that refers to an XML document somehow (either as a URL, or a local filename, or a hard-coded XML document in a string) and parses it. Listing 10-7 illustrates how openAnything is used in kgp.py, the sample program presented in Chapter 9 (in Listing 9-1).

Listing 10-7. Using openAnything in kgp.py

```
class KantGenerator:
    def _load(self, source):
        sock = toolbox.openAnything(source)
        xmldoc = minidom.parse(sock).documentElement
        sock.close()
        return xmldoc
```

Using Standard Input, Output, and Error

UNIX users are already familiar with the concept of standard input, standard output, and standard error. This section is for the rest of you.

Standard output and standard error (commonly abbreviated stdout and stderr) are pipes that are built into every UNIX system. When you print something, it goes to the stdout pipe. When your program crashes and prints debugging information (like a traceback in Python), it goes to the stderr pipe. Both of these pipes are ordinarily just connected to the terminal window where you are working. So, when a program prints, you see the output; when a program crashes, you see the debugging information. (If you're working on a system with a window-based Python IDE, stdout and stderr default to your interactive window.) Listing 10-8 demonstrates how standard output and error work.

Listing 10-8. Introducing stdout and stderr

```
>>> for i in range(3):                          (1)
...     print 'Dive in'
Dive in
Dive in
Dive in
>>> import sys
>>> for i in range(3):
...     sys.stdout.write('Dive in')             (2)
Dive inDive inDive in
>>> for i in range(3):
...     sys.stderr.write('Dive in')             (3)
Dive inDive inDive in
```

(1) As you saw back in Chapter 6, in Listing 6-9, "Simple Counters," you can use Python's built-in range function to build simple counter loops that repeat something a set number of times.

(2) stdout is a file-like object; calling its write function will print whatever string you give it. In fact, this is what the print function really does: it adds a carriage return to the end of the string you're printing and calls sys.stdout.write.

(3) In the simplest case, stdout and stderr send their output to the same place: the Python IDE (if you're in one), or the terminal (if you're running Python from the command line). Like stdout, stderr does not add carriage returns for you; if you want them, you must add them yourself.

Redirecting stdout and stderr Output

stdout and stderr are both file-like objects, like the ones we discussed in the previous section, "Abstracting Input Sources," but they are both write-only. They have no read method, only write. Still, they are file-like objects, and you can assign any other file or file-like object to them to redirect their output, as demonstrated in Listing 10-9.

Listing 10-9. Redirecting Output

```
[you@localhost kgp]$ python stdout.py
Dive in
[you@localhost kgp]$ cat out.log
This message will be logged instead of displayed
```

```
#stdout.py
import sys

print 'Dive in'                                             (1)
saveout = sys.stdout                                        (2)
fsock = open('out.log', 'w')                                (3)
sys.stdout = fsock                                          (4)
print 'This message will be logged instead of displayed'    (5)
sys.stdout = saveout                                        (6)
fsock.close()                                               (7)
```

> **NOTE** *On Windows, you can use* type *instead of* cat *to display the contents of a file.*

(1) This will print to the IDE interactive window (or the terminal, if you're running the script from the command line).

(2) Always save stdout before redirecting it, so you can set it back to its normal output location later.

(3) Open a file for writing. If the file doesn't exist, it will be created. If the file does exist, it will be overwritten.

(4) Redirect all further output to the new file you just opened.

(5) This will be "printed" to the log file only; it will not be visible in the IDE window or on the screen.

(6) Set stdout back to the way it was before you mucked with it.

(7) Close the log file.

Redirecting stderr works the same way, using sys.stderr instead of sys.stdout, as shown in Listing 10-10.

Listing 10-10. Redirecting Error Information

```
[you@localhost kgp]$ python stderr.py
[you@localhost kgp]$ cat error.log
Traceback (most recent line last):
  File "stderr.py", line 5, in ?
    raise Exception, 'this error will be logged'
```

```
Exception: this error will be logged
#stderr.py
import sys

fsock = open('error.log', 'w')                      (1)
sys.stderr = fsock                                  (2)
raise Exception, 'this error will be logged'        (3) (4)
```

(1) Open the log file where you want to store debugging information.

(2) Redirect stderr by assigning the file object of your newly opened log file to stderr.

(3) Raise an exception. Note from the screen output that this does *not* print anything on the screen. All the normal traceback information has been written to error.log.

(4) Also note that you're not explicitly closing your log file, nor are you setting stderr back to its original value. This is fine, since once the program crashes (due to your exception), Python will clean up and close the file for you, and it doesn't make any difference that stderr is never restored, since Python ends when the program crashes. Restoring the original is more important for stdout, if you expect to do other stuff within the same script afterwards.

Since it is so common to write error messages to standard error, there is a shorthand syntax that can be used instead of going through the hassle of redirecting it outright, as shown in Listing 10-11.

Listing 10-11. Printing to stderr

```
>>> print 'entering function'
entering function
>>> import sys
>>> print >> sys.stderr, 'entering function'        (1)
entering function
```

(1) This shorthand syntax of the print statement can be used to write to any open file or file-like object. In this case, you can redirect a single print statement to stderr without affecting subsequent print statements.

Reading from stdin

Standard input (stdin), on the other hand, is a read-only file object, and it represents the data flowing into the program from some previous program. This will likely not make much sense to classic Mac OS users, or even Windows users (unless you were ever fluent on the MS-DOS command line). To have data flow from one program to another, you can construct a chain of commands in a single line, so that one program's output becomes the input for the next program in the chain.

The program shown in Listing 10-12 simply outputs to standard output (without doing any special redirecting itself; just doing normal print statements or whatever).

Listing 10-12. Chaining Commands

```
[you@localhost kgp]$ python kgp.py -g binary.xml                    (1)
01100111
[you@localhost kgp]$ cat binary.xml                                 (2)
<?xml version="1.0"?>
<!DOCTYPE grammar PUBLIC "-//diveintopython.org//DTD Kant Generator Pro v1.0//EN" "kgp.dtd">
<grammar>
<ref id="bit">
  <p>0</p>
  <p>1</p>
</ref>
<ref id="byte">
  <p><xref id="bit"/><xref id="bit"/><xref id="bit"/><xref id="bit"/>\
<xref id="bit"/><xref id="bit"/><xref id="bit"/><xref id="bit"/></p>
</ref>
</grammar>
[you@localhost kgp]$ cat binary.xml | python kgp.py -g -           (3) (4)
10110001
```

(1) As you saw in the "Diving In" section of Chapter 9, this will print a string of eight random bits, 0 or 1.

(2) This simply prints the entire contents of binary.xml. (Windows users should use type instead of cat.)

(3) This prints the contents of binary.xml, but the | character, called the *pipe* character, means that the contents will not be printed to the screen. Instead, they will become the standard input of the next command, which, in this case, calls your Python script.

(4) Instead of specifying a module (like binary.xml), you specify -, which causes your script to load the grammar from standard input instead of from a specific file on disk (more on how this happens in the next example). So the effect is the same as the first syntax, where you specified the grammar filename directly, but think of the expansion possibilities here. Instead of simply doing cat binary.xml, you could run a script that dynamically generates the grammar, and then you can pipe it into your script. It could come from anywhere: a database, or some grammar-generating meta-script, or whatever. The point is that you don't need to change your kgp.py script at all to incorporate any of this functionality. All you need to do is be able to take grammar files from standard input, and you can separate all the other logic into another program.

So how does your script "know" to read from standard input when the grammar file is -? It's not magic; it's just code. Listing 10-13 shows how this works in kgp.py (the sample program presented in Chapter 9). This program reads from standard input, and the operating system takes care of connecting one program's output to the next program's input.

Listing 10-13. Reading from Standard Input in kgp.py

```
def openAnything(source):
    if source == "-":                              (1)
        import sys
        return sys.stdin

    # try to open with urllib (if source is http, ftp, or file URL)
    import urllib
    try:
```

[... snip ...]

(1) This is the openAnything function from toolbox.py, which you saw in the "Abstracting Input Sources" section earlier in the chapter. All you've done is add three lines of code at the beginning of the function to check if the source is "-"; if so, you return sys.stdin. Really, that's it! Remember, stdin is a file-like object with a read method, so the rest of the code (in kgp.py, where you call openAnything) doesn't change a bit.

Introducing Some XML Processing Techniques

Our sample program (introduced in Chapter 9), kgp.py, employs several tricks that may be useful to you in your XML processing. The first one takes advantage of the consistent structure of the input documents to build a cache of nodes. The next one finds all the direct child elements of a particular element. The third useful XML processing tip involves separating your code into logical functions, based on node types and element names.

Caching Node Lookups

A grammar file defines a series of ref elements. Each ref contains one or more p elements, which can contain a lot of different things, including xrefs. Whenever you encounter an xref, you look for a corresponding ref element with the same id attribute, and choose one of the ref element's children and parse it. (You'll see how this random choice is made in the next section.)

This is how you build up your grammar:

- Define ref elements for the smallest pieces.

- Then define ref elements that "include" the first ref elements by using xref, and so forth.

- Then parse the "largest" reference and follow each xref.

- Eventually, output real text. The text you output depends on the (random) decisions you make each time you fill in an xref, so the output is different each time.

This is all very flexible, but there is one downside: performance. When you find an xref and need to find the corresponding ref element, you have a problem. The xref has an id attribute, and you want to find the ref element that has that same id attribute, but there is no easy way to do that. The slow way to do it would be to get the entire list of ref elements each time, and then manually loop through and look at each id attribute. The fast way is to do that once and build a cache, in the form of a dictionary, as shown in Listing 10-14.

Listing 10-14. loadGrammar

```
def loadGrammar(self, grammar):
    self.grammar = self._load(grammar)
    self.refs = {}                                        (1)
    for ref in self.grammar.getElementsByTagName("ref"):  (2)
        self.refs[ref.attributes["id"].value] = ref       (3) (4)
```

(1) Start by creating an empty dictionary, self.refs.

(2) As you saw in the "Searching for Elements" section of Chapter 9, getElementsByTagName returns a list of all the elements of a particular name. You can easily get a list of all the ref elements, and then simply loop through that list.

(3) As you saw in the "Accessing Element Attributes" section of Chapter 9, you can access individual attributes of an element by name, using standard dictionary syntax. So, the keys of the self.refs dictionary will be the values of the id attribute of each ref element.

(4) The values of the self.refs dictionary will be the ref elements themselves. As you saw in the "Parsing XML" section of Chapter 9, each element, node, comment, and piece of text in a parsed XML document is an object.

Once you build this cache, whenever you come across an xref and need to find the ref element with the same id attribute, you can simply look it up in self.refs, as shown in Listing 10-15.

Listing 10-15. Using the ref Element Cache

```
def do_xref(self, node):
    id = node.attributes["id"].value
    self.parse(self.randomChildElement(self.refs[id]))
```

We'll explore the randomChildElement function in the next section.

Finding the Direct Children of a Node

Another useful techique when parsing XML documents is finding all the direct child elements of a particular element. For instance, in your grammar files, a ref element can have several p elements, each of which can contain many things, including other p elements. Suppose that you want to find just the p elements that are children of the ref, not p elements that are children of other p elements.

You might think you could simply use getElementsByTagName for this, but you can't. getElementsByTagName searches recursively and returns a single list for all the elements it finds. Since p elements can contain other p elements, you can't use getElementsByTagName, because it would return nested p elements that you don't want. To find only direct child elements, you'll need to do it yourself, as shown in Listing 10-16.

Listing 10-16. Finding Direct Child Elements

```
def randomChildElement(self, node):
    choices = [e for e in node.childNodes
                if e.nodeType == e.ELEMENT_NODE]   (1) (2) (3)
    chosen = random.choice(choices)                 (4)
    return chosen
```

(1) As you saw in Chapter 9, in Listing 9-6, "Getting Child Nodes," the childNodes attribute returns a list of all the child nodes of an element.

(2) However, as you saw in Listing 9-8, "Child Nodes Can Be Text," the list returned by childNodes contains all different types of nodes, including text nodes. That's not what you're looking for here. You want only the children that are elements.

(3) Each node has a `nodeType` attribute, which can be `ELEMENT_NODE`, `TEXT_NODE`, `COMMENT_NODE`, or any number of other values. The complete list of possible values is in the `__init__.py` file in the `xml.dom` package. (See the "Importing Python Packages" section in Chapter 9 for more information about packages.) But you're just interested in nodes that are elements, so you can filter the list to include only those nodes whose `nodeType` is `ELEMENT_NODE`.

(4) Once you have a list of actual elements, choosing a random one is easy. Python comes with a module called `random`, which includes several useful functions. The `random.choice` function takes a list of any number of items and returns a random item. For example, if the `ref` element contains several `p` elements, then `choices` would be a list of `p` elements, and `chosen` would end up being assigned exactly one of them, selected at random.

Creating Separate Handlers by Node Type

Parsed XML documents are made up of various types of nodes, each represented by a Python object. The root level of the document itself is represented by a `Document` object. The `Document` then contains one or more `Element` objects (for actual XML tags), each of which may contain other `Element` objects, `Text` objects (for bits of text), or `Comment` objects (for embedded comments). Python makes it easy to write a dispatcher to separate the logic for each node type.

Listing 10-17 shows how you can get the class name of a specific XML node.

Listing 10-17. Class Names of Parsed XML Objects

```
>>> from xml.dom import minidom
>>> xmldoc = minidom.parse('kant.xml')                    (1)
>>> xmldoc
<xml.dom.minidom.Document instance at 0x01359DE8>
>>> xmldoc.__class__                                       (2)
<class xml.dom.minidom.Document at 0x01105D40>
>>> xmldoc.__class__.__name__                              (3)
'Document'
```

(1) Assume for a moment that `kant.xml` is in the current directory.

(2) As you saw in the "Accessing Packages" section of Chapter 9, the object returned by parsing an XML document is a `Document` object, as defined in the `minidom.py` in the `xml.dom` package. As you saw in the "Instantiating Classes" section in Chapter 5, `__class__` is a built-in attribute of every Python object.

(3) Furthermore, `__name__` is a built-in attribute of every Python class, and it is a string. This string is not mysterious; it's the same as the class name you type when you define a class yourself (see the "Defining Classes" section in Chapter 5).

Fine, so now you can get the class name of any particular XML node (since each XML node is represented as a Python object). How can you use this to your advantage to separate the logic of parsing each node type? The answer is getattr, which you first saw in Chapter 4, in the "Getting Object References with getattr" section. Listing 10-18 shows the solution.

Listing 10-18. parse: A Generic XML Node Dispatcher

```
def parse(self, node):
    parseMethod = getattr(self, "parse_%s" % node.__class__.__name__)    (1) (2)
    parseMethod(node)                                                          (3)
```

(1) First, notice that you're constructing a larger string based on the class name of the node you were passed (in the node argument). So if you're passed a Document node, you're constructing the string 'parse_Document', and so forth.

(2) Now, you can treat that string as a function name and get a reference to the function itself using getattr.

(3) Finally, you can call that function and pass the node itself as an argument. Listing 10-19 shows the definitions of each of the functions called by parse.

Listing 10-19. Functions Called by the parse Dispatcher

```
def parse_Document(self, node):                    (1)
    self.parse(node.documentElement)

def parse_Text(self, node):                        (2)
    text = node.data
    if self.capitalizeNextWord:
        self.pieces.append(text[0].upper())
        self.pieces.append(text[1:])
        self.capitalizeNextWord = 0
    else:
        self.pieces.append(text)

def parse_Comment(self, node):                     (3)
    pass

def parse_Element(self, node):                     (4)
    handlerMethod = getattr(self, "do_%s" % node.tagName)
    handlerMethod(node)
```

(1) parse_Document is called only once, since there is only one Document node in an XML document and only one Document object in the parsed XML representation. It simply turns around and parses the root element of the grammar file.

(2) parse_Text is called on nodes that represent bits of text. The function itself does some special processing to handle automatic capitalization of the first word of a sentence, but otherwise simply appends the represented text to a list.

(3) parse_Comment is just a pass, since you don't care about embedded comments in your grammar files. Note, however, that you still need to define the function and explicitly make it do nothing. If the function did not exist, your generic parse function would fail as soon as it stumbled on a comment, because it would try to find the nonexistent parse_Comment function. Defining a separate function for every node type, even ones you don't use, allows the generic parse function to stay simple and dumb.

(4) The parse_Element method is actually itself a dispatcher, based on the name of the element's tag. The basic idea is the same: take what distinguishes elements from each other (their tag names) and dispatch to a separate function for each of them. You construct a string like 'do_xref' (for an <xref> tag), find a function of that name, call it, and so forth for each of the other tag names that might be found in the course of parsing a grammar file (like <p> tags and <choice> tags).

In this example, the dispatch functions parse and parse_Element simply find other methods in the same class. If your processing is very complex (or you have many different tag names), you could break up your code into separate modules and use dynamic importing to import each module and call whatever functions you needed. Dynamic importing will be discussed in Chapter 16.

Handling Command-Line Arguments

Python fully supports creating programs that can be run on the command line, complete with command-line arguments and either short- or long-style flags to specify various options. None of this is XML-specific, but kgp.py makes good use of command-line processing, so it seems like a good time to mention it.

It's difficult to talk about command-line processing without understanding how command-line arguments are exposed to your Python program, so let's write a simple program to see them. Listing 10-20 shows the program.

Listing 10-20. Introducing sys.argv

```
#argecho.py
import sys

for arg in sys.argv:                                    (1)
    print arg
```

(1) Each command-line argument passed to the program will be in sys.argv, which is just a list. Here, you are printing each argument on a separate line.

Listing 10-21 shows the contents of sys.argv.

Listing 10-21. sys.argv Contents

```
[you@localhost py]$ python argecho.py                (1)
argecho.py
[you@localhost py]$ python argecho.py abc def        (2)
argecho.py
abc
def
[you@localhost py]$ python argecho.py --help         (3)
argecho.py
--help
[you@localhost py]$ python argecho.py -m kant.xml     (4)
argecho.py
-m
kant.xml
```

(1) The first thing to know about sys.argv is that it contains the name of the script you're calling. You will actually use this knowledge to your advantage later, in Chapter 16. Don't worry about it for now.

(2) Command-line arguments are separated by spaces, and each shows up as a separate element in the sys.argv list.

(3) Command-line flags, like --help, also show up as their own element in the sys.argv list.

(4) To make things even more interesting, some command-line flags themselves take arguments. For instance, here you have a flag (-m) that takes an argument (kant.xml). Both the flag itself and the flag's argument are simply sequential elements in the sys.argv list. No attempt is made to associate one with the other; all you get is a list.

Getting Command-Line Arguments with getopt

So as you can see, you certainly have all the information passed on the command line. But then again, it doesn't look like it's going to be all that easy to actually use it. For simple programs that take only a single argument and have no flags, you can simply use sys.argv[1] to access the argument. There's no shame in this; I do it all the time. For more complex programs, you need the getopt module, as shown in Listing 10-22.

Listing 10-22. Introducing getopt

```
def main(argv):
    grammar = "kant.xml"                                          (1)
    try:
        opts, args = getopt.getopt(argv, "hg:d", ["help", "grammar="])    (2)
    except getopt.GetoptError:                                    (3)
        usage()                                                   (4)
        sys.exit(2)


...


if __name__ == "__main__":
    main(sys.argv[1:])
```

(1) First, look at the bottom of the example and notice that you're calling the main function with `sys.argv[1:]`. Remember, `sys.argv[0]` is the name of the script that you're running; you don't care about that for command-line processing, so chop it off and pass the rest of the list.

(2) This is where all the interesting processing happens. The `getopt` function of the `getopt` module takes three parameters: the argument list (which you got from `sys.argv[1:]`), a string containing all the possible single-character command-line flags that this program accepts, and a list of longer command-line flags that are equivalent to the single-character versions. This is quite confusing at first glance, and these parameters are explained in more detail in the following sections.

(3) If anything goes wrong trying to parse these command-line flags, `getopt` will raise an exception, which you catch. You told `getopt` all the flags you understand, so this probably means that the end user passed some command-line flag that you don't understand.

(4) As is standard practice in the UNIX world, when your script is passed flags it doesn't understand, you print a summary of proper usage and exit gracefully. Note that I haven't shown the `usage` function here. You would still need to code that somewhere and have it print the appropriate summary; it's not automatic.

So what are all those parameters you pass to the `getopt` function? Well, the first one is simply the raw list of command-line flags and arguments (not including the first element, the script name, which you already chopped off before calling the main function). The second is the list of short command-line flags that your script accepts. Let's take a closer look at these parameters.

The "hg:d" Parameter of getopt

The "hg:d" parameter consists of three flags:

- -h, to print a usage summary

- -g ... , to use a specified grammar file or URL

- -d, to show debugging information while parsing

The first and third flags are simply stand-alone flags; you specify them or you don't, and they do things (print help) or change state (turn on debugging). However, the second flag (-g) *must* be followed by an argument, which is the name of the grammar file to read from. In fact, it can be a filename or a web address, and you don't know which yet (you'll figure it out later), but you know it has to be *something*. So, you tell getopt this by putting a colon after the g in that second parameter to the getopt function.

To further complicate things, this script accepts either short flags (like -h) or long flags (like --help), and you want them to do the same thing. This is what the third parameter to getopt is for, to specify a list of the long flags that correspond to the short flags you specified in the second parameter.

The ["help", "grammar="] Parameter of getopt

The ["help", "grammar="] parameter has two flags: --help, to print a usage summary, and --grammar ..., to specify the grammar file or URL.

Note several points here:

- All long flags are preceded by two dashes on the command line, but you don't include those dashes when calling getopt. They are understood.

- The --grammar flag must always be followed by an additional argument, just like the -g flag. This is notated by an equal sign, "grammar=".

- The list of long flags is shorter than the list of short flags, because the -d flag does not have a corresponding long version. This is fine; only -d will turn on debugging. But the order of short and long flags must be the same, so you'll need to specify all the short flags that *do* have corresponding long flags first, and then all the rest of the short flags.

Confused yet? Let's look at the actual code and see if it makes sense in context.

Handling Command-Line Arguments in kgp.py

Listing 10-23 shows the portion of kgp.py that uses getopt to handle command-line arguments.

Listing 10-23. Handling Command-line Arguments in kgp.py

```
def main(argv):                                          (1)
    grammar = "kant.xml"
    try:
        opts, args = getopt.getopt(argv, "hg:d", ["help", "grammar="])
    except getopt.GetoptError:
        usage()
        sys.exit(2)
    for opt, arg in opts:                                (2)
        if opt in ("-h", "--help"):                      (3)
            usage()
            sys.exit()
        elif opt == '-d':                                (4)
            global _debug
            _debug = 1
        elif opt in ("-g", "--grammar"):                 (5)
            grammar = arg

    source = "".join(args)                               (6)

    k = KantGenerator(grammar, source)
    print k.output()
```

(1) The grammar variable will keep track of the grammar file you're using. You initialize it here in case it's not specified on the command line (using either the -g or the --grammar flag).

(2) The opts variable that you get back from getopt contains a list of tuples: flag and arg. If flag doesn't take an argument, arg will simply be None. This makes it easier to loop through the flags.

(3) getopt validates that the command-line flags are acceptable, but it doesn't do any sort of conversion between short and long flags. If you specify the -h flag, opt will contain "-h"; if you specify the --help flag, opt will contain "--help". So you need to check for both.

(4) Remember that the -d flag doesn't have a corresponding long flag, so you need to check for only the short form. If you find it, you set a global variable that you'll refer to later to print debugging information. (I used this during the development of the script. What, you thought all these examples worked on the first try?)

(5) If you find a grammar file, either with a -g flag or a --grammar flag, you save the argument that followed it (stored in arg) into your grammar variable, overwriting the default that you initialized at the top of the main function.

(6) That's it. You've looped through and dealt with all the command-line flags. That means that anything left must be command-line arguments. These come back from the getopt function in the args variable. In this case, you're treating them as source material for your parser. If there are no command-line arguments specified, args will be an empty list, and source will end up as the empty string.

Putting It All Together

We've covered a lot of ground. Let's step back and see how all the pieces fit together.

To start with, this is a script that takes its arguments on the command line, using the getopt module.

```
def main(argv):
...
    try:
        opts, args = getopt.getopt(argv, "hg:d", ["help", "grammar="])
    except getopt.GetoptError:
...
    for opt, arg in opts:
...
```

We create a new instance of the KantGenerator class, and pass it the grammar file and source that may or may not have been specified on the command line.

```
    k = KantGenerator(grammar, source)
```

The KantGenerator instance automatically loads the grammar, which is an XML file. We use our custom openAnything function to open the file (which could be stored in a local file or a remote web server), and then use the built-in minidom parsing functions to parse the XML into a tree of Python objects.

```
    def _load(self, source):
        sock = toolbox.openAnything(source)
        xmldoc = minidom.parse(sock).documentElement
        sock.close()
```

Oh, and along the way, we take advantage of our knowledge of the structure of the XML document to set up a little cache of references, which are just elements in the XML document.

```
def loadGrammar(self, grammar):
    for ref in self.grammar.getElementsByTagName("ref"):
        self.refs[ref.attributes["id"].value] = ref
```

If we specified some source material on the command line, we use that; otherwise we rip through the grammar looking for the "top-level" reference (that isn't referenced by anything else) and use that as a starting point.

```
def getDefaultSource(self):
    xrefs = {}
    for xref in self.grammar.getElementsByTagName("xref"):
        xrefs[xref.attributes["id"].value] = 1
    xrefs = xrefs.keys()
    standaloneXrefs = [e for e in self.refs.keys() if e not in xrefs]
    return '<xref id="%s"/>' % random.choice(standaloneXrefs)
```

Now, we rip through our source material. The source material is also XML, and we parse it one node at a time. To keep our code separated and more maintainable, we use separate handlers for each node type.

```
def parse_Element(self, node):
    handlerMethod = getattr(self, "do_%s" % node.tagName)
    handlerMethod(node)
```

We bounce through the grammar, parsing all the children of each p element,

```
def do_p(self, node):
    ...
    if doit:
        for child in node.childNodes: self.parse(child)
```

replacing choice elements with a random child:

```
def do_choice(self, node):
    self.parse(self.randomChildElement(node))
```

and replacing xref elements with a random child of the corresponding ref element, which we previously cached.

```
def do_xref(self, node):
    id = node.attributes["id"].value
    self.parse(self.randomChildElement(self.refs[id]))
```

Eventually, we parse our way down to plain text:

```
def parse_Text(self, node):
    text = node.data
...
        self.pieces.append(text)
```

which we print out.

```
def main(argv):
...
    k = KantGenerator(grammar, source)
    print k.output()
```

Summary

Python comes with powerful libraries for parsing and manipulating XML documents. `minidom` takes an XML file and parses it into Python objects, providing for random access to arbitrary elements. Furthermore, this chapter showed how Python can be used to create a "real" stand-alone command-line script, complete with command-line flags, command-line arguments, error handling, and even the ability to take input from the piped result of a previous program.

Before moving on to the next chapter, you should be comfortable doing all of these things:

- Using file-like objects

- Chaining programs with standard input and output

- Defining command-line flags and validating them with `getopt`

HTTP Web Services

WE'VE TALKED ABOUT **HTML** processing and XML processing, and along the way we've touched on how to download a web page and how to parse XML from a URL. Now, let's dive into the more general topic of HTTP web services.

Diving In

Simply stated, HTTP web services are programmatic ways of sending and receiving data from remote servers using the operations of HTTP directly. If you want to get data from the server, use a straight HTTP GET; if you want to send new data to the server, use HTTP POST. (Some more advanced HTTP web service APIs also define ways of modifying existing data and deleting data, using HTTP PUT and HTTP DELETE.) In other words, the "verbs" built into the HTTP protocol (GET, POST, PUT, and DELETE) map directly to application-level operations for receiving, sending, modifying, and deleting data.

The main advantage of this approach is simplicity, and its simplicity has proven popular with many different sites. Data—usually XML data—can be built and stored statically or generated dynamically by a server-side script, and all major languages include an HTTP library for downloading it. Debugging is also easier, because you can load the web service in any web browser and see the raw data. Modern browsers will even nicely format and pretty-print XML data for you, to allow you to quickly navigate through it.

Here are some examples of pure XML-over-HTTP web services:

- Amazon API (http://www.amazon.com/webservices) allows you to retrieve product information from the Amazon.com online store.

- National Weather Service (http://www.nws.noaa.gov/alerts/) (United States) and Hong Kong Observatory (http://demo.xml.weather.gov.hk/) (Hong Kong) offer weather alerts as a web service.

- Atom API (http://atomenabled.org/) provides tools and services for managing web-based content.

- Syndicated feeds (http://syndic8.com/) from weblogs and news sites bring you up-to-the-minute news from a variety of sites.

In Chapter 12, we'll explore an alternative to this approach: APIs that use HTTP as a transport for sending and receiving data, but don't map application semantics to the underlying HTTP semantics. But for now, we'll concentrate on using HTTP GET to get data from a remote server, and we'll explore several HTTP features you can use to get the maximum benefit out of pure HTTP web services.

Listing 11-1 shows a more advanced version of the openanything module that you saw in the previous chapter.

> **NOTE** *If you have not already done so, you can download this and other examples used in this book from the Downloads section of the Apress web site* (http://www.apress.com).

Listing 11-1. openanything.py

```
import urllib2, urlparse, gzip
from StringIO import StringIO

USER_AGENT = 'OpenAnything/1.0 +http://diveintopython.org/http_web_services/'

class SmartRedirectHandler(urllib2.HTTPRedirectHandler):
    def http_error_301(self, req, fp, code, msg, headers):
        result = urllib2.HTTPRedirectHandler.http_error_301(
            self, req, fp, code, msg, headers)
        result.status = code
        return result

    def http_error_302(self, req, fp, code, msg, headers):
        result = urllib2.HTTPRedirectHandler.http_error_302(
            self, req, fp, code, msg, headers)
        result.status = code
        return result

class DefaultErrorHandler(urllib2.HTTPDefaultErrorHandler):
    def http_error_default(self, req, fp, code, msg, headers):
        result = urllib2.HTTPError(
            req.get_full_url(), code, msg, headers, fp)
        result.status = code
        return result

def openAnything(source, etag=None, lastmodified=None, agent=USER_AGENT):
    '''URL, filename, or string --> stream
```

This function lets you define parsers that take any input source
(URL, pathname to local or network file, or actual data as a string)
and deal with it in a uniform manner. Returned object is guaranteed
to have all the basic stdio read methods (read, readline, readlines).
Just .close() the object when you're done with it.

If the etag argument is supplied, it will be used as the value of an
If-None-Match request header.

If the lastmodified argument is supplied, it must be a formatted
date/time string in GMT (as returned in the Last-Modified header of
a previous request). The formatted date/time will be used
as the value of an If-Modified-Since request header.

If the agent argument is supplied, it will be used as the value of a
User-Agent request header.
'''

```
if hasattr(source, 'read'):
    return source

if source == '-':
    return sys.stdin

if urlparse.urlparse(source)[0] == 'http':
    # open URL with urllib2
    request = urllib2.Request(source)
    request.add_header('User-Agent', agent)
    if etag:
        request.add_header('If-None-Match', etag)
    if lastmodified:
        request.add_header('If-Modified-Since', lastmodified)
    request.add_header('Accept-encoding', 'gzip')
    opener = urllib2.build_opener(SmartRedirectHandler(),
        DefaultErrorHandler())
    return opener.open(request)

# try to open with native open function (if source is a filename)
try:
    return open(source)
except (IOError, OSError):
    pass

# treat source as string
return StringIO(str(source))
```

```
def fetch(source, etag=None, last_modified=None, agent=USER_AGENT):
    '''Fetch data and metadata from a URL, file, stream, or string'''
    result = {}
    f = openAnything(source, etag, last_modified, agent)
    result['data'] = f.read()
    if hasattr(f, 'headers'):
        # save ETag, if the server sent one
        result['etag'] = f.headers.get('ETag')
        # save Last-Modified header, if the server sent one
        result['lastmodified'] = f.headers.get('Last-Modified')
        if f.headers.get('content-encoding', '') == 'gzip':
            # data came back gzip-compressed, decompress it
            result['data'] = gzip.GzipFile(
                fileobj=StringIO(result['data']])).read()
    if hasattr(f, 'url'):
        result['url'] = f.url
        result['status'] = 200
    if hasattr(f, 'status'):
        result['status'] = f.status
    f.close()
    return result
```

> **TIP** *Paul Prescod believes that pure HTTP web services are the future of the Internet* (http://webservices.xml.com/pub/a/ws/2002/02/06/rest.html).

How Not to Fetch Data Over HTTP

Let's say you want to download a resource over HTTP, such as a syndicated Atom feed. But you don't just want to download it once; you want to download it over and over again, every hour, to get the latest news from the site that's offering the news feed. Let's do it the quick-and-dirty way first, as shown in Listing 11-2, and then see how you can do better.

Listing 11-2. Downloading a Feed the Quick-and-Dirty Way

```
>>> import urllib
>>> data = urllib.urlopen('http://diveintomark.org/xml/atom.xml').read()    (1)
>>> print data
<?xml version="1.0" encoding="iso-8859-1"?>
<feed version="0.3"
  xmlns="http://purl.org/atom/ns#"
  xmlns:dc="http://purl.org/dc/elements/1.1/"
```

```
xml:lang="en">
<title mode="escaped">dive into mark</title>
<link rel="alternate" type="text/html" href="http://diveintomark.org/"/>
<-- rest of feed omitted for brevity -->
```

(1) Downloading anything over HTTP is incredibly easy in Python; in fact, it's a one-liner. The urllib module has a handy urlopen function that takes the address of the page you want and returns a file-like object that you can just read() from to get the full contents of the page. It just couldn't get much easier.

So what's wrong with this? Well, for a quick one-off during testing or development, there's nothing wrong with it. I do it all the time. I wanted the contents of the feed, and I got the contents of the feed. The same technique works for any web page. But once you start thinking in terms of a web service that you want to access on a regular basis—and remember that you want to retrieve this syndicated feed once an hour—then you're being inefficient, and you're being rude.

We'll work on improving this HTTP web services client throughout this chapter. First, let's talk about some of the basic features of HTTP.

Supporting HTTP Features

HTTP has five important features that you should support:

- User-Agent

- Redirects

- Last-Modified/If-Modified-Since

- ETag/If-None-Match

- Compression

User-Agent

The User-Agent is simply a way for a client to tell a server who it is when it requests a web page, a syndicated feed, or any sort of web service over HTTP. When the client requests a resource, it should always announce who it is, as specifically as possible. This allows the server-side administrator to get in touch with the client-side developer if anything goes fantastically wrong.

By default, Python sends a generic User-Agent: Python-urllib/1.15. In the next section, you'll see how to change this to something more specific.

Redirects

Sometimes resources move around: web sites get reorganized, pages move to new addresses, and even web services can reorganize. A syndicated feed at `http://example.com/index.xml` might be moved to `http://example.com/xml/atom.xml`, or an entire domain might move when an organization expands and reorganizes; for instance, `http://www.example.com/index.xml` might be redirected to `http://server-farm-1.example.com/index.xml`.

Every time you request any kind of resource from an HTTP server, the server includes a status code in its response. Status code 200 means "Everything is normal; here's the page you asked for." Status code 404 means "Page not found." (You've probably seen 404 errors while browsing the Web.)

HTTP has two different ways of signifying that a resource has moved:

- Status code 302 is a *temporary redirect*. It means "Oops, that got moved over here temporarily" (and then gives the temporary address in a `Location:` header). If you get a 302 status code and a new address, the HTTP specification says you should use the new address to get what you asked for, but the next time you want to access the same resource, you should retry the old address.

- Status code 301 is a *permanent redirect*. It means "Oops, that got moved permanently" (and then gives the new address in a `Location:` header). If you get a 301 status code and a new address, you're supposed to use the new address for subsequent access.

`urllib.urlopen` will automatically "follow" redirects when it receives the appropriate status code from the HTTP server, but unfortunately, it doesn't tell you when it does so. You'll end up getting data you asked for, but you'll never know that the underlying library "helpfully" followed a redirect for you. So you'll continue pounding away at the old address, and each time, you'll get redirected to the new address. That's two round-trips instead of one, which is not very efficient! Later in this chapter, in the "Handling Redirects" section, you'll see how to work around this so you can deal with permanent redirects properly and efficiently.

Last-Modified/If-Modified-Since

Some data changes all the time. The home page of CNN.com is constantly updating every few minutes. On the other hand, the home page of Google.com changes only once every few weeks (when the webmaster puts up a special holiday logo or advertises a new service). Web services are no different. Usually, the server knows when the data you requested last changed, and HTTP provides a way for the server to include this last-modified date along with the data you requested.

If you ask for the same data a second time (or third, or fourth), you can tell the server the last-modified date that you got last time: you send an If-Modified-Since header with your request, with the date you got back from the server last time. If the data hasn't changed since then, the server sends back a special HTTP status code 304, which means "This data hasn't changed since the last time you asked for it." Why is this an improvement? Because when the server sends a 304, *it doesn't resend the data*. All you get is the status code. So, you don't need to download the same data over and over again if it hasn't changed, because the server assumes you have the data cached locally.

All modern web browsers support last-modified-date checking. If you've ever visited a page, revisited the same page a day later, and found that it loaded much more quickly the second time, last-modified-date checking could be the reason. Your web browser cached the contents of the page locally the first time, and when you visited the second time, your browser automatically sent the last-modified date it got from the server the first time. If the data didn't change, the server simply says 304: Not Modified, so your browser knows to load the page from its cache. Web services can be this smart, too.

Python's URL library does not have any built-in support for last-modified-date checking, but since you can add arbitrary headers to each request and read arbitrary headers in each response, you can add support for it yourself.

ETag/If-None-Match

ETags are an alternate way to accomplish the same thing as the last-modified-date checking: don't re-download data that hasn't changed. The server sends some sort of hash of the data (in an ETag header) along with the data you requested. Exactly how this hash is determined is entirely up to the server. The second time you request the same data, you include the ETag hash in an If-None-Match: header, and if the data hasn't changed, the server will send you back a 304 status code.

As with the last-modified-date checking, the server sends *just* the 304; it doesn't send you the same data a second time. By including the ETag hash in your second request, you're telling the server that there's no need to resend the same data if it still matches this hash, since you still have the data from the last time.

Python's URL library has no built-in support for ETags. You'll see how to add ETag support later in this chapter, in the "Checking for ETag and Sending If-None-Match" section.

Compression

The other important HTTP feature is gzip compression. When we talk about HTTP web services, we're almost always talking about moving XML back and forth over the wire. XML is text, and quite verbose text at that, and text generally compresses well. When you request a resource over HTTP, you can ask the server, if it has any

new data to send you, to please send it in compressed format. You include the
Accept-encoding: gzip header in your request, and if the server supports compression,
it will send you back gzip-compressed data and mark it with a Content-encoding: gzip
header.

Python's URL library has no built-in support for gzip compression per se, but
you can add arbitrary headers to your request. And Python comes with a separate
gzip module, which has functions you can use to decompress the data yourself.

Notice that the one-line script (Listing 11-2) to download a syndicated feed
did not support any of these HTTP features. Let's see how we can improve it.

Debugging HTTP Web Services

First, let's turn on the debugging features of Python's HTTP library and see what's
being sent over the wire. This will be useful throughout the chapter, as you add
more features. Listing 11-3 shows how to turn on debugging for web services.

Listing 11-3. Debugging HTTP

```
>>> import httplib
>>> httplib.HTTPConnection.debuglevel = 1          (1)
>>> import urllib
>>> feeddata = urllib.urlopen('http://diveintomark.org/xml/atom.xml').read()
connect: (diveintomark.org, 80)                    (2)
send: '
GET /xml/atom.xml HTTP/1.0                          (3)
Host: diveintomark.org                              (4)
User-agent: Python-urllib/1.15                      (5)
'
reply: 'HTTP/1.1 200 OK\r\n'                        (6)
header: Date: Wed, 14 Apr 2004 22:27:30 GMT
header: Server: Apache/2.0.49 (Debian GNU/Linux)
header: Content-Type: application/atom+xml
header: Last-Modified: Wed, 14 Apr 2004 22:14:38 GMT  (7)
header: ETag: "e8284-68e0-4de30f80"                 (8)
header: Accept-Ranges: bytes
header: Content-Length: 26848
header: Connection: close
```

(1) urllib relies on another standard Python library, httplib. Normally, you
don't need to import httplib directly (urllib does that automatically), but you do
here, so you can set the debugging flag on the HTTPConnection class that urllib uses
internally to connect to the HTTP server. This is an incredibly useful technique.

Some other Python libraries have similar debug flags, but there's no particular standard for naming them or turning them on. You need to read the documentation for each library to see if such a feature is available.

(2) Now that the debugging flag is set, information on the HTTP request and response is printed in real time. The first thing it tells you is that you're connecting to the server diveintomark.org on port 80, which is the standard port for HTTP.

(3) When you request the Atom feed, urllib sends three lines to the server. The first line specifies the HTTP verb you're using and the path of the resource (minus the domain name). All the requests in this chapter will use GET, but in the next chapter on SOAP, you'll see that it uses POST for everything. The basic syntax is the same, regardless of the verb.

(4) The second line that urllib sends to the server is the Host header, which specifies the domain name of the service you're accessing. This is important, because a single HTTP server can host multiple separate domains. My server currently hosts 12 domains; other servers can host hundreds or even thousands.

(5) The third line that urllib sends to the server is the User-Agent header. What you see here is the generic User-Agent that the urllib library adds by default. In the next section, you'll see how to customize this to be more specific.

(6) The server replies with a status code and a bunch of headers (and possibly some data, which was stored in the feeddata variable). The status code here is 200, meaning "Everything is normal; here's the data you requested." The server also tells you the date it responded to your request, some information about the server itself, and the content type of the data it's giving you. Depending on your application, this may or may not be useful. It's certainly reassuring that you thought you were asking for an Atom feed, and lo and behold, you're getting an Atom feed (application/atom+xml, which is the registered content type for Atom feeds).

(7) The server tells you when this Atom feed was last modified (in this case, about 13 minutes ago). You can send this date back to the server the next time you request the same feed, and the server can do last-modified checking.

(8) The server also tells you that this Atom feed has an ETag hash of "e8284-68e0-4de30f80". The hash doesn't mean anything by itself; there's nothing you can do with it, except send it back to the server the next time you request this same feed. Then the server can use it to tell you whether the data has changed.

Setting the User-Agent

The first step to improving your HTTP web services client is to identify yourself properly with a User-Agent. To do that, you need to move beyond the basic urllib and dive into urllib2, as shown in Listing 11-4.

Listing 11-4. Introducing urllib2

```
>>> import httplib
>>> httplib.HTTPConnection.debuglevel = 1                              (1)
>>> import urllib2
>>> request = urllib2.Request('http://diveintomark.org/xml/atom.xml')  (2)
>>> opener = urllib2.build_opener()                                    (3)
>>> feeddata = opener.open(request).read()                            (4)
connect: (diveintomark.org, 80)
send: '
GET /xml/atom.xml HTTP/1.0
Host: diveintomark.org
User-agent: Python-urllib/2.1
'
reply: 'HTTP/1.1 200 OK\r\n'
header: Date: Wed, 14 Apr 2004 23:23:12 GMT
header: Server: Apache/2.0.49 (Debian GNU/Linux)
header: Content-Type: application/atom+xml
header: Last-Modified: Wed, 14 Apr 2004 22:14:38 GMT
header: ETag: "e8284-68e0-4de30f80"
header: Accept-Ranges: bytes
header: Content-Length: 26848
header: Connection: close
```

(1) If you still have your Python IDE open from the previous section's example, you can skip this. It turns on HTTP debugging, so you can see what you're actually sending over the wire and what is sent back.

(2) Fetching an HTTP resource with urllib2 is a three-step process, for good reasons that will become clear shortly. The first step is to create a Request object, which takes the URL of the resource you'll eventually get around to retrieving. Note that this step doesn't actually retrieve anything yet.

(3) The second step is to build a URL opener. This can take any number of handlers, which control how responses are handled. But you can also build an opener without any custom handlers, which is what you're doing here. You'll see how to define and use custom handlers later in this chapter, when we explore redirects.

(4) The final step is to tell the opener to open the URL, using the Request object you created. As you can see from all the debugging information that is printed, this step actually retrieves the resource and stores the returned data in feeddata.

The previous example created a Request object with the URL you want to access. Continuing, Listing 11-5 shows how to add headers with the Request object.

Listing 11-5. Adding Headers with the Request Object

```
>>> request
<urllib2.Request instance at 0x00250AA8>
>>> request.get_full_url()
http://diveintomark.org/xml/atom.xml
>>> request.add_header('User-Agent',
...       'OpenAnything/1.0 +http://diveintopython.org/')      (1)
>>> feeddata = opener.open(request).read()                     (2)
connect: (diveintomark.org, 80)
send: '
GET /xml/atom.xml HTTP/1.0
Host: diveintomark.org
User-agent: OpenAnything/1.0 +http://diveintopython.org/       (3)
'
reply: 'HTTP/1.1 200 OK\r\n'
header: Date: Wed, 14 Apr 2004 23:45:17 GMT
header: Server: Apache/2.0.49 (Debian GNU/Linux)
header: Content-Type: application/atom+xml
header: Last-Modified: Wed, 14 Apr 2004 22:14:38 GMT
header: ETag: "e8284-68e0-4de30f80"
header: Accept-Ranges: bytes
header: Content-Length: 26848
header: Connection: close
```

(1) Using the add_header method on the Request object, you can add arbitrary HTTP headers to your request. The first argument is the header, and the second is the value you're providing for that header. Convention dictates that a User-Agent should be in this specific format: an application name, followed by a slash, followed by a version number. The rest is free-form, and you'll see a lot of variation in the wild, but somewhere it should include a URL of your application. Along with other details of your request, the User-Agent is usually logged by the server, and including a URL of your application allows server administrators looking through their access logs to contact you if something is wrong.

(2) The opener object you created before can be reused, too, and it will retrieve the same feed again, but with your custom User-Agent header.

(3) And here you are sending your custom User-Agent, in place of the generic one that Python sends by default. If you look closely, you'll notice that although you defined a User-Agent header, you actually sent a User-agent header. See the difference? urllib2 changed the case so that only the first letter was capitalized. It doesn't really matter; HTTP specifies that header field names are completely case-insensitive.

Handling Last-Modified and ETag

Now that you know how to add custom HTTP headers to your web service requests, let's look at adding support for Last-Modified and ETag headers.

> **NOTE** *These examples show the output with debugging turned off. If you still have debugging turned on from the previous section, you can turn it off by setting* httplib.HTTPConnection.debuglevel = 0. *Or you can just leave debugging on, if that helps you.*

Checking for Last-Modified and Sending If-Modified-Since

Listing 11-6 demonstrates how to test for Last-Modified.

Listing 11-6. Testing Last-Modified

```
>>> import urllib2
>>> request = urllib2.Request('http://diveintomark.org/xml/atom.xml')
>>> opener = urllib2.build_opener()
>>> firstdatastream = opener.open(request)
>>> firstdatastream.headers.dict                              (1)
{'date': 'Thu, 15 Apr 2004 20:42:41 GMT',
 'server': 'Apache/2.0.49 (Debian GNU/Linux)',
 'content-type': 'application/atom+xml',
 'last-modified': 'Thu, 15 Apr 2004 19:45:21 GMT',
 'etag': '"e842a-3e53-55d97640"',
 'content-length': '15955',
 'accept-ranges': 'bytes',
 'connection': 'close'}
>>> request.add_header('If-Modified-Since',
...      firstdatastream.headers.get('Last-Modified'))        (2)
>>> seconddatastream = opener.open(request)                   (3)
Traceback (most recent call last):
  File "<stdin>", line 1, in ?
  File "c:\python23\lib\urllib2.py", line 326, in open
    '_open', req)
  File "c:\python23\lib\urllib2.py", line 306, in _call_chain
    result = func(*args)
  File "c:\python23\lib\urllib2.py", line 901, in http_open
    return self.do_open(httplib.HTTP, req)
  File "c:\python23\lib\urllib2.py", line 895, in do_open
    return self.parent.error('http', req, fp, code, msg, hdrs)
```

```
  File "c:\python23\lib\urllib2.py", line 352, in error
    return self._call_chain(*args)
  File "c:\python23\lib\urllib2.py", line 306, in _call_chain
    result = func(*args)
  File "c:\python23\lib\urllib2.py", line 412, in http_error_default
    raise HTTPError(req.get_full_url(), code, msg, hdrs, fp)
urllib2.HTTPError: HTTP Error 304: Not Modified
```

(1) Remember all those HTTP headers you saw printed when you turned on debugging? This is how you can access them programmatically. `firstdatastream.headers` is an object that acts like a dictionary and allows you to get any of the individual headers returned from the HTTP server.

(2) In the second request, you add the `If-Modified-Since` header with the last-modified date from your first request. If the data hasn't changed, the server should return a 304 status code.

(3) Sure enough, the data hasn't changed. You can see from the traceback that `urllib2` throws a special exception, `HTTPError`, in response to the 304 status code. This is a little unusual and not entirely helpful. It's not an error, so why is it throwing an exception? You specifically asked the server not to send any data if it hadn't changed, and the data didn't change, so the server told you it wasn't sending you any data. That's not an error; that's exactly what you were hoping for.

`urllib2` also raises an `HTTPError` exception for conditions that you would think of as errors, such as 404 (Page Not Found). In fact, it will raise `HTTPError` for *any* status code other than 200 (OK), 301 (permanent redirect), or 302 (temporary redirect). It would be more helpful to capture the status code and simply return it, without throwing an exception. To do that, you'll need to define a custom URL handler.

The custom URL handler shown in Listing 11-7 is part of `openanything.py`.

Listing 11-7. Defining a URL Handler

```
class DefaultErrorHandler(urllib2.HTTPDefaultErrorHandler):      (1)
    def http_error_default(self, req, fp, code, msg, headers):   (2)
        result = urllib2.HTTPError(
            req.get_full_url(), code, msg, headers, fp)
        result.status = code                                     (3)
        return result
```

(1) `urllib2` is designed around URL handlers. Each handler is just a class that can define any number of methods. When something happens—an HTTP error or even a 304 code—`urllib2` introspects into the list of defined handlers for a method that can handle it. You used a similar introspection in Chapter 9 to define handlers for different node types, but `urllib2` is more flexible and introspects over as many handlers as are defined for the current request.

(2) urllib2 searches through the defined handlers and calls the http_error_ default method when it encounters a 304 status code from the server. By defining a custom error handler, you can prevent urllib2 from raising an exception. Instead, you create the HTTPError object, but return it instead of raising it.

(3) This is the key part: before returning, save the status code returned by the HTTP server. This will allow you easy access to it from your calling program.

Continuing the previous example, with the Request object already set up and the If-Modified-Since header already added, Listing 11-8 shows how to use the custom URL handler.

Listing 11-8. Using a Custom URL Handler

```
>>> request.headers
{'If-modified-since': 'Thu, 15 Apr 2004 19:45:21 GMT'}
>>> import openanything
>>> opener = urllib2.build_opener(
...     openanything.DefaultErrorHandler())          (1)
>>> seconddatastream = opener.open(request)
>>> seconddatastream.status                           (2)
304
>>> seconddatastream.read()                           (3)
''
```

(1) This is the key: now that you've defined your custom URL handler, you need to tell urllib2 to use it. Remember how I said that urllib2 broke up the process of accessing an HTTP resource into three steps, and for good reason? This is why building the URL opener is its own step: because you can build it with your own custom URL handlers that override urllib2's default behavior.

(2) Now, you can quietly open the resource. You get back an object that, along with the usual headers (use seconddatastream.headers.dict to access them), also contains the HTTP status code. In this case, as expected, the status is 304, meaning this data hasn't changed since the last time you asked for it.

(3) Note that when the server sends back a 304 status code, it doesn't resend the data. That's the whole point: to save bandwidth by not re-downloading data that hasn't changed. So, if you actually want that data, you'll need to cache it locally the first time you get it.

Checking for ETag and Sending If-None-Match

Handling ETag works much the same way, but instead of checking for Last-Modified and sending If-Modified-Since, you check for ETag and send If-None-Match. Let's start with a fresh IDE session, as shown in Listing 11-9.

Listing 11-9. Supporting ETag/If-None-Match

```
>>> import urllib2, openanything
>>> request = urllib2.Request('http://diveintomark.org/xml/atom.xml')
>>> opener = urllib2.build_opener(
...     openanything.DefaultErrorHandler())
>>> firstdatastream = opener.open(request)
>>> firstdatastream.headers.get('ETag')              (1)
'"e842a-3e53-55d97640"'
>>> firstdata = firstdatastream.read()
>>> print firstdata                                   (2)
<?xml version="1.0" encoding="iso-8859-1"?>
<feed version="0.3"
  xmlns="http://purl.org/atom/ns#"
  xmlns:dc="http://purl.org/dc/elements/1.1/"
  xml:lang="en">
  <title mode="escaped">dive into mark</title>
  <link rel="alternate" type="text/html" href="http://diveintomark.org/"/>
  <-- rest of feed omitted for brevity -->
>>> request.add_header('If-None-Match',
...     firstdatastream.headers.get('ETag'))          (3)
>>> seconddatastream = opener.open(request)
>>> seconddatastream.status                           (4)
304
>>> seconddatastream.read()                           (5)
''
```

(1) Using the firstdatastream.headers pseudo-dictionary, you can get the ETag returned from the server. (What happens if the server didn't send back an ETag? Then this line would return None.)

(2) Okay, you got the data.

(3) Now, set up the second call by setting the If-None-Match header to the ETag you got from the first call.

(4) The second call succeeds quietly (without throwing an exception), and once again, you see that the server has sent back a 304 status code. Based on the ETag you sent the second time, it knows that the data hasn't changed.

(5) Regardless of whether the 304 is triggered by Last-Modified date checking or ETag hash matching, you'll never get the data along with the 304. That's the whole point.

> **CAUTION** *In these examples, the HTTP server has supported both* Last-Modified *and* ETag *headers, but not all servers do. As a web services client, you should be prepared to support both, but you must code defensively, in case a server supports only one or the other, or neither.*

Handling Redirects

You can support permanent and temporary redirects using a different kind of custom URL handler. First, let's see why a redirect handler is necessary in the first place. Take a look at Listing 11-10.

Listing 11-10. Accessing Web Services Without a Redirect Handler

```
>>> import urllib2, httplib
>>> httplib.HTTPConnection.debuglevel = 1                      (1)
>>> request = urllib2.Request(
...      'http://diveintomark.org/redir/example301.xml')       (2)
>>> opener = urllib2.build_opener()
>>> f = opener.open(request)
connect: (diveintomark.org, 80)
send: '
GET /redir/example301.xml HTTP/1.0
Host: diveintomark.org
User-agent: Python-urllib/2.1
'
reply: 'HTTP/1.1 301 Moved Permanently\r\n'                    (3)
header: Date: Thu, 15 Apr 2004 22:06:25 GMT
header: Server: Apache/2.0.49 (Debian GNU/Linux)
header: Location: http://diveintomark.org/xml/atom.xml         (4)
header: Content-Length: 338
header: Connection: close
header: Content-Type: text/html; charset=iso-8859-1
connect: (diveintomark.org, 80)
send: '
GET /xml/atom.xml HTTP/1.0                                     (5)
Host: diveintomark.org
User-agent: Python-urllib/2.1
'
reply: 'HTTP/1.1 200 OK\r\n'
header: Date: Thu, 15 Apr 2004 22:06:25 GMT
header: Server: Apache/2.0.49 (Debian GNU/Linux)
header: Last-Modified: Thu, 15 Apr 2004 19:45:21 GMT
header: ETag: "e842a-3e53-55d97640"
header: Accept-Ranges: bytes
header: Content-Length: 15955
header: Connection: close
header: Content-Type: application/atom+xml
>>> f.url                                                      (6)
'http://diveintomark.org/xml/atom.xml'
```

```
>>> f.headers.dict
{'content-length': '15955',
'accept-ranges': 'bytes',
'server': 'Apache/2.0.49 (Debian GNU/Linux)',
'last-modified': 'Thu, 15 Apr 2004 19:45:21 GMT',
'connection': 'close',
'etag': '"e842a-3e53-55d97640"',
'date': 'Thu, 15 Apr 2004 22:06:25 GMT',
'content-type': 'application/atom+xml'}
>>> f.status
Traceback (most recent call last):
  File "<stdin>", line 1, in ?
AttributeError: addinfourl instance has no attribute 'status'
```

(1) You'll be better able to see what's happening if you turn on debugging.

(2) This is a URL that I have set up to permanently redirect to my Atom feed at http://diveintomark.org/xml/atom.xml.

(3) Sure enough, when you try to download the data at that address, the server sends back a 301 status code, telling you that the resource has moved permanently.

(4) The server also sends back a Location: header that gives the new address of this data.

(5) urllib2 notices the redirect status code and automatically tries to retrieve the data at the new location specified in the Location: header.

(6) The object you get back from the opener contains the new permanent address and all the headers returned from the second request (retrieved from the new permanent address). But the status code is missing, so you have no way of knowing programmatically whether this redirect was temporary or permanent, and that matters very much. If it was a temporary redirect, you should continue to ask for the data at the old location. But if it was a permanent redirect (as this was), you should ask for the data at the new location from now on. This is sub-optimal, but easy to fix.

Defining a Redirect Handler

urllib2 doesn't behave exactly as you want it to when it encounters a 301 or 302, so let's override its behavior. How can you do that? By creating a custom URL handler, just as you did to handle 304 codes. Listing 11-11 shows the redirect handler, which references a class defined in openanything.py.

Listing 11-11. Defining the Redirect Handler

```
class SmartRedirectHandler(urllib2.HTTPRedirectHandler):       (1)
    def http_error_301(self, req, fp, code, msg, headers):
        result = urllib2.HTTPRedirectHandler.http_error_301(   (2)
            self, req, fp, code, msg, headers)
```

```
        result.status = code                              (3)
        return result


    def http_error_302(self, req, fp, code, msg, headers):    (4)
        result = urllib2.HTTPRedirectHandler.http_error_302(
            self, req, fp, code, msg, headers)
        result.status = code
        return result
```

(1) Redirect behavior is defined in urllib2 in a class called HTTPRedirectHandler. You don't want to completely override the behavior; you just want to extend it a little. You'll subclass HTTPRedirectHandler so that you can call the ancestor class to do all the hard work.

(2) When it encounters a 301 status code from the server, urllib2 will search through its handlers and call the http_error_301 method. The first thing this redirect handler does is just call the http_error_301 method in the ancestor, which handles the grunt work of looking for the Location: header and following the redirect to the new address.

(3) Here's the key: before you return, you store the status code (301), so that the calling program can access it later.

(4) Temporary redirects (status code 302) work the same way: override the http_error_302 method, call the ancestor, and save the status code before returning.

Detecting Permanent and Temporary Redirects

So what has this bought you? You can now build a URL opener with your custom redirect handler. It will still automatically follow redirects, but now it will also expose the redirect status code.

Listing 11-12 demonstrates how the redirect handler detects permanent redirects.

Listing 11-12. Using the Redirect Handler to Detect Permanent Redirects

```
>>> request = urllib2.Request('http://diveintomark.org/redir/example301.xml')
>>> import openanything, httplib
>>> httplib.HTTPConnection.debuglevel = 1
>>> opener = urllib2.build_opener(
...     openanything.SmartRedirectHandler())        (1)
>>> f = opener.open(request)
connect: (diveintomark.org, 80)
send: 'GET /redir/example301.xml HTTP/1.0
Host: diveintomark.org
User-agent: Python-urllib/2.1
'
```

```
reply: 'HTTP/1.1 301 Moved Permanently\r\n'          (2)
header: Date: Thu, 15 Apr 2004 22:13:21 GMT
header: Server: Apache/2.0.49 (Debian GNU/Linux)
header: Location: http://diveintomark.org/xml/atom.xml
header: Content-Length: 338
header: Connection: close
header: Content-Type: text/html; charset=iso-8859-1
connect: (diveintomark.org, 80)
send: '
GET /xml/atom.xml HTTP/1.0
Host: diveintomark.org
User-agent: Python-urllib/2.1
'
reply: 'HTTP/1.1 200 OK\r\n'
header: Date: Thu, 15 Apr 2004 22:13:21 GMT
header: Server: Apache/2.0.49 (Debian GNU/Linux)
header: Last-Modified: Thu, 15 Apr 2004 19:45:21 GMT
header: ETag: "e842a-3e53-55d97640"
header: Accept-Ranges: bytes
header: Content-Length: 15955
header: Connection: close
header: Content-Type: application/atom+xml
```

```
>>> f.status                                         (3)
301
>>> f.url
'http://diveintomark.org/xml/atom.xml'
```

(1) First, build a URL opener with the redirect handler you just defined (in Listing 11-11).

(2) You sent your request and got back a 301 status code in response. At this point, your http_error_301 method is called. You call the ancestor method, which follows the redirect and sends a request at the new location (http://diveintomark.org/xml/atom.xml).

(3) This is the payoff: now, not only do you have access to the new URL, but you also have access to the redirect status code, so you can tell that this was a permanent redirect. The next time you request this data, you should request it from the new location (http://diveintomark.org/xml/atom.xml, as specified in f.url). If you had the location stored in a configuration file or a database, you need to update that, so you don't keep pounding the server with requests at the old address. It's time to update your address book.

The same redirect handler can also tell you that you *shouldn't* update our address book. Listing 11-13 demonstrates using the custom redirect handler and finding a temporary redirect.

Listing 11-13. Using the Redirect Handler to Detect Temporary Redirects

```
>>> request = urllib2.Request(
...     'http://diveintomark.org/redir/example302.xml')          (1)
>>> f = opener.open(request)
connect: (diveintomark.org, 80)
send: '
GET /redir/example302.xml HTTP/1.0
Host: diveintomark.org
User-agent: Python-urllib/2.1
'
reply: 'HTTP/1.1 302 Found\r\n'                                  (2)
header: Date: Thu, 15 Apr 2004 22:18:21 GMT
header: Server: Apache/2.0.49 (Debian GNU/Linux)
header: Location: http://diveintomark.org/xml/atom.xml
header: Content-Length: 314
header: Connection: close
header: Content-Type: text/html; charset=iso-8859-1
connect: (diveintomark.org, 80)
send: '
GET /xml/atom.xml HTTP/1.0                                       (3)
Host: diveintomark.org
User-agent: Python-urllib/2.1
'
reply: 'HTTP/1.1 200 OK\r\n'
header: Date: Thu, 15 Apr 2004 22:18:21 GMT
header: Server: Apache/2.0.49 (Debian GNU/Linux)
header: Last-Modified: Thu, 15 Apr 2004 19:45:21 GMT
header: ETag: "e842a-3e53-55d97640"
header: Accept-Ranges: bytes
header: Content-Length: 15955
header: Connection: close
header: Content-Type: application/atom+xml
>>> f.status                                                     (4)
302
>>> f.url
http://diveintomark.org/xml/atom.xml
```

(1) This is a sample URL I've set up that is configured to tell clients to *temporarily* redirect to http://diveintomark.org/xml/atom.xml.

(2) The server sends back a 302 status code, indicating a temporary redirect. The temporary new location of the data is given in the Location: header.

(3) urllib2 calls the http_error_302 method, which calls the ancestor method of the same name in urllib2.HTTPRedirectHandler, which follows the redirect to the new location. Then the http_error_302 method stores the status code (302), so the calling application can get it later.

(4) And here you are, having successfully followed the redirect to http:// diveintomark.org/xml/atom.xml. f.status tells you that this was a temporary redirect, which means that you should continue to request data from the original address (http://diveintomark.org/redir/example302.xml). Maybe it will redirect next time; maybe not. Maybe it will redirect to a different address. It's not for us to say. The server said this redirect was only temporary, so you should respect that. And now you're exposing enough information that the calling application can respect that.

Handling Compressed Data

The other important HTTP feature that every HTTP web services client should support is compression. Many web services have the ability to send data compressed, which can reduce the amount of data sent over the wire by 60% or more. This is especially true of XML web services, since XML data compresses very well.

Getting Compressed Data

Servers won't give you compressed data unless you tell them you can handle it. Listing 11-14 shows how to do that.

Listing 11-14. Telling the Server You Want Compressed Data

```
>>> import urllib2, httplib
>>> httplib.HTTPConnection.debuglevel = 1
>>> request = urllib2.Request('http://diveintomark.org/xml/atom.xml')
>>> request.add_header('Accept-encoding', 'gzip')          (1)
>>> opener = urllib2.build_opener()
>>> f = opener.open(request)
connect: (diveintomark.org, 80)
send: '
GET /xml/atom.xml HTTP/1.0
Host: diveintomark.org
User-agent: Python-urllib/2.1
Accept-encoding: gzip                                      (2)
'
reply: 'HTTP/1.1 200 OK\r\n'
header: Date: Thu, 15 Apr 2004 22:24:39 GMT
header: Server: Apache/2.0.49 (Debian GNU/Linux)
header: Last-Modified: Thu, 15 Apr 2004 19:45:21 GMT
header: ETag: "e842a-3e53-55d97640"
```

```
header: Accept-Ranges: bytes
header: Vary: Accept-Encoding
header: Content-Encoding: gzip                                    (3)
header: Content-Length: 6289                                      (4)
header: Connection: close
header: Content-Type: application/atom+xml
```

(1) This is the key: once you've created your `Request` object, add an `Accept-encoding` header to tell the server you can accept gzip-encoded data. `gzip` is the name of the compression algorithm you're using. In theory, there could be other compression algorithms, but `gzip` is the compression algorithm used by 99% of web servers.

(2) There's your header going across the wire.

(3) And here's what the server sends back: the `Content-Encoding: gzip` header means that the data you're about to receive has been gzip-compressed.

(4) The `Content-Length` header is the length of the compressed data, not the uncompressed data. As you'll see in a minute, the actual length of the uncompressed data was 15955, so gzip compression cut the bandwidth by more than 60%!

Decompressing Data

After you get the compressed data, you'll need to decompress it. Listing 11-15 shows how that's done.

Listing 11-15. Decompressing the Data

```
>>> compresseddata = f.read()                                    (1)
>>> len(compresseddata)
6289
>>> import StringIO
>>> compressedstream = StringIO.StringIO(compresseddata)         (2)
>>> import gzip
>>> gzipper = gzip.GzipFile(fileobj=compressedstream)            (3)
>>> data = gzipper.read()                                        (4)
>>> print data                                                   (5)
<?xml version="1.0" encoding="iso-8859-1"?>
<feed version="0.3"
  xmlns="http://purl.org/atom/ns#"
  xmlns:dc="http://purl.org/dc/elements/1.1/"
  xml:lang="en">
  <title mode="escaped">dive into mark</title>
  <link rel="alternate" type="text/html" href="http://diveintomark.org/"/>
  <-- rest of feed omitted for brevity -->
>>> len(data)
15955
```

(1) Continuing from the previous example (Listing 11-14), f is the file-like object returned from the URL opener. Using its read() method would ordinarily get uncompressed data, but since this data has been gzip-compressed, this is just the first step toward getting the data you want.

(2) This step is a bit of a messy workaround. Python has a gzip module, which reads (and actually writes) gzip-compressed files on disk. But you don't have a file on disk. You have a gzip-compressed buffer in memory, and you don't want to write out a temporary file just so you can uncompress it. So, you'll create a file-like object from your in-memory data (compresseddata), using the StringIO module. You first saw the StringIO module in the previous chapter, but now you'll see another use for it.

(3) Now, you can create an instance of GzipFile and tell it that its "file" is the file-like object compressedstream.

(4) This is the line that does all the actual work: "reading" from GzipFile will decompress the data. Is this strange? Yes, but it makes sense in a twisted kind of way. gzipper is a file-like object that represents a gzip-compressed file. That "file" is not a real file on disk, though. gzipper is really just "reading" from the file-like object you created with StringIO to wrap your compressed data, which is only in memory in the variable compresseddata. And where did that compressed data come from? You originally downloaded it from a remote HTTP server by "reading" from the file-like object you built with urllib2.build_opener. And amazingly, this all works. Every step in the chain has no idea that the previous step is faking it.

(5) Look ma, real data (15,955 bytes of it, in fact).

"But wait!" I hear you cry. "This could be even easier!" I know what you're thinking. You're thinking that opener.open returns a file-like object, so why not cut out the StringIO middleman and just pass f directly to GzipFile? Okay, maybe you aren't thinking that, but don't worry about it, because it doesn't work. Listing 11-16 shows why.

Listing 11-16. Decompressing the Data Directly from the Server

```
>>> f = opener.open(request)                    (1)
>>> f.headers.get('Content-Encoding')           (2)
'gzip'
>>> data = gzip.GzipFile(fileobj=f).read()      (3)
Traceback (most recent call last):
  File "<stdin>", line 1, in ?
  File "c:\python23\lib\gzip.py", line 217, in read
    self._read(readsize)
  File "c:\python23\lib\gzip.py", line 252, in _read
    pos = self.fileobj.tell()   # Save current position
AttributeError: addinfourl instance has no attribute 'tell'
```

(1) Continuing from the previous example, you already have a Request object set up with an Accept-encoding: gzip header.

(2) Simply opening the request will get the headers (though not download any data yet). As you can see from the returned Content-Encoding header, this data has been sent gzip-compressed.

(3) Since opener.open returns a file-like object, and you know from the headers that when you read it, you're going to get gzip-compressed data, why not simply pass that file-like object directly to GzipFile? As you "read" from the GzipFile instance, it will "read" compressed data from the remote HTTP server and decompress it on the fly. It's a good idea, but unfortunately it doesn't work. Because of the way gzip compression works, GzipFile needs to save its position and move forwards and backwards through the compressed file. This doesn't work when the "file" is a stream of bytes coming from a remote server; all you can do with it is retrieve bytes one at a time, not move back and forth through the data stream.

So the inelegant hack of using StringIO is the best solution: download the compressed data, create a file-like object out of it with StringIO, and then decompress the data from that.

Putting It All Together

You've seen all the pieces for building an intelligent HTTP web services client. Now, let's see how they all fit together.

Listing 11-17 shows the openanything function, which is defined in openanything.py.

Listing 11-17. The openanything Function

```
def openAnything(source, etag=None, lastmodified=None, agent=USER_AGENT):
    # non-HTTP code omitted for brevity
    if urlparse.urlparse(source)[0] == 'http':          (1)
        # open URL with urllib2
        request = urllib2.Request(source)
        request.add_header('User-Agent',                (2)
        if etag:
            request.add_header('If-None-Match',         (3)
        if lastmodified:
            request.add_header('If-Modified-Since',
                lastmodified)                           (4)
        request.add_header('Accept-encoding', 'gzip')   (5)
        opener = urllib2.build_opener(
            SmartRedirectHandler(),
            DefaultErrorHandler())                      (6)
        return opener.open(request)                     (7)
```

(1) urlparse is a handy utility module for, you guessed it, parsing URLs. Its primary function, also called urlparse, takes a URL and splits it into a tuple of scheme, domain, path, parameters, query string parameters, and fragment identifier. Of these, the only thing you care about is the scheme, to make sure that you're dealing with an HTTP URL (which urllib2 can handle).

(2) You identify yourself to the HTTP server with the User-Agent passed in by the calling function. If no User-Agent was specified, you use a default one defined earlier in the openanything.py module. You never use the default one defined by urllib2.

(3) If an ETag hash was given, send it in the If-None-Match header.

(4) If a last-modified date was given, send it in the If-Modified-Since header.

(5) Tell the server you would like compressed data if possible.

(6) Build a URL opener that uses *both* of your custom URL handlers: SmartRedirectHandler for handling 301 and 302 redirects, and DefaultErrorHandler for handling 304, 404, and other error conditions gracefully.

(7) That's it! Open the URL and return a file-like object to the caller.

Listing 11-18 shows the fetch function, which is defined in openanything.py.

Listing 11-18. The fetch Function

```
def fetch(source, etag=None, last_modified=None, agent=USER_AGENT):
    '''Fetch data and metadata from a URL, file, stream, or string'''
    result = {}
    f = openAnything(source, etag, last_modified, agent)        (1)
    result['data'] = f.read()                                   (2)
    if hasattr(f, 'headers'):
        # save ETag, if the server sent one
        result['etag'] = f.headers.get('ETag')                  (3)
        # save Last-Modified header, if the server sent one
        result['lastmodified'] = f.headers.get('Last-Modified') (4)
        if f.headers.get('content-encoding', '') == 'gzip':     (5)
            # data came back gzip-compressed, decompress it
            result['data'] = gzip.GzipFile(
                fileobj=StringIO(result['data'])).read()
    if hasattr(f, 'url'):                                        (6)
        result['url'] = f.url
        result['status'] = 200
    if hasattr(f, 'status'):                                     (7)
        result['status'] = f.status
    f.close()
    return result
```

(1) First, call the `openAnything` function with a URL, `ETag` hash, `Last-Modified` date, and `User-Agent`.

(2) Read the actual data returned from the server. This may be compressed; if so, you'll decompress it later.

(3) Save the `ETag` hash returned from the server, so the calling application can pass it back to you next time, and you can pass it on to `openAnything`, which can stick it in the `If-None-Match` header and send it to the remote server.

(4) Save the `Last-Modified` date, too.

(5) If the server says that it sent compressed data, decompress it.

(6) If you got a URL back from the server, save it, and assume that the status code is `200` until you find out otherwise.

(7) If one of your custom URL handlers captured a status code, then save that, too.

And, finally, Listing 11-19 demonstrates using `openanything.py`.

Listing 11-19. Using openanything.py

```
>>> import openanything
>>> useragent = 'MyHTTPWebServicesApp/1.0'
>>> url = 'http://diveintopython.org/redir/example301.xml'
>>> params = openanything.fetch(url, agent=useragent)          (1)
>>> params                                                      (2)
{'url': 'http://diveintomark.org/xml/atom.xml',
'lastmodified': 'Thu, 15 Apr 2004 19:45:21 GMT',
'etag': '"e842a-3e53-55d97640"',
'status': 301,
'data': '<?xml version="1.0" encoding="iso-8859-1"?>
<feed version="0.3"
<-- rest of data omitted for brevity -->'}
>>> if params['status'] == 301:                                (3)
...     url = params['url']
>>> newparams = openanything.fetch(
...     url, params['etag'], params['lastmodified'], useragent) (4)
>>> newparams
{'url': 'http://diveintomark.org/xml/atom.xml',
'lastmodified': None,
'etag': '"e842a-3e53-55d97640"',
'status': 304,
'data': ''}                                                    (5)
```

(1) The very first time you fetch a resource, you don't have an ETag hash or Last-Modified date, so you'll leave those out. (They're optional parameters.)

(2) What you get back is a dictionary of several useful headers, the HTTP status code, and the actual data returned from the server. openanything handles the gzip compression internally; you don't care about that at this level.

(3) If you get a 301 status code, that's a permanent redirect, and you need to update your URL to the new address.

(4) The second time you fetch the same resource, you have all sorts of information to pass back: a (possibly updated) URL, the ETag from the last time, the Last-Modified date from the last time, and, of course, your User-Agent.

(5) Again, you get back a dictionary, but the data hasn't changed, so all you get is a 304 status code and no data.

Summary

The openanything.py script and its functions should now make perfect sense.

There are five important features of HTTP web services that every client should include:

- Identifying your application by setting a proper User-Agent

- Handling permanent redirects properly

- Supporting last-modified-date checking to avoid re-downloading data that hasn't changed

- Supporting ETag hashes to avoid re-downloading data that hasn't changed

- Supporting gzip compression to reduce bandwidth even when data *has* changed

CHAPTER 12

SOAP Web Services

CHAPTER 11 FOCUSED ON document-oriented web services over HTTP. The "input parameter" was the URL, and the "return value" was an actual XML document, which it was your responsibility to parse.

This chapter will focus on SOAP web services, which take a more structured approach. Rather than dealing with HTTP requests and XML documents directly, SOAP allows you to simulate calling functions that return native datatypes. As you'll see, the illusion is almost perfect; you can "call" a function through a SOAP library, with the standard Python calling syntax, and the function appears to return Python objects and values. But under the covers, the SOAP library has actually performed a complex transaction involving multiple XML documents and a remote server.

SOAP is a complex specification, and it is somewhat misleading to say that SOAP is all about calling remote functions. Some people would pipe up to add that SOAP allows for one-way asynchronous message passing and document-oriented web services. And those people would be correct; SOAP can be used that way and in many different ways. But this chapter will focus on so-called RPC-style SOAP—calling a remote function and getting results back.

Diving In

You use Google, right? It's a popular search engine. Have you ever wished you could programmatically access Google search results? Now you can. Listing 12-1 is a program to search Google from Python.

> **NOTE** *If you have not already done so, you can download this and other examples used in this book from the Downloads section of the Apress web site (*http://www.apress.com*).*

Listing 12-1. search.py

```
from SOAPpy import WSDL

# you'll need to configure these two values;
# see http://www.google.com/apis/
WSDLFILE = '/path/to/copy/of/GoogleSearch.wsdl'
APIKEY = 'YOUR_GOOGLE_API_KEY'
```

```
_server = WSDL.Proxy(WSDLFILE)
def search(q):
    """Search Google and return list of {title, link, description}"""
    results = _server.doGoogleSearch(
        APIKEY, q, 0, 10, False, "", False, "", "utf-8", "utf-8")
    return [{"title": r.title.encode("utf-8"),
             "link": r.URL.encode("utf-8"),
             "description": r.snippet.encode("utf-8")}
            for r in results.resultElements]

if __name__ == '__main__':
    import sys
    for r in search(sys.argv[1])[:5]:
        print r['title']
        print r['link']
        print r['description']
        print
```

You can import this as a module and use it from a larger program, or you can run the script from the command line. On the command line, you give the search query as a command-line argument, and it prints the URL, title, and description of the top-five Google search results.

Listing 12-2 shows the sample output for a search for the word *python*.

Listing 12-2. Sample Usage of search.py

```
C:\diveintopython\common\py> python search.py "python"
<b>Python</b> Programming Language
http://www.python.org/
Home page for <b>Python</b>, an interpreted, interactive, object-oriented,
extensible<br> programming language. <b>...</b> <b>Python</b>
is OSI Certified Open Source: OSI Certified.

<b>Python</b> Documentation Index
http://www.python.org/doc/
 <b>...</b> New-style classes (aka descrintro). Regular expressions. Database
API. Email Us.<br> docs@<b>python</b>.org. (c) 2004. <b>Python</b>
Software Foundation. <b>Python</b> Documentation. <b>...</b>

Download <b>Python</b> Software
http://www.python.org/download/
Download Standard <b>Python</b> Software. <b>Python</b> 2.3.3 is the
current production<br> version of <b>Python</b>. <b>...</b>
<b>Python</b> is OSI Certified Open Source:
```

Pythonline
http://www.pythonline.com/

Dive Into Python
http://diveintopython.org/
Dive Into Python. Python from novice to pro. Find:
... It is also available in multiple
 languages. Read
Dive Into Python. This book is still being written. ...

Installing the SOAP Libraries

Unlike the other code in this book, this chapter relies on libraries that do not come preinstalled with Python. Before you can dive into SOAP web services, you'll need to install three libraries: PyXML, fpconst, and SOAPpy.

Installing PyXML

The first library you need is PyXML, which is an advanced set of XML libraries that provide more functionality than the built-in XML libraries we studied in Chapter 9.
Here is the procedure for installing PyXML:

1. Go to http://pyxml.sourceforge.net, click Downloads, and download the latest version for your operating system. If you are using Windows, there are several choices. Make sure to download the version of PyXML that matches the version of Python you are using.

2. Double-click the installer. If you download PyXML 0.8.3 for Windows and Python 2.3, the installer program will be PyXML-0.8.3.win32-py2.3.exe.

3. Step through the installer program.

4. After the installation is complete, close the installer. There will not be any visible indication of success (no programs installed on the Start menu or shortcuts installed on the desktop). PyXML is simply a collection of XML libraries used by other programs.

To verify that you installed PyXML correctly, run your Python IDE and check the version of the XML libraries you have installed, as shown here:

```
>>> import xml
>>> xml.__version__
'0.8.3'
```

This version number should match the version number of the PyXML installer program you downloaded and ran.

Installing *fpconst*

The second library you need is fpconst, a set of constants and functions for working with IEEE 754 (the standard for binary floating-point arithmetic) double-precision special values. This provides support for the special values Not-a-Number (NaN), Positive Infinity (Inf), and Negative Infinity (-Inf), which are part of the SOAP datatype specification.

Here is the procedure for installing fpconst:

1. Download the latest version of fpconst from http:// www.analytics.washington.edu/statcomp/projects/rzope/fpconst. There are two downloads available: one in .tar.gz format and another in .zip format. If you are using Windows, download the .zip file; otherwise, download the .tar.gz file.

2. Decompress the downloaded file. On Windows XP, you can right-click the file and choose Extract All; on earlier versions of Windows, you will need a third-party program such as WinZip. On Mac OS X, you can double-click the compressed file to decompress it with Stuffit Expander.

3. Open a command prompt and navigate to the directory where you decompressed the fpconst files.

4. Type python setup.py install to run the installation program.

To verify that you installed fpconst correctly, run your Python IDE and check the version number, as follows:

```
>>> import fpconst
>>> fpconst.__version__
'0.6.0'
```

This version number should match the version number of the fpconst archive you downloaded and installed.

Installing SOAPpy

The third and final requirement is the SOAP library itself: SOAPpy. Here is the procedure for installing SOAPpy:

1. Go to `http://pywebsvcs.sourceforge.net` and select Latest Official Release under the SOAPpy section. There are two downloads available. If you are using Windows, download the `.zip` file; otherwise, download the `.tar.gz` file.

2. Decompress the downloaded file, just as you did with fpconst.

3. Open a command prompt and navigate to the directory where you decompressed the SOAPpy files.

4. Type `python setup.py install` to run the installation program.

To verify that you installed SOAPpy correctly, run your Python IDE and check the version number, as follows:

```
>>> import SOAPpy
>>> SOAPpy.__version__
'0.11.4'
```

This version number should match the version number of the SOAPpy archive you downloaded and installed.

Taking Your First Steps with SOAP

The heart of SOAP is the ability to call remote functions. A number of public-access SOAP servers provide simple functions for demonstration purposes. The most popular public-access SOAP server is `http://www.xmethods.net/`. The example shown in Listing 12-3 uses a demonstration function that takes a United States zip code and returns the current temperature in that region.

Listing 12-3. Getting the Current Temperature

```
>>> from SOAPpy import SOAPProxy                                    (1)
>>> url = 'http://services.xmethods.net:80/soap/servlet/rpcrouter' (2)
>>> namespace = 'urn:xmethods-Temperature'                         (3)
>>> server = SOAPProxy(url, namespace)                             (4)
>>> server.getTemp('27502')                                        (5)
80.0
```

(1) You access the remote SOAP server through a proxy class, SOAPProxy. The proxy handles all the internals of SOAP for you, including creating the XML request document out of the function name and argument list, sending the request over HTTP to the remote SOAP server, parsing the XML response document, and creating native Python values to return. You'll see what these XML documents look like in the next section.

(2) Every SOAP service has a URL that handles all the requests. The same URL is used for all function calls. This particular service has only a single function, but later in this chapter, you'll see examples of the Google API, which has several functions. The service URL is shared by all functions.

(3) Each SOAP service also has a namespace, which is defined by the server and is completely arbitrary. It's simply part of the configuration required to call SOAP methods. It allows the server to share a single service URL and route requests between several unrelated services. It's like dividing Python modules into packages.

(4) You're creating the SOAPProxy with the service URL and the service namespace. This doesn't make any connection to the SOAP server; it simply creates a local Python object.

(5) Now, with everything configured properly, you can actually call remote SOAP methods as if they were local functions. You pass arguments just as you do with a normal function, and you get a return value just as you do with a normal function. But under the covers, there's a heck of a lot going on.

Let's peek under those covers.

Debugging SOAP Web Services

The SOAP libraries provide an easy way to see what's going on behind the scenes. Turning on debugging is a simple matter of setting two flags in the SOAPProxy's configuration, as shown in Listing 12-4.

Listing 12-4. Debugging SOAP Web Services

```
>>> from SOAPpy import SOAPProxy
>>> url = 'http://services.xmethods.net:80/soap/servlet/rpcrouter'
>>> n = 'urn:xmethods-Temperature'
>>> server = SOAPProxy(url, namespace=n)              (1)
>>> server.config.dumpSOAPOut = 1                      (2)
>>> server.config.dumpSOAPIn = 1
>>> temperature = server.getTemp('27502')              (3)
*** Outgoing SOAP ******************************************************
<?xml version="1.0" encoding="UTF-8"?>
<SOAP-ENV:Envelope SOAP-
ENV:encodingStyle="http://schemas.xmlsoap.org/soap/encoding/"
   xmlns:SOAP-ENC="http://schemas.xmlsoap.org/soap/encoding/"
   xmlns:xsi="http://www.w3.org/1999/XMLSchema-instance"
```

```
   xmlns:SOAP-ENV="http://schemas.xmlsoap.org/soap/envelope/"
   xmlns:xsd="http://www.w3.org/1999/XMLSchema">
<SOAP-ENV:Body>
<ns1:getTemp xmlns:ns1="urn:xmethods-Temperature" SOAP-ENC:root="1">
<v1 xsi:type="xsd:string">27502</v1>
</ns1:getTemp>
</SOAP-ENV:Body>
</SOAP-ENV:Envelope>
*************************************************************************
*** Incoming SOAP ****************************************************
<?xml version='1.0' encoding='UTF-8'?>
<SOAP-ENV:Envelope xmlns:SOAP-ENV="http://schemas.xmlsoap.org/soap/envelope/"
   xmlns:xsi="http://www.w3.org/2001/XMLSchema-instance"
   xmlns:xsd="http://www.w3.org/2001/XMLSchema">
<SOAP-ENV:Body>
<ns1:getTempResponse xmlns:ns1="urn:xmethods-Temperature"
   SOAP-ENV:encodingStyle="http://schemas.xmlsoap.org/soap/encoding/">
<return xsi:type="xsd:float">80.0</return>
</ns1:getTempResponse>

</SOAP-ENV:Body>
</SOAP-ENV:Envelope>
*************************************************************************


>>> temperature
80.0
```

(1) First, create the SOAPProxy in the normal way, with the service URL and the namespace.

(2) Second, turn on debugging by setting server.config.dumpSOAPIn and server.config.dumpSOAPOut.

(3) Third, call the remote SOAP method as usual. The SOAP library will print both the outgoing XML request document and the incoming XML response document. This is all the hard work that SOAPProxy is doing for you. Intimidating, isn't it? Let's break it down.

Most of the XML request document that is sent to the server is just boilerplate. Ignore all the namespace declarations, since they're going to be the same (or similar) for all SOAP calls. The heart of the "function call" is this fragment within the <Body> element:

```
<ns1:getTemp                                    (1)
   xmlns:ns1="urn:xmethods-Temperature"         (2)
   SOAP-ENC:root="1">
<v1 xsi:type="xsd:string">27502</v1>            (3)
</ns1:getTemp>
```

(1) The element name is the function name, getTemp. SOAPProxy uses getattr as a dispatcher. Instead of calling separate local methods based on the method name, it actually uses the method name to construct the XML request document.

(2) The function's XML element is contained in a specific namespace, which is the namespace you specified when you created the SOAPProxy object. Don't worry about the SOAP-ENC:root; that's boilerplate, too.

(3) The arguments of the function also are translated into XML. SOAPProxy introspects each argument to determine its datatype (in this case, it's a string). The argument datatype goes into the xsi:type attribute, followed by the actual string value.

The XML return document is equally easy to understand, once you know what to ignore. Focus on this fragment within the <Body>:

```
<ns1:getTempResponse                              (1)
  xmlns:ns1="urn:xmethods-Temperature"            (2)
  SOAP-ENV:encodingStyle="http://schemas.xmlsoap.org/soap/encoding/">
<return xsi:type="xsd:float">80.0</return>        (3)
</ns1:getTempResponse>
```

(1) The server wraps the function return value within a <getTempResponse> element. By convention, this wrapper element is the name of the function, plus Response. But it could be almost anything. The important item that SOAPProxy notices is not the element name, but the namespace.

(2) The server returns the response in the same namespace you used in the request, which is the same namespace you specified when you first created the SOAPProxy. Later in this chapter, in the "Troubleshooting SOAP Web Services" section, you'll see what happens if you forget to specify the namespace when creating the SOAPProxy.

(3) The return value is specified, along with its datatype (it's a float). SOAPProxy uses this explicit datatype to create a Python object of the correct, native datatype and return that object.

Further Reading on SOAP

For more information about SOAP, refer to the following:

- http://www.xmethods.net/ is a repository of public-access SOAP web services.

- The SOAP specification (http://www.w3.org/TR/soap) is surprisingly readable, if you like that sort of thing.

Introducing WSDL

The SOAPProxy class proxies local method calls and transparently turns then into invocations of remote SOAP methods. As you've seen, this is a lot of work, and SOAPProxy does it quickly and transparently. What it doesn't do is provide any means of method introspection.

Consider this: the previous section showed an example of calling a simple remote SOAP method with one argument and one return value, both of simple datatypes. This required knowing, and keeping track of, the service URL, the service namespace, the function name, the number of arguments, and the datatype of each argument. If any of these is missing or wrong, the whole thing falls apart.

That shouldn't come as a big surprise. If you wanted to call a local function, you would need to know which package or module it was in (the equivalent of service URL and namespace). You would need to know the correct function name and the correct number of arguments. Python deftly handles datatyping without explicit types, but you would still need to know how many arguments to pass and how many return values to expect.

The big difference is introspection. As you saw in Chapter 4, Python excels at letting you discover things about modules and functions at runtime. You can list the available functions within a module, and with a little work, drill down to individual function declarations and arguments. WSDL lets you do that with SOAP web services.

WSDL stands for Web Services Description Language. Although WSDL is designed to be flexible enough to describe many types of web services, it is most often used to describe SOAP web services. Like many things in the web services arena, WSDL has a long and checkered history, full of political strife and intrigue. I will skip over this history entirely, since it bores me to tears. There were other standards that tried to do similar things, but WSDL won, so let's learn how to use it.

Using a WSDL File

A WSDL file is just that: a file. More specifically, it's an XML file. It usually lives on the same server you use to access the SOAP web services it describes, although there's nothing special about it. Later in this chapter, in the "Searching Google" section, you'll download the WSDL file for the Google API and use it locally. That doesn't mean you're calling Google locally; the WSDL file still describes the remote functions sitting on Google's server.

A WSDL file contains a description of everything involved in calling a SOAP web service:

- The service URL and namespace

- The type of web service (probably function calls using SOAP, although as I mentioned, WSDL is flexible enough to describe a wide variety of web services)

- The list of available functions

- The arguments for each function

- The datatype of each argument

- The return values of each function and the datatype of each return value

In other words, a WSDL file tells you everything you need to know to be able to call a SOAP web service.

Introspecting SOAP Web Services with WSDL

The most fundamental thing that WSDL allows you to do is discover the available methods offered by a SOAP server, as demonstrated in Listing 12-5.

Listing 12-5. Discovering the Available Methods

```
>>> from SOAPpy import WSDL                             (1)
>>> wsdlFile = 'http://www.xmethods.net/sd/2001/TemperatureService.wsdl')
>>> server = WSDL.Proxy(wsdlFile)                       (2)
>>> server.methods.keys()                               (3)
[u'getTemp']
```

(1) SOAPpy includes a WSDL parser. At the time of this writing, it was labeled as being in the early stages of development, but I had no problem parsing any of the WSDL files I tried.

(2) To use a WSDL file, you again use a proxy class, WSDL.Proxy, which takes a single argument: the WSDL file. Notice that, in this case, you are passing in the URL of a WSDL file stored on the remote server, but the proxy class works just as well with a local copy of the WSDL file. The act of creating the WSDL proxy will download the WSDL file and parse it, so if there are any errors in the WSDL file (or it can't be fetched due to networking problems), you'll know about it immediately.

(3) The WSDL proxy class exposes the available functions as a Python dictionary, server.methods. So getting the list of available methods is as simple as calling the dictionary method keys().

Okay, so you know that this SOAP server offers a single method: getTemp. But how do you call it? The WSDL proxy object can tell you that, too, as shown in Listing 12-6.

Listing 12-6. Discovering a Method's Arguments

```
>>> callInfo = server.methods['getTemp']          (1)
>>> callInfo.inparams                             (2)
[<SOAPpy.wstools.WSDLTools.ParameterInfo instance at 0x00CF3AD0>]
>>> callInfo.inparams[0].name                     (3)
u'zipcode'
>>> callInfo.inparams[0].type                     (4)
(u'http://www.w3.org/2001/XMLSchema', u'string')
```

(1) The server.methods dictionary is filled with a SOAPpy-specific structure called CallInfo. A CallInfo object contains information about one specific function, including the function arguments.

(2) The function arguments are stored in callInfo.inparams, which is a Python list of ParameterInfo objects that hold information about each parameter.

(3) Each ParameterInfo object contains a name attribute, which is the argument name. You are not required to know the argument name to call the function through SOAP, but SOAP does support calling functions with named arguments (just like Python), and WSDL.Proxy will correctly handle mapping named arguments to the remote function, if you choose to use them.

(4) Each parameter is also explicitly typed, using datatypes defined in XML Schema. You saw this in the wire trace in the previous section. The XML Schema namespace was part of the "boilerplate" I told you to ignore. For our purposes here, you may continue to ignore it. The zipcode parameter is a string, and if you pass in a Python string to the WSDL.Proxy object, it will map it correctly and send it to the server.

WSDL also lets you introspect into a function's return values, as shown in Listing 12-7.

Listing 12-7. Discovering a Method's Return Values

```
>>> callInfo.outparams                            (1)
[<SOAPpy.wstools.WSDLTools.ParameterInfo instance at 0x00CF3AF8>]
>>> callInfo.outparams[0].name                    (2)
u'return'
>>> callInfo.outparams[0].type
(u'http://www.w3.org/2001/XMLSchema', u'float')
```

(1) The adjunct to callInfo.inparams for function arguments is callInfo.outparams for return values. It is also a list, because functions called through SOAP can return multiple values, just like Python functions.

(2) Each `ParameterInfo` object contains `name` and `type`. This function returns a single value, named `return`, which is a float.

Calling a SOAP Web Service Through a WSDL Proxy

Let's put it all together and call a SOAP web service through a WSDL proxy. Listing 12-8 shows how to do this.

Listing 12-8. Calling a Web Service Through a WSDL Proxy

```
>>> from SOAPpy import WSDL
>>> wsdlFile = 'http://www.xmethods.net/sd/2001/TemperatureService.wsdl')
>>> server = WSDL.Proxy(wsdlFile)                    (1)
>>> server.getTemp('90210')                          (2)
66.0
>>> server.soapproxy.config.dumpSOAPOut = 1          (3)
>>> server.soapproxy.config.dumpSOAPIn = 1
>>> temperature = server.getTemp('90210')
*** Outgoing SOAP ******************************************************
<?xml version="1.0" encoding="UTF-8"?>
<SOAP-ENV:Envelope SOAP-
ENV:encodingStyle="http://schemas.xmlsoap.org/soap/encoding/"
  xmlns:SOAP-ENC="http://schemas.xmlsoap.org/soap/encoding/"
  xmlns:xsi="http://www.w3.org/1999/XMLSchema-instance"
  xmlns:SOAP-ENV="http://schemas.xmlsoap.org/soap/envelope/"
  xmlns:xsd="http://www.w3.org/1999/XMLSchema">
<SOAP-ENV:Body>
<ns1:getTemp xmlns:ns1="urn:xmethods-Temperature" SOAP-ENC:root="1">
<v1 xsi:type="xsd:string">90210</v1>
</ns1:getTemp>
</SOAP-ENV:Body>
</SOAP-ENV:Envelope>
************************************************************************
*** Incoming SOAP ******************************************************
<?xml version='1.0' encoding='UTF-8'?>
<SOAP-ENV:Envelope xmlns:SOAP-ENV="http://schemas.xmlsoap.org/soap/envelope/"
  xmlns:xsi="http://www.w3.org/2001/XMLSchema-instance"
  xmlns:xsd="http://www.w3.org/2001/XMLSchema">
<SOAP-ENV:Body>
<ns1:getTempResponse xmlns:ns1="urn:xmethods-Temperature"
  SOAP-ENV:encodingStyle="http://schemas.xmlsoap.org/soap/encoding/">
<return xsi:type="xsd:float">66.0</return>
</ns1:getTempResponse>
```

```
</SOAP-ENV:Body>
</SOAP-ENV:Envelope>
**********************************************************************
```

```
>>> temperature
66.0
```

(1) The configuration is slightly simpler than calling the SOAP service directly, since the WSDL file contains both the service URL and namespace you need to call the service. Creating the WSDL.Proxy object downloads the WSDL file, parses it, and configures a SOAPProxy object that it uses to call the actual SOAP web service.

(2) Once the WSDL.Proxy object is created, you can call a function as easily as you did with the SOAPProxy object. This is not surprising; the WSDL.Proxy is just a wrapper around the SOAPProxy with some introspection methods added, so the syntax for calling functions is the same.

(3) You can access the WSDL.Proxy's SOAPProxy with server.soapproxy. This is useful to turn on debugging, so that when you call functions through the WSDL proxy, its SOAPProxy will dump the outgoing and incoming XML documents that are going over the wire.

Searching Google

Let's finally turn to the sample code that you saw at the beginning of this chapter (Listing 12-1), which does something more useful and exciting than getting the current temperature.

Google provides a SOAP API for programmatically accessing Google search results. To use it, you will need to sign up for Google Web Services, as follows:

1. Go to http://www.google.com/apis and create a Google account. This requires only an e-mail address. After you sign up, you will receive your Google API license key by e-mail. You will need this key to pass as a parameter whenever you call Google's search functions.

2. Also on http://www.google.com/apis, download the Google Web APIs developer kit. This includes some sample code in several programming languages (but not Python), and more important, it includes the WSDL file.

3. Decompress the developer kit file and find GoogleSearch.wsdl. Copy this file to some permanent location on your local drive. You will need it for the example in this chapter.

Once you have your developer key and your Google WSDL file in a known place, you can start poking around with Google Web Services. Listing 12-9 shows how to get started.

Listing 12-9. Introspecting Google Web Services

```
>>> from SOAPpy import WSDL
>>> server = WSDL.Proxy('/path/to/your/GoogleSearch.wsdl')          (1)
>>> server.methods.keys()                                          (2)
[u'doGoogleSearch', u'doGetCachedPage', u'doSpellingSuggestion']
>>> callInfo = server.methods['doGoogleSearch']
>>> for arg in callInfo.inparams:                                  (3)
...     print arg.name.ljust(15), arg.type
key             (u'http://www.w3.org/2001/XMLSchema', u'string')
q               (u'http://www.w3.org/2001/XMLSchema', u'string')
start           (u'http://www.w3.org/2001/XMLSchema', u'int')
maxResults      (u'http://www.w3.org/2001/XMLSchema', u'int')
filter          (u'http://www.w3.org/2001/XMLSchema', u'boolean')
restrict        (u'http://www.w3.org/2001/XMLSchema', u'string')
safeSearch      (u'http://www.w3.org/2001/XMLSchema', u'boolean')
lr              (u'http://www.w3.org/2001/XMLSchema', u'string')
ie              (u'http://www.w3.org/2001/XMLSchema', u'string')
oe              (u'http://www.w3.org/2001/XMLSchema', u'string')
```

(1) Getting started with Google Web Services is easy: just create a WSDL.Proxy object and point it at your local copy of Google's WSDL file.

(2) According to the WSDL file, Google offers three functions: doGoogleSearch, doGetCachedPage, and doSpellingSuggestion. These do exactly what they sound like: perform a Google search and return the results programmatically, get access to the cached version of a page from the last time Google saw it, and offer spelling suggestions for commonly misspelled search words.

(3) The doGoogleSearch function takes a number of parameters of various types. Note that while the WSDL file can tell you what the arguments are called and what datatype they are, it can't tell you what they mean or how to use them. It could theoretically tell you the acceptable range of values for each parameter, if only specific values were allowed, but Google's WSDL file is not that detailed. WSDL.Proxy can't work magic; it can only give you the information provided in the WSDL file.

Here is a brief synopsis of all the parameters to the doGoogleSearch function:

- key: Your Google API key, which you received when you signed up for Google Web Services.

- q: The search word or phrase you're looking for. The syntax is exactly the same as Google's web form, so if you know any advanced search syntax or tricks, those work here as well.

- **start**: The index of the result to start on. Like the interactive web version of Google, this function returns ten results at a time. If you wanted to get the second "page" of results, you would set start to 10.

- **maxResults**: The number of results to return. Currently capped at 10, although you can specify fewer if you are interested in only a few results and want to save a little bandwidth.

- **filter**: If True, Google will filter out duplicate pages from the results.

- **restrict**: Set this to country plus a country code to get results from only a particular country. An example is countryUK to search pages in the United Kingdom. You can also specify linux, mac, or bsd to search a Google-defined set of technical sites, or unclesam to search sites about the United States government.

- **safeSearch**: If True, Google will filter out porn sites.

- **lr**: For *language restrict*, set this to a language code to get results in only a particular language.

- **ie** and oe: For *input encoding* and *output encoding*, these are deprecated; both must be utf-8.

Now, you can search Google, as shown in Listing 12-10.

Listing 12-10. Searching Google

```
>>> from SOAPpy import WSDL
>>> server = WSDL.Proxy('/path/to/your/GoogleSearch.wsdl')
>>> key = 'YOUR_GOOGLE_API_KEY'
>>> results = server.doGoogleSearch(key, 'mark', 0, 10, False, "",
...     False, "", "utf-8", "utf-8")                        (1)
>>> len(results.resultElements)                             (2)
10
>>> results.resultElements[0].URL                           (3)
'http://diveintomark.org/'
>>> results.resultElements[0].title
'dive into <b>mark</b>'
```

(1) After setting up the WSDL.Proxy object, you can call server.doGoogleSearch with all ten parameters. Remember to use your own Google API key that you received when you signed up for Google Web Services. Although SOAP can theoretically support optional arguments, Google has defined this function so that all ten arguments are required, including the last two, which are ignored.

(2) There's a lot of information returned, but let's look at the actual search results first. They're stored in results.resultElements, and you can access them in the same way you access a normal Python list.

(3) Each element in the resultElements is an object that has a URL, title, snippet, and other useful attributes. At this point, you can use normal Python introspection techniques like dir(results.resultElements[0]) to see the available attributes. Or you can introspect through the WSDL proxy object and look through the function's outparams. Both techniques will give you the same information.

The results object contains more than the actual search results. It also contains information about the search itself, such as how long it took and how many results were found (even though only ten results were returned). The Google web interface shows this information, and you can access it programmatically, too, as shown in Listing 12-11.

Listing 12-11. Accessing Secondary Information from Google

```
>>> results.searchTime                                    (1)
0.224919
>>> results.estimatedTotalResultsCount                    (2)
29800000
>>> results.directoryCategories                           (3)
[<SOAPpy.Types.structType item at 14367400>:
 {'fullViewableName':
  'Top/Arts/Literature/World_Literature/American/19th_Century/Twain,_Mark',
  'specialEncoding': ''}]
>>> results.directoryCategories[0].fullViewableName
'Top/Arts/Literature/World_Literature/American/19th_Century/Twain,_Mark'
```

(1) This search took 0.224919 seconds. That does not include the time spent sending and receiving the actual SOAP XML documents. It's just the time that Google spent processing your request once the server received it.

(2) In total, there were approximately 30 million results. You can access them ten at a time by changing the start parameter and calling server.doGoogleSearch again.

(3) For some queries, Google also returns a list of related categories in the Google Directory (http://directory.google.com). You can append these URLs to http://directory.google.com to construct the link to the directory category page.

Troubleshooting SOAP Web Services

Of course, the world of SOAP web services is not all happiness and light. Sometimes things go wrong.

As you've seen throughout this chapter, SOAP involves several layers. There's the HTTP layer, since SOAP is sending XML documents to, and receiving XML documents from, an HTTP server. So, all the debugging techniques you learned in Chapter 11 come into play here. You can `import httplib`, and then set `httplib.HTTPConnection.debuglevel = 1` to see the underlying HTTP traffic.

Beyond the underlying HTTP layer, there are a number of things that can go wrong. SOAPpy does an admirable job hiding the SOAP syntax from you, but that also means it can be difficult to determine where the problem is when things don't work.

Here, I'll show you a few examples of common mistakes that I've made in using SOAP web services and the errors they generated.

Misconfigured Proxy

What happens when you don't set up the proxy correctly? Listing 12-12 answers that question.

Listing 12-12. Calling a Method with an Incorrectly Configured Proxy

```
>>> from SOAPpy import SOAPProxy
>>> url = 'http://services.xmethods.net:80/soap/servlet/rpcrouter'
>>> server = SOAPProxy(url)                                          (1)
>>> server.getTemp('27502')                                         (2)
<Fault SOAP-ENV:Server.BadTargetObjectURI:
Unable to determine object id from call: is the method element namespaced?>
Traceback (most recent call last):
  File "<stdin>", line 1, in ?
  File "c:\python23\Lib\site-packages\SOAPpy\Client.py", line 453, in __call__
    return self.__r_call(*args, **kw)
  File "c:\python23\Lib\site-packages\SOAPpy\Client.py", line 475, in __r_call
    self.__hd, self.__ma)
  File "c:\python23\Lib\site-packages\SOAPpy\Client.py", line 389, in __call
    raise p
SOAPpy.Types.faultType: <Fault SOAP-ENV:Server.BadTargetObjectURI:
Unable to determine object id from call: is the method element namespaced?>
```

(1) Did you spot the mistake? You're creating a `SOAPProxy` manually, and you've correctly specified the service URL, but you haven't specified the namespace. Since multiple services may be routed through the same service URL, the namespace is essential to determine which service you're trying to talk to, and therefore which method you're really calling.

(2) The server responds by sending a SOAP Fault, which SOAPpy turns into a Python exception of type SOAPpy.Types.faultType. All errors returned from any SOAP server will always be SOAP Faults, so you can easily catch this exception. In this case, the human-readable part of the SOAP Fault gives a clue to the problem: the method element is not namespaced, because the original SOAPProxy object was not configured with a service namespace.

Misconfiguring the basic elements of the SOAP service is one of the problems that WSDL aims to solve. The WSDL file contains the service URL and namespace, so you can't get it wrong. Of course, there are still other things you can get wrong.

Incorrect Method Calls

Listing 12-13 shows an example of another common SOAP-related error.

Listing 12-13. Calling a Method with the Wrong Arguments

```
>>> from SOAPpy import WSDL
>>> wsdlFile = 'http://www.xmethods.net/sd/2001/TemperatureService.wsdl'
>>> server = WSDL.Proxy(wsdlFile)
>>> temperature = server.getTemp(27502)                              (1)
<Fault SOAP-ENV:Server: Exception while handling service request:
services.temperature.TempService.getTemp(int) -- no signature match>  (2)
Traceback (most recent call last):
  File "<stdin>", line 1, in ?
  File "c:\python23\Lib\site-packages\SOAPpy\Client.py", line 453, in __call__
    return self.__r_call(*args, **kw)
  File "c:\python23\Lib\site-packages\SOAPpy\Client.py", line 475, in __r_call
    self.__hd, self.__ma)
  File "c:\python23\Lib\site-packages\SOAPpy\Client.py", line 389, in __call
    raise p
SOAPpy.Types.faultType: <Fault SOAP-ENV:Server:
    Exception while handling service request:
services.temperature.TempService.getTemp(int) -- no signature match>
```

(1) Did you spot the mistake? It's a subtle one: you're calling server.getTemp with an integer instead of a string. As you saw from introspecting the WSDL file, the getTemp() SOAP function takes a single argument, zipcode, which must be a string. WSDL.Proxy will *not* coerce datatypes for you. You need to pass the exact datatypes that the server expects.

(2) Again, the server returns a SOAP Fault, and the human-readable part of the error gives a clue as to the problem: you're calling a getTemp function with an integer value, but there is no function defined with that name that takes an integer. In theory, SOAP allows you to *overload* functions, so you could have two functions in the same SOAP service with the same name and the same number of arguments. However, the arguments here are of different datatypes. This is why it's important to match the datatypes exactly, and why `WSDL.Proxy` doesn't coerce datatypes for you. If it did, you could end up calling a completely different function! Good luck debugging that one. It's much easier to be picky about datatypes and fail as quickly as possible if you get them wrong.

It's also possible to write Python code that expects a different number of return values than the remote function actually returns, as you can see in Listing 12-14.

Listing 12-14. Calling a Method and Expecting the Wrong Number of Return Values

```
>>> from SOAPpy import WSDL
>>> wsdlFile = 'http://www.xmethods.net/sd/2001/TemperatureService.wsdl'
>>> server = WSDL.Proxy(wsdlFile)
>>> (city, temperature) = server.getTemp('27502')                    (1)
Traceback (most recent call last):
  File "<stdin>", line 1, in ?
TypeError: unpack non-sequence
```

(1) Did you spot the mistake? `server.getTemp` returns only one value, a float, but you've written code that assumes you're getting two values and trying to assign them to two different variables. Note that this does not fail with a SOAP Fault. As far as the remote server is concerned, nothing went wrong. The error occurred only *after* the SOAP transaction was complete, `WSDL.Proxy` returned a float, and your local Python interpreter tried to accommodate your request to split it into two different variables. Since the function returned only one value, you get a Python exception, not a SOAP Fault.

Intermittent Failures

There is one other type of problem, which can be maddening to debug: intermittent failures due to heavy server load. Listing 12-15 shows an example.

Listing 12-15. Spotting Intermittent Failures

```
>>> from SOAPpy import WSDL
>>> wsdlFile = 'http://www.xmethods.net/sd/2001/TemperatureService.wsdl'
>>> server = WSDL.Proxy(wsdlFile)
>>> temperature = server.getTemp('27502')
<Fault SOAP-ENV:Server: Exception from service object:
Connection refused>                                                  (1)
Traceback (most recent call last):
  File "<stdin>", line 1, in ?
  File "c:\python23\Lib\site-packages\SOAPpy\Client.py", line 453, in __call__
    return self.__r_call(*args, **kw)
```

```
  File "c:\python23\Lib\site-packages\SOAPpy\Client.py", line 475, in __r_call
    self.__hd, self.__ma)
  File "c:\python23\Lib\site-packages\SOAPpy\Client.py", line 389, in __call
    raise p
SOAPpy.Types.faultType: <Fault SOAP-ENV:Server: Exception from service object:
Connection refused>
```

(1) You did nothing wrong here. The problem is entirely on the server. When the server is overloaded (as is common for a public-access demonstration server), it refuses to process requests. The error comes back as a SOAP Fault that says `Connection refused`. There is no way to fix this yourself. Try the same query again a few seconds later, and it will probably work correctly.

Application Errors

What about Google's web service? I've never had the server intermittently fail on me. The most common problem I've had with it is that I forgot to set the application key properly. Listing 12-16 shows what happens.

Listing 12-16. Calling a Method with an Application-Specific Error

```
>>> from SOAPpy import WSDL
>>> server = WSDL.Proxy(r'/path/to/local/GoogleSearch.wsdl')
>>> results = server.doGoogleSearch('foo', 'mark', 0, 10, False, "",      (1)
...      False, "", "utf-8", "utf-8")
<Fault SOAP-ENV:Server:                                                   (2)
 Exception from service object: Invalid authorization key: foo:
 <SOAPpy.Types.structType detail at 14164616>:
 {'stackTrace':
  'com.google.soap.search.GoogleSearchFault: Invalid authorization key: foo
   at com.google.soap.search.QueryLimits.lookUpAndLoadFromINSIfNeedBe(
     QueryLimits.java:220)
   at com.google.soap.search.QueryLimits.validateKey(QueryLimits.java:127)
   at com.google.soap.search.GoogleSearchService.doPublicMethodChecks(
     GoogleSearchService.java:825)
   at com.google.soap.search.GoogleSearchService.doGoogleSearch(
     GoogleSearchService.java:121)
   at sun.reflect.GeneratedMethodAccessor13.invoke(Unknown Source)
   at sun.reflect.DelegatingMethodAccessorImpl.invoke(Unknown Source)
   at java.lang.reflect.Method.invoke(Unknown Source)
   at org.apache.soap.server.RPCRouter.invoke(RPCRouter.java:146)
   at org.apache.soap.providers.RPCJavaProvider.invoke(
     RPCJavaProvider.java:129)
```

```
    at org.apache.soap.server.http.RPCRouterServlet.doPost(
      RPCRouterServlet.java:288)
    at javax.servlet.http.HttpServlet.service(HttpServlet.java:760)
    at javax.servlet.http.HttpServlet.service(HttpServlet.java:853)
    at com.google.gse.HttpConnection.runServlet(HttpConnection.java:237)
    at com.google.gse.HttpConnection.run(HttpConnection.java:195)
    at com.google.gse.DispatchQueue$WorkerThread.run(DispatchQueue.java:201)
Caused by: com.google.soap.search.UserKeyInvalidException: Key was of wrong size.
    at com.google.soap.search.UserKey.<init>(UserKey.java:59)
    at com.google.soap.search.QueryLimits.lookUpAndLoadFromINSIfNeedBe(
      QueryLimits.java:217)
    ... 14 more
'}>
Traceback (most recent call last):
  File "<stdin>", line 1, in ?
  File "c:\python23\Lib\site-packages\SOAPpy\Client.py", line 453, in __call__
    return self.__r_call(*args, **kw)
  File "c:\python23\Lib\site-packages\SOAPpy\Client.py", line 475, in __r_call
    self.__hd, self.__ma)
  File "c:\python23\Lib\site-packages\SOAPpy\Client.py", line 389, in __call
    raise p
SOAPpy.Types.faultType: <Fault SOAP-ENV:Server: Exception from service object:
Invalid authorization key: foo:
<SOAPpy.Types.structType detail at 14164616>:
{'stackTrace':
  'com.google.soap.search.GoogleSearchFault: Invalid authorization key: foo
    at com.google.soap.search.QueryLimits.lookUpAndLoadFromINSIfNeedBe(
      QueryLimits.java:220)
    at com.google.soap.search.QueryLimits.validateKey(QueryLimits.java:127)
    at com.google.soap.search.GoogleSearchService.doPublicMethodChecks(
      GoogleSearchService.java:825)
    at com.google.soap.search.GoogleSearchService.doGoogleSearch(
      GoogleSearchService.java:121)
    at sun.reflect.GeneratedMethodAccessor13.invoke(Unknown Source)
    at sun.reflect.DelegatingMethodAccessorImpl.invoke(Unknown Source)
    at java.lang.reflect.Method.invoke(Unknown Source)
    at org.apache.soap.server.RPCRouter.invoke(RPCRouter.java:146)
    at org.apache.soap.providers.RPCJavaProvider.invoke(
      RPCJavaProvider.java:129)
    at org.apache.soap.server.http.RPCRouterServlet.doPost(
      RPCRouterServlet.java:288)
    at javax.servlet.http.HttpServlet.service(HttpServlet.java:760)
    at javax.servlet.http.HttpServlet.service(HttpServlet.java:853)
    at com.google.gse.HttpConnection.runServlet(HttpConnection.java:237)
```

```
    at com.google.gse.HttpConnection.run(HttpConnection.java:195)
    at com.google.gse.DispatchQueue$WorkerThread.run(DispatchQueue.java:201)
Caused by: com.google.soap.search.UserKeyInvalidException: Key was of wrong size.
    at com.google.soap.search.UserKey.<init>(UserKey.java:59)
    at com.google.soap.search.QueryLimits.lookUpAndLoadFromINSIfNeedBe(
    QueryLimits.java:217)
    ... 14 more
'}>
```

(1) Can you spot the mistake? There's nothing wrong with the calling syntax, the number of arguments, or the datatypes. The problem is application-specific: the first argument is supposed to be my application key, but foo is not a valid Google key.

(2) The Google server responds with a SOAP Fault and an incredibly long error message, which includes a complete Java stack trace. Remember that *all* SOAP errors are signified by SOAP Faults: errors in configuration, errors in function arguments, and application-specific errors like this. Buried in there somewhere is the crucial piece of information: Invalid authorization key: foo.

Further Reading on Troubleshooting SOAP

For more information about troubleshooting SOAP, refer to the following:

- New developments for SOAPpy (http://www-106.ibm.com/developerworks/ webservices/library/ws-pyth17.html) steps through trying to connect to another SOAP service that doesn't quite work as advertised.

Summary

SOAP web services are complicated. The specification is ambitious and tries to cover many different use cases for web services. This chapter has touched on some of the simpler use cases.

Before diving into the next chapter, make sure you're comfortable doing all of these things:

- Connecting to a SOAP server and calling remote methods

- Loading a WSDL file and introspecting remote methods

- Debugging SOAP calls with wire traces

- Troubleshooting common SOAP-related errors

CHAPTER 13

Unit Testing

IN PREVIOUS CHAPTERS, we "dived in" by immediately looking at code and trying to understand it as quickly as possible. Now that you have some Python under your belt, we're going to look at the steps that happen *before* the code gets written.

In this and the next few chapters, we're going to write, debug, and optimize a set of utility functions to convert to and from Roman numerals. We discussed the mechanics of constructing and validating Roman numerals in Chapter 7, but now let's step back and consider what it would take to expand that into a two-way utility.

Diving In

The rules for Roman numerals lead to a number of interesting observations:

- There is only one correct way to represent a particular number as a Roman numeral.

- The converse is also true: if a string of characters is a valid Roman numeral, it represents only one number (that is, it can be read only one way).

- A limited range of numbers can be expressed as Roman numerals, specifically 1 through 3,999.

- There is no way to represent zero in Roman numerals.

- There is no way to represent negative numbers in Roman numerals.

- There is no way to represent fractions or noninteger numbers in Roman numerals.

> **NOTE** *Amazingly, the ancient Romans had no concept of zero as a number. Numbers were for counting things you had; how can you count what you don't have? However, the Romans did have several ways of expressing larger numbers, such as by having a bar over a numeral to represent that its normal value should be multiplied by 1,000, but we're not going to deal with that. For our purposes, we will stipulate that Roman numerals go from 1 to 3,999.*

Given all of this, what would we expect out of a set of functions to convert to and from Roman numerals? Here are our requirements:

Requirement #1: toRoman should return the Roman numeral representation for all integers 1 to 3,999.

Requirement #2: toRoman should fail when given an integer outside the range 1 to 3,999.

Requirement #3: toRoman should fail when given a noninteger number.

Requirement #4: fromRoman should take a valid Roman numeral and return the number that it represents.

Requirement #5: fromRoman should fail when given an invalid Roman numeral.

Requirement #6: If you take a number, convert it to Roman numerals, then convert that back to a number, you should end up with the number you started with. So fromRoman(toRoman(n)) == n for all n in 1..3999.

Requirement #7: toRoman should always return a Roman numeral using uppercase letters.

Requirement #8: fromRoman should accept only uppercase Roman numerals (it should fail when given lowercase input).

> **TIP** http://www.wilkiecollins.demon.co.uk/roman/front.htm *has more on Roman numerals, including a fascinating history of how Romans and other civilizations really used them (short answer: haphazardly and inconsistently).*

Introducing the Test Suite

Now that we've completely defined the behavior we expect from our conversion functions, we're going to do something a little unexpected: we're going to write a test suite that puts these functions through their paces and makes sure that they behave the way we want them to behave. You read that right: we're going to write code that tests code that we haven't written yet.

This is called *unit testing*, since the set of two conversion functions can be written and tested as a unit, separate from any larger program they may become part of later. Python has a framework for unit testing, the appropriately named unittest module. unittest is included with Python 2.1 and later. Python 2.0 users can download it from pyunit.sourceforge.net http://pyunit.sourceforge.net.

Unit testing is an important part of an overall testing-centric development strategy. If you write unit tests, it is important to write them early (preferably before writing the code that they test) and to keep them updated as code and requirements change. Unit testing is not a replacement for higher-level functional or system testing, but it is important in all phases of development:

- Before writing code, it forces you to detail your requirements in a useful fashion.

- While writing code, it keeps you from overcoding. When all the test cases pass, the function is complete.

- When refactoring code, it assures you that the new version behaves the same way as the old version.

- When maintaining code, it protects you when someone comes screaming that your latest change broke their old code. ("But *sir*, all the unit tests passed when I checked it in....").

- When writing code in a team, it increases confidence that the code you're about to commit isn't going to break other people's code, because you can run their unit tests first.

> **NOTE** *I've seen this sort of thing in code sprints (where developers get together and rapidly prototype a new feature or requirement): A team breaks up the assignment, everybody takes the specifications for their task, writes unit tests for it, and then shares their unit tests with the rest of the team. That way, no one goes off too far into developing code that won't play well with others.*

Listing 13-1 shows the complete test suite for our Roman numeral conversion functions, which are yet to be written but will eventually be in roman.py. It is not immediately obvious how it all fits together; none of these classes or methods reference any of the others. There are good reasons for this, as you'll see shortly.

> **NOTE** *If you have not already done so, you can download this and other examples used in this book from the Downloads section of the Apress web site (http://www.apress.com).*

Listing 13-1. romantest.py

```
"""Unit test for roman.py"""

import roman
import unittest
```

```
class KnownValues(unittest.TestCase):
    knownValues = ( (1, 'I'),
                    (2, 'II'),
                    (3, 'III'),
                    (4, 'IV'),
                    (5, 'V'),
                    (6, 'VI'),
                    (7, 'VII'),
                    (8, 'VIII'),
                    (9, 'IX'),
                    (10, 'X'),
                    (50, 'L'),
                    (100, 'C'),
                    (500, 'D'),
                    (1000, 'M'),
                    (31, 'XXXI'),
                    (148, 'CXLVIII'),
                    (294, 'CCXCIV'),
                    (312, 'CCCXII'),
                    (421, 'CDXXI'),
                    (528, 'DXXVIII'),
                    (621, 'DCXXI'),
                    (782, 'DCCLXXXII'),
                    (870, 'DCCCLXX'),
                    (941, 'CMXLI'),
                    (1043, 'MXLIII'),
                    (1110, 'MCX'),
                    (1226, 'MCCXXVI'),
                    (1301, 'MCCCI'),
                    (1485, 'MCDLXXXV'),
                    (1509, 'MDIX'),
                    (1607, 'MDCVII'),
                    (1754, 'MDCCLIV'),
                    (1832, 'MDCCCXXXII'),
                    (1993, 'MCMXCIII'),
                    (2074, 'MMLXXIV'),
                    (2152, 'MMCLII'),
                    (2212, 'MMCCXII'),
                    (2343, 'MMCCCXLIII'),
                    (2499, 'MMCDXCIX'),
                    (2574, 'MMDLXXIV'),
                    (2646, 'MMDCXLVI'),
                    (2723, 'MMDCCXXIII'),
                    (2892, 'MMDCCCXCII'),
```

```
                        (2975, 'MMCMLXXV'),
                        (3051, 'MMMLI'),
                        (3185, 'MMMCLXXXV'),
                        (3250, 'MMMCCL'),
                        (3313, 'MMMCCCXIII'),
                        (3408, 'MMMCDVIII'),
                        (3501, 'MMMDI'),
                        (3610, 'MMMDCX'),
                        (3743, 'MMMDCCXLIII'),
                        (3844, 'MMMDCCCXLIV'),
                        (3888, 'MMMDCCCLXXXVIII'),
                        (3940, 'MMMCMXL'),
                        (3999, 'MMMCMXCIX'))

    def testToRomanKnownValues(self):
        """toRoman should give known result with known input"""
        for integer, numeral in self.knownValues:
            result = roman.toRoman(integer)
            self.assertEqual(numeral, result)

    def testFromRomanKnownValues(self):
        """fromRoman should give known result with known input"""
        for integer, numeral in self.knownValues:
            result = roman.fromRoman(numeral)
            self.assertEqual(integer, result)

class ToRomanBadInput(unittest.TestCase):
    def testTooLarge(self):
        """toRoman should fail with large input"""
        self.assertRaises(roman.OutOfRangeError, roman.toRoman, 4000)

    def testZero(self):
        """toRoman should fail with 0 input"""
        self.assertRaises(roman.OutOfRangeError, roman.toRoman, 0)

    def testNegative(self):
        """toRoman should fail with negative input"""
        self.assertRaises(roman.OutOfRangeError, roman.toRoman, -1)

    def testNonInteger(self):
        """toRoman should fail with non-integer input"""
        self.assertRaises(roman.NotIntegerError, roman.toRoman, 0.5)
```

```
class FromRomanBadInput(unittest.TestCase):
    def testTooManyRepeatedNumerals(self):
        """fromRoman should fail with too many repeated numerals"""
        for s in ('MMMM', 'DD', 'CCCC', 'LL', 'XXXX', 'VV', 'IIII'):
            self.assertRaises(roman.InvalidRomanNumeralError, roman.fromRoman, s)

    def testRepeatedPairs(self):
        """fromRoman should fail with repeated pairs of numerals"""
        for s in ('CMCM', 'CDCD', 'XCXC', 'XLXL', 'IXIX', 'IVIV'):
            self.assertRaises(roman.InvalidRomanNumeralError, roman.fromRoman, s)

    def testMalformedAntecedent(self):
        """fromRoman should fail with malformed antecedents"""
        for s in ('IIMXCC', 'VX', 'DCM', 'CMM', 'IXIV',
                  'MCMC', 'XCX', 'IVI', 'LM', 'LD', 'LC'):
            self.assertRaises(roman.InvalidRomanNumeralError, roman.fromRoman, s)

class SanityCheck(unittest.TestCase):
    def testSanity(self):
        """fromRoman(toRoman(n))==n for all n"""
        for integer in range(1, 4000):
            numeral = roman.toRoman(integer)
            result = roman.fromRoman(numeral)
            self.assertEqual(integer, result)

class CaseCheck(unittest.TestCase):
    def testToRomanCase(self):
        """toRoman should always return uppercase"""
        for integer in range(1, 4000):
            numeral = roman.toRoman(integer)
            self.assertEqual(numeral, numeral.upper())

    def testFromRomanCase(self):
        """fromRoman should only accept uppercase input"""
        for integer in range(1, 4000):
            numeral = roman.toRoman(integer)
            roman.fromRoman(numeral.upper())
            self.assertRaises(roman.InvalidRomanNumeralError,
                              roman.fromRoman, numeral.lower())

if __name__ == "__main__":
    unittest.main()
```

Further Reading on Python Unit Testing

For more information aboutwriting unit tests, refer to the following:

- The PyUnit home page (`http://pyunit.sourceforge.net`) has an in-depth discussion of using the `unittest` framework, including advanced features not covered in this chapter (`http://pyunit.sourceforge.net/pyunit.html`).

- The PyUnit FAQ (`http://pyunit.sourceforge.net/pyunit.html`) explains why test cases are stored separately from the code they test (`http://pyunit.sourceforge.net/pyunit.html#WHERE`).

- *Python Library Reference* (`http://www.python.org/doc/current/lib`) summarizes the `unittest` module (`http://www.python.org/doc/current/lib/module-unittest.html`).

- ExtremeProgramming.org (`http://www.extremeprogramming.org/`) discusses why you should write unit tests (`http://www.extremeprogramming.org/rules/unittests.html`).

- The Portland Pattern Repository (`http://www.c2.com/cgi/wiki`) has an ongoing discussion of unit tests (`http://www.c2.com/cgi/wiki?UnitTests`), including a standard definition (`http://www.c2.com/cgi/wiki?StandardDefinitionOfUnitTest`), why you should code unit tests first (`http://www.c2.com/cgi/wiki?CodeUnitTestFirst`), and several in-depth case studies (`http://www.c2.com/cgi/wiki?UnitTestTrial`).

Constructing Test Cases

The most fundamental part of unit testing is constructing individual test cases. A test case answers a single question about the code it is testing.

A test case should be able to do the following:

- Run completely by itself, without any human input. Unit testing is about automation.

- Determine by itself whether the function it is testing has passed or failed, without a human interpreting the results.

- Run in isolation, separate from any other test cases (even if they test the same functions). Each test case is an island.

Given that, let's build our test cases.

Testing for Success

As identified in the "Diving In" section at the beginning of the chapter, we have the following requirement:

- **Requirement #1:** toRoman should return the Roman numeral representation for all integers 1 to 3,999.

Listing 13-2 shows the test case for this requirement.

Listing 13-2. testToRomanKnownValues

```
class KnownValues(unittest.TestCase):                    (1)
    knownValues = ( (1, 'I'),
                    (2, 'II'),
                    (3, 'III'),
                    (4, 'IV'),
                    (5, 'V'),
                    (6, 'VI'),
                    (7, 'VII'),
                    (8, 'VIII'),
                    (9, 'IX'),
                    (10, 'X'),
                    (50, 'L'),
                    (100, 'C'),
                    (500, 'D'),
                    (1000, 'M'),
                    (31, 'XXXI'),
                    (148, 'CXLVIII'),
                    (294, 'CCXCIV'),
                    (312, 'CCCXII'),
                    (421, 'CDXXI'),
                    (528, 'DXXVIII'),
                    (621, 'DCXXI'),
                    (782, 'DCCLXXXII'),
                    (870, 'DCCCLXX'),
                    (941, 'CMXLI'),
                    (1043, 'MXLIII'),
                    (1110, 'MCX'),
                    (1226, 'MCCXXVI'),
                    (1301, 'MCCCI'),
                    (1485, 'MCDLXXXV'),
                    (1509, 'MDIX'),
                    (1607, 'MDCVII'),
```

```
                (1754, 'MDCCLIV'),
                (1832, 'MDCCCXXXII'),
                (1993, 'MCMXCIII'),
                (2074, 'MMLXXIV'),
                (2152, 'MMCLII'),
                (2212, 'MMCCXII'),
                (2343, 'MMCCCXLIII'),
                (2499, 'MMCDXCIX'),
                (2574, 'MMDLXXIV'),
                (2646, 'MMDCXLVI'),
                (2723, 'MMDCCXXIII'),
                (2892, 'MMDCCCXCII'),
                (2975, 'MMCMLXXV'),
                (3051, 'MMMLI'),
                (3185, 'MMMCLXXXV'),
                (3250, 'MMMCCL'),
                (3313, 'MMMCCCXIII'),
                (3408, 'MMMCDVIII'),
                (3501, 'MMMDI'),
                (3610, 'MMMDCX'),
                (3743, 'MMMDCCXLIII'),
                (3844, 'MMMDCCCXLIV'),
                (3888, 'MMMDCCCLXXXVIII'),
                (3940, 'MMMCMXL'),
                (3999, 'MMMCMXCIX'))                          (2)


    def testToRomanKnownValues(self):                          (3)
        """toRoman should give known result with known input"""
        for integer, numeral in self.knownValues:
            result = roman.toRoman(integer)                    (4) (5)
            self.assertEqual(numeral, result)                  (6)
```

(1) To write a test case, first subclass the `TestCase` class of the `unittest` module. This class provides many useful methods that you can use in your test case to test specific conditions.

(2) This is a list of integer/numeral pairs that I verified manually. It includes the lowest ten numbers, the highest number, every number that translates to a single-character Roman numeral, and a random sampling of other valid numbers. The point of a unit test is not to test every possible input, but to test a representative sample.

(3) Every individual test is its own method, which must take no parameters and return no value. If the method exits normally without raising an exception, the test is considered passed; if the method raises an exception, the test is considered failed.

(4) Here, we call the actual toRoman function. (Well, the function hasn't been written yet, but once it is, this is the line that will call it.) Notice that we have now defined the API for the toRoman function: it must take an integer (the number to convert) and return a string (the Roman numeral representation). If the API is different, this test is considered failed.

(5) Also notice that we are not trapping any exceptions when we call toRoman. This is intentional. toRoman shouldn't raise an exception when we call it with valid input, and these input values are all valid. If toRoman raises an exception, this test is considered failed.

(6) Assuming the toRoman function was defined correctly, called correctly, completed successfully, and returned a value, the last step is to check whether it returned the *right* value. This is a common question, and the TestCase class provides a method, assertEqual, to check whether two values are equal. If the result returned from toRoman (result) does not match the known value we were expecting (numeral), assertEqual will raise an exception, and the test will fail. If the two values are equal, assertEqual will do nothing. If every value returned from toRoman matches the known value we expect, assertEqual never raises an exception, so testToRomanKnownValues eventually exits normally, which means toRoman has passed this test.

Testing for Failure

It is not enough to test that your functions succeed when given good input; you must also test that they fail when given bad input. And not just any sort of failure—they must fail in the way we expect.

Remember two of our other requirements for toRoman:

- **Requirement #2:** toRoman should fail when given an integer outside the range 1 to 3,999.

- **Requirement #3:** toRoman should fail when given a noninteger number.

In Python, functions indicate failure by raising exceptions. The unittest module provides methods for testing whether a function raises a particular exception when given bad input. Listing 13-3 shows the test for bad input to the toRoman function.

Listing 13-3. Testing Bad Input to toRoman

```
class ToRomanBadInput(unittest.TestCase):
    def testTooLarge(self):
        """toRoman should fail with large input"""
        self.assertRaises(roman.OutOfRangeError, roman.toRoman, 4000)    (1)
```

```
    def testZero(self):
        """toRoman should fail with 0 input"""
        self.assertRaises(roman.OutOfRangeError, roman.toRoman, 0)          (2)

    def testNegative(self):
        """toRoman should fail with negative input"""
        self.assertRaises(roman.OutOfRangeError, roman.toRoman, -1)

    def testNonInteger(self):
        """toRoman should fail with non-integer input"""
        self.assertRaises(roman.NotIntegerError, roman.toRoman, 0.5)        (3)
```

(1) The `TestCase` class of the `unittest` provides the `assertRaises` method, which takes the following arguments: the exception you're expecting, the function you're testing, and the arguments you're passing that function. (If the function you're testing takes more than one argument, pass all of the arguments to `assertRaises`, in order, and it will pass them right along to the function you're testing.) Pay close attention to what we're doing here: instead of calling `toRoman` directly and manually checking that it raises a particular exception (by wrapping it in a `try...except` block), `assertRaises` has encapsulated all of that for us. All we do is give it the exception (`roman.OutOfRangeError`), the function (`toRoman`), and `toRoman`'s arguments (4000), and `assertRaises` takes care of calling `toRoman` and checking to make sure that it raises `roman.OutOfRangeError`. Also notice that we're passing the `toRoman` function itself as an argument; we're not calling it, and we're not passing the name of it as a string. (Have I mentioned recently how handy it is that everything in Python is an object, including functions and exceptions?)

(2) Along with testing numbers that are too large, we need to test numbers that are too small. Remember, Roman numerals cannot express zero or negative numbers, so we have a test case for each of those (`testZero` and `testNegative`). In `testZero`, we are testing that `toRoman` raises a `roman.OutOfRangeError` exception when called with 0. If it does *not* raise a `roman.OutOfRangeError` (either because it returns an actual value or because it raises some other exception), this test is considered failed.

(3) Requirement #3 specifies that `toRoman` cannot accept a noninteger number, so here we test to make sure that `toRoman` raises a `roman.NotIntegerError` exception when called with 0.5. If `toRoman` does not raise a `roman.NotIntegerError`, this test is considered failed.

The next two requirements are similar to the first three, except they apply to `fromRoman` instead of `toRoman`:

- **Requirement #4:** `fromRoman` should take a valid Roman numeral and return the number that it represents.

- **Requirement #5:** `fromRoman` should fail when given an invalid Roman numeral.

Requirement #4 is handled in the same way as requirement #1, iterating through a sampling of known values and testing each in turn. Requirement #5 is handled in the same way as requirements #2 and #3, by testing a series of bad inputs and making sure fromRoman raises the appropriate exception, as shown in Listing 13-4.

Listing 13-4. Testing Bad Input to fromRoman

```
class FromRomanBadInput(unittest.TestCase):
  def testTooManyRepeatedNumerals(self):
      """fromRoman should fail with too many repeated numerals"""
      for s in ('MMMM', 'DD', 'CCCC', 'LL', 'XXXX', 'VV', 'IIII'):
          self.assertRaises(roman.InvalidRomanNumeralError, roman.fromRoman, s) (1)

  def testRepeatedPairs(self):
      """fromRoman should fail with repeated pairs of numerals"""
      for s in ('CMCM', 'CDCD', 'XCXC', 'XLXL', 'IXIX', 'IVIV'):
          self.assertRaises(roman.InvalidRomanNumeralError, roman.fromRoman, s)

  def testMalformedAntecedent(self):
      """fromRoman should fail with malformed antecedents"""
      for s in ('IIMXCC', 'VX', 'DCM', 'CMM', 'IXIV',
                'MCMC', 'XCX', 'IVI', 'LM', 'LD', 'LC'):
          self.assertRaises(roman.InvalidRomanNumeralError, roman.fromRoman, s)
```

(1) Not much new to say here. The pattern is exactly the same as the one we used to test bad input to toRoman. However, notice that we have another exception: roman.InvalidRomanNumeralError. That makes a total of three custom exceptions that will need to be defined in roman.py: InvalidRomanNumeralError, roman.OutOfRangeError and roman.NotIntegerError. You'll see how to define these custom exceptions when we actually start writing roman.py in Chapter 14.

Testing for Sanity

Often, you will find that a unit of code contains a set of reciprocal functions, usually in the form of conversion functions, where one converts A to B and the other converts B to A. In these cases, it is useful to create a "sanity check" to make sure that you can convert A to B and back to A without losing precision, incurring rounding errors, or triggering any other sort of bug.

Consider this requirement:

- **Requirement #6:** If you take a number, convert it to Roman numerals, and then convert that back to a number, you should end up with the number you started with. So fromRoman(toRoman(n)) == n for all n in 1..3999.

Listing 13-5 shows the sanity check test.

Listing 13-5. Testing toRoman *against* fromRoman

```
class SanityCheck(unittest.TestCase):
    def testSanity(self):
        """fromRoman(toRoman(n))==n for all n"""
        for integer in range(1, 4000):                    (1) (2)
            numeral = roman.toRoman(integer)
            result = roman.fromRoman(numeral)
            self.assertEqual(integer, result)             (3)
```

(1) You've seen the range function before, but here it is called with two arguments. This form returns a list of integers starting at the first argument (1) and counting consecutively up to *but not including* the second argument (4000). Thus, it counts 1..3999, which is the valid range for converting to Roman numerals.

(2) I just wanted to mention in passing that integer is not a keyword in Python. Here it's just a variable name like any other.

(3) The actual testing logic here is straightforward: take a number (integer), convert it to a Roman numeral (numeral), and then convert it back to a number (result) and make sure you end up with the same number you started with. If not, assertEqual will raise an exception, and the test will immediately be considered failed. If all the numbers match, assertEqual will always return silently, the entire testSanity method will eventually return silently, and the test will be considered passed.

The last two requirements are different from the others because they seem both arbitrary and trivial:

- **Requirement #7:** toRoman should always return a Roman numeral using uppercase letters.

- **Requirement #8:** fromRoman should only accept uppercase Roman numerals (that is, it should fail when given lowercase input).

In fact, they are somewhat arbitrary. We could, for instance, have stipulated that fromRoman accept lowercase and mixed-case input. But they are not completely arbitrary; if toRoman is always returning uppercase output, then fromRoman must at least accept uppercase input, or our sanity check (requirement #6) would fail. The fact that it accepts *only* uppercase input is arbitrary, but as any systems integrator will tell you, case always matters, so it's worth specifying the behavior up front. And if it's worth specifying, it's worth testing. Listing 13-6 shows the test for case.

Listing 13-6. Testing for Case

```
class CaseCheck(unittest.TestCase):
    def testToRomanCase(self):
        """toRoman should always return uppercase"""
        for integer in range(1, 4000):
            numeral = roman.toRoman(integer)
            self.assertEqual(numeral, numeral.upper())              (1)

    def testFromRomanCase(self):
        """fromRoman should only accept uppercase input"""
        for integer in range(1, 4000):
            numeral = roman.toRoman(integer)
            roman.fromRoman(numeral.upper())                        (2) (3)
            self.assertRaises(roman.InvalidRomanNumeralError,
                              roman.fromRoman, numeral.lower())     (4)
```

(1) The most interesting thing about this test case is all the things it doesn't test. It doesn't test that the value returned from toRoman is correct or even consistent; those questions are answered by separate test cases. We have a whole test case just to test for uppercase-ness. You might be tempted to combine this with the sanity check, since both run through the entire range of values and call toRoman. But that would violate one of the fundamental rules: each test case should answer only a single question. Suppose that you combined this case check with the sanity check, and then that test case failed. You would need to do further analysis to figure out which part of the test case failed to determine what the problem was. If you need to analyze the results of your unit testing just to figure out what they mean, it's a sure sign that you've designed your test cases incorrectly.

(2) There's a similar lesson to be learned here: even though "we know" that toRoman always returns uppercase, we are explicitly converting its return value to uppercase here to test that fromRoman accepts uppercase input. Why? Because the fact that toRoman always returns uppercase is an independent requirement. If we changed that requirement so that, for instance, it always returned lowercase, the testToRomanCase test case would need to change, but this test case would still work. This is another fundamental rule: each test case must be able to work in isolation from any of the others. Every test case is an island.

(3) Notice that we're not assigning the return value of fromRoman to anything. This is legal syntax in Python. If a function returns a value but nobody is listening, Python just throws away the return value. In this case, that's what we want. This test case doesn't test anything about the return value—it just tests that fromRoman accepts the uppercase input without raising an exception.

(4) This is a complicated line, but it's very similar to what we did in the ToRomanBadInput and FromRomanBadInput tests. We are testing to make sure that calling a particular function (roman.fromRoman) with a particular value (numeral.lower(), the lowercase version of the current Roman numeral in the loop) raises a particular exception (`roman.InvalidRomanNumeralError`). If it does (each time through the loop), the test passes. If even one time it does something else (like raises a different exception or returns a value without raising an exception at all), the test fails.

Summary

You've identified your requirements and written test cases to test them. In the next chapter, you'll see how to write code that passes these tests.

CHAPTER 14

Test-First Programming

THE PREVIOUS CHAPTER introduced unit testing and test cases for roman.py, a set of functions to convert to and from Roman numerals. In that chapter, we wrote the tests. In this chapter, we'll write the code that those tests validate.

Diving In (Stage 1)

Now that our unit tests are complete, it's time to start writing the code that our test cases are attempting to test. We're going to do this in stages—five of them—so we can see all the unit tests fail, and then watch them pass one by one as we fill in the gaps in roman.py.

Listing 14-1 shows stage 1 of the roman.py module. This file is available in py/roman/stage1/ in the examples directory.

> **NOTE** *If you have not already done so, you can download this and other examples used in this book from the Downloads section of the Apress web site (*http://www.apress.com*).*

Listing 14-1. roman1.py

```
"""Convert to and from Roman numerals"""

#Define exceptions
class RomanError(Exception): pass                        (1)
class OutOfRangeError(RomanError): pass                   (2)
class NotIntegerError(RomanError): pass
class InvalidRomanNumeralError(RomanError): pass          (3)

def toRoman(n):
    """convert integer to Roman numeral"""
    pass                                                  (4)

def fromRoman(s):
    """convert Roman numeral to integer"""
    pass
```

(1) This is how you define your own custom exceptions in Python. Exceptions are classes, and you create your own by subclassing existing exceptions. It is strongly recommended (but not required) that you subclass `Exception`, which is the base class that all built-in exceptions inherit from. Here, we are defining `RomanError` (inherited from `Exception`) to act as the base class for all the other custom exceptions to follow. This is a matter of style; we could just as easily have inherited each individual exception from the `Exception` class directly.

(2) The `OutOfRangeError` and `NotIntegerError` exceptions will eventually be used by `toRoman` to flag various forms of invalid input, as specified in `ToRomanBadInput` (Listing 13-3 in Chapter 13).

(3) The `InvalidRomanNumeralError` exception will eventually be used by `fromRoman` to flag invalid input, as specified in `FromRomanBadInput` (Listing 13-4 in Chapter 13).

(4) At this stage, we want to define the API of each of our functions, but we don't want to code them yet, so we stub them out using the Python reserved word `pass`.

Now for the big moment (drum roll please): we're finally going to run our unit test against this stubby little module. At this point, every test case should fail. In fact, if any test case passes in stage 1, we should go back to `romantest.py` and reevaluate why we coded a test so useless that it passes with do-nothing functions.

Run `romantest1.py` with the `-v` command-line option, which will give verbose output, so you can see exactly what's going on as each test case runs. With any luck, your output should look like Listing 14-2.

Listing 14-2. Output of romantest1.py Against roman1.py

```
fromRoman should only accept uppercase input ... ERROR
toRoman should always return uppercase ... ERROR
fromRoman should fail with malformed antecedents ... FAIL
fromRoman should fail with repeated pairs of numerals ... FAIL
fromRoman should fail with too many repeated numerals ... FAIL
fromRoman should give known result with known input ... FAIL
toRoman should give known result with known input ... FAIL
fromRoman(toRoman(n))==n for all n ... FAIL
toRoman should fail with non-integer input ... FAIL
toRoman should fail with negative input ... FAIL
toRoman should fail with large input ... FAIL
toRoman should fail with 0 input ... FAIL


======================================================================
ERROR: fromRoman should only accept uppercase input
----------------------------------------------------------------------
Traceback (most recent call last):
  File "C:\diveintopython\py\roman\stage1\romantest1.py", line 154,
```

```
    in testFromRomanCase
    roman1.fromRoman(numeral.upper())
AttributeError: 'None' object has no attribute 'upper'
======================================================================
ERROR: toRoman should always return uppercase
----------------------------------------------------------------------
Traceback (most recent call last):
  File "C:\diveintopython\py\roman\stage1\romantest1.py", line 148,
    in testToRomanCase
    self.assertEqual(numeral, numeral.upper())
AttributeError: 'None' object has no attribute 'upper'
======================================================================
FAIL: fromRoman should fail with malformed antecedents
----------------------------------------------------------------------
Traceback (most recent call last):
  File "C:\diveintopython\py\roman\stage1\romantest1.py", line 133,
    in testMalformedAntecedent
    self.assertRaises(roman1.InvalidRomanNumeralError, roman1.fromRoman, s)
  File "c:\python21\lib\unittest.py", line 266, in failUnlessRaises
    raise self.failureException, excName
AssertionError: InvalidRomanNumeralError
======================================================================
FAIL: fromRoman should fail with repeated pairs of numerals
----------------------------------------------------------------------
Traceback (most recent call last):
  File "C:\diveintopython\py\roman\stage1\romantest1.py", line 127,
    in testRepeatedPairs
    self.assertRaises(roman1.InvalidRomanNumeralError, roman1.fromRoman, s)
  File "c:\python21\lib\unittest.py", line 266, in failUnlessRaises
    raise self.failureException, excName
AssertionError: InvalidRomanNumeralError
======================================================================
FAIL: fromRoman should fail with too many repeated numerals
----------------------------------------------------------------------
Traceback (most recent call last):
  File "C:\diveintopython\py\roman\stage1\romantest1.py", line 122,
    in testTooManyRepeatedNumerals
    self.assertRaises(roman1.InvalidRomanNumeralError, roman1.fromRoman, s)
  File "c:\python21\lib\unittest.py", line 266, in failUnlessRaises
    raise self.failureException, excName
AssertionError: InvalidRomanNumeralError
```

```
===========================================================================
FAIL: fromRoman should give known result with known input
---------------------------------------------------------------------------
Traceback (most recent call last):
  File "C:\diveintopython\py\roman\stage1\romantest1.py", line 99,
    in testFromRomanKnownValues
    self.assertEqual(integer, result)
  File "c:\python21\lib\unittest.py", line 273, in failUnlessEqual
    raise self.failureException, (msg or '%s != %s' % (first, second))
AssertionError: 1 != None
===========================================================================
FAIL: toRoman should give known result with known input
---------------------------------------------------------------------------
Traceback (most recent call last):
  File "C:\diveintopython\py\roman\stage1\romantest1.py", line 93,
    in testToRomanKnownValues
    self.assertEqual(numeral, result)
  File "c:\python21\lib\unittest.py", line 273, in failUnlessEqual
    raise self.failureException, (msg or '%s != %s' % (first, second))
AssertionError: I != None
===========================================================================
FAIL: fromRoman(toRoman(n))==n for all n
---------------------------------------------------------------------------
Traceback (most recent call last):
  File "C:\diveintopython\py\roman\stage1\romantest1.py", line 141,
    in testSanity
    self.assertEqual(integer, result)
  File "c:\python21\lib\unittest.py", line 273, in failUnlessEqual
    raise self.failureException, (msg or '%s != %s' % (first, second))
AssertionError: 1 != None
===========================================================================
FAIL: toRoman should fail with non-integer input
---------------------------------------------------------------------------
Traceback (most recent call last):
  File "C:\diveintopython\py\roman\stage1\romantest1.py", line 116,
    in testNonInteger
    self.assertRaises(roman1.NotIntegerError, roman1.toRoman, 0.5)
  File "c:\python21\lib\unittest.py", line 266, in failUnlessRaises
    raise self.failureException, excName
AssertionError: NotIntegerError
```

```
========================================================================
FAIL: toRoman should fail with negative input
------------------------------------------------------------------------
Traceback (most recent call last):
  File "C:\diveintopython\py\roman\stage1\romantest1.py", line 112,
    in testNegative
    self.assertRaises(roman1.OutOfRangeError, roman1.toRoman, -1)
  File "c:\python21\lib\unittest.py", line 266, in failUnlessRaises
    raise self.failureException, excName
AssertionError: OutOfRangeError
========================================================================
FAIL: toRoman should fail with large input
------------------------------------------------------------------------
Traceback (most recent call last):
  File "C:\diveintopython\py\roman\stage1\romantest1.py", line 104,
    in testTooLarge
    self.assertRaises(roman1.OutOfRangeError, roman1.toRoman, 4000)
  File "c:\python21\lib\unittest.py", line 266, in failUnlessRaises
    raise self.failureException, excName
AssertionError: OutOfRangeError
========================================================================
FAIL: toRoman should fail with 0 input                             (1)
------------------------------------------------------------------------
Traceback (most recent call last):
  File "C:\diveintopython\py\roman\stage1\romantest1.py", line 108, in testZero
    self.assertRaises(roman1.OutOfRangeError, roman1.toRoman, 0)
  File "c:\python21\lib\unittest.py", line 266, in failUnlessRaises
    raise self.failureException, excName
AssertionError: OutOfRangeError                                    (2)
------------------------------------------------------------------------
Ran 12 tests in 0.040s                                             (3)

FAILED (failures=10, errors=2)                                     (4)
```

(1) Running the script runs unittest.main(), which executes each test case, or each method defined in each class within romantest.py. For each test case, it prints the doc string of the method and whether that test passed or failed. As expected, none of our test cases passed.

(2) For each failed test case, unittest displays the trace information showing exactly what happened. In this case, our call to assertRaises (also called failUnlessRaises) raised an AssertionError because it was expecting toRoman to raise an OutOfRangeError and it didn't.

(3) After the detail, unittest displays a summary of how many tests were performed and how long the testing took.

(4) Overall, the test run failed because at least one test case did not pass. When a test case doesn't pass, unittest distinguishes between failures and errors.

A failure is a call to an `assertXYZ` method, like `assertEqual` or `assertRaises`, that fails because the asserted condition is not true or the expected exception was not raised. An error is any other sort of exception raised in the code we're testing or the unit test case itself. For instance, the `testFromRomanCase` method ("`fromRoman` should only accept uppercase input") was an error, because the call to `numeral.upper()` raised an `AttributeError` exception when `toRoman` didn't return a string. But `testZero` ("`toRoman` should fail with 0 input") was a failure, because the call to `fromRoman` did not raise the `InvalidRomanNumeral` exception that `assertRaises` was looking for.

Converting Roman Numerals, Stage 2

Now that we have the framework of our `roman` module laid out, it's time to start writing code and passing test cases. Listing 14-3 shows the "stage 2" code. This file is available in `py/roman/stage2/` in the examples directory.

Listing 14-3. roman2.py

```python
"""Convert to and from Roman numerals"""

#Define exceptions
class RomanError(Exception): pass
class OutOfRangeError(RomanError): pass
class NotIntegerError(RomanError): pass
class InvalidRomanNumeralError(RomanError): pass

#Define digit mapping
romanNumeralMap = (('M',  1000),                    (1)
                   ('CM', 900),
                   ('D',  500),
                   ('CD', 400),
                   ('C',  100),
                   ('XC', 90),
                   ('L',  50),
                   ('XL', 40),
                   ('X',  10),
                   ('IX', 9),
                   ('V',  5),
                   ('IV', 4),
                   ('I',  1))

def toRoman(n):
    """convert integer to Roman numeral"""
    result = ""
    for numeral, integer in romanNumeralMap:
```

```
        while n >= integer:                              (2)
            result += numeral
            n -= integer
    return result

def fromRoman(s):
    """convert Roman numeral to integer"""
    pass
```

(1) romanNumeralMap is a tuple of tuples that defines three things:

- The character representations of the most basic Roman numerals. Note that this is not just the single-character Roman numerals; we're also defining two-character pairs like CM (one hundred less than one thousand). This will make our toRoman code simpler later.

- The order of the Roman numerals. They are listed in descending value order, from M all the way down to I.

- The value of each Roman numeral. Each inner tuple is a pair of *(numeral, value)*.

(2) Here's where our rich data structure pays off, because we don't need any special logic to handle the subtraction rule. To convert to Roman numerals, we simply iterate through romanNumeralMap looking for the largest integer value less than or equal to our input. Once found, we add the Roman numeral representation to the end of the output, subtract the corresponding integer value from the input, lather, rinse, and repeat.

If you're not clear how toRoman works, add a print statement to the end of the while loop:

```
        while n >= integer:
            result += numeral
            n -= integer
            print 'subtracting', integer, 'from input, adding', numeral, 'to output'
```

```
>>> import roman2
>>> roman2.toRoman(1424)
subtracting 1000 from input, adding M to output
subtracting 400 from input, adding CD to output
subtracting 10 from input, adding X to output
subtracting 10 from input, adding X to output
subtracting 4 from input, adding IV to output
'MCDXXIV'
```

So toRoman appears to work, at least in our manual spot check. But will it pass the unit testing? Well no, not entirely, as shown in Listing 14-4.

> **NOTE**   *Remember to run* `romantest2.py` *with the* `-v` *command-line flag to enable verbose mode.*

Listing 14-4. Output of romantest2.py Against roman2.py

```
fromRoman should only accept uppercase input ... FAIL
toRoman should always return uppercase ... ok                              (1)
fromRoman should fail with malformed antecedents ... FAIL
fromRoman should fail with repeated pairs of numerals ... FAIL
fromRoman should fail with too many repeated numerals ... FAIL
fromRoman should give known result with known input ... FAIL
toRoman should give known result with known input ... ok                   (2)
fromRoman(toRoman(n))==n for all n ... FAIL
toRoman should fail with non-integer input ... FAIL                        (3)
toRoman should fail with negative input ... FAIL
toRoman should fail with large input ... FAIL
toRoman should fail with 0 input ... FAIL
```

(1) `toRoman` does, in fact, always return uppercase, because our `romanNumeralMap` defines the Roman numeral representations as uppercase. So this test passes.

(2) Here's the big news: this version of the `toRoman` function passes the known-values test. Remember, it's not comprehensive, but it does put the function through its paces with a variety of good inputs, including inputs that produce every single-character Roman numeral, the largest possible input (3999), and the input that produces the longest possible Roman numeral (3888). At this point, we can be reasonably confident that the function works for any good input value you could throw at it.

(3) However, the function does not "work" for bad values; it fails every single bad-input test. That makes sense, because we didn't include any checks for bad input. Those test cases look for specific exceptions to be raised (via `assertRaises`), and we're never raising them. We'll do that in the next stage.

Here's the rest of the output of the unit test, listing the details of all the failures. We're down to ten failures.

```
======================================================================
FAIL: fromRoman should only accept uppercase input
----------------------------------------------------------------------
Traceback (most recent call last):
  File "C:\diveintopython\py\roman\stage2\romantest2.py", line 156,
    in testFromRomanCase
    roman2.fromRoman, numeral.lower())
  File "c:\python21\lib\unittest.py", line 266, in failUnlessRaises
    raise self.failureException, excName
AssertionError: InvalidRomanNumeralError
```

```
=======================================================================
FAIL: fromRoman should fail with malformed antecedents
-----------------------------------------------------------------------
Traceback (most recent call last):
  File "C:\diveintopython\py\roman\stage2\romantest2.py", line 133,
    in testMalformedAntecedent
    self.assertRaises(roman2.InvalidRomanNumeralError, roman2.fromRoman, s)
  File "c:\python21\lib\unittest.py", line 266, in failUnlessRaises
    raise self.failureException, excName
AssertionError: InvalidRomanNumeralError
=======================================================================
FAIL: fromRoman should fail with repeated pairs of numerals
-----------------------------------------------------------------------
Traceback (most recent call last):
  File "C:\diveintopython\py\roman\stage2\romantest2.py", line 127,
    in testRepeatedPairs
    self.assertRaises(roman2.InvalidRomanNumeralError, roman2.fromRoman, s)
  File "c:\python21\lib\unittest.py", line 266, in failUnlessRaises
    raise self.failureException, excName
AssertionError: InvalidRomanNumeralError
=======================================================================
FAIL: fromRoman should fail with too many repeated numerals
-----------------------------------------------------------------------
Traceback (most recent call last):
  File "C:\diveintopython\py\roman\stage2\romantest2.py", line 122,
    in testTooManyRepeatedNumerals
    self.assertRaises(roman2.InvalidRomanNumeralError, roman2.fromRoman, s)
  File "c:\python21\lib\unittest.py", line 266, in failUnlessRaises
    raise self.failureException, excName
AssertionError: InvalidRomanNumeralError
=======================================================================
FAIL: fromRoman should give known result with known input
-----------------------------------------------------------------------
Traceback (most recent call last):
  File "C:\diveintopython\py\roman\stage2\romantest2.py", line 99,
    in testFromRomanKnownValues
    self.assertEqual(integer, result)
  File "c:\python21\lib\unittest.py", line 273, in failUnlessEqual
    raise self.failureException, (msg or '%s != %s' % (first, second))
AssertionError: 1 != None
```

```
=========================================================================
FAIL: fromRoman(toRoman(n))==n for all n
-------------------------------------------------------------------------
Traceback (most recent call last):
  File "C:\diveintopython\py\roman\stage2\romantest2.py", line 141,
    in testSanity
    self.assertEqual(integer, result)
  File "c:\python21\lib\unittest.py", line 273, in failUnlessEqual
    raise self.failureException, (msg or '%s != %s' % (first, second))
AssertionError: 1 != None
=========================================================================
FAIL: toRoman should fail with non-integer input
-------------------------------------------------------------------------
Traceback (most recent call last):
  File "C:\diveintopython\py\roman\stage2\romantest2.py", line 116,
    in testNonInteger
    self.assertRaises(roman2.NotIntegerError, roman2.toRoman, 0.5)
  File "c:\python21\lib\unittest.py", line 266, in failUnlessRaises
    raise self.failureException, excName
AssertionError: NotIntegerError
=========================================================================
FAIL: toRoman should fail with negative input
-------------------------------------------------------------------------
Traceback (most recent call last):
  File "C:\diveintopython\py\roman\stage2\romantest2.py", line 112,
    in testNegative
    self.assertRaises(roman2.OutOfRangeError, roman2.toRoman, -1)
  File "c:\python21\lib\unittest.py", line 266, in failUnlessRaises
    raise self.failureException, excName
AssertionError: OutOfRangeError
=========================================================================
FAIL: toRoman should fail with large input
-------------------------------------------------------------------------
Traceback (most recent call last):
  File "C:\diveintopython\py\roman\stage2\romantest2.py", line 104,
    in testTooLarge
    self.assertRaises(roman2.OutOfRangeError, roman2.toRoman, 4000)
  File "c:\python21\lib\unittest.py", line 266, in failUnlessRaises
    raise self.failureException, excName
AssertionError: OutOfRangeError
=========================================================================
FAIL: toRoman should fail with 0 input
-------------------------------------------------------------------------
Traceback (most recent call last):
  File "C:\diveintopython\py\roman\stage2\romantest2.py", line 108,
```

```
    in testZero
    self.assertRaises(roman2.OutOfRangeError, roman2.toRoman, 0)
  File "c:\python21\lib\unittest.py", line 266, in failUnlessRaises
    raise self.failureException, excName
AssertionError: OutOfRangeError
----------------------------------------------------------------------
Ran 12 tests in 0.320s

FAILED (failures=10)
```

Converting Roman Numerals, Stage 3

Now that toRoman behaves correctly with good input (integers from 1 to 3999), it's
time to make it behave correctly with bad input (everything else). Listing 14-5 shows
the "stage 3" code. This file is available in py/roman/stage3/ in the examples directory.

Listing 14-5. roman3.py

```
"""Convert to and from Roman numerals"""

#Define exceptions
class RomanError(Exception): pass
class OutOfRangeError(RomanError): pass
class NotIntegerError(RomanError): pass
class InvalidRomanNumeralError(RomanError): pass

#Define digit mapping
romanNumeralMap = (('M',  1000),
                   ('CM', 900),
                   ('D',  500),
                   ('CD', 400),
                   ('C',  100),
                   ('XC', 90),
                   ('L',  50),
                   ('XL', 40),
                   ('X',  10),
                   ('IX', 9),
                   ('V',  5),
                   ('IV', 4),
                   ('I',  1))

def toRoman(n):
    """convert integer to Roman numeral"""
```

```
    if not (0 < n < 4000):                                          (1)
        raise OutOfRangeError, "number out of range (must be 1..3999)"   (2)
    if int(n) <> n:                                                 (3)
        raise NotIntegerError, "non-integers can not be converted"

    result = ""                                                     (4)
    for numeral, integer in romanNumeralMap:
        while n >= integer:
            result += numeral
            n -= integer
    return result

def fromRoman(s):
    """convert Roman numeral to integer"""
    pass
```

(1) This is a nice Pythonic shortcut: multiple comparisons at once. This is equivalent to if not ((0 < n) and (n < 4000)), but it's much easier to read. This is our range check, and it should catch inputs that are too large, negative, or zero.

(2) You raise exceptions yourself with the raise statement. You can raise any of the built-in exceptions, or you can raise any of your custom exceptions that you've defined. The second parameter, the error message, is optional; if given, it's displayed in the traceback that is printed if the exception is never handled.

(3) This is our noninteger check. Nonintegers cannot be converted to Roman numerals.

(4) The rest of the function is unchanged.

Let's watch toRoman handle bad input:

```
>>> import roman3
>>> roman3.toRoman(4000)
Traceback (most recent call last):
  File "<interactive input>", line 1, in ?
  File "roman3.py", line 27, in toRoman
    raise OutOfRangeError, "number out of range (must be 1..3999)"
OutOfRangeError: number out of range (must be 1..3999)
>>> roman3.toRoman(1.5)
Traceback (most recent call last):
  File "<interactive input>", line 1, in ?
  File "roman3.py", line 29, in toRoman
    raise NotIntegerError, "non-integers can not be converted"
NotIntegerError: non-integers can not be converted
```

Listing 14-6 shows the results of unit testing stage 3.

Listing 14-6. Output of romantest3.py Against roman3.py

```
fromRoman should only accept uppercase input ... FAIL
toRoman should always return uppercase ... ok
fromRoman should fail with malformed antecedents ... FAIL
fromRoman should fail with repeated pairs of numerals ... FAIL
fromRoman should fail with too many repeated numerals ... FAIL
fromRoman should give known result with known input ... FAIL
toRoman should give known result with known input ... ok          (1)
fromRoman(toRoman(n))==n for all n ... FAIL
toRoman should fail with non-integer input ... ok                 (2)
toRoman should fail with negative input ... ok                    (3)
toRoman should fail with large input ... ok
toRoman should fail with 0 input ... ok
```

(1) toRoman still passes the known-values test, which is comforting. All the tests that passed in stage 2 still pass, so our latest code hasn't broken anything.

(2) More exciting is the fact that all of our bad-input tests now pass. This test, testNonInteger, passes because of the int(n) <> n check. When a noninteger is passed to toRoman, the int(n) <> n check notices it and raises the NotIntegerError exception, which is what testNonInteger is looking for.

(3) This test, testNegative, passes because of the not (0 < n < 4000) check, which raises an OutOfRangeError exception, which is what testNegative is looking for.

Looking at the rest of the output of the unit test, you can see that we're down to six failures, all of them involving fromRoman: the known-values test, the three separate bad-input tests, the case check, and the sanity check.

```
======================================================================
FAIL: fromRoman should only accept uppercase input
----------------------------------------------------------------------
Traceback (most recent call last):
  File "C:\diveintopython\py\roman\stage3\romantest3.py", line 156,
    in testFromRomanCase
    roman3.fromRoman, numeral.lower())
  File "c:\python21\lib\unittest.py", line 266, in failUnlessRaises
    raise self.failureException, excName
AssertionError: InvalidRomanNumeralError
======================================================================
FAIL: fromRoman should fail with malformed antecedents
----------------------------------------------------------------------
Traceback (most recent call last):
  File "C:\diveintopython\py\roman\stage3\romantest3.py", line 133,
    in testMalformedAntecedent
    self.assertRaises(roman3.InvalidRomanNumeralError, roman3.fromRoman, s)
```

```
    File "c:\python21\lib\unittest.py", line 266, in failUnlessRaises
      raise self.failureException, excName
AssertionError: InvalidRomanNumeralError
=========================================================================
FAIL: fromRoman should fail with repeated pairs of numerals
-------------------------------------------------------------------------
Traceback (most recent call last):
  File "C:\diveintopython\py\roman\stage3\romantest3.py", line 127,
    in testRepeatedPairs
    self.assertRaises(roman3.InvalidRomanNumeralError, roman3.fromRoman, s)
  File "c:\python21\lib\unittest.py", line 266, in failUnlessRaises
    raise self.failureException, excName
AssertionError: InvalidRomanNumeralError
=========================================================================
FAIL: fromRoman should fail with too many repeated numerals
-------------------------------------------------------------------------
Traceback (most recent call last):
  File "C:\diveintopython\py\roman\stage3\romantest3.py", line 122,
    in testTooManyRepeatedNumerals
    self.assertRaises(roman3.InvalidRomanNumeralError, roman3.fromRoman, s)
  File "c:\python21\lib\unittest.py", line 266, in failUnlessRaises
    raise self.failureException, excName
AssertionError: InvalidRomanNumeralError
=========================================================================
FAIL: fromRoman should give known result with known input
-------------------------------------------------------------------------
Traceback (most recent call last):
  File "C:\diveintopython\py\roman\stage3\romantest3.py", line 99,
    in testFromRomanKnownValues
    self.assertEqual(integer, result)
  File "c:\python21\lib\unittest.py", line 273, in failUnlessEqual
    raise self.failureException, (msg or '%s != %s' % (first, second))
AssertionError: 1 != None
=========================================================================
FAIL: fromRoman(toRoman(n))==n for all n
-------------------------------------------------------------------------
Traceback (most recent call last):
  File "C:\diveintopython\py\roman\stage3\romantest3.py", line 141,
    in testSanity
    self.assertEqual(integer, result)
  File "c:\python21\lib\unittest.py", line 273, in failUnlessEqual
    raise self.failureException, (msg or '%s != %s' % (first, second))
AssertionError: 1 != None
-------------------------------------------------------------------------
```

```
Ran 12 tests in 0.401s
```

```
FAILED (failures=6)
```

That means that toRoman has passed all the tests it can pass by itself. (It's involved in the sanity check, but that also requires that fromRoman be written, which it isn't yet.) And that means that we must stop coding toRoman now—no tweaking, no twiddling, no extra checks "just in case." Just stop now. Back away from the keyboard.

> **NOTE** *The most important thing that comprehensive unit testing can tell you is when to stop coding. When all the unit tests for a function pass, stop coding the function. When all the unit tests for an entire module pass, stop coding the module.*

Converting Roman Numerals, Stage 4

Now that toRoman is done, it's time to start coding fromRoman, as shown in Listing 14-7. Thanks to our rich data structure that maps individual Roman numerals to integer values, this is no more difficult than the toRoman function. This file is available in py/roman/stage4/ in the examples directory.

Listing 14-7. roman4.py

```python
"""Convert to and from Roman numerals"""

#Define exceptions
class RomanError(Exception): pass
class OutOfRangeError(RomanError): pass
class NotIntegerError(RomanError): pass
class InvalidRomanNumeralError(RomanError): pass

#Define digit mapping
romanNumeralMap = (('M',  1000),
                   ('CM', 900),
                   ('D',  500),
                   ('CD', 400),
                   ('C',  100),
                   ('XC', 90),
                   ('L',  50),
                   ('XL', 40),
                   ('X',  10),
                   ('IX', 9),
```

```
                          ('V',  5),
                          ('IV', 4),
                          ('I',  1))

# toRoman function omitted for clarity (it hasn't changed)

def fromRoman(s):
    """convert Roman numeral to integer"""
    result = 0
    index = 0
    for numeral, integer in romanNumeralMap:
        while s[index:index+len(numeral)] == numeral:          (1)
            result += integer
            index += len(numeral)
    return result
```

(1) The pattern here is the same as toRoman. We iterate through our Roman numeral data structure (a tuple of tuples), and instead of matching the highest integer values as often as possible, we match the "highest" Roman numeral character strings as often as possible.

If you're not clear how fromRoman works, add a print statement to the end of the while loop:

```
while s[index:index+len(numeral)] == numeral:
    result += integer
    index += len(numeral)
    print 'found', numeral, 'of length', len(numeral), ', adding', integer
```

```
>>> import roman4
>>> roman4.fromRoman('MCMLXXII')
found M , of length 1, adding 1000
found CM , of length 2, adding 900
found L , of length 1, adding 50
found X , of length 1, adding 10
found X , of length 1, adding 10
found I , of length 1, adding 1
found I , of length 1, adding 1
1972
```

Listing 14-8 shows the results of unit testing stage 4.

Listing 14-8. Output of romantest4.py Against roman4.py

```
fromRoman should only accept uppercase input ... FAIL
toRoman should always return uppercase ... ok
fromRoman should fail with malformed antecedents ... FAIL
fromRoman should fail with repeated pairs of numerals ... FAIL
fromRoman should fail with too many repeated numerals ... FAIL
fromRoman should give known result with known input ... ok          (1)
toRoman should give known result with known input ... ok
fromRoman(toRoman(n))==n for all n ... ok                           (2)
toRoman should fail with non-integer input ... ok
toRoman should fail with negative input ... ok
toRoman should fail with large input ... ok
toRoman should fail with 0 input ... ok
```

(1) Two pieces of exciting news here. The first is that fromRoman works for good input, at least for all the known values we test.

(2) The second is that our sanity check also passed. Combined with the known-values tests, we can be reasonably sure that both toRoman and fromRoman work properly for all possible good values.

> **NOTE** *Although toRoman and fromRoman probably work properly for all good values, this is not guaranteed. It is theoretically possible that toRoman has a bug that produces the wrong Roman numeral for some particular set of inputs, and that fromRoman has a reciprocal bug that produces the same wrong integer values for exactly that set of Roman numerals that toRoman generated incorrectly. Depending on your application and your requirements, this possibility may bother you. If so, write more comprehensive test cases until it doesn't bother you anymore.*

The rest of the output shows we're down to four failures.

```
======================================================================
FAIL: fromRoman should only accept uppercase input
----------------------------------------------------------------------
Traceback (most recent call last):
  File "C:\diveintopython\py\roman\stage4\romantest4.py", line 156,
    in testFromRomanCase
    roman4.fromRoman, numeral.lower())
  File "c:\python21\lib\unittest.py", line 266, in failUnlessRaises
    raise self.failureException, excName
AssertionError: InvalidRomanNumeralError
```

```
=======================================================================
FAIL: fromRoman should fail with malformed antecedents
-----------------------------------------------------------------------
Traceback (most recent call last):
  File "C:\diveintopython\py\roman\stage4\romantest4.py", line 133,
    in testMalformedAntecedent
    self.assertRaises(roman4.InvalidRomanNumeralError, roman4.fromRoman, s)
  File "c:\python21\lib\unittest.py", line 266, in failUnlessRaises
    raise self.failureException, excName
AssertionError: InvalidRomanNumeralError
=======================================================================
FAIL: fromRoman should fail with repeated pairs of numerals
-----------------------------------------------------------------------
Traceback (most recent call last):
  File "C:\diveintopython\py\roman\stage4\romantest4.py", line 127,
    in testRepeatedPairs
    self.assertRaises(roman4.InvalidRomanNumeralError, roman4.fromRoman, s)
  File "c:\python21\lib\unittest.py", line 266, in failUnlessRaises
    raise self.failureException, excName
AssertionError: InvalidRomanNumeralError
=======================================================================
FAIL: fromRoman should fail with too many repeated numerals
-----------------------------------------------------------------------
Traceback (most recent call last):
  File "C:\diveintopython\py\roman\stage4\romantest4.py", line 122,
    in testTooManyRepeatedNumerals
    self.assertRaises(roman4.InvalidRomanNumeralError, roman4.fromRoman, s)
  File "c:\python21\lib\unittest.py", line 266, in failUnlessRaises
    raise self.failureException, excName
AssertionError: InvalidRomanNumeralError
-----------------------------------------------------------------------
Ran 12 tests in 1.222s

FAILED (failures=4)
```

Converting Roman Numerals, Stage 5

Now that fromRoman works properly with good input, it's time to fit in the last piece of the puzzle: making it work properly with bad input. That means finding a way to look at a string and determine if it's a valid Roman numeral. This is inherently more difficult than validating numeric input in toRoman, but we have a powerful tool at our disposal: regular expressions. (If you're not familiar with regular expressions and didn't read Chapter 7, now would be a good time to do that.)

As you saw in Chapter 7, there are several simple rules for constructing a Roman numeral, using the letters M, D, C, L, X, V, and I. Let's review the rules:

- Characters are additive. I is 1, II is 2, and III is 3. VI is 6 (literally, 5 and 1), VII is 7, and VIII is 8.

- The tens characters (I, X, C, and M) can be repeated up to three times. At 4, you need to subtract from the next highest fives character. You can't represent 4 as IIII; instead, it is represented as IV (1 less than 5). The number 40 is written as XL (10 less than 50), 41 as XLI, 42 as XLII, 43 as XLIII, and then 44 as XLIV (10 less than 50, then 1 less than 5).

- Similarly, at 9, you need to subtract from the next highest tens character: 8 is VIII, but 9 is IX (1 less than 10), not VIIII (since the I character cannot be repeated four times). The number 90 is XC, and 900 is CM.

- The fives characters cannot be repeated. The number 10 is always represented as X, never as VV. The number 100 is always C, never LL.

- Roman numerals are always written highest to lowest, and read left to right, so the order of characters matters very much. DC is 600; CD is a completely different number (400, or 100 less than 500). CI is 101; IC is not even a valid Roman numeral, because you can't subtract 1 directly from 100 (you would write it as XCIX, for 10 less than 100, then 1 less than 10).

Listing 14-9 shows the fifth stage of building roman.py. This file is available in py/roman/stage5/ in the examples directory.

Listing 14-9. roman5.py

```
"""Convert to and from Roman numerals"""
import re

#Define exceptions
class RomanError(Exception): pass
class OutOfRangeError(RomanError): pass
class NotIntegerError(RomanError): pass
class InvalidRomanNumeralError(RomanError): pass

#Define digit mapping
romanNumeralMap = (('M',  1000),
                   ('CM', 900),
                   ('D',  500),
                   ('CD', 400),
                   ('C',  100),
                   ('XC', 90),
```

```
                            ('L',  50),
                            ('XL', 40),
                            ('X',  10),
                            ('IX', 9),
                            ('V',  5),
                            ('IV', 4),
                            ('I',  1))

def toRoman(n):
    """convert integer to Roman numeral"""
    if not (0 < n < 4000):
        raise OutOfRangeError, "number out of range (must be 1..3999)"
    if int(n) <> n:
        raise NotIntegerError, "non-integers can not be converted"

    result = ""
    for numeral, integer in romanNumeralMap:
        while n >= integer:
            result += numeral
            n -= integer
    return result


#Define pattern to detect valid Roman numerals
romanNumeralPattern = \
    '^M?M?M?(CM|CD|D?C?C?C?)(XC|XL|L?X?X?X?)(IX|IV|V?I?I?I?)$'        (1)


def fromRoman(s):
    """convert Roman numeral to integer"""
    if not re.search(romanNumeralPattern, s):                        (2)
        raise InvalidRomanNumeralError, \
            'Invalid Roman numeral: %s' % s

    result = 0
    index = 0
    for numeral, integer in romanNumeralMap:
        while s[index:index+len(numeral)] == numeral:
            result += integer
            index += len(numeral)
    return result
```

(1) This is just a continuation of the pattern we discussed in the "Case Study: Roman Numerals" section of Chapter 7. The tens place is XC (90), XL (40), or an optional L followed by zero to three optional X characters. The ones place is IX (9), IV (4), or an optional V followed by zero to three optional I characters.

(2) Having encoded all that logic into our regular expression, the code to check for invalid Roman numerals becomes trivial. If re.search returns an object, then the regular expression matched and our input is valid; otherwise, our input is invalid.

At this point, you are allowed to be skeptical that the big, ugly regular expression could possibly catch all the types of invalid Roman numerals. But don't take my word for it, look at the results shown in Listing 14-10.

Listing 14-10. Output of romantest5.py Against roman5.py

```
fromRoman should only accept uppercase input ... ok                    (1)
toRoman should always return uppercase ... ok
fromRoman should fail with malformed antecedents ... ok                (2)
fromRoman should fail with repeated pairs of numerals ... ok           (3)
fromRoman should fail with too many repeated numerals ... ok
fromRoman should give known result with known input ... ok
toRoman should give known result with known input ... ok
fromRoman(toRoman(n))==n for all n ... ok
toRoman should fail with non-integer input ... ok
toRoman should fail with negative input ... ok
toRoman should fail with large input ... ok
toRoman should fail with 0 input ... ok


----------------------------------------------------------------------
Ran 12 tests in 2.864s

OK                                                                     (4)
```

(1) One thing I didn't mention about regular expressions is that, by default, they are case-sensitive. Since our regular expression romanNumeralPattern was expressed in uppercase characters, our re.search check will reject any input that isn't completely uppercase. So our uppercase-input test passes.

(2) More important, our bad-input tests pass. For instance, the malformed antecedents test checks cases like MCMC. As you've seen, this does not match our regular expression, so fromRoman raises an InvalidRomanNumeralError exception, which is what the malformed antecedents test case is looking for, so the test passes.

(3) In fact, all the bad-input tests pass. This regular expression catches everything we could think of when we made our test cases.

(4) And the anticlimax award of the year goes to the word OK, which is printed by the unittest module when all of the tests pass.

Summary

What should you do when all of your tests pass? When all of your tests pass, stop coding!

CHAPTER 15

Refactoring

DESPITE YOUR BEST EFFORTS to write comprehensive unit tests, bugs happen. What do I mean by *bug*? A bug is a test case you haven't written yet.

Diving In

You may not realize it, but there's a bug lurking in the Roman numeral conversion module we've been working with in the previous two chapters. Take a look at Listing 15-1 to see it in action.

Listing 15-1. The Bug

```
>>> import roman5
>>> roman5.fromRoman("")         (1)
0
```

(1) Remember in the previous chapter when we saw that an empty string would match the regular expression we were using to check for valid Roman numerals? Well, it turns out that this is still true for the final version of the regular expression. And that's a bug; we want an empty string to raise an InvalidRomanNumeralError exception, just like any other sequence of characters that don't represent a valid Roman numeral.

Writing the Test Case First

After reproducing the bug, and before fixing it, you should write a test case that fails, thus demonstrating the bug. Listing 15-2 shows the test case for the bug in Listing 15-1.

Listing 15-2. Testing for the Bug (romantest61.py)

```
class FromRomanBadInput(unittest.TestCase):

    # previous test cases omitted for clarity (they haven't changed)

    def testBlank(self):
```

```
        """fromRoman should fail with blank string"""
        self.assertRaises(roman.InvalidRomanNumeralError, roman.fromRoman, "")   (1)
```

(1) This is fairly straightforward. Call fromRoman with an empty string and make sure it raises an InvalidRomanNumeralError exception. The hard part was finding the bug. Now that we know about it, testing for it is the easy part.

Since our code has a bug, and we now have a test case that tests this bug, the test case will fail, as shown in Listing 15-3.

Listing 15-3. Output of romantest61.py Against roman61.py

```
fromRoman should only accept uppercase input ... ok
toRoman should always return uppercase ... ok
fromRoman should fail with blank string ... FAIL
fromRoman should fail with malformed antecedents ... ok
fromRoman should fail with repeated pairs of numerals ... ok
fromRoman should fail with too many repeated numerals ... ok
fromRoman should give known result with known input ... ok
toRoman should give known result with known input ... ok
fromRoman(toRoman(n))==n for all n ... ok
toRoman should fail with non-integer input ... ok
toRoman should fail with negative input ... ok
toRoman should fail with large input ... ok
toRoman should fail with 0 input ... ok


======================================================================
FAIL: fromRoman should fail with blank string
----------------------------------------------------------------------
Traceback (most recent call last):
  File "C:\diveintopython\py\roman\stage6\romantest61.py", line 137,
    in testBlank
    self.assertRaises(roman61.InvalidRomanNumeralError, roman61.fromRoman, "")
  File "c:\python21\lib\unittest.py", line 266, in failUnlessRaises
    raise self.failureException, excName
AssertionError: InvalidRomanNumeralError
----------------------------------------------------------------------

Ran 13 tests in 2.864s

FAILED (failures=1)
```

Fixing the New Bug

Now you can fix the bug. Listing 15-4 shows how. This file is available in py/roman/stage6/ in the examples directory.

Listing 15-4. Fixing the New Bug (roman62.py)

```
def fromRoman(s):
    """convert Roman numeral to integer"""
    if not s:                                        (1)
        raise InvalidRomanNumeralError, 'Input can not be blank'
    if not re.search(romanNumeralPattern, s):
        raise InvalidRomanNumeralError, 'Invalid Roman numeral: %s' % s

    result = 0
    index = 0
    for numeral, integer in romanNumeralMap:
        while s[index:index+len(numeral)] == numeral:
            result += integer
            index += len(numeral)
    return result
```

(1) Only two lines of code are required: an explicit check for an empty string and a raise statement.

Listing 15-5 shows the results of running the test cases again.

Listing 15-5. Output of romantest62.py Against roman62.py

```
fromRoman should only accept uppercase input ... ok
toRoman should always return uppercase ... ok
fromRoman should fail with blank string ... ok            (1)
fromRoman should fail with malformed antecedents ... ok
fromRoman should fail with repeated pairs of numerals ... ok
fromRoman should fail with too many repeated numerals ... ok
fromRoman should give known result with known input ... ok
toRoman should give known result with known input ... ok
fromRoman(toRoman(n))==n for all n ... ok
toRoman should fail with non-integer input ... ok
toRoman should fail with negative input ... ok
toRoman should fail with large input ... ok
toRoman should fail with 0 input ... ok

----------------------------------------------------------------------
```

```
Ran 13 tests in 2.834s

OK                                                    (2)
```

(1) The blank string test case now passes, so the bug is fixed.

(2) All the other test cases still pass, which means that this bug fix didn't break anything else. Stop coding.

Coding this way does not make fixing bugs any easier. Simple bugs (like this one) require simple test cases; complex bugs will require complex test cases.

In a testing-centric environment, it may *seem* like it takes longer to fix a bug, since you need to articulate in code exactly what the bug is (to write the test case), and then fix the bug itself. Then if the test case doesn't pass right away, you need to figure out whether the fix was wrong or whether the test case itself has a bug in it. However, in the long run, this back-and-forth between test code and code tested pays for itself, because it makes it more likely that bugs are fixed correctly the first time. Also, since you can easily rerun *all* the test cases along with your new one, you are much less likely to break old code when fixing new code. Today's unit test is tomorrow's regression test.

Handling Changing Requirements

Despite your best efforts to pin your customers to the ground and extract exact requirements from them on pain of horrible nasty things involving scissors and hot wax, requirements will change. Most customers don't know what they want until they see it, and even if they do, they aren't that good at articulating what they want precisely enough to be useful. And even if they do, they'll want more in the next release anyway. So, be prepared to update your test cases as requirements change.

Updating the Test Cases

Suppose, for instance, that we wanted to expand the range of our Roman numeral conversion functions. Remember the rule that said that no character could be repeated more than three times? Well, the Romans were willing to make an exception to that rule by having four M characters in a row to represent 4,000. If we make this change, we'll be able to expand our range of convertible numbers from 1 through 3,999 to 1 through 4,999. But first, we need to make some changes to our test cases, as shown in Listing 15-6. This file is available in `py/roman/stage7/` in the examples directory.

312

Listing 15-6. Modifying Test Cases for New Requirements (romantest71.py)

```
import roman71
import unittest

class KnownValues(unittest.TestCase):
    knownValues = ( (1, 'I'),
                    (2, 'II'),
                    (3, 'III'),
                    (4, 'IV'),
                    (5, 'V'),
                    (6, 'VI'),
                    (7, 'VII'),
                    (8, 'VIII'),
                    (9, 'IX'),
                    (10, 'X'),
                    (50, 'L'),
                    (100, 'C'),
                    (500, 'D'),
                    (1000, 'M'),
                    (31, 'XXXI'),
                    (148, 'CXLVIII'),
                    (294, 'CCXCIV'),
                    (312, 'CCCXII'),
                    (421, 'CDXXI'),
                    (528, 'DXXVIII'),
                    (621, 'DCXXI'),
                    (782, 'DCCLXXXII'),
                    (870, 'DCCCLXX'),
                    (941, 'CMXLI'),
                    (1043, 'MXLIII'),
                    (1110, 'MCX'),
                    (1226, 'MCCXXVI'),
                    (1301, 'MCCCI'),
                    (1485, 'MCDLXXXV'),
                    (1509, 'MDIX'),
                    (1607, 'MDCVII'),
                    (1754, 'MDCCLIV'),
                    (1832, 'MDCCCXXXII'),
                    (1993, 'MCMXCIII'),
                    (2074, 'MMLXXIV'),
                    (2152, 'MMCLII'),
                    (2212, 'MMCCXII'),
                    (2343, 'MMCCCXLIII'),
```

```
                    (2499, 'MMCDXCIX'),
                    (2574, 'MMDLXXIV'),
                    (2646, 'MMDCXLVI'),
                    (2723, 'MMDCCXXIII'),
                    (2892, 'MMDCCCXCII'),
                    (2975, 'MMCMLXXV'),
                    (3051, 'MMMLI'),
                    (3185, 'MMMCLXXXV'),
                    (3250, 'MMMCCL'),
                    (3313, 'MMMCCCXIII'),
                    (3408, 'MMMCDVIII'),
                    (3501, 'MMMDI'),
                    (3610, 'MMMDCX'),
                    (3743, 'MMMDCCXLIII'),
                    (3844, 'MMMDCCCXLIV'),
                    (3888, 'MMMDCCCLXXXVIII'),
                    (3940, 'MMMCMXL'),
                    (3999, 'MMMCMXCIX'),
                    (4000, 'MMMM'),                          (1)
                    (4500, 'MMMMD'),
                    (4888, 'MMMMDCCCLXXXVIII'),
                    (4999, 'MMMMCMXCIX'))

    def testToRomanKnownValues(self):
        """toRoman should give known result with known input"""
        for integer, numeral in self.knownValues:
            result = roman71.toRoman(integer)
            self.assertEqual(numeral, result)

    def testFromRomanKnownValues(self):
        """fromRoman should give known result with known input"""
        for integer, numeral in self.knownValues:
            result = roman71.fromRoman(numeral)
            self.assertEqual(integer, result)

class ToRomanBadInput(unittest.TestCase):
    def testTooLarge(self):
        """toRoman should fail with large input"""
        self.assertRaises(roman71.OutOfRangeError, roman71.toRoman, 5000) (2)

    def testZero(self):
        """toRoman should fail with 0 input"""
        self.assertRaises(roman71.OutOfRangeError, roman71.toRoman, 0)
```

```python
    def testNegative(self):
        """toRoman should fail with negative input"""
        self.assertRaises(roman71.OutOfRangeError, roman71.toRoman, -1)

    def testNonInteger(self):
        """toRoman should fail with non-integer input"""
        self.assertRaises(roman71.NotIntegerError, roman71.toRoman, 0.5)

class FromRomanBadInput(unittest.TestCase):
    def testTooManyRepeatedNumerals(self):
        """fromRoman should fail with too many repeated numerals"""
        for s in ('MMMMM', 'DD', 'CCCC', 'LL', 'XXXX', 'VV', 'IIII'):      (3)
            self.assertRaises(roman71.InvalidRomanNumeralError,
                roman71.fromRoman, s)

    def testRepeatedPairs(self):
        """fromRoman should fail with repeated pairs of numerals"""
        for s in ('CMCM', 'CDCD', 'XCXC', 'XLXL', 'IXIX', 'IVIV'):
            self.assertRaises(roman71.InvalidRomanNumeralError,
                roman71.fromRoman, s)

    def testMalformedAntecedent(self):
        """fromRoman should fail with malformed antecedents"""
        for s in ('IIMXCC', 'VX', 'DCM', 'CMM', 'IXIV',
                    'MCMC', 'XCX', 'IVI', 'LM', 'LD', 'LC'):
            self.assertRaises(roman71.InvalidRomanNumeralError,
                roman71.fromRoman, s)

    def testBlank(self):
        """fromRoman should fail with blank string"""
        self.assertRaises(roman71.InvalidRomanNumeralError, roman71.fromRoman, "")

class SanityCheck(unittest.TestCase):
    def testSanity(self):
        """fromRoman(toRoman(n))==n for all n"""
        for integer in range(1, 5000):                                    (4)
            numeral = roman71.toRoman(integer)
            result = roman71.fromRoman(numeral)
            self.assertEqual(integer, result)

class CaseCheck(unittest.TestCase):
    def testToRomanCase(self):
        """toRoman should always return uppercase"""
        for integer in range(1, 5000):
```

```
                numeral = roman71.toRoman(integer)
                self.assertEqual(numeral, numeral.upper())

        def testFromRomanCase(self):
            """fromRoman should only accept uppercase input"""
            for integer in range(1, 5000):
                numeral = roman71.toRoman(integer)
                roman71.fromRoman(numeral.upper())
                self.assertRaises(roman71.InvalidRomanNumeralError,
                                  roman71.fromRoman, numeral.lower())

if __name__ == "__main__":
    unittest.main()
```

(1) The existing known values don't change (they're all still reasonable values to test), but we need to add a few more in the 4,000 range. Here, I've included 4000 (the shortest), 4500 (the second shortest), 4888 (the longest), and 4999 (the largest).

(2) The definition of "large input" has changed. This test used to call toRoman with 4000 and expect an error. Now that 4,000 to 4,999 are good values, we need to bump this up to 5000.

(3) The definition of "too many repeated numerals" has also changed. This test used to call fromRoman with 'MMMM' and expect an error. Now that MMMM is considered a valid Roman numeral, we need to bump this up to 'MMMMM'.

(4) The sanity check and case checks loop through every number in the range, from 1 to 3999. Since the range has now expanded, these for loops need to be updated as well to go up to 4999.

Now our test cases are up to date with our new requirements, but our code is not, so we expect several of our test cases to fail. Listing 15-7 confirms this.

Listing 15-7. Output of romantest71.py Against roman71.py

```
fromRoman should only accept uppercase input ... ERROR        (1)
toRoman should always return uppercase ... ERROR
fromRoman should fail with blank string ... ok
fromRoman should fail with malformed antecedents ... ok
fromRoman should fail with repeated pairs of numerals ... ok
fromRoman should fail with too many repeated numerals ... ok
fromRoman should give known result with known input ... ERROR  (2)
toRoman should give known result with known input ... ERROR    (3)
fromRoman(toRoman(n))==n for all n ... ERROR                    (4)
toRoman should fail with non-integer input ... ok
toRoman should fail with negative input ... ok
toRoman should fail with large input ... ok
toRoman should fail with 0 input ... ok
```

(1) Our case checks loop from 1 to 4999, but toRoman accepts numbers only from 1 to 3999, so the checks will fail as soon the test case hits 4000.

(2) The fromRoman known-values test fails as soon as it hits 'MMMM', because fromRoman still thinks this is an invalid Roman numeral.

(3) The toRoman known-values test fails as soon as it hits 4000, because toRoman still thinks this is out of range.

(4) The sanity check also fails as soon as it hits 4000, because toRoman still thinks this is out of range.

Here's the rest of the output of the unit test, listing the details of the failures:

```
======================================================================
ERROR: fromRoman should only accept uppercase input
----------------------------------------------------------------------
Traceback (most recent call last):
  File "C:\diveintopython\py\roman\stage7\romantest71.py", line 161,
    in testFromRomanCase
    numeral = roman71.toRoman(integer)
  File "roman71.py", line 28, in toRoman
    raise OutOfRangeError, "number out of range (must be 1..3999)"
OutOfRangeError: number out of range (must be 1..3999)
======================================================================
ERROR: toRoman should always return uppercase
----------------------------------------------------------------------
Traceback (most recent call last):
  File "C:\diveintopython\py\roman\stage7\romantest71.py", line 155,
    in testToRomanCase
    numeral = roman71.toRoman(integer)
  File "roman71.py", line 28, in toRoman
    raise OutOfRangeError, "number out of range (must be 1..3999)"
OutOfRangeError: number out of range (must be 1..3999)
======================================================================
ERROR: fromRoman should give known result with known input
----------------------------------------------------------------------
Traceback (most recent call last):
  File "C:\diveintopython\py\roman\stage7\romantest71.py", line 102,
    in testFromRomanKnownValues
    result = roman71.fromRoman(numeral)
  File "roman71.py", line 47, in fromRoman
    raise InvalidRomanNumeralError, 'Invalid Roman numeral: %s' % s
InvalidRomanNumeralError: Invalid Roman numeral: MMMM
======================================================================
ERROR: toRoman should give known result with known input
----------------------------------------------------------------------
Traceback (most recent call last):
  File "C:\diveintopython\py\roman\stage7\romantest71.py", line 96,
```

```
    in testToRomanKnownValues
    result = roman71.toRoman(integer)
  File "roman71.py", line 28, in toRoman
    raise OutOfRangeError, "number out of range (must be 1..3999)"
OutOfRangeError: number out of range (must be 1..3999)
======================================================================
ERROR: fromRoman(toRoman(n))==n for all n
----------------------------------------------------------------------
Traceback (most recent call last):
  File "C:\diveintopython\py\roman\stage7\romantest71.py", line 147,
    in testSanity
    numeral = roman71.toRoman(integer)
  File "roman71.py", line 28, in toRoman
    raise OutOfRangeError, "number out of range (must be 1..3999)"
OutOfRangeError: number out of range (must be 1..3999)
----------------------------------------------------------------------
Ran 13 tests in 2.213s

FAILED (errors=5)
```

Updating the Code

Now that we have test cases that fail due to the new requirements, we can think about fixing the code to bring it in line with the test cases. One thing that takes some getting used to when you first start coding unit tests is that the code being tested is never "ahead" of the test cases. While it's behind, you still have some work to do, and as soon as it catches up to the test cases, you stop coding.

Listing 15-8 demonstrates how to code the new requirements. This file is available in py/roman/stage7/ in the examples directory.

Listing 15-8. Coding the New Requirements (roman72.py)

```python
"""Convert to and from Roman numerals"""

import re

#Define exceptions
class RomanError(Exception): pass
class OutOfRangeError(RomanError): pass
class NotIntegerError(RomanError): pass
class InvalidRomanNumeralError(RomanError): pass

#Define digit mapping
romanNumeralMap = (('M',  1000),
```

```
                    ('CM', 900),
                    ('D',  500),
                    ('CD', 400),
                    ('C',  100),
                    ('XC', 90),
                    ('L',  50),
                    ('XL', 40),
                    ('X',  10),
                    ('IX', 9),
                    ('V',  5),
                    ('IV', 4),
                    ('I',  1))

def toRoman(n):
    """convert integer to Roman numeral"""
    if not (0 < n < 5000):                                          (1)
        raise OutOfRangeError, "number out of range (must be 1..4999)"
    if int(n) <> n:
        raise NotIntegerError, "non-integers can not be converted"

    result = ""
    for numeral, integer in romanNumeralMap:
        while n >= integer:
            result += numeral
            n -= integer
    return result


#Define pattern to detect valid Roman numerals
romanNumeralPattern = \
    '^M?M?M?M?(CM|CD|D?C?C?C?)(XC|XL|L?X?X?X?)(IX|IV|V?I?I?I?)$'     (2)


def fromRoman(s):
    """convert Roman numeral to integer"""
    if not s:
        raise InvalidRomanNumeralError, 'Input can not be blank'
    if not re.search(romanNumeralPattern, s):
        raise InvalidRomanNumeralError, 'Invalid Roman numeral: %s' % s

    result = 0
    index = 0
    for numeral, integer in romanNumeralMap:
        while s[index:index+len(numeral)] == numeral:
            result += integer
            index += len(numeral)
    return result
```

(1) toRoman needs only one small change, in the range check. Where we used to check 0 < n < 4000, we now check 0 < n < 5000. And we change the error message that we raise to reflect the new acceptable range (1..4999 instead of 1..3999). We don't need to make any changes to the rest of the function; it handles the new cases already. It merrily adds 'M' for each thousand that it finds; given 4000, it will spit out 'MMMM'. The only reason it didn't do this before is that we explicitly stopped it with the range check.

(2) We don't need to make any changes to fromRoman at all. The only change is to romanNumeralPattern. If you look closely, you'll notice that we added another optional M in the first section of the regular expression. This will allow up to four M characters instead of three, meaning we will allow the Roman numeral equivalents of 4,999 instead of 3,999. The actual fromRoman function is completely general; it just looks for repeated Roman numeral characters and adds them up, without caring how many times they repeat. The only reason it didn't handle 'MMMM' before is that we explicitly stopped it with the regular expression pattern matching.

You may be skeptical that these two small changes are all that we need. Hey, don't take my word for it—see for yourself in Listing 15-9.

Listing 15-9. Output of romantest72.py Against roman72.py

```
fromRoman should only accept uppercase input ... ok
toRoman should always return uppercase ... ok
fromRoman should fail with blank string ... ok
fromRoman should fail with malformed antecedents ... ok
fromRoman should fail with repeated pairs of numerals ... ok
fromRoman should fail with too many repeated numerals ... ok
fromRoman should give known result with known input ... ok
toRoman should give known result with known input ... ok
fromRoman(toRoman(n))==n for all n ... ok
toRoman should fail with non-integer input ... ok
toRoman should fail with negative input ... ok
toRoman should fail with large input ... ok
toRoman should fail with 0 input ... ok


----------------------------------------------------------------------
Ran 13 tests in 3.685s

OK                                                                  (1)
```

(1) All the test cases pass. Stop coding.

Comprehensive unit testing means never having to rely on a programmer who says, "Trust me."

Refactoring for Performance

The best thing about comprehensive unit testing is not the feeling you get when all your test cases finally pass, or even the feeling you get when someone else blames you for breaking their code and you can actually *prove* that you didn't. The best thing about unit testing is that it gives you the freedom to refactor mercilessly.

Refactoring is the process of taking working code and making it work better. Usually, "better" means faster, although it can also mean using less memory, using less disk space, or simply running more elegantly. Whatever it means to you and to your project in your environment, refactoring is important to the long-term health of any program.

For our example, better means faster. Specifically, the fromRoman function is slower than it needs to be, because of that big, nasty regular expression that we use to validate Roman numerals.

Compiling Regular Expressions

It's probably not worth trying to do away with the regular expression altogether (it would be difficult, and the code might not end up being any faster), but we can speed up the function by compiling the regular expression, as shown in Listing 15-10.

Listing 15-10. Compiling Regular Expressions

```
>>> import re
>>> pattern = '^M?M?M?$'
>>> re.search(pattern, 'M')                    (1)
<SRE_Match object at 01090490>
>>> compiledPattern = re.compile(pattern)      (2)
>>> compiledPattern
<SRE_Pattern object at 00F06E28>
>>> dir(compiledPattern)                        (3)
['findall', 'match', 'scanner', 'search', 'split', 'sub', 'subn']
>>> compiledPattern.search('M')                 (4)
<SRE_Match object at 01104928>
```

(1) This is the syntax you've seen before: re.search takes a regular expression as a string (pattern) and a string to match against it ('M'). If the pattern matches, the function returns a match object that can be queried to find out exactly what matched and how.

(2) This is the new syntax: re.compile takes a regular expression as a string and returns a pattern object. Notice there is no string to match here. Compiling a regular expression has nothing to do with matching it against any specific strings (like 'M'); it involves only the regular expression itself.

(3) The compiled pattern object returned from re.compile has several useful-looking functions, including some (like search and sub) that are available directly in the re module.

(4) Calling the compiled pattern object's search function with the string 'M' accomplishes the same thing as calling re.search with both the regular expression and the string 'M'—only much, much faster. (In fact, the re.search function simply compiles the regular expression and calls the resulting pattern object's search method for you.)

> **TIP** *Whenever you are going to use a regular expression more than once, you should compile it to get a pattern object, and then call the methods on the pattern object directly.*

Listing 15-11 shows how compiled regular expressions work in the the fromRoman function. This file is available in py/roman/stage8/ in the examples directory.

Listing 15-11. Compiled Regular Expressions in roman81.py

```
# toRoman and rest of module omitted for clarity

romanNumeralPattern = \
    re.compile('^M?M?M?M?(CM|CD|D?C?C?C?)(XC|XL|L?X?X?X?)(IX|IV|V?I?I?I?)$')     (1)

def fromRoman(s):
    """convert Roman numeral to integer"""
    if not s:
        raise InvalidRomanNumeralError, 'Input can not be blank'
    if not romanNumeralPattern.search(s):                                        (2)
        raise InvalidRomanNumeralError, 'Invalid Roman numeral: %s' % s

    result = 0
    index = 0
    for numeral, integer in romanNumeralMap:
        while s[index:index+len(numeral)] == numeral:
            result += integer
            index += len(numeral)
    return result
```

(1) This looks very similar, but, in fact, a lot has changed. `romanNumeralPattern` is no longer a string; it is a pattern object that was returned from `re.compile`.

(2) That means that we can call methods on `romanNumeralPattern` directly. This will be much, much faster than calling `re.search` every time. The regular expression is compiled once and stored in `romanNumeralPattern` when the module is first imported. Then every time we call `fromRoman`, we can immediately match the input string against the regular expression, without any intermediate steps occurring under the covers.

So how much faster is it to compile our regular expressions? See for yourself. Listing 15-12 shows the results of running the test case.

Listing 15-12. Output of romantest81.py Against roman81.py

```
. . . . . . . . . . . .                                                    (1)
----------------------------------------------------------------------
Ran 13 tests in 3.385s                                                 (2)

OK                                                                     (3)
```

(1) Just a note in passing here: this time, I ran the unit test *without* the -v option, so instead of the full `doc string` for each test, we get only a dot for each test that passes. If a test failed, we would get an F, and if it had an error, we would get an E. We would still get complete tracebacks for each failure and error, so we could track down any problems.

(2) We ran 13 tests in 3.385 seconds, compared to 3.685 seconds without compiling the regular expressions. That's an 8% improvement overall, and remember that most of the time spent during the unit test is used doing other things. (Separately, I time-tested the regular expressions by themselves, apart from the rest of the unit tests, and found that compiling this regular expression speeds up the `search` by an average of 54%.) That's not bad for such a simple fix.

(3) Oh, and in case you were wondering, compiling our regular expression didn't break anything, and we just proved it.

Using the {n, m} Syntax

Let's try another performance optimization. Given the complexity of regular expression syntax, it should come as no surprise that there is frequently more than one way to write the same expression. After some discussion about this module on comp.lang.python (http://groups.google.com/groups?group=comp.lang.python), someone suggested that I try using the {*n, m*} syntax for the optional repeated characters. You saw this alternative syntax in Chapter 7. Listing 15-13 shows this version. This file is available in py/roman/stage8/ in the examples directory.

Listing 15-13. roman82.py

```
# rest of program omitted for clarity

#old version
#romanNumeralPattern = \
#    re.compile('^M?M?M?M?(CM|CD|D?C?C?C?)(XC|XL|L?X?X?X?)(IX|IV|V?I?I?I?)$')

#new version
romanNumeralPattern = \
    re.compile('^M{0,4}(CM|CD|D?C{0,3})(XC|XL|L?X{0,3})(IX|IV|V?I{0,3})$')      (1)
```

(1) We have replaced M?M?M?M? with M{0,4}. Both mean the same thing: match zero to four M characters. Similarly, C?C?C? became C{0,3} (match zero to three C characters), and so forth for X and I.

This form of the regular expression is a little shorter (although not any more readable). Is it any faster? Listing 15-14 answers that question.

Listing 15-14. Output of romantest82.py Against roman82.py

```
. . . . . . . . . . . . .
---------------------------------------------------------------------
Ran 13 tests in 3.315s                                          (1)

OK                                                              (2)
```

(1) Overall, the unit tests run 2% faster with this form of regular expression. That doesn't sound exciting, but remember that the search function is a small part of the overall unit test; most of the time is spent doing other things. (Separately, I time-tested just the regular expressions, and found that the search function is 11% faster with this syntax.) By compiling the regular expression and rewriting part of it to use this new syntax, we've improved the regular expression performance by more than 60% and improved the overall performance of the entire unit test by over 10%. You'll learn more about performance-testing techniques in Chapter 18.

(2) More important than any performance boost is the fact that the module still works perfectly. This is the freedom I was talking about earlier: the freedom to tweak, change, or rewrite any piece of it and verify that you haven't messed up anything in the process. This is not a license to endlessly tweak your code just for the sake of tweaking it. Here, we had a very specific objective (to make fromRoman faster), and we were able to accomplish that objective without any lingering doubts about whether we introduced new bugs in the process.

Using Verbose Regular Expressions

There is one other tweak I would like to make, and then I promise I'll stop refactoring and put this module to bed. As you've seen, regular expressions can quickly get pretty hairy and unreadable. I wouldn't like to come back to this module in six months and try to maintain it. Sure, the test cases pass, so I know that it works. But if I can't figure out *how* the code works, it's still going to be difficult to add new features, fix new bugs, or otherwise maintain the code. As you saw in Chapter 7, in the "Verbose Regular Expressions" section, Python provides a way to document your logic line by line.

Listing 15-15 shows the module with a verbose regular expression. This file is available in py/roman/stage8/ in the examples directory.

Listing 15-15. roman83.py

```
# rest of program omitted for clarity

#old version
#romanNumeralPattern = \
#    re.compile('^M{0,4}(CM|CD|D?C{0,3})(XC|XL|L?X{0,3})(IX|IV|V?I{0,3})$')

#new version
romanNumeralPattern = re.compile('''
    ^                      # beginning of string
    M{0,4}                 # thousands - 0 to 4 M's
    (CM|CD|D?C{0,3})       # hundreds - 900 (CM), 400 (CD), 0-300 (0 to 3 C's),
                           #            or 500-800 (D, followed by 0 to 3 C's)
    (XC|XL|L?X{0,3})       # tens - 90 (XC), 40 (XL), 0-30 (0 to 3 X's),
                           #        or 50-80 (L, followed by 0 to 3 X's)
    (IX|IV|V?I{0,3})       # ones - 9 (IX), 4 (IV), 0-3 (0 to 3 I's),
                           #        or 5-8 (V, followed by 0 to 3 I's)
    $                      # end of string
    ''', re.VERBOSE)                                          (1)
```

(1) The re.compile function can take an optional second argument, which is a set of one or more flags that control various options about the compiled regular expression. Here, we're specifying the re.VERBOSE flag, which tells Python that there are in-line comments within the regular expression itself. The comments and all the whitespace around them are *not* considered part of the regular expression; the re.compile function simply strips them all out when it compiles the expression. This new, "verbose" version is identical to the old version, but it's infinitely more readable.

Now, let's test the refactored version. Listing 15-16 shows the results.

Listing 15-16. Output of romantest83.py Against roman83.py

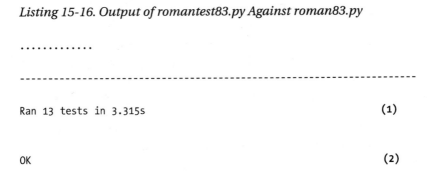

```
Ran 13 tests in 3.315s                                      (1)


OK                                                          (2)
```

(1) This new, verbose version runs at exactly the same speed as the old version. In fact, the compiled pattern objects are the same, since the re.compile function strips out all the stuff we added.

(2) This new, verbose version passes all the same tests as the old version. Nothing has changed, except that the programmer who comes back to this module in six months stands a fighting chance of understanding how the function works.

Postscript

A clever reader read the previous section on refactoring and took it to the next level. The biggest headache (and performance drain) in the program as it is currently written is the regular expression, which is required because we have no other way of breaking down a Roman numeral. But there are only 5,000 of these numerals, so why don't we just build a lookup table once, and then simply read that? This idea gets even better when you realize that you don't need to use regular expressions at all. As you build the lookup table for converting integers to Roman numerals, you can build the reverse lookup table to convert Roman numerals to integers. And best of all, the reader who suggested it already had a complete set of unit tests. He changed more than half the code in the module, but the unit tests stayed the same, so he could prove that his code worked just as well as the original.

Listing 15-17 shows the version of roman.py using a lookup table. This file is available in py/roman/stage9/ in the examples directory.

Listing 15-17. roman9.py

```
#Define exceptions
class RomanError(Exception): pass
class OutOfRangeError(RomanError): pass
class NotIntegerError(RomanError): pass
class InvalidRomanNumeralError(RomanError): pass

#Roman numerals must be less than 5000
MAX_ROMAN_NUMERAL = 4999
```

```
#Define digit mapping
romanNumeralMap = (('M',  1000),
                   ('CM', 900),
                   ('D',  500),
                   ('CD', 400),
                   ('C',  100),
                   ('XC', 90),
                   ('L',  50),
                   ('XL', 40),
                   ('X',  10),
                   ('IX', 9),
                   ('V',  5),
                   ('IV', 4),
                   ('I',  1))


#Create tables for fast conversion of roman numerals.
#See fillLookupTables() below.
toRomanTable = [ None ]  # Skip an index since Roman numerals have no zero
fromRomanTable = {}


def toRoman(n):
    """convert integer to Roman numeral"""
    if not (0 < n <= MAX_ROMAN_NUMERAL):
        raise OutOfRangeError, \
            "number out of range (must be 1..%s)" % MAX_ROMAN_NUMERAL
    if int(n) <> n:
        raise NotIntegerError, "non-integers can not be converted"
    return toRomanTable[n]


def fromRoman(s):
    """convert Roman numeral to integer"""
    if not s:
        raise InvalidRomanNumeralError, "Input can not be blank"
    if not fromRomarTable.has_key(s):
        raise InvalidRomanNumeralError, "Invalid Roman numeral: %s" % s
    return fromRomanTable[s]


def toRomanDynamic(n):
    """convert integer to Roman numeral using dynamic programming"""
    result = ""
    for numeral, integer in romanNumeralMap:
        if n >= integer:
            result = numeral
            n -= integer
            break
```

```
        if n > 0:
            result += toRomanTable[n]
        return result

def fillLookupTables():
    """compute all the possible roman numerals"""
    #Save the values in two global tables to convert to and from integers.
    for integer in range(1, MAX_ROMAN_NUMERAL + 1):
        romanNumber = toRomanDynamic(integer)
        toRomanTable.append(romanNumber)
        fromRomanTable[romanNumber] = integer

fillLookupTables()
```

So how fast is it? Here's the output of `romantest9.py` against `roman9.py`:

```
. . . . . . . . . . . . .
-----------------------------------------------------------------------
Ran 13 tests in 0.791s

OK
```

Remember that the best performance we ever got in the original version was 13 tests in 3.315 seconds. Of course, it's not entirely a fair comparison, because this version will take longer to import (when it fills the lookup tables). But since importing is done only once, this is negligible in the long run.

What's the moral of the story?

- Simplicity is a virtue.

- Especially when regular expressions are involved.

- And unit tests can give you the confidence to do large-scale refactoring, even if you didn't write the original code.

Summary

Unit testing is a powerful concept, which, if properly implemented, can both reduce maintenance costs and increase flexibility in any long-term project. It is also important to understand that unit testing is not a panacea, a magic problem solver, or a silver bullet. Writing good test cases is hard, and keeping them up to date takes discipline (especially when customers are screaming for critical bug fixes). Unit testing is not a replacement for other forms of testing, including functional testing, integration testing, and user-acceptance testing. But it is feasible, and it does work, and once you've seen it work, you'll wonder how you ever got along without it.

These last few chapters have covered a lot of ground, and much of it wasn't even Python-specific. There are unit testing frameworks for many languages, all of which require you to understand the same basic concepts:

- Designing test cases that are specific, automated, and independent

- Writing test cases *before* writing the code they are testing

- Writing tests that test good input and check for proper results

- Writing tests that test bad input and check for proper failures

- Writing and updating test cases to illustrate bugs or reflect new requirements

- Refactoring mercilessly to improve performance, scalability, readability, maintainability, or whatever other "ility" you're lacking

> **TIP** *XProgramming.com* (http://www.xprogramming.com) *has links to download unit testing frameworks for many different languages* (http://www.xprogramming.com/software.htm).

Additionally, you should be comfortable doing all of the following Python-specific things:

- Subclassing unittest.TestCase and writing methods for individual test cases

- Using assertEqual to check that a function returns a known value

- Using assertRaises to check that a function raises a known exception

- Calling unittest.main() in your if __name__ clause to run all your test cases at once

- Running unit tests in verbose or regular mode

Functional Programming

IN CHAPTER 13, you learned about the philosophy of unit testing. In Chapter 14, you stepped through the implementation of basic unit tests in Python. In Chapter 15, you saw how unit testing makes large-scale refactoring easier. This chapter will build on those sample programs, but here, we will focus on advanced Python-specific techniques, rather than on unit testing itself.

Diving In

Listing 16-1 is a complete Python program that acts as a cheap and simple regression testing framework. It takes unit tests that you've written for individual modules, collects them into one big test suite, and runs them all at once.

> **NOTE** *I actually used this script as part of the build process for this book. I have unit tests for several of the example programs (not just the* roman.py *module featured in Chapter 13), and the first thing my automated build script does is run this program to make sure all my examples still work. If this regression test fails, the build immediately stops. I don't want to release examples that don't work any more than you want to download them.*

Listing 16-1. regression.py

```
"""Regression testing framework

This module will search for scripts in the same directory named
XYZtest.py.  Each such script should be a test suite that tests a
module through PyUnit.  (As of Python 2.1, PyUnit is included in
the standard library as "unittest".)  This script will aggregate all
found test suites into one big test suite and run them all at once.
"""

import sys, os, re, unittest

def regressionTest():
    path = os.path.abspath(os.path.dirname(sys.argv[0]))
    files = os.listdir(path)
```

```
    test = re.compile("test\.py$", re.IGNORECASE)
    files = filter(test.search, files)
    filenameToModuleName = lambda f: os.path.splitext(f)[0]
    moduleNames = map(filenameToModuleName, files)
    modules = map(__import__, moduleNames)
    load = unittest.defaultTestLoader.loadTestsFromModule
    return unittest.TestSuite(map(load, modules))

if __name__ == "__main__":
    unittest.main(defaultTest="regressionTest")
```

> **NOTE** *If you have not already done so, you can download this and other
> examples used in this book from the Downloads section of the Apress web site
> (http://www.apress.com).*

Running this script in the same directory as the rest of the example scripts
that come with this book will find all the unit tests, named *module*test.py, run
them as a single test, and pass or fail them all at once. Listing 16-2 shows some
sample output of this script.

Listing 16-2. Sample Output of regression.py

```
[you@localhost py]$ python regression.py -v
help should fail with no object ... ok                          (1)
help should return known result for apihelper ... ok
help should honor collapse argument ... ok
help should honor spacing argument ... ok
buildConnectionString should fail with list input ... ok        (2)
buildConnectionString should fail with string input ... ok
buildConnectionString should fail with tuple input ... ok
buildConnectionString handles empty dictionary ... ok
buildConnectionString returns known result with known input ... ok
fromRoman should only accept uppercase input ... ok             (3)
toRoman should always return uppercase ... ok
fromRoman should fail with blank string ... ok
fromRoman should fail with malformed antecedents ... ok
fromRoman should fail with repeated pairs of numerals ... ok
fromRoman should fail with too many repeated numerals ... ok
fromRoman should give known result with known input ... ok
toRoman should give known result with known input ... ok
fromRoman(toRoman(n))==n for all n ... ok
toRoman should fail with non-integer input ... ok
```

```
toRoman should fail with negative input ... ok
toRoman should fail with large input ... ok
toRoman should fail with 0 input ... ok
kgp a ref test ... ok
kgp b ref test ... ok
kgp c ref test ... ok
kgp d ref test ... ok
kgp e ref test ... ok
kgp f ref test ... ok
kgp g ref test ... ok


----------------------------------------------------------------------
Ran 29 tests in 2.799s

OK
```

(1) The first five tests are from `apihelpertest.py`, which tests the sample script from Chapter 4.

(2) The next five tests are from `odbchelpertest.py`, which tests the sample script from Chapter 2.

(3) The rest are from `kgp.py`, which you studied in Chapter 9, and `romantest.py`, which you studied in depth in Chapters 13 and 14.

Finding the Path

When running Python scripts from the command line, it is sometimes useful to know where the currently running script is located on disk.

This is one of those obscure little tricks that is virtually impossible to figure out on your own, but it's simple to remember once you see it. The key to it is `sys.argv`. As you saw in Chapter 9, `sys.argv` is a list that holds the command-line arguments. However, it also holds the name of the running script, exactly as it was called from the command line, and this is enough information to determine its location, as shown in Listing 16-3.

Listing 16-3. fullpath.py

```
import sys, os

print 'sys.argv[0] =', sys.argv[0]                    (1)
pathname = os.path.dirname(sys.argv[0])               (2)
print 'path =', pathname
print 'full path =', os.path.abspath(pathname)        (3)
```

(1) Regardless of how you run a script, `sys.argv[0]` will always contain the name of the script, exactly as it appears on the command line. This may or may not include any path information, as you'll see shortly.

(2) `os.path.dirname` takes a filename as a string and returns the directory path portion. If the given filename does not include any path information, `os.path.dirname` returns an empty string.

(3) `os.path.abspath` is the key here. It takes a pathname, which can be partial or even blank, and returns a fully qualified pathname.

`os.path.abspath` deserves further explanation and is demonstrated in Listing 16-4. It is very flexible and can take any kind of pathname.

Listing 16-4. Further Explanation of os.path.abspath

```
>>> import os
>>> os.getcwd()                               (1)
/home/you
>>> os.path.abspath('')                       (2)
/home/you
>>> os.path.abspath('.ssh')                   (3)
/home/you/.ssh
>>> os.path.abspath('/home/you/.ssh')         (4)
/home/you/.ssh
>>> os.path.abspath('.ssh/../foo/')           (5)
/home/you/foo
```

(1) `os.getcwd()` returns the current working directory.

(2) Calling `os.path.abspath` with an empty string returns the current working directory—the same result as calling `os.getcwd()`.

(3) Calling `os.path.abspath` with a partial pathname constructs a fully qualified pathname from it, based on the current working directory.

(4) Calling `os.path.abspath` with a full pathname simply returns it.

(5) `os.path.abspath` also *normalizes* the pathname it returns. That means that if you are in the `/usr/` directory, `os.path.abspath('bin/../local/bin')` will return `/usr/local/bin`. It normalizes the path by making it as simple as possible. If you just want to normalize a pathname like this without turning it into a full pathname, use `os.path.normpath` instead. Note that this example worked even though I don't actually have a foo directory. `os.path.abspath` never checks your actual disk; this is all just string manipulation. In other words, `os.path.abspath` does not validate pathnames; the pathnames and filenames you pass to `os.path.abspath` do not need to exist.

Listing 16-5 shows some sample output from `fullpath.py`.

Listing 16-5. Sample Output from fullpath.py

```
[you@localhost py]$ python /home/you/diveintopython/common/py/fullpath.py      (1)
sys.argv[0] = /home/you/diveintopython/common/py/fullpath.py
path = /home/you/diveintopython/common/py
full path = /home/you/diveintopython/common/py
[you@localhost diveintopython]$ python common/py/fullpath.py                    (2)
sys.argv[0] = common/py/fullpath.py
path = common/py
full path = /home/you/diveintopython/common/py
[you@localhost diveintopython]$ cd common/py
[you@localhost py]$ python fullpath.py                                          (3)
sys.argv[0] = fullpath.py
path =
full path = /home/you/diveintopython/common/py
```

(1) In the first case, sys.argv[0] includes the full path of the script. You can then use the os.path.dirname function to strip off the script name and return the full directory name, and os.path.abspath simply returns what you give it.

(2) If you run the script by using a partial pathname, sys.argv[0] will still contain exactly what appears on the command line. os.path.dirname will then give you a partial pathname (relative to the current directory), and os.path.abspath will construct a full pathname from the partial pathname.

(3) If you run the script from the current directory without giving any path, os.path.dirname will simply return an empty string. Given an empty string, os.path.abspath returns the current directory, which is what you want, since the script was run from the current directory.

> **NOTE** *Like the other functions in the os and os.path modules, os.path.abspath is cross-platform. Your results will look slightly different than my examples if you're running on Windows (which uses the backslash as a path separator) or Mac OS (which uses colons), but they'll still work. That's the whole point of the os module.*

One reader was dissatisfied with this solution. He wanted to be able to run all the unit tests in the current directory, not the directory where regression.py is located. He suggested the approach shown in Listing 16-6 instead.

Listing 16-6. Running Scripts in the Current Directory

```
import sys, os, re, unittest

def regressionTest():
    path = os.getcwd()                  (1)
    sys.path.append(path)               (2)
    files = os.listdir(path)            (3)
```

(1) Instead of setting `path` to the directory where the currently running script is located, you set it to the current working directory. This will be whatever directory you were in before you ran the script, which is not necessarily the same as the directory where the script is located. (Read that sentence a few times until you get it.)

(2) Append this directory to the Python library search path, so that when you dynamically import the unit test modules later, Python can find them. You didn't need to do this when `path` was the directory of the currently running script, because Python always looks in that directory.

(3) The rest of the function is the same.

This technique will allow you to reuse this `regression.py` script on multiple projects. Just put the script in a common directory, and then change to the project's directory before running it. All of that project's unit tests will be found and tested, instead of the unit tests in the common directory where `regression.py` is located.

Filtering Lists Revisited

You're already familiar with using list comprehensions to filter lists (introduced in Chapter 4). There is another way to accomplish this same thing, which some people feel is more expressive.

Python has a built-in `filter` function, which takes two arguments—a function and a list—and returns a list. The function passed as the first argument to `filter` must itself take one argument, and the list that `filter` returns will contain all the elements from the list passed to `filter` for which the function passed to `filter` returns true.

> **NOTE** *Technically, the second argument to* `filter` *can be any sequence, including lists, tuples, and custom classes that act like lists, by defining the* `__getitem__` *special method. If possible,* `filter` *will return the same datatype as you give it, so filtering a list returns a list, but filtering a tuple returns a tuple.*

Got all that? It's not as difficult as it sounds, as you can see in Listing 16-7.

Listing 16-7. Introducing filter

```
>>> def odd(n):                                    (1)
...     return n % 2
...
>>> li = [1, 2, 3, 5, 9, 10, 256, -3]
>>> filter(odd, li)                                (2)
[1, 3, 5, 9, -3]
>>> [e for e in li if odd(e)]                      (3)
[1, 3, 5, 9, -3]
>>> filteredList = []
>>> for n in li:                                   (4)
...     if odd(n):
...         filteredList.append(n)
...
>>> filteredList
[1, 3, 5, 9, -3]
```

(1) odd uses the built-in modulus function % to return True if n is odd and False if n is even.

(2) filter takes two arguments: a function (odd) and a list (li). It loops through the list and calls odd with each element. If odd returns a true value (remember that any nonzero value is true in Python), then the element is included in the returned list; otherwise, it is filtered out. The result is a list of only the odd numbers from the original list, in the same order as they appeared in the original.

(3) You could accomplish the same thing using list comprehensions, as you saw in the "Filtering Lists" section in Chapter 4.

(4) You could also accomplish the same thing with a for loop. Depending on your programming background, this may seem more straightforward, but functions like filter are much more expressive. Not only is the function easier to write, it's easier to read, too. Reading the for loop is like standing too close to a painting: you see all the details, but it may take a few seconds to be able to step back and see the bigger picture ("Oh, you're just filtering the list!").

Listing 16-8 shows the use of the filter function in regression.py.

Listing 16-8. Using filter in regression.py

```
files = os.listdir(path)                           (1)
test = re.compile("test\.py$", re.IGNORECASE)      (2)
files = filter(test.search, files)                 (3)
```

(1) As you saw in the previous section of this chapter, path may contain the full or partial pathname of the directory of the currently running script, or it may contain an empty string if the script is being run from the current directory.

Either way, `files` will end up with the names of the files in the same directory as the script you're running.

(2) This is a compiled regular expression. As you saw in the "Refactoring for Performance" section in Chapter 15, if you're going to use the same regular expression over and over, you should compile it for faster performance. The compiled object has a `search` method, which takes a single argument: the string to search. If the regular expression matches the string, the `search` method returns a `Match` object containing information about the regular expression match; otherwise, it returns `None`, the Python null value.

(3) For each element in the `files` list, you're going to call the `search` method of the compiled regular expression object, `test`. If the regular expression matches, the method will return a `Match` object, which Python considers to be true, so the element will be included in the list returned by `filter`. If the regular expression does not match, the `search` method will return `None`, which Python considers to be false, so the element will not be included.

> **NOTE** *Versions of Python prior to 2.0 did not have list comprehensions, so you couldn't filter using list comprehensions; the* `filter` *function was the only game in town. Even with the introduction of list comprehensions in 2.0, some people still prefer the old-style* `filter` *(and its companion function,* `map`, *which you'll see in the next section of this chapter). Both techniques work at the moment, so which one you use is a matter of style. There is discussion that* `map` *and* `filter` *might be deprecated in a future version of Python, but no decision has been made yet.*

Listing 16-9 demonstrates filtering using list comprehensions rather than `filter`.

Listing 16-9. Filtering Using List Comprehensions

```
files = os.listdir(path)
test = re.compile("test\.py$", re.IGNORECASE)
files = [f for f in files if test.search(f)]        (1)
```

(1) This will accomplish exactly the same result as using the `filter` function. Which way is more expressive? That's up to you.

Mapping Lists Revisited

You're already familiar with using list comprehensions to map one list into another (introduced in Chapter 4). There is another way to accomplish the same thing, using the built-in `map` function, as shown in Listing 16-10. It works much the same way as the `filter` function.

Listing 16-10. Introducing map

```
>>> def double(n):
...      return n*2
...
>>> li = [1, 2, 3, 5, 9, 10, 256, -3]
>>> map(double, li)                            (1)
[2, 4, 6, 10, 18, 20, 512, -6]
>>> [double(n) for n in li]                    (2)
[2, 4, 6, 10, 18, 20, 512, -6]
>>> newlist = []
>>> for n in li:                               (3)
...      newlist.append(double(n))
...
>>> newlist
[2, 4, 6, 10, 18, 20, 512, -6]
```

(1) map takes a function and a list and returns a new list by calling the function with each element of the list in order. In this case, the function simply multiplies each element by 2.

(2) You could accomplish the same thing with a list comprehension. List comprehensions were first introduced in Python 2.0; map has been around forever.

(3) You could, if you insist on thinking like a Visual Basic programmer, use a for loop to accomplish the same thing.

> **NOTE** *Similar to* filter, map *can take a list, a tuple, or any object that acts like a sequence.*

As a side note, I would like to point out that map works just as well with lists of mixed datatypes, as long as the function you're using correctly handles each type. Listing 16-11 demonstrates this use.

Listing 16-11. Using map with Lists of Mixed Datatypes

```
>>> li = [5, 'a', (2, 'b')]
>>> map(double, li)                            (1)
[10, 'aa', (2, 'b', 2, 'b')]
```

(1) In this case, the double function simply multiplies the given argument by 2, and Python does the right thing, depending on the datatype of the argument. For integers, this means actually multiplying it by 2; for strings, it means concatenating the string with itself; for tuples, it means making a new tuple that has all of the elements of the original, then all of the elements of the original again.

All right, enough play time. Let's look at some real code, in Listing 16-12.

Listing 16-12. map in regression.py

```
filenameToModuleName = lambda f: os.path.splitext(f)[0]     (1)
moduleNames = map(filenameToModuleName, files)              (2)
```

(1) As you saw in the "Using lambda Functions" in Chapter 4, `lambda` defines an in-line function. And as you saw in Chapter 6 (Listing 6-17, "Splitting Pathnames"), `os.path.splitext` takes a filename and returns a tuple (*name, extension*). So, `filenameToModuleName` is a function that will take a filename, strip off the file extension, and return just the name.

(2) Calling `map` takes each filename listed in `files`, passes it to the function `filenameToModuleName`, and returns a list of the return values of each of those function calls. In other words, you strip the file extension off each filename and store the list of all those stripped filenames in `moduleNames`.

As you'll see in the rest of the chapter, you can extend this type of data-centric thinking all the way to the final goal, which is to define and execute a single test suite that contains the tests from all of those individual test suites.

Data-centric Programming

By now, you're probably scratching your head wondering why using `map` and `filter` is better than using `for` loops and straight function calls. And that's a perfectly valid question. Mostly, it's a matter of perspective. Using `map` and `filter` forces you to center your thinking around your data.

In this case, you started with no data at all. You began by getting the directory path of the current script, and then you got a list of files in that directory. That was the bootstrap, and it gave you real data to work with: a list of filenames.

However, you knew you didn't care about all of those files; you were interested in only the ones that were actually test suites. You had *too much data*, so you needed to *filter* it. How did you know which data to keep? You needed a test to decide, so you defined one and passed it to the `filter` function. In this case, you used a regular expression to decide, but the concept would be the same, regardless of how you constructed the test.

After filtering, you had the filenames of each of the test suites (and only the test suites, since everything else had been filtered out), but you really wanted module names instead. You had the right amount of data, but it was *in the wrong format*. So you defined a function that would transform a single filename into a module name, and you mapped that function onto the entire list. From one filename, you can get a module name; from a list of filenames, you can get a list of module names.

Instead of `filter`, you could have used a `for` loop with an `if` statement. Instead of `map`, you could have used a `for` loop with a function call. But using `for` loops like that is busywork. At best, it simply wastes time; at worst, it introduces obscure bugs. For instance, you need to figure out how to test for the condition "is this file a test suite?" That's the application-specific logic, and no language can write that for you. But once you've figured that out, do you really want to go to all the trouble of defining a new empty list, writing a `for` loop and an `if` statement, manually calling `append` to add each element to the new list if it passes the condition, and then keeping track of which variable holds the new filtered data and which one holds the old unfiltered data? Why not just define the test condition, and then let Python do the rest of that work for you?

Leave the Busywork Behind

Oh sure, you could try to be fancy and delete elements in place without creating a new list. But you've been burned by that before. Trying to modify a data structure that you're looping through can be tricky. You delete an element, then loop to the next element, and suddenly you've skipped one. Is Python one of the languages that works that way? How long would it take you to figure it out? Would you remember for certain whether it was safe the next time you tried?

Programmers spend a lot of time and make many mistakes dealing with purely technical issues like this, and it's all pointless. It doesn't advance your program at all; it's just busywork.

I resisted list comprehensions when I first learned Python, and I resisted `filter` and `map` even longer. I insisted on making my life more difficult, sticking to the familiar way of `for` loops and `if` statements and step-by-step code-centric programming. And my Python programs looked a lot like Visual Basic programs, detailing every step of every operation in every function. And they had all the same types of little problems and obscure bugs. And it was all pointless.

Let it all go. Busywork code is not important. Data is important. And data is not difficult. It's only data. If you have too much, filter it. If it's not what you want, map it. Focus on the data, and leave the busywork behind.

Dynamically Importing Modules

Now, let's talk about dynamically importing modules. First, let's look at how you normally import modules.

The `import` *module* syntax looks in the search path for the named module and imports it by name. You can even import multiple modules at once this way, with a comma-separated list. You did this on the very first line of this chapter's script:

```
import sys, os, re, unittest
```

This imports four modules at once: `sys` (for system functions and access to the command-line parameters), `os` (for operating system functions like directory listings), `re` (for regular expressions), and `unittest` (for unit testing).

Now, let's do the same thing, but with dynamic imports, as shown in Listing 16-13.

Listing 16-13. Importing Modules Dynamically

```
>>> sys = __import__('sys')                         (1)
>>> os = __import__('os')
>>> re = __import__('re')
>>> unittest = __import__('unittest')
>>> sys                                             (2)
>>> <module 'sys' (built-in)>
>>> os
>>> <module 'os' from 'c:\Python23\lib\os.pyc'>
```

(1) The built-in `__import__` function accomplishes the same goal as using the `import` statement, but it's an actual function, and it takes a string as an argument.

(2) The variable `sys` is now the `sys` module, just as if you had said `import sys`. The variable `os` is now the `os` module, and so forth.

So `__import__` imports a module, but takes a string argument to do it. In this case, the module you imported was just a hard-coded string, but it could just as easily be a variable or the result of a function call. And the variable that you assign the module to doesn't need to match the module name, either. You could import a series of modules and assign them to a list, as shown in Listing 16-14.

Listing 16-14. Importing a List of Modules Dynamically

```
>>> moduleNames = ['sys', 'os', 're', 'unittest']      (1)
>>> moduleNames
['sys', 'os', 're', 'unittest']
>>> modules = map(__import__, moduleNames)             (2)
>>> modules                                            (3)
[<module 'sys' (built-in)>,
<module 'os' from 'c:\Python23\lib\os.pyc'>,
<module 're' from 'c:\Python23\lib\re.pyc'>,
<module 'unittest' from 'c:\Python23\lib\unittest.pyc'>]
```

```
>>> modules[0].version                                    (4)
'2.3.3 (#51, Dec 18 2003, 20:22:39) [MSC v.1200 32 bit (Intel)]'
>>> import sys
>>> sys.version
'2.3.3 (#51, Dec 18 2003, 20:22:39) [MSC v.1200 32 bit (Intel)]'
```

(1) moduleNames is just a list of strings. There is nothing fancy here, except that the strings happen to be names of modules that you could import, if you wanted to.

(2) Surprise, you wanted to import them, and you did just that, by mapping the __import__ function onto the list. Remember that this takes each element of the list (moduleNames) and calls the function (__import__) over and over, once with each element of the list; builds a list of the return values; and returns the result.

(3) So, now from a list of strings, you've created a list of actual modules. (Your paths may be different, depending on your operating system, where you installed Python, the phase of the moon, and so on.)

(4) To drive home the point that these are real modules, let's look at some module attributes. Remember that modules[0] *is* the sys module, so modules[0].version *is* sys.version. All the other attributes and methods of these modules are also available. There's nothing magic about the import statement, and there's nothing magic about modules. Modules are objects. Everything is an object.

Now, you should be able to put this all together and figure out what most of this chapter's code sample is doing.

Putting It All Together

You've learned enough now to deconstruct the first seven lines of this chapter's code sample: reading a directory and importing selected modules within it. This portion is shown again in Listing 16-15.

Listing 16-15. The regressionTest Function

```
def regressionTest():
    path = os.path.abspath(os.path.dirname(sys.argv[0]))
    files = os.listdir(path)
    test = re.compile("test\.py$", re.IGNORECASE)
    files = filter(test.search, files)
    filenameToModuleName = lambda f: os.path.splitext(f)[0]
    moduleNames = map(filenameToModuleName, files)
    modules = map(__import__, moduleNames)
load = unittest.defaultTestLoader.loadTestsFromModule
return unittest.TestSuite(map(load, modules))
```

Let's look at it line by line, interactively. Assume that the current directory is c:\diveintopython\py, which contains the examples that come with this book, including this chapter's script. As you saw in the "Finding the Path" section earlier in this chapter, the script directory will end up in the path variable, so let's start hard-code and go from there. Listing 16-16 shows step 1 in the process.

Listing 16-16. Step 1: Get All the Files

```
>>> import sys, os, re, unittest
>>> path = r'c:\diveintopython\py'
>>> files = os.listdir(path)
>>> files                                         (1)
['BaseHTMLProcessor.py', 'LICENSE.txt', 'apihelper.py', 'apihelpertest.py',
 'argecho.py', 'autosize.py', 'builddialectexamples.py', 'dialect.py',
 'fileinfo.py', 'fullpath.py', 'kgptest.py', 'makerealworddoc.py',
 'odbchelper.py', 'odbchelpertest.py', 'parsephone.py', 'piglatin.py',
 'plural.py', 'pluraltest.py', 'pyfontify.py', 'regression.py', 'roman.py',
 'romantest.py',
 'uncurly.py', 'unicode2koi8r.py', 'urllister.py', 'kgp', 'plural', 'roman',
 'colorize.py']
```

(1) files is a list of all the files and directories in the script's directory. (If you've been running some of the examples already, you may also see some .pyc files in there as well.)

On to step 2, shown in Listing 16-17.

Listing 16-17. Step 2: Filter to Find the Files You Care About

```
>>> test = re.compile("test\.py$", re.IGNORECASE)     (1)
>>> files = filter(test.search, files)                (2)
>>> files                                             (3)
['apihelpertest.py', 'kgptest.py', 'odbchelpertest.py',
 'pluraltest.py', 'romantest.py']
```

(1) This regular expression will match any string that ends with test.py. Note that you need to escape the period, since a period in a regular expression usually means "match any single character," but you actually want to match a literal period instead.

(2) The compiled regular expression acts like a function, so you can use it to filter the large list of files and directories, to find the ones that match the regular expression.

(3) And you're left with the list of unit testing scripts, because they are the only ones named *something*test.py.

Next, the third step is shown in Listing 16-18.

Listing 16-18. Step 3: Map Filenames to Module Names

```
>>> filenameToModuleName = lambda f: os.path.splitext(f)[0]      (1)
>>> filenameToModuleName('romantest.py')                          (2)
'romantest'
>>> filenameToModuleName('odchelpertest.py')
'odbchelpertest'
>>> moduleNames = map(filenameToModuleName, files)                (3)
>>> moduleNames                                                   (4)
['apihelpertest', 'kgptest', 'odbchelpertest', 'pluraltest', 'romantest']
```

(**1**) As you saw in the "Using lambda Functions" section in Chapter 4, `lambda` is a quick-and-dirty way of creating an in-line, one-line function. This one takes a filename with an extension and returns just the filename part, using the standard library function `os.path.splitext` that you saw in Chapter 6 (Listing 6-17, "Splitting Pathnames").

(**2**) `filenameToModuleName` is a function. There's nothing magic about `lambda` functions as opposed to regular functions that you define with a `def` statement. You can call the `filenameToModuleName` function like any other function, and it does just what you wanted it to do: strips the file extension off its argument.

(**3**) Now, you can apply this function to each file in the list of unit test files, using `map`.

(**4**) And the result is just what you wanted: a list of modules, as strings.

Now, you're ready for step 4, which is to map module names to modules, as shown in Listing 16-19.

Listing 16-19. Step 4: Mapping Module Names to Modules

```
>>> modules = map(__import__, moduleNames)                        (1)
>>> modules                                                       (2)
[<module 'apihelpertest' from 'apihelpertest.py'>,
<module 'kgptest' from 'kgptest.py'>,
<module 'odbchelpertest' from 'odbchelpertest.py'>,
<module 'pluraltest' from 'pluraltest.py'>,
<module 'romantest' from 'romantest.py'>]
>>> modules[-1]                                                   (3)
<module 'romantest' from 'romantest.py'>
```

(**1**) As you saw in the previous section of this chapter, you can use a combination of `map` and `__import__` to map a list of module names (as strings) into actual modules (which you can call or access like any other module).

(**2**) `modules` is now a list of modules, fully accessible like any other module.

(**3**) The last module in the list *is* the `romantest` module, just as if you had said `import romantest`.

Next, load the modules, as shown in Listing 16-20.

Listing 16-20. Step 5: Loading the Modules into a Test Suite

```
>>> load = unittest.defaultTestLoader.loadTestsFromModule
>>> map(load, modules)                                        (1)
[<unittest.TestSuite tests=[
  <unittest.TestSuite tests=[<apihelpertest.BadInput testMethod=testNoObject>]>,
  <unittest.TestSuite tests=[
    <apihelpertest.KnownValues testMethod=testApiHelper>
  ]>,
  <unittest.TestSuite tests=[
    <apihelpertest.ParamChecks testMethod=testCollapse>,
    <apihelpertest.ParamChecks testMethod=testSpacing>]>,
  ...
  ]
]
>>> unittest.TestSuite(map(load, modules))                    (2)
```

(1) These are real module objects. Not only can you access them like any other module, instantiate classes, and call functions, but you can also introspect into the module to figure out which classes and functions it has in the first place. That's what the `loadTestsFromModule` method does: it introspects into each module and returns a `unittest.TestSuite` object for each module. Each `TestSuite` object actually contains a list of `TestSuite` objects: one for each `TestCase` class in your module. And each of those `TestSuite` objects contains a list of tests: one for each test method in your module.

(2) Finally, you wrap the list of `TestSuite` objects into one big test suite. The `unittest` module has no problem traversing this tree of nested test suites within test suites. Eventually, it gets down to an individual test method and executes it, verifies that it passes or fails, and moves on to the next one.

This introspection process is what the `unittest` module usually does for you. Remember that magic-looking `unittest.main()` function that your individual test modules called to kick the whole thing off? `unittest.main()` actually creates an instance of `unittest.TestProgram`, which, in turn, creates an instance of a `unittest.defaultTestLoader` and loads it with the module that called it. How does it get a reference to the module that called it if you don't give it one? By using the equally magic `__import__('__main__')` command, which dynamically imports the currently running module. (I could write a book on all the tricks and techniques used in the `unittest` module, but then I would never finish this one.)

Finally, the last step in the process is shown in Listing 16-21.

Listing 16-21. Step 6: Telling unittest to Use Your Test Suite

```
if __name__ == "__main__":
    unittest.main(defaultTest="regressionTest")               (1)
```

(1) Instead of letting the unittest module do all its magic for you, you've done most of it yourself. You've created a function (regressionTest) that imports the modules, calls unittest.defaultTestLoader, and wraps it all up in a test suite. Now, all you need to do is tell unittest that, instead of looking for tests and building a test suite in the usual way, it should just call the regressionTest function, which returns a ready-to-use TestSuite.

Summary

The regression.py program and its output should make perfect sense to you. You should now feel comfortable doing all of these things:

- Manipulating path information from the command line

- Filtering lists using filter instead of list comprehensions

- Mapping lists using map instead of list comprehensions

- Dynamically importing modules

CHAPTER 17

Dynamic Functions

I want to talk about plural nouns. Also, I want to discuss functions that return other functions, advanced regular expressions, and generators, which are new in Python 2.3. But first, let's talk about how to make plural nouns.

Note that this chapter assumes you understand the basics of regular expressions, and it focuses on more advanced uses. If you haven't read Chapter 7, which covers regular expressions, now would be a good time to do that.

Diving In

English is a schizophrenic language that borrows from a lot of other languages, and the rules for making singular nouns into plural nouns are varied and complex. There are rules, and then there are exceptions to those rules, and then there are exceptions to the exceptions.

If you grew up in an English-speaking country or learned English in a formal school setting, you're probably familiar with the basic rules:

- If a word ends in *s*, *x*, or *z*, add *es*. *Bass* becomes *basses*, *fax* becomes *faxes*, and *waltz* becomes *waltzes*.

- If a word ends in a noisy *h*, add *es*; if it ends in a silent *h*, just add *s*. What's a noisy *h*? It's one that gets combined with other letters to make a sound that you can hear. So, *coach* becomes *coaches* and *rash* becomes *rashes*, because you can hear the *ch* and *sh* sounds when you say them. But *cheetah* becomes *cheetahs*, because the *h* is silent.

- If a word ends in *y* that sounds like *i*, change the *y* to *ies*; if the *y* is combined with a vowel to sound like something else, just add *s*. So *vacancy* becomes *vacancies*, but *day* becomes *days*.

- If all else fails, just add *s* and hope for the best.

> **NOTE** *Of course, there are many exceptions and special cases when it comes to plurals. Man becomes men, and woman becomes women, but human becomes humans. Mouse becomes mice and louse becomes lice, but house becomes houses. Knife becomes knives, and wife becomes wives, but lowlife becomes lowlifes. And don't even get me started on words that are their own plural, like sheep, deer, and haiku.*

Let's design a module that pluralizes nouns. We'll start with just English nouns and just these four rules, but keep in mind that we'll inevitably need to add more rules, and we may eventually need to add more languages. And, of course, other languages are completely different.

Pluralizing Nouns, Stage 1

So we're looking at words, which, at least in English, are strings of characters. And we have rules that say we need to find different combinations of characters, and then do different things to them. This sounds like a job for regular expressions. Listing 17-1 shows the first version of plural.py, which we'll develop in six stages in this chapter.

> **NOTE** *If you have not already done so, you can download this and other examples used in this book from the Downloads section of the Apress web site (http://www.apress.com).*

Listing 17-1. plural1.py

```
import re

def plural(noun):
    if re.search('[sxz]$', noun):              (1)
        return re.sub('$', 'es', noun)          (2)
    elif re.search('[^aeioudgkprt]h$', noun):
        return re.sub('$', 'es', noun)
    elif re.search('[^aeiou]y$', noun):
        return re.sub('y$', 'ies', noun)
    else:
        return noun + 's'
```

(1) This is a regular expression, but it uses a syntax you didn't see in Chapter 7. The square brackets mean "match exactly one of these characters." So [sxz] means *s* or *x*, or *z*, but only one of them. The $ should be familiar; it matches the end of string. So we're checking to see if noun ends with *s*, *x*, or *z*.

(2) This re.sub function performs regular expression-based string substitutions. Let's look at it in more detail.

Listing 17-2 introduces the re.sub function.

Listing 17-2. Introducing re.sub

```
>>> import re
>>> re.search('[abc]', 'Mark')                    (1)
<_sre.SRE_Match object at 0x001C1FA8>
>>> re.sub('[abc]', 'o', 'Mark')                  (2)
'Mork'
>>> re.sub('[abc]', 'o', 'rock')                  (3)
'rook'
>>> re.sub('[abc]', 'o', 'caps')                  (4)
'oops'
```

(1) Does the string Mark contain *a*, *b*, or *c*? Yes, it contains *a*.

(2) Okay, now find *a*, *b*, or *c*, and replace it with *o*. *Mark* becomes *Mork*.

(3) The same function turns *rock* into *rook*.

(4) You might think this would turn *caps* into *oaps*, but it doesn't. re.sub replaces *all* of the matches, not just the first one. So this regular expression turns *caps* into *oops*, because both the *c* and the *a* are turned into *o*.

Now, let's get back to the plural function, as shown in Listing 17-3.

Listing 17-3. Back to plural1.py

```
import re

def plural(noun):
    if re.search('[sxz]$', noun):
        return re.sub('$', 'es', noun)            (1)
    elif re.search('[^aeioudgkprt]h$', noun):     (2)
        return re.sub('$', 'es', noun)            (3)
    elif re.search('[^aeiou]y$', noun):
        return re.sub('y$', 'ies', noun)
    else:
        return noun + 's'
```

(1) What are we doing? We're replacing the end of string with *es*. In other words, we're adding *es* to the string. You could accomplish the same thing with string concatenation (for example, noun + 'es'), but here, we're using regular expressions for consistency and for other reasons that will become clear later in the chapter.

(2) Look closely—this is another new variation. The ^ as the first character inside the square brackets means something special: negation. [^abc] means "any single character *except a*, *b*, or *c*." So [^aeioudgkprt] means any character except *a, e, i, o, u, d, g, k, p, r,* or *t*. Then that character needs to be followed by *h*, followed by the end of the string. We're looking for words that end in *h* where the *h* can be heard.

(3) This is the same pattern here: match words that end in *y*, where the character before the *y* is not *a, e, i, o,* or *u*. We're looking for words that end in a *y* that sounds like an *i*.

Listing 17-4 shows how negation regular expressions work.

Listing 17-4. More on Negation Regular Expressions

```
>>> import re
>>> re.search('[^aeiou]y$', 'vacancy')          (1)
<_sre.SRE_Match object at 0x001C1FA8>
>>> re.search('[^aeiou]y$', 'boy')              (2)
>>>
>>> re.search('[^aeiou]y$', 'day')
>>>
>>> re.search('[^aeiou]y$', 'pita')             (3)
>>>
```

(1) vacancy matches this regular expression, because it ends in *cy*, and *c* is not *a, e, i, o,* or *u*.

(2) boy does not match, because it ends in *oy*, and we specifically said that the character before the *y* could not be *o*. day does not match, because it ends in *ay*.

(3) pita does not match, because it does not end in *y*.

Listing 17-5 shows how re.sub works in the function.

Listing 17-5. More on re.sub

```
>>> re.sub('y$', 'ies', 'vacancy')              (1)
'vacancies'
>>> re.sub('y$', 'ies', 'agency')
'agencies'
>>> re.sub('([^aeiou])y$', r'\1ies', 'vacancy') (2)
'vacancies'
```

(1) This regular expression turns vacancy into vacancies and agency into agencies, which is what we wanted. Note that it would also turn boy into boies, but that will never happen in our function, because we did that re.search first to find out whether we should do this re.sub.

(2) Just in passing, I want to point out that it is possible to combine these two regular expressions (one to find out whether the rule applies and another to actually apply it) into a single regular expression. Here's what that would look like. Most of it should look familiar: we're using a remembered group (which

you learned about in the "Case Study: Parsing Phone Numbers" section in Chapter 7) to remember the character before the *y*. Then in the substitution string, we use a new syntax, \1, which means "hey, that first group you remembered? Put it here." In this case, we remember the c before the y, and then when we do the substitution, we substitute c in place of c, and ies in place of y. (If you have more than one remembered group, you can use \2, \3, and so on.)

Regular expression substitutions are extremely powerful, and the \1 syntax makes them even more powerful. But combining the entire operation into one regular expression is also much harder to read, and it doesn't directly map to the way we first described the pluralizing rules. We originally laid out rules like "if the word ends in *s*, *x*, or *z*, then add *es*." And if you look at this function, we have two lines of code that say, "if the word ends in *s*, *x*, or *z*, then add *es*." It doesn't get much more direct than that.

Pluralizing Nouns, Stage 2

Now we're going to add a level of abstraction. We started by defining a list of rules: if this, then do that; otherwise, go to the next rule. Let's temporarily complicate part of our program so we can simplify another part. Listing 17-6 shows this temporary modification.

Listing 17-6. plural2.py

```python
import re

def match_sxz(noun):
    return re.search('[sxz]$', noun)

def apply_sxz(noun):
    return re.sub('$', 'es', noun)

def match_h(noun):
    return re.search('[^aeioudgkprt]h$', noun)

def apply_h(noun):
    return re.sub('$', 'es', noun)

def match_y(noun):
    return re.search('[^aeiou]y$', noun)

def apply_y(noun):
    return re.sub('y$', 'ies', noun)
```

```
def match_default(noun):
    return 1

def apply_default(noun):
    return noun + 's'

rules = ((match_sxz, apply_sxz),
         (match_h, apply_h),
         (match_y, apply_y),
         (match_default, apply_default)
         )                                          (1)

def plural(noun):
    for matchesRule, applyRule in rules:            (2)
        if matchesRule(noun):                       (3)
            return applyRule(noun)                  (4)
```

(1) This version looks more complicated (it's certainly longer), but it does the same thing: try to match four different rules, in order, and apply the appropriate regular expression when a match is found. The difference is that each individual match and apply rule is defined in its own function, and the functions are then listed in this rules variable, which is a tuple of tuples.

(2) Using a for loop, we can pull out the match and apply rules two at a time (one match, one apply) from the rules tuple. On the first iteration of the for loop, matchesRule will get match_sxz, and applyRule will get apply_sxz. On the second iteration (assuming we get that far), matchesRule will be assigned match_h, and applyRule will be assigned apply_h.

(3) Remember that everything in Python, including functions, is an object. rules contains actual functions—not names of functions, but actual functions. When they get assigned in the for loop, matchesRule and applyRule are actual functions that we can call. So, on the first iteration of the for loop, this is equivalent to calling matches_sxz(noun).

(4) On the first iteration of the for loop, this is equivalent to calling apply_sxz(noun), and so forth.

If this additional level of abstraction is confusing, try unrolling the function to see the equivalence. This for loop is equivalent to the following:

```
def plural(noun):
    if match_sxz(noun):
        return apply_sxz(noun)
    if match_h(noun):
        return apply_h(noun)
    if match_y(noun):
        return apply_y(noun)
    if match_default(noun):
        return apply_default(noun)
```

The benefit here is that our `plural` function is now simplified. It takes a list of rules, defined elsewhere, and iterates through them in a generic fashion. Get a match rule; does it match? Then call the apply rule. The rules could be defined anywhere, in any way. The `plural` function doesn't care.

Now, was adding this level of abstraction worth it? Well, not yet. Let's consider what it would take to add a new rule to this function. Well, in the previous example, it would require adding an `if` statement to the `plural` function. In this example, it would require adding two functions, `match_foo` and `apply_foo`, and then updating the `rules` list to specify where in the order the new match and apply functions should be called relative to the other rules.

This is really just a stepping-stone to the next section. Let's move on.

Pluralizing Nouns, Stage 3

Defining separate named functions for each match and apply rule isn't really necessary. We never call them directly; we define them in the `rules` list and call them through there. Let's streamline our rules definition by anonymizing those functions, as shown in Listing 17-7.

Listing 17-7. plural3.py

```
import re

rules = \
  (
    (
     lambda word: re.search('[sxz]$', word),
     lambda word: re.sub('$', 'es', word)
    ),
    (
     lambda word: re.search('[^aeioudgkprt]h$', word),
     lambda word: re.sub('$', 'es', word)
    ),
    (
     lambda word: re.search('[^aeiou]y$', word),
     lambda word: re.sub('y$', 'ies', word)
    ),
    (
     lambda word: re.search('$', word),
     lambda word: re.sub('$', 's', word)
    )
  )                                           (1)
```

```
def plural(noun):
    for matchesRule, applyRule in rules:          (2)
        if matchesRule(noun):
            return applyRule(noun)
```

(1) This is the same set of rules as we defined in stage 2. The only difference is that, instead of defining named functions like match_sxz and apply_sxz, we have "in-lined" those function definitions directly into the rules list itself, using lambda functions.

(2) Note that the plural function hasn't changed at all. It iterates through a set of rule functions, checks the first rule, and if it returns a true value, calls the second rule and returns the value. This is the same as the previous version, word for word. The only difference is that the rule functions were defined in-line, anonymously, using lambda functions. But the plural function doesn't care how the rule functions were defined; it just gets a list of rules and blindly works through them.

Now to add a new rule, all we need to do is define the functions directly in the rules list itself: one match rule and one apply rule. But defining the rule functions in-line like this makes it very clear that we have some unnecessary duplication here. We have four pairs of functions, and they all follow the same pattern. The match function is a single call to re.search, and the apply function is a single call to re.sub. Let's factor out these similarities.

Pluralizing Nouns, Stage 4

Listing 17-8 demonstrates how to factor out the duplication in the code so that defining new rules can be easier.

Listing 17-8. plural4.py

```
import re

def buildMatchAndApplyFunctions((pattern, search, replace)):
    matchFunction = lambda word: re.search(pattern, word)          (1)
    applyFunction = lambda word: re.sub(search, replace, word)     (2)
    return (matchFunction, applyFunction)                          (3)
```

(1) buildMatchAndApplyFunctions is a function that builds other functions dynamically. It takes pattern, search, and replace (actually it takes a tuple, but more on that in a minute). We can build the match function, using the lambda syntax, to be a function that takes one parameter (word), and calls re.search with the pattern that was passed to the buildMatchAndApplyFunctions function and the word that was passed to the match function we're building. Whoa.

(2) Building the apply function works the same way. The apply function takes one parameter, and calls re.sub with the search and replace parameters that were passed to the buildMatchAndApplyFunctions function and the word that was passed to the apply function we're building. This technique of using the values of outside parameters within a dynamic function is called *closures*. We're essentially defining constants within the apply function we're building. It takes one parameter (word), but it then acts on that plus two other values (search and replace), which were set when we defined the apply function.

(3) Finally, the buildMatchAndApplyFunctions function returns a tuple of two values: the two functions we just created. The constants we defined within those functions (pattern within matchFunction, and search and replace within applyFunction) stay with those functions, even after we return from buildMatchAndApplyFunctions. That's insanely cool.

If this is incredibly confusing (and it should be, since this is weird stuff), it may become clearer when you see how to use it, in Listing 17-9.

Listing 17-9. plural4.py Continued

```
patterns = \
  (
    ('[sxz]$', '$', 'es'),
    ('[^aeioudgkprt]h$', '$', 'es'),
    ('(qu|[^aeiou])y$', 'y$', 'ies'),
    ('$', '$', 's')
  )                                             (1)
rules = map(buildMatchAndApplyFunctions, patterns)    (2)
```

(1) The pluralization rules are now defined as a series of strings (not functions). The first string is the regular expression that we would use in re.search to see if this rule matches. The second and third are the search and replace expressions we would use in re.sub to actually apply the rule to turn a noun into its plural.

(2) This line is magic. It takes the list of strings in patterns and turns them into a list of functions. How? By mapping the strings to the buildMatchAndApplyFunctions function, which just happens to take three strings as parameters and return a tuple of two functions. This means that rules ends up being exactly the same as the previous example: a list of tuples, where each tuple is a pair of functions, where the first function is our match function that calls re.search and the second function is our apply function that calls re.sub.

I swear I am not making this up: rules ends up with exactly the same list of functions as the previous example. Unroll the rules definition, and you'll get this:

```
rules = \
  (
    (
     lambda word: re.search('[sxz]$', word),
     lambda word: re.sub('$', 'es', word)
    ),
    (
     lambda word: re.search('[^aeioudgkprt]h$', word),
     lambda word: re.sub('$', 'es', word)
    ),
    (
     lambda word: re.search('[^aeiou]y$', word),
     lambda word: re.sub('y$', 'ies', word)
    ),
    (
     lambda word: re.search('$', word),
     lambda word: re.sub('$', 's', word)
    )
  )
```

Now, let's finish up with this version of `plural.py`, as shown in Listing 17-10.

Listing 17-10. plural4.py, Finishing Up

```
def plural(noun):
    for matchesRule, applyRule in rules:          (1)
        if matchesRule(noun):
            return applyRule(noun)
```

(1) Since the `rules` list is the same as the previous example, it should come as no surprise that the `plural` function hasn't changed. Remember, it's completely generic. It takes a list of rule functions and calls them in order. It doesn't care how the rules are defined. In stage 2, they were defined as separate, named functions. In stage 3, they were defined as anonymous `lambda` functions. Now, in stage 4, they are built dynamically by mapping the `buildMatchAndApplyFunctions` function onto a list of raw strings. It doesn't matter—the `plural` function still works the same way.

Just in case that wasn't mind-blowing enough, I must confess that there was a subtlety in the definition of `buildMatchAndApplyFunctions` that I skipped over. Let's go back and take another look:

```
def buildMatchAndApplyFunctions((pattern, search, replace)):
```

Notice the double parentheses? This function doesn't really take three parameters; it actually takes one parameter: a tuple of three elements. But the tuple is expanded when the function is called, and the three elements of the tuple are each assigned to different variables: pattern, search, and replace. Confused yet? Let's see it in action, in Listing 17-11.

Listing 17-11. Expanding Tuples When Calling Functions

```
>>> def foo((a, b, c)):
...     print c
...     print b
...     print a
>>> parameters = ('apple', 'bear', 'catnap')
>>> foo(parameters)                              (1)
catnap
bear
apple
```

(1) The proper way to call the function foo is with a tuple of three elements. When the function is called, the elements are assigned to different local variables within foo.

Now, let's go back and see why this auto-tuple-expansion trick was necessary. patterns was a list of tuples, and each tuple had three elements. That means when we call map(buildMatchAndApplyFunctions, patterns), buildMatchAndApplyFunctions is *not* getting called with three parameters. Using map to map a single list onto a function always calls the function with a single parameter: each element of the list. In the case of patterns, each element of the list is a tuple, so buildMatchAndApplyFunctions always gets called with the tuple, and we use the auto-tuple-expansion trick in the definition of buildMatchAndApplyFunctions to assign the elements of that tuple to named variables.

Pluralizing Nouns, Stage 5

We've factored out all the duplicate code and added enough abstractions so that the pluralization rules are defined in a list of strings. The next logical step is to take these strings and put them in a separate file, where they can be maintained separately from the code that uses them.

First, let's create a text file that contains the rules we want. No fancy data structures—just space-delimited (or tab-delimited) strings in three columns. We'll call it rules.en (en stands for English), as shown in Listing 17-12. These are the rules for pluralizing English nouns. We could add other rule files for other languages later.

Listing 17-12. rules.en

```
[sxz]$                  $           es
[^aeioudgkprt]h$        $           es
[^aeiou]y$              y$          ies
$                       $           s
```

Now, let's see how we can use this rules file. Listing 17-13 shows the next version of plural.py.

Listing 17-13. plural5.py
```
import re
import string
def buildRule((pattern, search, replace)):
    return lambda word: re.search(pattern, word) and \
        re.sub(search, replace, word)                      (1)

def plural(noun, language='en'):                           (2)
    lines = file('rules.%s' % language).readlines()        (3)
    patterns = map(string.split, lines)                    (4)
    rules = map(buildRule, patterns)                       (5)
    for rule in rules:
        result = rule(noun)                                (6)
        if result: return result
```

(1) We're still using the closures technique here (building a function dynamically that uses variables defined outside the function), but now we've combined the separate match and apply functions into one. (The reason for this change will become clear in the next section.) This will let us accomplish the same thing as having two functions, but we'll need to call it differently, as you'll see in a minute.

(2) The plural function now takes an optional second parameter, language, which defaults to en.

(3) We use the language parameter to construct a filename, then open the file and read the contents into a list. If language is en, then we'll open the rules.en file, read the entire thing, break it up by carriage returns, and return a list. Each line of the file will be one element in the list.

(4) As you saw, each line in the file really has three values, but they're separated by whitespace (tabs or spaces—it makes no difference). Mapping the string.split function onto this list will create a new list where each element is a tuple of three strings. So, a line like [sxz]$ $ es will be broken up into the tuple ('[sxz]$', '$', 'es'). This means that patterns will end up as a list of tuples, just as we hard-coded it in stage 4.

(5) If patterns is a list of tuples, then rules will be a list of the functions created dynamically by each call to buildRule. Calling buildRule(('[sxz]$', '$', 'es')) returns a function that takes a single parameter: word. When this returned function is called, it will execute re.search('[sxz]$', word) and re.sub('$', 'es', word).

(6) Because we're now building a combined match-and-apply function, we need to call it differently. Just call the function, and if it returns something, then that's the plural; if it returns nothing (None), then the rule didn't match and we need to try another rule.

So, the improvement here is that we've completely separated our pluralization rules into an external file. Not only can the file be maintained separately from the code, but we've set up a naming scheme where the same plural function can use different rule files, based on the language parameter.

The downside here is that we're reading that file every time we call the plural function. I thought I could get through this entire book without using the phrase "left as an exercise for the reader," but here you go: building a caching mechanism for the language-specific rule files that auto-refreshes itself if the rule files change between calls *is left as an exercise for the reader*. Have fun.

Pluralizing Nouns, Stage 6

Now we're ready to talk about generators. Take a look at the final version of plural.py shown in Listing 17-14.

Listing 17-14. plural6.py

```
import re

def rules(language):
    for line in file('rules.%s' % language):
        pattern, search, replace = line.split()
        yield lambda word: re.search(pattern, word) and \
            re.sub(search, replace, word)

def plural(noun, language='en'):
    for applyRule in rules(language):
        result = applyRule(noun)
        if result: return result
```

This uses a technique called *generators*, which I'm not even going to try to explain until we look at a simpler example first, in Listing 17-15.

Listing 17-15. Introducing Generators

```
>>> def make_counter(x):
...     print 'entering make_counter'
...     while 1:
```

```
...          yield x                              (1)
...          print 'incrementing x'
...          x = x + 1
...
>>> counter = make_counter(2)                     (2)
>>> counter                                       (3)
<generator object at 0x001C9C10>
>>> counter.next()                                (4)
entering make_counter
2
>>> counter.next()                                (5)
incrementing x
3
>>> counter.next()                                (6)
incrementing x
4
```

(1) The presence of the yield keyword in make_counter means that this is not a normal function. It is a special kind of function that generates values one at a time. You can think of it as a resumable function. Calling it will return a generator that can be used to generate successive values of x.

(2) To create an instance of the make_counter generator, just call it like any other function. Note that this does not actually execute the function code. You can tell this because the first line of make_counter is a print statement, but nothing has been printed yet.

(3) The make_counter function returns a generator object.

(4) The first time we call the next() method on the generator object, it executes the code in make_counter up to the first yield statement, and then returns the value that was yielded. In this case, that will be 2, because we originally created the generator by calling make_counter(2).

(5) Repeatedly calling next() on the generator object *resumes where we left off* and continues until we hit the next yield statement. The next line of code waiting to be executed is the print statement that prints incrementing x, and then after that the x = x + 1 statement that actually increments it. Then we loop through the while loop again, and the first thing we do is yield x, which returns the current value of x (now 3).

(6) The second time we call counter.next(), we do all the same things again, but this time x is now 4, and so on. Since make_counter sets up an infinite loop, you could theoretically do this forever, and it would just keep incrementing x and spitting out values. But let's look at more productive uses of generators instead.

Listing 17-16 demonstrates the usefulness of generators.

Listing 17-16. Using Generators Instead of Recursion

```
def fibonacci(max):
    a, b = 0, 1                                    (1)
    while a < max:
        yield a                                    (2)
        a, b = b, a+b                              (3)
```

(1) The Fibonacci sequence is a sequence of numbers where each number is the sum of the two numbers before it. It starts with 0 and 1, goes up slowly at first, then more and more rapidly. To start the sequence, we need two variables: a starts at 0, and b starts at 1.

(2) a is the current number in the sequence, so yield it.

(3) b is the next number in the sequence, so assign that to a, but also calculate the next value (a+b) and assign that to b for later use. Note that this happens in parallel. If a is 3 and b is 5, then a, b = b, a+b will set a to 5 (the previous value of b) and b to 8 (the sum of the previous values of a and b).

So, we have a function that spits out successive Fibonacci numbers. Sure, you could do that with recursion, but this way is easier to read. Also, it works well with for loops, as shown in Listing 17-17.

Listing 17-17. Generators in for Loops

```
>>> for n in fibonacci(1000):                      (1)
...     print n,                                    (2)
0 1 1 2 3 5 8 13 21 34 55 89 144 233 377 610 987
```

(1) You can use a generator like fibonacci in a for loop directly. The for loop will create the generator object and successively call the next() method to get values to assign to the for loop index variable (n).

(2) Each time through the for loop, n gets a new value from the yield statement in fibonacci, and all we do is print it. Once fibonacci runs out of numbers (a gets bigger than max, which in this case is 1000), then the for loop exits gracefully.

Okay, let's go back to the plural function and see how we're using this, as shown in Listing 17-18.

Listing 17-18. Generators That Generate Dynamic Functions

```
def rules(language):
    for line in file('rules.%s' % language):       (1)
        pattern, search, replace = line.split()    (2)
        yield lambda word: re.search(pattern, word) and \
            re.sub(search, replace, word)          (3)
```

```
def plural(noun, language='en'):
    for applyRule in rules(language):          (4)
        result = applyRule(noun)
        if result: return result
```

(1) `for line in file(...)` is a common idiom for reading lines from a file, one line at a time. It works because `file` *actually returns a generator* whose `next()` method returns the next line of the file. That is so insanely cool.

(2) There's no magic here. Remember that the lines of our rules file have three values separated by whitespace, so `line.split()` returns a tuple of three values, and we assign those values to three local variables.

(3) *And then we yield.* What do we yield? A function, built dynamically with `lambda`, that is actually a closure (it uses the local variables `pattern`, `search`, and `replace` as constants). In other words, `rules` is a generator that spits our rule functions.

(4) Since `rules` is a generator, we can use it directly in a `for` loop. The first time through the `for` loop, we will call the `rules` function, which will open the rules file, read the first line from it, dynamically build a function that matches and applies the first rule defined in the rules file, and yield the dynamically built function. The second time through the `for` loop, we will pick up where we left off in `rules` (which was in the middle of the `for line in file(...)` loop), read the second line of the rules file, dynamically build another function that matches and applies the second rule defined in the rules file, yields it, and so forth.

What have we gained over stage 5? In stage 5, we read the entire rules file and built a list of all the possible rules before we even tried the first one. With generators, we can do everything lazily: we open the file and read the first rule, and create a function to try it. If that works, we don't ever read the rest of the file or create any other functions.

Further Reading on Generators

For more information about Python generators, refer to the following:

- PEP 255 (`http://www.python.org/peps/pep-0255.html`) defines generators.

- Python Cookbook (`http://www.activestate.com/ASPN/Python/Cookbook`) has many more examples of generators (`http://www.google.com/search?q=generators+cookbook+site:aspn.activestate.com`).

Summary

We talked about several different advanced techniques in this chapter. Not all of them are appropriate for every situation.

You should now be comfortable with all of these techniques:

- Performing string substitution with regular expressions

- Treating functions as objects, storing them in lists, assigning them to variables, and calling them through those variables

- Building dynamic functions with `lambda`

- Building closures—dynamic functions that contain surrounding variables as constants

- Building generators—resumable functions that perform incremental logic and return different values each time you call them

Adding abstractions, building functions dynamically, building closures, and using generators can make your code simpler, more readable, and more flexible. But they can also end up making your code more difficult to debug later. It's up to you to find the right balance between simplicity and power.

CHAPTER 18

Performance Tuning

PERFORMANCE TUNING IS A many-splendored thing. Just because Python is an interpreted language doesn't mean you shouldn't worry about code optimization. But don't worry about it *too* much.

Diving In

There are so many pitfalls involved in optimizing your code that it's hard to know where to start.

Let's start here: *are you sure you need to do it at all?* Is your code really so bad? Is it worth the time to tune it? Over the lifetime of your application, how much time is going to be spent running that code, compared to the time spent waiting for a remote database server or waiting for user input?

Second, *are you sure you're finished coding?* Premature optimization is like spreading frosting on a half-baked cake. You spend hours or days (or more) optimizing your code for performance, only to discover it doesn't do what you need it to do. That's time down the drain.

This is not to say that code optimization is worthless, but you need to look at the whole system and decide whether it's the best use of your time. Every minute you spend optimizing code is a minute you're not spending adding new features, writing documentation, playing with your kids, or writing unit tests.

Oh yes, there are those unit tests. It should go without saying that you need a complete set of unit tests before you begin performance tuning. The last thing you need is to introduce new bugs while fiddling with your algorithms.

With these caveats in place, let's look at some techniques for optimizing Python code. The code in question is an implementation of the Soundex algorithm. Soundex was a method used in the early twentieth century for categorizing surnames in the United States census. It grouped similar-sounding names together, so even if a name was misspelled, researchers had a chance of finding it. Soundex is still used today for much the same reason, although, of course, we use computerized database servers now. Most database servers include a Soundex function.

There are several subtle variations of the Soundex algorithm. This is the one used in this chapter:

1. Keep the first letter of the name as-is.

2. Convert the remaining letters to digits, according to a specific table:

    *   *B*, *F*, *P*, and *V* become 1.

    *   *C*, *G*, *J*, *K*, *Q*, *S*, *X*, and *Z* become 2.

    *   *D* and *T* become 3.

    *   *L* becomes 4.

    *   *M* and *N* become 5.

    *   *R* becomes 6.

    *   All other letters become 9.

3. Remove consecutive duplicates.

4. Remove all 9s.

5. If the result is shorter than four characters (the first letter plus three digits), pad the result with trailing zeros.

6. If the result is longer than four characters, discard everything after the fourth character.

For example, my last name, Pilgrim, becomes P942695. That has no consecutive duplicates, so there is nothing to do here. Then you remove the 9s, leaving P4265. That's too long, so you discard the excess character, leaving P426.

Here's another example: Woo becomes W99, which becomes W9, which becomes W, which gets padded with zeros to become W000.

Listing 18.1 presents a first attempt at a Soundex function.

> **NOTE**   *If you have not already done so, you can download this and other examples used in this book from the Downloads section of the Apress web site* (http://www.apress.com).

Listing 18-1. soundex/stage1/soundex1a.py

```python
import string, re

charToSoundex = {"A": "9",
                 "B": "1",
                 "C": "2",
                 "D": "3",
                 "E": "9",
                 "F": "1",
                 "G": "2",
                 "H": "9",
                 "I": "9",
                 "J": "2",
                 "K": "2",
                 "L": "4",
                 "M": "5",
                 "N": "5",
                 "O": "9",
                 "P": "1",
                 "Q": "2",
                 "R": "6",
                 "S": "2",
                 "T": "3",
                 "U": "9",
                 "V": "1",
                 "W": "9",
                 "X": "2",
                 "Y": "9",
                 "Z": "2"}

def soundex(source):
    "convert string to Soundex equivalent"

    # Soundex requirements:
    # source string must be at least 1 character
    # and must consist entirely of letters
    allChars = string.uppercase + string.lowercase
    if not re.search('^[%s]+$' % allChars, source):
        return "0000"
```

```
# Soundex algorithm:
# 1. make first character uppercase
source = source[0].upper() + source[1:]

# 2. translate all other characters to Soundex digits
digits = source[0]
for s in source[1:]:
    s = s.upper()
    digits += charToSoundex[s]

# 3. remove consecutive duplicates
digits2 = digits[0]
for d in digits[1:]:
    if digits2[-1] != d:
        digits2 += d

# 4. remove all "9"s
digits3 = re.sub('9', '', digits2)

# 5. pad end with "0"s to 4 characters
while len(digits3) < 4:
    digits3 += "0"

# 6. return first 4 characters
return digits3[:4]

if __name__ == '__main__':
    from timeit import Timer
    names = ('Woo', 'Pilgrim', 'Flingjingwaller')
    for name in names:
        statement = "soundex('%s')" % name
        t = Timer(statement, "from __main__ import soundex")
        print name.ljust(15), soundex(name), min(t.repeat())
```

> **TIP** *Soundexing and Genealogy* (http://www.avotaynu.com/soundex.html)
> *gives a chronology of the evolution of the Soundex and its regional variations.*

Using the timeit Module

Timing short pieces of code is incredibly complex. How much processor time is your computer devoting to running this code? Are there things running in the background? Are you sure? Every modern computer has background processes running—some all the time and some intermittently. Cron jobs fire off at consistent intervals; background services occasionally "wake up" to do useful things like check for new mail, connect to instant messaging servers, check for application updates, scan for viruses, check whether a disk has been inserted into your CD drive in the last 100 nanoseconds, and so on.

Before you start your timing tests, turn off everything and disconnect from the network. Then turn off all the things you forgot to turn off the first time, then turn off the service that's incessantly checking whether the network has come back yet, then... well, you get the idea.

And then there's the matter of the variations introduced by the timing framework itself. Does the Python interpreter cache method-name lookups? Does it cache code-block compilations? How about regular expressions? Will your code have side effects if run more than once? Don't forget that you're dealing with small fractions of a second, so small mistakes in your timing framework will irreparably skew your results.

The Python community has a saying: "Python comes with batteries included." Don't write your own timing framework! Python 2.3 comes with a perfectly good one called `timeit`, demonstrated in Listing 18-2.

Listing 18-2. Introducing timeit

```
>>> import timeit
>>> t = timeit.Timer("soundex.soundex('Pilgrim')",
...     "import soundex")          (1)
>>> t.timeit()                     (2)
8.21683733547
>>> t.repeat(3, 2000000)           (3)
[16.48319309109, 16.46128984923, 16.44203948912]
```

(1) The `timeit` module defines one class, `Timer`, which takes two arguments. Both arguments are strings. The first argument is the statement you wish to time; in this case, you are timing a call to the Soundex function within the `soundex` module with an argument of `'Pilgrim'`. The second argument to the `Timer` class is the `import` statement that sets up the environment for the statement. Internally, `timeit` sets up an isolated virtual environment, manually executes the setup statement (importing the `soundex` module), and then manually compiles and executes the timed statement (calling the Soundex function).

(2) Once you have the `Timer` object, the easiest thing to do is call `timeit()`, which calls your function one million times and returns the number of seconds it took to do it.

(3) The other major method of the `Timer` object is `repeat()`, which takes two optional arguments. The first argument is the number of times to repeat the entire test, and the second argument is the number of times to call the timed statement within each test. Both arguments are optional, and they default to 3 and 1000000,

respectively. The repeat() method returns a list of the times each test cycle took, in seconds.

> **TIP** *You can use the* timeit *module on the command line to test an existing Python program, without modifying the code. See* http://docs.python.org/ lib/node396.html *for documentation on the command-line flags.*

Note that repeat() returns a list of times. The times will almost never be identical, due to slight variations in how much processor time the Python interpreter is getting (and those pesky background processes that you can't eliminate).

Your first thought might be to say, "Let's take the average and call that The True Number." In fact, that's almost certainly wrong. The tests that took longer didn't take longer because of variations in your code or in the Python interpreter; they took longer because of those pesky background processes or other factors outside the Python interpreter that you can't fully eliminate. If the different timing results differ by more than a few percent, you still have too much variability to trust the results. Otherwise, take the minimum time and discard the rest.

Python has a handy min function that takes a list and returns the smallest value:

```
>>> min(t.repeat(3, 1000000))
8.22203948912
```

> **TIP** *The* timeit *module works only if you already know what piece of code you need to optimize. If you have a larger Python program and don't know where your performance problems are, check out the* hotshot *module (*http://docs.python.org/lib/module-hotshot.html*).*

Optimizing Regular Expressions

The first thing the Soundex function checks is whether the input is a nonempty string of letters. What's the best way to do this?

If you answered "regular expressions," go sit in the corner and contemplate your bad instincts. Regular expressions are almost never the right answer. They should be avoided whenever possible, not only for performance reasons (which are good reasons), but also because they're difficult to debug and maintain.

This code fragment from soundex/stage1/soundex1a.py checks whether the function argument source is a word made entirely of letters, with at least one letter (not the empty string):

```
allChars = string.uppercase + string.lowercase
if not re.search('^[%s]+$' % allChars, source):
    return "0000"
```

How does `soundex1a.py` perform? For convenience, the `__main__` section of the script contains this code that calls the `timeit` module, sets up a timing test with three different names, tests each name three times, and displays the minimum time for each:

```
if __name__ == '__main__':
    from timeit import Timer
    names = ('Woo', 'Pilgrim', 'Flingjingwaller')
    for name in names:
        statement = "soundex('%s')" % name
        t = Timer(statement, "from __main__ import soundex")
        print name.ljust(15), soundex(name), min(t.repeat())
```

So how does `soundex1a.py` perform with this regular expression?

```
C:\samples\soundex\stage1>python soundex1a.py
Woo             W000 19.3356647283
Pilgrim         P426 24.0772053431
Flingjingwaller F452 35.0463220884
```

As you might expect, the algorithm takes significantly longer when called with longer names. You can do some things to narrow that gap (make the function take less relative time for longer input), but the nature of the algorithm dictates that it will never run in constant time.

The other thing to keep in mind is that you are testing a representative sample of names. Woo is a kind of trivial case, in that it gets shortened to a single letter and then padded with zeros. Pilgrim is a normal case, of average length and a mixture of significant and ignored letters. Flingjingwaller is extraordinarily long and contains consecutive duplicates. Other tests might also be helpful, but this covers a good range of different cases.

So, what about that regular expression? Well, it's inefficient. Since the expression is testing for ranges of characters (*A* to *Z* in uppercase and *a* to *z* in lowercase), you can use a shorthand regular expression syntax. Here is `soundex/stage1/soundex1b.py`:

```
if not re.search('^[A-Za-z]+$', source):
    return "0000"
```

`timeit` says `soundex1b.py` is slightly faster than `soundex1a.py`, but nothing to get terribly excited about:

```
C:\samples\soundex\stage1>python soundex1b.py
Woo            WOOO 17.1361133887
Pilgrim        P426 21.8201693232
Flingjingwaller F452 32.7262294509
```

As you saw in the "Refactoring for Performance" section of Chapter 15, regular expressions can be compiled and reused for faster results. Since this regular expression never changes across function calls, you can compile it once and use the compiled version. Here is soundex/stage1/soundex1c.py:

```
isOnlyChars = re.compile('^[A-Za-z]+$').search
def soundex(source):
    if not isOnlyChars(source):
        return "0000"
```

Using a compiled regular expression in soundex1c.py is significantly faster:

```
C:\samples\soundex\stage1>python soundex1c.py
Woo            WOOO 14.5348347346
Pilgrim        P426 19.2784703084
Flingjingwaller F452 30.0893873383
```

But is this the wrong path? The logic here is simple: the input source needs to be nonempty, and it needs to be composed entirely of letters. Wouldn't it be faster to write a loop checking each character, and do away with regular expressions altogether?

Here is soundex/stage1/soundex1d.py:

```
    if not source:
        return "0000"
    for c in source:
        if not ('A' <= c <= 'Z') and not ('a' <= c <= 'z'):
            return "0000"
```

It turns out that this technique in soundex1d.py is *not* faster than using a compiled regular expression (although it is faster than using a noncompiled regular expression):

```
    C:\samples\soundex\stage1>python soundex1d.py
Woo            WOOO 15.4065058548
Pilgrim        P426 22.2753567842
Flingjingwaller F452 37.5845122774
```

Why isn't soundex1d.py faster? The answer lies in the interpreted nature of Python. The regular expression engine is written in C and compiled to run natively on your computer. On the other hand, this loop is written in Python and runs through the Python interpreter. Even though the loop is relatively simple, it's not simple enough to make up for the overhead of being interpreted. Regular expressions are never the right answer... except when they are.

It turns out that Python offers an obscure string method. You can be excused for not knowing about it, since I haven't mentioned it in this book. The method is called isalpha(), and it checks whether a string contains only letters.

This is soundex/stage1/soundex1e.py:

```
if (not source) and (not source.isalpha()):
    return "0000"
```

How much did we gain by using this specific method in soundex1e.py? Quite a bit.

```
C:\samples\soundex\stage1>python soundex1e.py
Woo             W000 13.5069504644
Pilgrim         P426 18.2199394057
Flingjingwaller F452 28.9975225902
```

Listing 18-3 shows this version.

Listing 18-3. Best Result So Far: soundex/stage1/soundex1e.py

```
import string, re

charToSoundex = {"A": "9",
                 "B": "1",
                 "C": "2",
                 "D": "3",
                 "E": "9",
                 "F": "1",
                 "G": "2",
                 "H": "9",
                 "I": "9",
                 "J": "2",
                 "K": "2",
                 "L": "4",
                 "M": "5",
                 "N": "5",
                 "O": "9",
                 "P": "1",
                 "Q": "2",
                 "R": "6",
                 "S": "2",
```

```
                        "T": "3",
                        "U": "9",
                        "V": "1",
                        "W": "9",
                        "X": "2",
                        "Y": "9",
                        "Z": "2"}

def soundex(source):
    if (not source) and (not source.isalpha()):
        return "0000"
    source = source[0].upper() + source[1:]
    digits = source[0]
    for s in source[1:]:
        s = s.upper()
        digits += charToSoundex[s]
    digits2 = digits[0]
    for d in digits[1:]:
        if digits2[-1] != d:
            digits2 += d
    digits3 = re.sub('9', '', digits2)
    while len(digits3) < 4:
        digits3 += "0"
    return digits3[:4]

if __name__ == '__main__':
    from timeit import Timer
    names = ('Woo', 'Pilgrim', 'Flingjingwaller')
    for name in names:
        statement = "soundex('%s')" % name
        t = Timer(statement, "from __main__ import soundex")
        print name.ljust(15), soundex(name), min(t.repeat())
```

Optimizing Dictionary Lookups

The second step of the Soundex algorithm is to convert characters to digits in a specific pattern. What's the best way to do this?

The most obvious solution is to define a dictionary with individual characters as keys and their corresponding digits as values, and do dictionary lookups on each character. This is what we have in soundex/stage1/soundex1c.py (the current best result so far):

```
charToSoundex = {"A": "9",
                 "B": "1",
                 "C": "2",
                 "D": "3",
                 "E": "9",
                 "F": "1",
                 "G": "2",
                 "H": "9",
                 "I": "9",
                 "J": "2",
                 "K": "2",
                 "L": "4",
                 "M": "5",
                 "N": "5",
                 "O": "9",
                 "P": "1",
                 "Q": "2",
                 "R": "6",
                 "S": "2",
                 "T": "3",
                 "U": "9",
                 "V": "1",
                 "W": "9",
                 "X": "2",
                 "Y": "9",
                 "Z": "2"}

def soundex(source):
    # ... input check omitted for brevity ...
    source = source[0].upper() + source[1:]
    digits = source[0]
    for s in source[1:]:
        s = s.upper()
        digits += charToSoundex[s]
```

You timed soundex1c.py already; this is how it performs:

```
C:\samples\soundex\stage1>python soundex1c.py
Woo             W000 14.5341678901
Pilgrim         P426 19.2650071448
Flingjingwaller F452 30.1003563302
```

This code is straightforward, but is it the best solution? Calling upper() on each individual character seems inefficient. It would probably be better to call upper() once on the entire string.

Then there's the matter of incrementally building the digits string. Incrementally building strings like this is horribly inefficient. Internally, the Python interpreter needs to create a new string each time through the loop, and then discard the old one.

Python is good at lists, though. It can treat a string as a list of characters automatically. And lists are easy to combine into strings again, using the string method join().

Here is soundex/stage2/soundex2a.py, which converts letters to digits by using map and lambda:

```
def soundex(source):
    # ...
    source = source.upper()
    digits = source[0] + "".join(map(lambda c: charToSoundex[c], source[1:]))
```

Surprisingly, soundex2a.py is not faster:

```
C:\samples\soundex\stage2>python soundex2a.py
Woo             WOOO 15.0097526362
Pilgrim         P426 19.254806407
Flingjingwaller F452 29.3790847719
```

The overhead of the anonymous lambda function defeats any performance you gain by dealing with the string as a list of characters.

soundex/stage2/soundex2b.py uses a list comprehension instead of map and lambda:

```
    source = source.upper()
    digits = source[0] + "".join([charToSoundex[c] for c in source[1:]])
```

Using a list comprehension in soundex2b.py is faster than using map and lambda in soundex2a.py, but still not faster than the original code (incrementally building a string in soundex1c.py):

```
C:\samples\soundex\stage2>python soundex2b.py
Woo             WOOO 13.4221324219
Pilgrim         P426 16.4901234654
Flingjingwaller F452 25.8186157738
```

It's time for a radically different approach. Dictionary lookups are a general-purpose tool. Dictionary keys can be any length string (or many other datatypes), but, in this case, we are dealing only with single-character keys *and* single-character values. It turns out that Python has a specialized function for handling exactly this situation: the `string.maketrans` function.

This is soundex/stage2/soundex2c.py:

```
allChar = string.uppercase + string.lowercase
charToSoundex = string.maketrans(allChar, "91239129922455912623919292" * 2)
def soundex(source):
    # ...
    digits = source[0].upper() + source[1:].translate(charToSoundex)
```

What the heck is going on here? `string.maketrans` creates a translation matrix between two strings: the first argument and the second argument. In this case, the first argument is the string ABCDEFGHIJKLMNOPQRSTUVWXYZabcdefghijklmnopqrstuvwxyz, and the second argument is the string 9123912992245591262391929291239129922455912623919292. See the pattern? It's the same conversion pattern you were setting up longhand with a dictionary. *A* maps to 9, *B* maps to 1, *C* maps to 2, and so forth. But it's not a dictionary; it's a specialized data structure that you can access using the string method `translate`, which translates each character into the corresponding digit, according to the matrix defined by `string.maketrans`.

`timeit` shows that soundex2c.py is significantly faster than defining a dictionary, looping through the input, and building the output incrementally:

```
C:\samples\soundex\stage2>python soundex2c.py
Woo              W000 11.437645008
Pilgrim          P426 13.2825062962
Flingjingwaller  F452 18.5570110168
```

You're not going to get much better results than that. Python has a specialized function that does exactly what you want to do, so use it and move on. Listing 18-4 shows the optimized version so far.

Listing 18-4. Best Result So Far: soundex/stage2/soundex2c.py

```
import string, re

allChar = string.uppercase + string.lowercase
charToSoundex = string.maketrans(allChar, "91239129922455912623919292" * 2)
isOnlyChars = re.compile('^[A-Za-z]+$').search

def soundex(source):
    if not isOnlyChars(source):
        return "0000"
    digits = source[0].upper() + source[1:].translate(charToSoundex)
    digits2 = digits[0]
    for d in digits[1:]:
```

```
            if digits2[-1] != d:
                digits2 += d
    digits3 = re.sub('9', '', digits2)
    while len(digits3) < 4:
        digits3 += "0"
    return digits3[:4]

if __name__ == '__main__':
    from timeit import Timer
    names = ('Woo', 'Pilgrim', 'Flingjingwaller')
    for name in names:
        statement = "soundex('%s')" % name
        t = Timer(statement, "from __main__ import soundex")
        print name.ljust(15), soundex(name), min(t.repeat())
```

Optimizing List Operations

The third step in the Soundex algorithm is eliminating consecutive duplicate digits. What's the best way to do this?

Here's the code we have so far, in soundex/stage2/soundex2c.py:

```
digits2 = digits[0]
for d in digits[1:]:
    if digits2[-1] != d:
        digits2 += d
```

Here are the performance results for soundex2c.py:

```
C:\samples\soundex\stage2>python soundex2c.py
Woo             WO00 12.6070768771
Pilgrim         P426 14.4033353401
Flingjingwaller F452 19.7774882003
```

The first thing to consider is whether it's efficient to check digits[-1] each time through the loop. Are list indexes expensive? Would you be better off maintaining the last digit in a separate variable and checking that instead? To answer this question, here is soundex/stage3/soundex3a.py:

```
digits2 = ''
last_digit = ''
for d in digits:
    if d != last_digit:
        digits2 += d
        last_digit = d
```

soundex3a.py does not run any faster than soundex2c.py, and it may even be slightly slower (although it's not enough of a difference to say for sure):

```
C:\samples\soundex\stage3>python soundex3a.py
Woo              WO00 11.5346048171
Pilgrim          P426 13.3950636184
Flingjingwaller F452 18.6108927252
```

Why isn't soundex3a.py faster? It turns out that list indexes in Python are extremely efficient. Repeatedly accessing digits2[-1] is no problem at all. On the other hand, manually maintaining the last-seen digit in a separate variable means you have *two* variable assignments for each digit you're storing, which wipes out any small gains you might have gotten from eliminating the list lookup.

Let's try something radically different (again). If it's possible to treat a string as a list of characters, it should be possible to use a list comprehension to iterate through the list. The problem is that the code needs access to the previous character in the list, and that's not easy to do with a straightforward list comprehension. However, it is possible to create a list of index numbers using the built-in range() function, and then use those index numbers to progressively search through the list and pull out each character that is different from the previous character. That will give you a list of characters, and you can use the string method join() to reconstruct a string from that.

Here is soundex/stage3/soundex3b.py:

```
digits2 = "".join([digits[i] for i in range(len(digits))
                   if i == 0 or digits[i-1] != digits[i]])
```

Is this faster? In a word, no.

```
C:\samples\soundex\stage3>python soundex3b.py
Woo              WO00 14.2245271396
Pilgrim          P426 17.8337165757
Flingjingwaller F452 25.9954005327
```

It's possible that the techniques so far have been "string-centric." Python can convert a string into a list of characters with a single command: list('abc') returns ['a', 'b', 'c']. Furthermore, lists can be *modified in place* very quickly. Instead of incrementally building a new list (or string) from the source string, why not move elements around within a single list?

Here is soundex/stage3/soundex3c.py, which modifies a list in place to remove consecutive duplicate elements:

```
digits = list(source[0].upper() + source[1:].translate(charToSoundex))
i=0
for item in digits:
```

```
        if item==digits[i]: continue
        i+=1
        digits[i]=item
    del digits[i+1:]
    digits2 = "".join(digits)
```

Is this faster than soundex3a.py or soundex3b.py? No, in fact, it's the slowest method yet:

```
C:\samples\soundex\stage3>python soundex3c.py
Woo             W000 14.1662554878
Pilgrim         P426 16.0397885765
Flingjingwaller F452 22.1789341942
```

You haven't made any progress here at all, except to try and rule out several "clever" techniques. The fastest code you've seen so far was the original, most straightforward method (soundex2c.py). Sometimes, it doesn't pay to be clever. Listing 18-5 shows the optimized code so far.

Listing 18-5. Best Result So Far: soundex/stage2/soundex2c.py

```python
import string, re

allChar = string.uppercase + string.lowercase
charToSoundex = string.maketrans(allChar, "91239129922455912623919292" * 2)
isOnlyChars = re.compile('^[A-Za-z]+$').search

def soundex(source):
    if not isOnlyChars(source):
        return "0000"
    digits = source[0].upper() + source[1:].translate(charToSoundex)
    digits2 = digits[0]
    for d in digits[1:]:
        if digits2[-1] != d:
            digits2 += d
    digits3 = re.sub('9', '', digits2)
    while len(digits3) < 4:
        digits3 += "0"
    return digits3[:4]

if __name__ == '__main__':
```

```
from timeit import Timer
names = ('Woo', 'Pilgrim', 'Flingjingwaller')
for name in names:
    statement = "soundex('%s')" % name
    t = Timer(statement, "from __main__ import soundex")
    print name.ljust(15), soundex(name), min(t.repeat())
```

Optimizing String Manipulation

The final step of the Soundex algorithm is padding short results with zeros and truncating long results. What is the best way to do this?

This is what we have so far, taken from soundex/stage2/soundex2c.py:

```
digits3 = re.sub('9', '', digits2)
while len(digits3) < 4:
    digits3 += "0"
return digits3[:4]
```

These are the results for soundex2c.py:

```
C:\samples\soundex\stage2>python soundex2c.py
Woo           W000 12.6070768771
Pilgrim       P426 14.4033353401
Flingjingwaller F452 19.7774882003
```

The first thing to consider is replacing that regular expression with a loop. This code is from soundex/stage4/soundex4a.py:

```
digits3 = ''
for d in digits2:
    if d != '9':
        digits3 += d
```

Is soundex4a.py faster? Yes, it is:

```
C:\samples\soundex\stage4>python soundex4a.py
Woo           W000 6.62865531792
Pilgrim       P426 9.02247576158
Flingjingwaller F452 13.6328416042
```

But wait a minute. Why use a loop to remove characters from a string? You can use a simple string method for that. Here's soundex/stage4/soundex4b.py:

```
digits3 = digits2.replace('9', '')
```

Is soundex4b.py faster? That's an interesting question. It depends on the input:

```
C:\samples\soundex\stage4>python soundex4b.py
Woo             WOOO 6.75477414029
Pilgrim         P426 7.56652144337
Flingjingwaller F452 10.8727729362
```

The string method in soundex4b.py is faster than the loop for most names, but it's actually slightly slower than soundex4a.py in the trivial case (a very short name). Performance optimizations aren't always uniform; tuning that makes one case faster can sometimes make other cases slower. In this case, the majority of cases will benefit from the change, so let's leave it at that, but the principle is an important one to remember.

Last but not least, let's examine the final two steps of the algorithm: padding short results with zeros and truncating long results to four characters. The code you see in soundex4b.py does just that, but it's horribly inefficient. Take a look at soundex/stage4/soundex4c.py to see why:

```
digits3 += '000'
return digits3[:4]
```

Why do you need a while loop to pad the result? You know in advance that you're going to truncate the result to four characters, and you know that you already have at least one character (the initial letter, which is passed unchanged from the original source variable). That means you can simply add three zeros to the output, and then truncate it. Don't get stuck in a rut over the exact wording of the problem; looking at the problem slightly differently can lead to a simpler solution.

How much speed do you gain in soundex4c.py by dropping the while loop? It's significant:

```
C:\samples\soundex\stage4>python soundex4c.py
Woo             WOOO 4.89129791636
Pilgrim         P426 7.30642134685
Flingjingwaller F452 10.689832367
```

Finally, one more step you might take is to combine these three lines of code into one line. Take a look at soundex/stage4/soundex4d.py:

```
return (digits2.replace('9', '') + '000')[:4]
```

But putting all this code on one line in `soundex4d.py` is barely faster than `soundex4c.py`:

```
C:\samples\soundex\stage4>python soundex4d.py
Woo             W000 4.93624105857
Pilgrim         P426 7.19747593619
Flingjingwaller F452 10.5490700634
```

It is also significantly less readable, and for not much performance gain. Is that worth it? I hope you have good comments. Performance isn't everything. Your optimization efforts must always be balanced against threats to your program's readability and maintainability.

Summary

This chapter has illustrated several important aspects of performance tuning in Python and performance tuning in general.

- If you need to choose between regular expressions and writing a loop, choose regular expressions. The regular expression engine is compiled in C and runs natively on your computer. Your loop is written in Python and runs through the Python interpreter.

- If you need to choose between regular expressions and string methods, choose string methods. Both are compiled in C, so choose the simpler one.

- General-purpose dictionary lookups are fast, but specialty functions, such as `string.maketrans`, and string methods, such as `isalpha()`, are faster. If Python has a custom-tailored function for your purposes, use it.

- Don't be too clever. Sometimes the most obvious algorithm is also the fastest.

- Don't sweat it too much. Performance isn't everything.

I can't emphasize that last point strongly enough. Over the course of this chapter, you made this function three times faster and saved 20 seconds over one million function calls. That's great. Now think: over the course of those million function calls, how many seconds will your surrounding application wait for a database connection? Or wait for disk I/O? Or wait for user input? Don't spend too much time overoptimizing one algorithm, or you'll ignore obvious improvements somewhere else. Develop an instinct for the sort of code that Python runs well, correct obvious blunders if you find them, and leave the rest alone.

APPENDIX A
Python License

All of the sample code in this book is licensed under the Python license.

A. History of the Software

PYTHON WAS CREATED in the early 1990s by Guido van Rossum, at Stichting Mathematisch Centrum (CWI) in the Netherlands, as a successor of a language called ABC. Guido is Python's principal author, although it includes many contributions from others. The last version released from CWI was Python 1.2. In 1995, Guido continued his work on Python at the Corporation for National Research Initiatives (CNRI) in Reston, Virginia, where he released several versions of the software. Python 1.6 was the last of the versions released by CNRI. In 2000, Guido and the Python core development team moved to BeOpen.com to form the BeOpen PythonLabs team. Python 2.0 was the first and only release from BeOpen.com.

Following the release of Python 1.6, and after Guido van Rossum left CNRI to work with commercial software developers, it became clear that the ability to use Python with software available under the GNU Public License (GPL) was very desirable. CNRI and the Free Software Foundation (FSF) interacted to develop enabling wording changes to the Python license. Python 1.6.1 is essentially the same as Python 1.6, with a few minor bug fixes and with a different license that enables later versions to be GPL-compatible. Python 2.1 is a derivative work of Python 1.6.1 as well as of Python 2.0.

After Python 2.0 was released by BeOpen.com, Guido van Rossum and the other PythonLabs developers joined Digital Creations. All intellectual property added from this point on, starting with Python 2.1 and its alpha and beta releases, is owned by the Python Software Foundation (PSF), a nonprofit modeled after the Apache Software Foundation. See http://www.python.org/psf for more information about the PSF.

Thanks to the many outside volunteers who have worked under Guido's direction to make these releases possible.

B. Terms and Conditions for Accessing or Otherwise Using Python

PSF License Agreement

1. This LICENSE AGREEMENT is between the Python Software Foundation ("PSF"), and the Individual or Organization ("Licensee") accessing and otherwise using Python 2.1.1 software in source or binary form and its associated documentation.

2. Subject to the terms and conditions of this License Agreement, PSF hereby grants Licensee a nonexclusive, royalty-free, world-wide license to reproduce, analyze, test, perform and/or display publicly, prepare derivative works, distribute, and otherwise use Python 2.1.1 alone or in any derivative version, provided, however, that PSF's License Agreement and PSF's notice of copyright, i.e., "Copyright © 2001 Python Software Foundation; All Rights Reserved" are retained in Python 2.1.1 alone or in any derivative version prepared by Licensee.

3. In the event Licensee prepares a derivative work that is based on or incorporates Python 2.1.1 or any part thereof, and wants to make the derivative work available to others as provided herein, then Licensee hereby agrees to include in any such work a brief summary of the changes made to Python 2.1.1.

4. PSF is making Python 2.1.1 available to Licensee on an "AS IS" basis. PSF MAKES NO REPRESENTATIONS OR WARRANTIES, EXPRESS OR IMPLIED. BY WAY OF EXAMPLE, BUT NOT LIMITATION, PSF MAKES NO AND DISCLAIMS ANY REPRESENTATION OR WARRANTY OF MERCHANTABILITY OR FITNESS FOR ANY PARTICULAR PURPOSE OR THAT THE USE OF PYTHON 2.1.1 WILL NOT INFRINGE ANY THIRD PARTY RIGHTS.

5. PSF SHALL NOT BE LIABLE TO LICENSEE OR ANY OTHER USERS OF PYTHON 2.1.1 FOR ANY INCIDENTAL, SPECIAL, OR CONSEQUENTIAL DAMAGES OR LOSS AS A RESULT OF MODIFYING, DISTRIBUTING, OR OTHERWISE USING PYTHON 2.1.1, OR ANY DERIVATIVE THEREOF, EVEN IF ADVISED OF THE POSSIBILITY THEREOF.

6. This License Agreement will automatically terminate upon a material breach of its terms and conditions.

7. Nothing in this License Agreement shall be deemed to create any relationship of agency, partnership, or joint venture between PSF and Licensee. This License Agreement does not grant permission to use PSF trademarks or trade name in a trademark sense to endorse or promote products or services of Licensee, or any third party.

8. By copying, installing or otherwise using Python 2.1.1, Licensee agrees to be bound by the terms and conditions of this License Agreement.

BeOpen Python Open Source License Agreement Version 1

1. This LICENSE AGREEMENT is between BeOpen.com ("BeOpen"), having an office at 160 Saratoga Avenue, Santa Clara, CA 95051, and the Individual or Organization ("Licensee") accessing and otherwise using this software in source or binary form and its associated documentation ("the Software").

2. Subject to the terms and conditions of this BeOpen Python License Agreement, BeOpen hereby grants Licensee a non-exclusive, royalty-free, world-wide license to reproduce, analyze, test, perform and/or display publicly, prepare derivative works, distribute, and otherwise use the Software alone or in any derivative version, provided, however, that the BeOpen Python License is retained in the Software, alone or in any derivative version prepared by Licensee.

3. BeOpen is making the Software available to Licensee on an "AS IS" basis. BEOPEN MAKES NO REPRESENTATIONS OR WARRANTIES, EXPRESS OR IMPLIED. BY WAY OF EXAMPLE, BUT NOT LIMITATION, BEOPEN MAKES NO AND DISCLAIMS ANY REPRESENTATION OR WARRANTY OF MERCHANTABILITY OR FITNESS FOR ANY PARTICULAR PURPOSE OR THAT THE USE OF THE SOFTWARE WILL NOT INFRINGE ANY THIRD PARTY RIGHTS.

4. BEOPEN SHALL NOT BE LIABLE TO LICENSEE OR ANY OTHER USERS OF THE SOFTWARE FOR ANY INCIDENTAL, SPECIAL, OR CONSEQUENTIAL DAMAGES OR LOSS AS A RESULT OF USING, MODIFYING OR DISTRIBUTING THE SOFTWARE, OR ANY DERIVATIVE THEREOF, EVEN IF ADVISED OF THE POSSIBILITY THEREOF.

5. This License Agreement will automatically terminate upon a material breach of its terms and conditions.

6. This License Agreement shall be governed by and interpreted in all respects by the law of the State of California, excluding conflict of law provisions. Nothing in this License Agreement shall be deemed to create any relationship of agency, partnership, or joint venture between BeOpen and Licensee. This License Agreement does not grant permission to use BeOpen trademarks or trade names in a trademark sense to endorse or promote products or services of Licensee, or any third party. As an exception, the "BeOpen Python" logos available at http://www.pythonlabs.com/logos.html may be used according to the permissions granted on that web page.

7. By copying, installing or otherwise using the software, Licensee agrees to be bound by the terms and conditions of this License Agreement.

CNRI Open Source GPL-Compatible License Agreement

1. This LICENSE AGREEMENT is between the Corporation for National Research Initiatives, having an office at 1895 Preston White Drive, Reston, VA 20191 ("CNRI"), and the Individual or Organization ("Licensee") accessing and otherwise using Python 1.6.1 software in source or binary form and its associated documentation.

2. Subject to the terms and conditions of this License Agreement, CNRI hereby grants Licensee a nonexclusive, royalty-free, world-wide license to reproduce, analyze, test, perform and/or display publicly, prepare derivative works, distribute, and otherwise use Python 1.6.1 alone or in any derivative version, provided, however, that CNRI's License Agreement and CNRI's notice of copyright, i.e., "Copyright © 1995-2001 Corporation for National Research Initiatives; All Rights Reserved" are retained in Python 1.6.1 alone or in any derivative version prepared by Licensee. Alternately, in lieu of CNRI's License Agreement, Licensee may substitute the following text (omitting the quotes): "Python 1.6.1 is made available subject to the terms and conditions in CNRI's License Agreement. This Agreement together with Python 1.6.1 may be located on the Internet using the following unique, persistent identifier (known as a handle): 1895.22/1013. This Agreement may also be obtained from a proxy server on the Internet using the following URL: http://hdl.handle.net/1895.22/1013."

3. In the event Licensee prepares a derivative work that is based on or incorporates Python 1.6.1 or any part thereof, and wants to make the derivative work available to others as provided herein, then Licensee hereby agrees to include in any such work a brief summary of the changes made to Python 1.6.1.

4. CNRI is making Python 1.6.1 available to Licensee on an "AS IS" basis. CNRI MAKES NO REPRESENTATIONS OR WARRANTIES, EXPRESS OR IMPLIED. BY WAY OF EXAMPLE, BUT NOT LIMITATION, CNRI MAKES NO AND DISCLAIMS ANY REPRESENTATION OR WARRANTY OF MERCHANTABILITY OR FITNESS FOR ANY PARTICULAR PURPOSE OR THAT THE USE OF PYTHON 1.6.1 WILL NOT INFRINGE ANY THIRD PARTY RIGHTS.

5. CNRI SHALL NOT BE LIABLE TO LICENSEE OR ANY OTHER USERS OF PYTHON 1.6.1 FOR ANY INCIDENTAL, SPECIAL, OR CONSEQUENTIAL DAMAGES OR LOSS AS A RESULT OF MODIFYING, DISTRIBUTING, OR OTHERWISE USING PYTHON 1.6.1, OR ANY DERIVATIVE THEREOF, EVEN IF ADVISED OF THE POSSIBILITY THEREOF.

6. This License Agreement will automatically terminate upon a material breach of its terms and conditions.

7. This License Agreement shall be governed by the federal intellectual property law of the United States, including without limitation the federal copyright law, and, to the extent such U.S. federal law does not apply, by the law of the Commonwealth of Virginia, excluding Virginia's conflict of law provisions. Notwithstanding the foregoing, with regard to derivative works based on Python 1.6.1 that incorporate non-separable material that was previously distributed under the GNU General Public License (GPL), the law of the Commonwealth of Virginia shall govern this License Agreement only as to issues arising under or with respect to Paragraphs 4, 5, and 7 of this License Agreement. Nothing in this License Agreement shall be deemed to create any relationship of agency, partnership, or joint venture between CNRI and Licensee. This License Agreement does not grant permission to use CNRI trademarks or trade name in a trademark sense to endorse or promote products or services of Licensee, or any third party.

8. By clicking on the "ACCEPT" button where indicated, or by copying, installing or otherwise using Python 1.6.1, Licensee agrees to be bound by the terms and conditions of this License Agreement.

CWI Permissions Statement and Disclaimer

Copyright © 1991–1995, Stichting Mathematisch Centrum Amsterdam, The Netherlands. All rights reserved.

Permission to use, copy, modify, and distribute this software and its documentation for any purpose and without fee is hereby granted, provided that the above copyright notice appear in all copies and that both that copyright notice and this permission notice appear in supporting documentation, and that the name of Stichting Mathematisch Centrum or CWI not be used in advertising or publicity pertaining to distribution of the software without specific, written prior permission.

STICHTING MATHEMATISCH CENTRUM DISCLAIMS ALL WARRANTIES WITH REGARD TO THIS SOFTWARE, INCLUDING ALL IMPLIED WARRANTIES OF MERCHANTABILITY AND FITNESS, IN NO EVENT SHALL STICHTING MATHEMATISCH CENTRUM BE LIABLE FOR ANY SPECIAL, INDIRECT OR CONSEQUENTIAL DAMAGES OR ANY DAMAGES WHATSOEVER RESULTING FROM LOSS OF USE, DATA OR PROFITS, WHETHER IN AN ACTION OF CONTRACT, NEGLIGENCE OR OTHER TORTIOUS ACTION, ARISING OUT OF OR IN CONNECTION WITH THE USE OR PERFORMANCE OF THIS SOFTWARE.

APPENDIX B

GNU Free Documentation License

THE TEXT OF THIS BOOK is licensed under the GNU Free Documentation License, Version 1.1, written March 2000.

0. Preamble

The purpose of this License is to make a manual, textbook, or other written document "free" in the sense of freedom: to assure everyone the effective freedom to copy and redistribute it, with or without modifying it, either commercially or noncommercially. Secondarily, this License preserves for the author and publisher a way to get credit for their work, while not being considered responsible for modifications made by others.

This License is a kind of "copyleft," which means that derivative works of the document must themselves be free in the same sense. It complements the GNU General Public License, which is a copyleft license designed for free software.

We have designed this License in order to use it for manuals for free software, because free software needs free documentation: a free program should come with manuals providing the same freedoms that the software does. But this License is not limited to software manuals; it can be used for any textual work, regardless of subject matter or whether it is published as a printed book. We recommend this License principally for works whose purpose is instruction or reference.

1. Applicability and Definitions

This License applies to any manual or other work that contains a notice placed by the copyright holder saying it can be distributed under the terms of this License. The "Document," below, refers to any such manual or work. Any member of the public is a licensee, and is addressed as "you."

A "Modified Version" of the Document means any work containing the Document or a portion of it, either copied verbatim, or with modifications and/or translated into another language.

A "Secondary Section" is a named appendix or a front-matter section of the Document that deals exclusively with the relationship of the publishers or authors of the Document to the Document's overall subject (or to related matters) and contains nothing that could fall directly within that overall subject. (For example, if the Document is in part a textbook of mathematics, a Secondary Section may not explain any mathematics.) The relationship could be a matter of historical connection with the subject or with related matters, or of legal, commercial, philosophical, ethical, or political position regarding them.

The "Invariant Sections" are certain Secondary Sections whose titles are designated, as being those of Invariant Sections, in the notice that says that the Document is released under this License.

The "Cover Texts" are certain short passages of text that are listed, as Front-Cover Texts or Back-Cover Texts, in the notice that says that the Document is released under this License.

A "Transparent" copy of the Document means a machine-readable copy, represented in a format whose specification is available to the general public, whose contents can be viewed and edited directly and straightforwardly with generic text editors or (for images composed of pixels) generic paint programs or (for drawings) some widely available drawing editor, and that is suitable for input to text formatters or for automatic translation to a variety of formats suitable for input to text formatters. A copy made in an otherwise Transparent file format whose markup has been designed to thwart or discourage subsequent modification by readers is not Transparent. A copy that is not "Transparent" is called "Opaque."

Examples of suitable formats for Transparent copies include plain ASCII without markup, Texinfo input format, LaTeX input format, SGML or XML using a publicly available DTD, and standard-conforming simple HTML designed for human modification. Opaque formats include PostScript, PDF, proprietary formats that can be read and edited only by proprietary word processors, SGML or XML for which the DTD and/or processing tools are not generally available, and the machine-generated HTML produced by some word processors for output purposes only.

The "Title Page" means, for a printed book, the title page itself, plus such following pages as are needed to hold, legibly, the material this License requires to appear in the title page. For works in formats which do not have any title page as such, "Title Page" means the text near the most prominent appearance of the work's title, preceding the beginning of the body of the text.

2. Verbatim Copying

You may copy and distribute the Document in any medium, either commercially or noncommercially, provided that this License, the copyright notices, and the license notice saying this License applies to the Document are reproduced in all copies, and that you add no other conditions whatsoever to those of this License. You may not use technical measures to obstruct or control the reading or further copying of the copies you make or distribute. However, you may accept compensation in exchange for copies. If you distribute a large enough number of copies you must also follow the conditions in section 3.

You may also lend copies, under the same conditions stated above, and you may publicly display copies.

3. Copying in Quantity

If you publish printed copies of the Document numbering more than 100, and the Document's license notice requires Cover Texts, you must enclose the copies in covers that carry, clearly and legibly, all these Cover Texts: Front-Cover Texts on the front cover, and Back-Cover Texts on the back cover. Both covers must also clearly and legibly identify you as the publisher of these copies. The front cover must present the full title with all words of the title equally prominent and visible. You may add other material on the covers in addition. Copying with changes limited to the covers, as long as they preserve the title of the Document and satisfy these conditions, can be treated as verbatim copying in other respects.

If the required texts for either cover are too voluminous to fit legibly, you should put the first ones listed (as many as fit reasonably) on the actual cover, and continue the rest onto adjacent pages.

If you publish or distribute Opaque copies of the Document numbering more than 100, you must either include a machine-readable Transparent copy along with each Opaque copy, or state in or with each Opaque copy a publicly accessible computer-network location containing a complete Transparent copy of the Document, free of added material, which the general network-using public has access to download anonymously at no charge using public-standard network protocols. If you use the latter option, you must take reasonably prudent steps, when you begin distribution of Opaque copies in quantity, to ensure that this Transparent copy will remain thus accessible at the stated location until at least one year after the last time you distribute an Opaque copy (directly or through your agents or retailers) of that edition to the public.

It is requested, but not required, that you contact the authors of the Document well before redistributing any large number of copies, to give them a chance to provide you with an updated version of the Document.

4. Modifications

You may copy and distribute a Modified Version of the Document under the conditions of sections 2 and 3 above, provided that you release the Modified Version under precisely this License, with the Modified Version filling the role of the Document, thus licensing distribution and modification of the Modified Version to whoever possesses a copy of it. In addition, you must do these things in the Modified Version:

A. Use in the Title Page (and on the covers, if any) a title distinct from that of the Document, and from those of previous versions (which should, if there were any, be listed in the History section of the Document). You may use the same title as a previous version if the original publisher of that version gives permission.

B. List on the Title Page, as authors, one or more persons or entities responsible for authorship of the modifications in the Modified Version, together with at least five of the principal authors of the Document (all of its principal authors, if it has less than five).

C. State on the Title page the name of the publisher of the Modified Version, as the publisher.

D. Preserve all the copyright notices of the Document.

E. Add an appropriate copyright notice for your modifications adjacent to the other copyright notices.

F. Include, immediately after the copyright notices, a license notice giving the public permission to use the Modified Version under the terms of this License, in the form shown in the Addendum below.

G. Preserve in that license notice the full lists of Invariant Sections and required Cover Texts given in the Document's license notice.

H. Include an unaltered copy of this License.

I. Preserve the section entitled "History", and its title, and add to it an item stating at least the title, year, new authors, and publisher of the Modified Version as given on the Title Page. If there is no section entitled "History" in the Document, create one stating the title, year, authors, and publisher of the Document as given on its Title Page, then add an item describing the Modified Version as stated in the previous sentence.

J. Preserve the network location, if any, given in the Document for public access to a Transparent copy of the Document, and likewise the network locations given in the Document for previous versions it was based on. These may be placed in the "History" section. You may omit a network location for a work that was published at least four years before the Document itself, or if the original publisher of the version it refers to gives permission.

K. In any section entitled "Acknowledgements" or "Dedications," preserve the section's title, and preserve in the section all the substance and tone of each of the contributor acknowledgements and/or dedications given therein.

L. Preserve all the Invariant Sections of the Document, unaltered in their text and in their titles. Section numbers or the equivalent are not considered part of the section titles.

M. Delete any section entitled "Endorsements." Such a section may not be included in the Modified Version.

N. Do not retitle any existing section as "Endorsements" or to conflict in title with any Invariant Section.

If the Modified Version includes new front-matter sections or appendices that qualify as Secondary Sections and contain no material copied from the Document, you may at your option designate some or all of these sections as invariant. To do this, add their titles to the list of Invariant Sections in the Modified Version's license notice. These titles must be distinct from any other section titles.

You may add a section entitled "Endorsements," provided it contains nothing but endorsements of your Modified Version by various parties—for example, statements of peer review or that the text has been approved by an organization as the authoritative definition of a standard.

You may add a passage of up to five words as a Front-Cover Text, and a passage of up to 25 words as a Back-Cover Text, to the end of the list of Cover Texts in the Modified Version. Only one passage of Front-Cover Text and one of Back-Cover Text may be added by (or through arrangements made by) any one entity. If the Document already includes a cover text for the same cover, previously added by you or by arrangement made by the same entity you are acting on behalf of, you may not add another; but you may replace the old one, on explicit permission from the previous publisher that added the old one.

The author(s) and publisher(s) of the Document do not by this License give permission to use their names for publicity for or to assert or imply endorsement of any Modified Version.

5. Combining Documents

You may combine the Document with other documents released under this License, under the terms defined in section 4 above for modified versions, provided that you include in the combination all of the Invariant Sections of all of the original documents, unmodified, and list them all as Invariant Sections of your combined work in its license notice.

The combined work need only contain one copy of this License, and multiple identical Invariant Sections may be replaced with a single copy. If there are multiple Invariant Sections with the same name but different contents, make the title of each such section unique by adding at the end of it, in parentheses, the name of the original author or publisher of that section if known, or else a unique number. Make the same adjustment to the section titles in the list of Invariant Sections in the license notice of the combined work.

In the combination, you must combine any sections entitled "History" in the various original documents, forming one section entitled "History"; likewise combine any sections entitled "Acknowledgements," and any sections entitled "Dedications." You must delete all sections entitled "Endorsements."

6. Collections of Documents

You may make a collection consisting of the Document and other documents released under this License, and replace the individual copies of this License in the various documents with a single copy that is included in the collection, provided that you follow the rules of this License for verbatim copying of each of the documents in all other respects.

You may extract a single document from such a collection, and distribute it individually under this License, provided you insert a copy of this License into the extracted document, and follow this License in all other respects regarding verbatim copying of that document.

7. Aggregation with Independent Works

A compilation of the Document or its derivatives with other separate and independent documents or works, in or on a volume of a storage or distribution medium, does not as a whole count as a Modified Version of the Document, provided no compilation copyright is claimed for the compilation. Such a compilation is called an "aggregate", and this License does not apply to the other self-contained works thus compiled with the Document, on account of their being thus compiled, if they are not themselves derivative works of the Document.

If the Cover Text requirement of section 3 is applicable to these copies of the Document, then if the Document is less than one quarter of the entire aggregate, the Document's Cover Texts may be placed on covers that surround only the Document within the aggregate. Otherwise they must appear on covers around the whole aggregate.

8. Translation

Translation is considered a kind of modification, so you may distribute translations of the Document under the terms of section 4. Replacing Invariant Sections with translations requires special permission from their copyright holders, but you may include translations of some or all Invariant Sections in addition to the original versions of these Invariant Sections. You may include a translation of this License provided that you also include the original English version of this License. In case of a disagreement between the translation and the original English version of this License, the original English version will prevail.

9. Termination

You may not copy, modify, sublicense, or distribute the Document except as expressly provided for under this License. Any other attempt to copy, modify, sublicense or distribute the Document is void, and will automatically terminate your rights under this License. However, parties who have received copies, or rights, from you under this License will not have their licenses terminated so long as such parties remain in full compliance.

10. Future Revisions of This License

The Free Software Foundation may publish new, revised versions of the GNU Free Documentation License from time to time. Such new versions will be similar in spirit to the present version, but may differ in detail to address new problems or concerns. See http://www.gnu.org/copyleft/.

Each version of the License is given a distinguishing version number. If the Document specifies that a particular numbered version of this License "or any later version" applies to it, you have the option of following the terms and conditions either of that specified version or of any later version that has been published (not as a draft) by the Free Software Foundation. If the Document does not specify a version number of this License, you may choose any version ever published (not as a draft) by the Free Software Foundation.

Addendum: How to Use This License for Your Documents

To use this License in a document you have written, include a copy of the License in the document and put the following copyright and license notices just after the title page:

> *Copyright © YEAR YOUR NAME. Permission is granted to copy, distribute and/or modify this document under the terms of the GNU Free Documentation License, Version 1.1 or any later version published by the Free Software Foundation; with the Invariant Sections being LIST THEIR TITLES, with the Front-Cover Texts being LIST, and with the Back-Cover Texts being LIST. A copy of the license is included in the section entitled "GNU Free Documentation License."*

If you have no Invariant Sections, write "with no Invariant Sections" instead of saying which ones are invariant. If you have no Front-Cover Texts, write "no Front-Cover Texts" instead of "Front-Cover Texts being LIST"; likewise for Back-Cover Texts.

If your document contains nontrivial examples of program code, we recommend releasing these examples in parallel under your choice of free software license, such as the GNU General Public License, to permit their use in free software.

Index

Symbols

A

B

C

U

forums.apress.com

JOIN THE APRESS FORUMS AND BE PART OF OUR COMMUNITY. You'll find discussions that cover topics of interest to IT professionals, programmers, and enthusiasts just like you. If you post a query to one of our forums, you can expect that some of the best minds in the business—especially Apress authors, who all write with *The Expert's Voice*™—will chime in to help you. Why not aim to become one of our most valuable participants (MVPs) and win cool stuff? Here's a sampling of what you'll find:

DATABASES
Data drives everything.

Share information, exchange ideas, and discuss any database programming or administration issues.

INTERNET TECHNOLOGIES AND NETWORKING
Try living without plumbing (and eventually IPv6).

Talk about networking topics including protocols, design, administration, wireless, wired, storage, backup, certifications, trends, and new technologies.

JAVA
We've come a long way from the old Oak tree.

Hang out and discuss Java in whatever flavor you choose: J2SE, J2EE, J2ME, Jakarta, and so on.

MAC OS X
All about the Zen of OS X.

OS X is both the present and the future for Mac apps. Make suggestions, offer up ideas, or boast about your new hardware.

OPEN SOURCE
Source code is good; understanding (open) source is better.

Discuss open source technologies and related topics such as PHP, MySQL, Linux, Perl, Apache, Python, and more.

PROGRAMMING/BUSINESS
Unfortunately, it is.

Talk about the Apress line of books that cover software methodology, best practices, and how programmers interact with the "suits."

WEB DEVELOPMENT/DESIGN
Ugly doesn't cut it anymore, and CGI is absurd.

Help is in sight for your site. Find design solutions for your projects and get ideas for building an interactive Web site.

SECURITY
Lots of bad guys out there—the good guys need help.

Discuss computer and network security issues here. Just don't let anyone else know the answers!

TECHNOLOGY IN ACTION
Cool things. Fun things.

It's after hours. It's time to play. Whether you're into LEGO® MINDSTORMS™ or turning an old PC into a DVR, this is where technology turns into fun.

WINDOWS
No defenestration here.

Ask questions about all aspects of Windows programming, get help on Microsoft technologies covered in Apress books, or provide feedback on any Apress Windows book.

HOW TO PARTICIPATE:
Go to the Apress Forums site at **http://forums.apress.com/**.
Click the New User link.